"*Reckless Grace* is a heart-wrenching memoir by the mother of a daughter struggling with type 1 diabetes, an eating disorder, and a severe substance abuse disorder. Carolyn DiPasquale describes her own experience, but also uses her daughter's rich diaries to help readers appreciate her daughter's suffering. DiPasquale recounts the pain that influenced her whole family as her daughter distanced herself from them while sinking deeper and deeper into her downward spiral."

—Ann Goebel-Fabbri, PhD, whose ground-breaking research on diabulimia has been featured on *BBC Radio*, *Good Morning America*, *National Public Radio*, the *Huffington Post*, *CNN*, and *The New York Times*.

"*Reckless Grace* tells the story of a common struggle—one of a family navigating a loved one's mental illness—through a powerful, unique lens. Carolyn DiPasquale's firsthand narrative, punctuated by actual passages from her daughter's journals, offers an intimate perspective on self-medication through substance use. It's exactly what we need to help normalize a much-needed national conversation on mental health and addiction."

—Former U.S. Congressman Patrick J. Kennedy

"As a woman who has healed from diabulimia, this memoir spoke to me. Rachel's death was the result of many colliding toxicities, many colliding illnesses."

—Maryjeanne Hunt, author of *Eating to Lose: healing from a life of diabulimia*, featured on ABC News and Oprah Radio.

"Struggling to understand how she and multiple trained medical professionals failed to notice three major mental illnesses, the author contrasts her own limited observations with the harder truths found in the pages of Rachel's journals. Beautiful in its simplicity and execution, *Reckless Grace* . . . helps bridge the gap between the torment of mental illness and what the outside world sees."

—K.C. Finn, *Readers' Favorite*

# RECKLESS GRACE

# RECKLESS GRACE

## A MOTHER'S CRASH COURSE IN MENTAL ILLNESS

CAROLYN DIPASQUALE

E. L. Marker
Salt Lake City

E. L. Marker, an imprint of WiDo Publishing
Salt Lake City, Utah
widopublishing.com

This is a true story told from my perspective, as well as hundreds of pages of Rachel's journals. Some names have been changed to protect people's privacy, and certain incidents may be slightly out of sequence; otherwise, I have made every effort to ensure that events, locales, and conversations from my memories are as accurate as possible.

Cover design by Steven Novak
Book design by Marny K. Parkin
Photographs of Rachel's art by Michael Osean

ISBN 978-1-947966-55-0

I will be beautiful.
My hair will be platinum blond.
My arms will be skinny.
My waist will be thin.
I will not be disappointed
when I look in the mirror.
When he looks at me,
he will be proud
I will own the world
People will open up
I will last though
I will feel so internally full
Life will be like warm sunlight
once I'm well.
   —dated July 12, 2000 (16 years old)

# Part I

*November 10–17, 2012*

# UNTHINKABLE TASK

STALLING, I STARE OUT my bedroom window at sinister black trees. Bleak sky. No sun. Three weeks ago, these trees were on fire—explosions of orange, copper, crimson, gold on a storybook blue sky. Lit by a luminous sun, fluorescent leaves fluttered with strobe effect, some floating to the ground. Musky notes of burning foliage wafted through the open window. Struck by the glory of fall, I lingered here, as before a campfire.

Now, except for a few tattered leaves, the branches are bare. Shivering, I turn.

I sink to the carpet, where I sit cross-legged, surrounded by boxes of loose photos and family albums pillowed in fabric and trimmed with lace. Two trifold poster boards lean against my bed, blank and inescapable.

I reach for my reading glasses, then drop my hand. I don't want to see these photos up close. Sharp images slash.

I sort through fuzzy pictures of my three children as swaddled infants, chubby, smiling toddlers, grinning school kids, and lanky teens, willing myself not to remember, not to feel.

There's too much to do in one week. I must select the luncheon menu, table linens, and music. I must decorate the church fellowship hall with Chinese lanterns, white string lights, votive candles in crystal bowls. I must also write a eulogy, for as little as I know, I know more than anyone else. This is the most pressing task. It precedes writing an obituary, scouring the Internet for a cremation urn that doesn't scream funeral, displaying a collection of Rachel's paintings on easels around the sanctuary.

On October 14, 2012, my only daughter, Rachel, had fallen into a drug-induced diabetic coma. Her boyfriend called 911 but did not follow the ambulance to the hospital. I would learn that paramedics carried her stretcher down the three flights of perpetually dusty stairs in her Bristol, Rhode Island, apartment building, past broken windows held together with duct tape, past her lovely paintings, hung on each floor, I often thought, to offset the squalor.

Rachel arrived at the hospital ER unconscious and alone, to the perplexity of the attending physician who found my number in her cell phone.

She died on November seventh and was cremated the next day. Two days later, my ex-husband, Perry, suggested we hold the memorial service on November 17 so it didn't interfere with the holidays. My husband Phil agreed. I told them I needed to grieve. "We must think of our guests," they said.

Therefore, I search through albums and boxes for photographs of Rachel from every phase in her life to arrange on the boards in some meaningful order. Her sweet face smiles up at me in photo after photo. Blond bangs and pigtails blur. I wipe my eyes and nose, swallowing the pain rising in my throat.

How is it that the mother, the one most crushed by the death of the first child she carried and bore, must plan the service? But who else could? My mother and three sisters are in Wisconsin booking flights. I can't entrust these preparations to Perry or our two adult sons, Matthew and Ryan, or Phil and his two adult daughters, Nikki and Krissy. No one knows Rachel's tastes like I do. No one but her mother would get every detail right.

Our dear neighbor, Maria, offered to help.

"What can I do?" she asked, appearing at our front door with red eyes.

Though Maria always had a heaping plate, she was the first to help someone hurting.

"I've got it," I lied, my own eyes dry.

What must friends and neighbors with pained faces and wet eyes make of my blank face and dry eyes when they bring casseroles and flowers? My heart feels frozen like it's been shot with Novocain. Only, unlike the dentist's numbing needle, this anesthetic doesn't fade.

Maria stood her ground until I gave up half the food and agreed to let her print the programs. The day of the memorial service, I would find her stunning flower arrangements, mums, and gladiolas in rich autumnal tones, displayed on the altar and banquet tables.

I organize the photos into piles—infancy, siblings, vacations, school. I should be drafting Rachel's eulogy. Shaken guests at her memorial service will want answers. But that will require focus. That will require reading glasses. Therefore, I stall.

A photo of Rachel taken a day after her birth—fat cheeks, doll lips, eyes sealed in post-fetal sleep—arrests me. As I pick it up, its colors bleed. In spite of myself, I flash back to her birth.

✦　✦　✦

PACING ON INDEPENDENCE DAY during the Bristol, Rhode Island, parade while bands played patriotic tunes and fireworks popped and whistled. Pain ripping from pelvis to spine. Pushing so hard, arms braced against cold steel bars, I feared rupturing something. Perry enthralled, watching from the foot of the bed with the doctor and nurses.

I didn't care where he stood. I had once adored him, his sense of humor, his tender blue eyes. But that man retreated when the smell of fresh coffee nauseated me one morning. I assured him he'd be a wonderful father, but his eyes dodged mine. The bigger I grew, the more he withdrew from me. So, this moment was mine. I would have my prize.

Bearing down for the last time, I commanded every muscle and cell of energy to push, and though I tried not to scream, the sound escaped, along with something warm and solid that slid out from between my legs. A foreign smell of birth filled the room.

"It's a girl!" the nurses sang.

Incomparable joy washed over me.

The doctor swung my infant daughter onto my chest, cord still attached. She did not cry. Her alert blue eyes passed from me to Perry and back to me.

Hands whisked her away, then returned my sleeping infant, wrapped in pink flannel. She received a perfect Apgar score, which one nurse had not seen in twenty years. As I breastfed my newborn, I studied the delicate eyelids and blue vein on her fair brow. Blond duck down hair, wintry pink skin. She could not have been more exquisite. After feeding, as I held her up, she opened her blue eyes. Her mouth also remained wide open, head bobbing like a baby bird seeking more food.

While amused, something about the dark pink mysteries inside her mouth arrested me. Her outward perfection was already too much. I couldn't begin to fathom God's inner workmanship—the number and wonder of all her perfectly working parts. While I was marveling at the miracle of human life, her mouth somehow found the stretch of skin between my forefinger and thumb, and she noisily resumed sucking.

Smiling, I pressed her to my heart.

I named her Rachel Grace after God's grace because I didn't deserve this child. Hadn't I stopped trusting Him, stopped counting the days till her birth—allowing myself, I supposed, to be sucked into the undertow of Perry's fears? But that was grace: getting something outrageously wonderful when you least expect it.

✦   ✦   ✦

SITTING ON MY BEDROOM floor, I stare at the photo of my flawless infant, struck by how far Rachel had fallen from that state.

How had this happened?

I repeat this question the night before Rachel's memorial service while scrambling to finish her eulogy. I can piece together the facts—what I think occurred, but the truth is buried in her journals, which I have not read yet. Wouldn't scanning some entries help me understand Rachel's struggles and write a truer speech? Besides, I've included a sample of her adolescent voice, and I'd like to balance it with her adult voice. I snatch two volumes from the storage cabinet in Rachel's room where I'd stowed her journals.

What I read appalls me. Flipping page after page, I search for some positive words that capture the spirit of the young woman I thought I knew. The text is jarring and dark. Tears streak my face, grotesquely distorting words. My heart pounds in my ears. If I continue, I will not be able to complete my speech, much less read it tomorrow. Abandoning my plan, I return the journals to their cabinet.

I work until my speech is acceptable. It's not perfect, but it provides context and tells Rachel's story, which pleases me. At the same time, my heart feels heavy, like I've failed my daughter by oversimplifying her demise, making assumptions, and drawing conclusions about things I do not know.

✦   ✦   ✦

THE NEXT MORNING, AS I stand at the podium in Middletown Baptist Church, I am struck by the sheer volume of people whose sober eyes lock mine. I begin by thanking them for their beautiful cards, words, meals, tears, and other loving gestures, which have sustained my family during this tragedy. Then, with trembling hands, I read my eulogy:

"Rachel was diagnosed with diabetes her first week of high school. She was barely fourteen. Because of her whimsical personality type—she hated rules and schedules—this was a difficult disease for her to manage, as she explains in an excerpt of a letter to her Aunt Dolores and family, written shortly after her diagnosis:

*Dear Dolores, Dale, Ben, and Emma,*

*Sorry it's taken so long to write. I've been making up tons of schoolwork and adjusting to my new schedule. These past few weeks have been so hard.*

*I guess I was in denial at first. I kept thinking, "This has got to be a dream. I'll wake up any minute now." And when I finally didn't, it all just fell on me—I would be controlled by this illness until the day I die. I'm the kind of person who, well, used to live very freely—and it's like now I have all these restrictions. I can't live the way I want to, and, well, it pisses me off because I want to eat sugar. I want to sleep late. I want to pig out at buffets. I want to go trick-or-treating . . ."*

I tell the mourners how, as a result of her strict diet, Rachel developed an eating disorder (ED), bulimia nervosa, which would control her life. Several times a day, she secretly gorged on junk food, vomiting to avoid weight gain.

Rachel attended multiple ED rehabs, including one of the finest Christian facilities in the nation. Days after her discharge, at age twenty, she relapsed. She could have used the tools she'd acquired to fight her bulimia. However, this would take time; it would require discipline and consistency. Instead, she took the easy route, using heroin to suppress her appetite. This triggered a downward spiral, replete with multiple arrests and imprisonment for possession.

I share how, after many years, Rachel recovered from heroin; however, she traded it for alcohol and prescription drugs. She also remained enslaved to bulimia. Her body image so consumed her she discovered another risky way to lose weight, by restricting her insulin. This cost her dearly. She acquired neuropathy, excruciating nerve damage, in both feet. Still, she continued to practice her EDs and self-medicate, resulting in a fatal overdose.

"Despite Rachel's addictions, she loved life, especially simple pleasures, like sunbathing, writing, reading good literature, and playing with her Boston terrier, Lola. She also loved to make people laugh with her irreverent sense of humor. As you can see from Rachel's paintings displayed here, she became an accomplished artist, whose work was exhibited in fine dining restaurants in Bristol and Newport."

I close my eulogy by telling the audience how much I will miss my daughter. As I walk off the stage, relief trickles through me. This task is over. At the same time, a strange weight descends, like it did the night before. Sitting beside Phil and our children in the front pew, I cannot help thinking I let Rachel down. I did not tell her true story.

# PART II

October 16–17, 2012
age twenty-eight
+
December 20, 2012–January 2013

# THE JOURNALS

RACHEL LAY IN A crisp hospital bed, her pale face blank. The clear tube in her mouth was attached to a ventilator that was breathing for her, moving her belly up and down beneath the white cotton blanket. Other beeping, hissing machines surrounding her bed assisted in life support. We had hoped these would be removed. Rachel would miraculously open her eyes, like charmed patients in movies and dreams. But we had recently learned her brain injury was too extreme. She would never lift her head from that pillow. Days earlier, Mom, my friend Lu, and I had spoken in hushed tones. Now we were silent. I stared at my lifeless daughter as if from a back row while hospital personnel floated in and out of the damp, dimly lit room.

When we got home, Mom brewed strong coffee. Like clockwork, the doorbell rang at four-thirty p.m. A sad church lady with a foil-covered pan. I worried that Lu had burdened our small congregation by asking women to bring meals every night of our three-week vigil. Now, as I smelled shepherd's pie, I was grateful. How could I have cooked when even drinking coffee felt taxing? We sat back down, no sooner lifting our mugs when I heard Phil's boots tromping up the basement stairs.

"I think these are Rachel's journals," he announced, holding a large blue bin. "Where do you want 'em?"

Rachel never hid her collection of journals. I knew they were in our basement, too precious for her to store in the community cellar of her apartment building. But they were hers, private, off-limits—until now.

Mom and I exchanged glances. "In her room," I said.

Grabbing our mugs, we followed Phil upstairs.

Mom and I unpacked the bin, spreading out the journals on her bed. They nearly covered her rosebud quilt. Still quite strong, the late afternoon sun streamed through her window and sky light, illuminating this sundry haul of spiral, hardbound, leather, even two juvenile journals. We counted twenty volumes.

I had no idea she'd filled so many books. I moved in closer to examine them, but Mom halted me.

"You can't read these until you heal," she said, moving diaries to sit down. "Give it a good year." Meanwhile, she picked one up and started reading.

I knew she was right. I stroked this cover, ran my fingers along that spine. I could only inventory these journals right now. Of course, I longed to read them. Rachel kept so many secrets. These diaries would finally let me in. Give me full access to her life, but I had to wait.

Scanning book after book, Mom clucked and shook her head, stopping only to remove her glasses and wipe her red eyes. "Oh, Rachel Gracie!"

She would read the volumes cover to cover before returning to Wisconsin, beginning with Rachel's juvenile journals.

"I think I bought her this," Mom said, lifting the Ariel the Little Mermaid diary. "Listen to what she wrote on the inside cover," she said, smiling: 'KEEP OUT! SCRAM!!! MINE! TOUCH THIS AND BE PREPARED TO GET HURT!!!! GO AWAY: GET YOUR BUTT OUT OF HERE! KEEP YOUR PAWS OFF MY STUFF! PRIVATE PROPERTY! SCRAM! NO ONE ALLOWED BEYOND THIS POINT! NO ADULTS! NO KIDS! NO ANYTHING! PISS OFF!!'"

"Here's an entry Rachel wrote right after Ryan was born," Mom remarked moments later. "She would have been eight years old. It's called Mustard Bath." She cleared her throat and began: "'Last night, mom got up to change Ryan. As soon as she took off his diaper, he squirted a liquid mustard poop all over the wall, the counter, and in the sink. Mom was so surprised she screamed. Dad woke up to help, but when he got there, Ryan whizzed all over him, the wall, counter, and sink!'"

We both smiled. It also stabbed. Her sweetness. Her innocence. Her potential.

If a juvenile entry undid me, how would I endure her adult journals? Later, when I would mention my intention to read these, friends and family would admonish me not to. "I'd read the journals once, then burn 'em in a big bonfire," my sister, Anna, would advise. Looking deeply into my eyes, my cousin, Marilyn, a retired social worker and mother of three grown children, would say, "I would not read those journals at all. What Rachel wrote will only hurt you."

No doubt, but nothing would stop me. I had to know what happened to my daughter; therefore, as Mom read, I labeled and numbered the volumes chronologically, so I could read them sequentially when the time was right.

I recognized every cover. I recalled seeing the Ariel journal and its yellow calico sequel, written respectively at ages eight and nine, on Rachel's desk or dresser when I was stripping her bed or returning clean clothes to her room. The Keep Out warnings written on the covers in bold black marker in her childish print had pinched. First: Why would this child of my body shut me out? Then: Didn't every human being deserve privacy?

I never peeked.

Touching the lavender tooled leather journal, I remembered how at age seventeen, Rachel used to write in this while working third shift as a desk clerk at the Seaside Manor. The burgundy journal she had filled one fall, often writing on the deck in the waning sun till it was so dark, all I saw was the glowing tip of her cigarette.

The black hardbound journal I had found once too often on the couch, coffee table, or deck steps to be coincidental. Each time I trotted it back to her room, I wondered, Has she left this out for me to read? And if so, what holds me back? I liked to think it was respect for her privacy, but fear might have played a part.

One sunny afternoon, after returning the diary to her room, I froze: What if she was seeking help? No one was home. A sunbeam, with dancing dust motes, cast a slanted square of light on her bed. Sitting down, I opened the book. Flipping to the last few entries, I began reading about a dalliance she was having with Stan, a co-worker at the Seaside Manor. At nineteen, Rachel had just broken up with Lance, her high school boyfriend of two years. Stan was older and ruggedly handsome. Lonely and bored, she seduced him. Following their first sexual encounter, she compared her new lover to Lance. Feeling like a voyeur, I clapped the book closed.

Among the journals, I noticed nine Pen-Tab PRO pocket spiral notebooks, identical except in color, their covers faded, with frayed corners. A glimpse inside confirmed my hunch: this was a subset called the "Everything Journals." Numbered with roman numerals, they had been written between April of 1999, when fourteen-year-old Rachel had her first boyfriend, to February of 2001, when the romance ended. Juvenile in nature, I assumed these were not as important as the rest. They would be syrupy and dramatic—Rachel's puppy love ramblings.

I was more interested in the adult journals, especially the most recent volumes. These would disclose what role drugs played in her demise. They would also reveal how much I hurt or helped her. I imagined scouring each page for the word "Mom." As I checked the dates on the final pages of the remaining journals, I noted that the volumes ended in 2009.

"Mom, we're missing the last three years!"

"Are you sure?" Emerging dreamily from the last page of Rachel's Ariel journal, she closed it to recheck the dates.

"You're right. We're missing 2010 to 2012," she said. "They've got to be here."

We searched through Rachel's built-in bookshelves—so many titles on eating disorders. Checked the closet and storage cabinet. Mom lifted the eyelet lace dust ruffle to look under the bed.

"I wonder if they're still at her apartment," Mom mused. Moving journals and propping pillows against the headboard, she stretched out, reaching for Rachel's calico juvenile sequel.

"It makes sense." Sitting back down, I felt a surge of hope. "We'll go to Bristol tomorrow."

Mom nodded without looking up, already lost in part two of Rachel's childhood.

I didn't want to return. Up those three flights of filthy stairs, past fractured windows. Last week, Phil and I had gone to the apartment to pick up some of Rachel's things, mainly her paintings, which I feared her boyfriend Josh would hock for drug money. He had moved most of Rachel's belongings into her studio, cordoning off the rest of their shared apartment though she owned nearly everything. Josh had only lived there eight months. While Phil and I sorted through Rachel's things, Josh stood in the doorway like an unshaven troll. He resembled a younger, brunette version of Bo Bridges, with sleepy hazel eyes and bushy, sloping brows that now followed us around the room. He wore a wrinkled long-sleeved oxford shirt and faded blue jeans with torn knees.

Rachel's clothes were heaped over her worktable. Removing them from their hangers, I packed them in heavy-duty garbage bags. I would keep some items and donate the rest. Certain clothes—her ruffled gauze chartreuse skirt, pink maxi skirt, worn jean jacket—evoked smiling images of her wearing them. They smelled like cigarette smoke and Victoria's Secret Pink cologne. Agony rose in my throat. I picked up her Aldo flip-flops with the abalone disks. I was with her at the Warwick Mall when she bought them. Inside, I saw the imprint of her toes.

While Phil and Josh carried Rachel's paintings to the car, I yielded to my grief, crying so hard it felt like my eyelids would turn inside out. This was my pattern—numb spans lasting days until reality poked through like an ice pick.

That day, we grabbed the paintings and got out of there. Our search tomorrow would take hours. We would have to leave the hospital early. As if Rachel knew the difference.

The only sound in Rachel's childhood room was the flipping of pages as Mom continued to read. The light had shifted, casting a pink lace pattern on Rachel's wall. I picked up a journal, then set it back down. I picked it up and opened it, heart swooping at the sight of Rachel's neat, round handwriting. I set it down, leaving the room.

✦  ✦  ✦

MY KNOCK ON THE apartment door triggered a cacophony of yipping and woofing from Rachel's Boston terrier, Lola, and Josh's golden retriever, Red. Why Josh had named this massive yellow dog "Red," I would never know. When he opened the door, both barking dogs jumped up to greet us, Red's tail flapping like a high-speed wiper blade. Standing on his hind legs, Red was easily our height. We both jumped back.

"Oh, my! You're a big fellow!" Mom said, trying to pet Red while backing out the door.

"Down, Red!" Josh roared, grabbing his collar and yanking him away from us.

Red was the largest, most undisciplined retriever I'd ever seen. Rachel said Josh had never trained him; he rarely even walked Red. When I learned about Rachel's vegetative coma, I told Josh I was taking Lola. He begged me to reconsider, insisting she was attached to him and Red.

"At least let me keep her a couple of weeks," he begged. "She's my last tie to Rachel."

Softening, I agreed. I couldn't take Lola then anyway as I spent eight-hour days at the hospital.

Josh dragged Red into another room and closed the door, ignoring his whines and howls. Lola continued to dance around the room, her uncut nails clicking against the floor.

"Can I have a kiss?" Josh leaned over Lola and stuck out his wagging tongue. Mom and I watched in horror as their tongues mingled for a good ten seconds. "Don't mind me. We like to French kiss," he said, laughing.

"We brought you stuffed shells." I handed him the aluminum plate, feigning nonchalance though I was still reeling from this spectacle.

"Oh, thank you!" He gleefully peeled off the foil, got a fork from the sink— there were no clean ones—and started eating them cold. "You don't have to keep feeding me," he said as he chewed, referring to the pepperoni pizza I'd brought the time before.

"We figured you're probably not eating much," Mom said.

Apparently, he wasn't doing much of anything. He wore the same white—well, now gray—shirt and ripped jeans, his stubble now a beard.

"How are you handling all of this, Josh?" Mom gently asked.

"Not very well, to be perfectly honest." Spearing a shell, Josh sucked it into his mouth whole. He opened the fridge for a carton of milk, releasing a foul smell. Spoiled meat? Even Red howled from the back room.

While Josh rummaged through the cupboards for a clean glass, Mom shot me a tortured look, her sharp olfactory senses assaulted by the stench.

"Do you have friends you can talk to?" she inquired, still grimacing behind his back.

"A few."

According to Rachel, his only friends were the drug dealers across the hall.

Locating what looked like the last clean coffee mug, Josh filled it with milk. "Just don't feel like talking." As he reached for the fridge handle to return the carton, we both held our breath.

Josh and Mom's dialog receded as I surveyed the room—sink brimming with dirty dishes, scorched pans on the stove. Empty carry-out containers and used paper plates on the white pedestal table. Dust, dog hair, and dog food nuggets littered the usually pristine linoleum floor. Even the two large windows, with their airy white floor-length Ikea curtains, were smudged and streaked, probably with Red's slobber.

It hurt to see Rachel's kitchen like this. Though outdated, she'd transformed it into a lovely room, with dove gray walls, white cabinets with whimsical glass pulls, and cobalt accents—fruit bowl, chair cushions, and paintings of fluid betta fish. Her kitchen had always struck me as an oasis after entering the rundown building and ascending the dusty stairs.

I had told Josh we were looking for Rachel's liquid silver bracelet and would need to search the whole place. A gift from Perry in our early marriage, I'd rediscovered the elegant multistrand bracelet in my jewelry box, slipped it on, and kept it on until Rachel requested it. It was the one piece I hated to part with, and now I wanted it back. I did not mention our interest in her Apple iPad, which had mysteriously disappeared. Nor that we were ultimately after her journals. Maybe I was paranoid, but I thought he might realize they contained incriminating information about their drug usage and destroy them.

We started in Rachel's room, the most likely place to find both the journals and bracelet. I sorted through the snarl of earrings and necklaces in her two jewelry boxes, with no luck. When we lifted her mattress, out slid the iPad. I set it aside, pleased to recover this gift Perry and I had bought for Rachel's twenty-eighth birthday four months earlier. We peered under her bed. Searched the drawer and cabinet of her nightstand. I even checked behind the headboard, thinking she might have attached a utility holder there to hide her journal, but found nothing. The art cabinet on rollers, with its multiple shelves and deep side pockets, was also empty.

Next, we searched the storage room, where we found Red reclining in a giant crate. He looked up with pleading chocolate eyes, giving his tail a demi-wag while emitting the faintest whine before dropping his dejected head. We rummaged through a tall walnut armoire and two storage chests, to no avail. Standing on a chair, I groped the top shelf of the closet, feeling all four corners as I had in her room. All I found was dust.

We struck out in the kitchen and living room, as well.

Before leaving, we rechecked Rachel's studio. In the closet, I glimpsed what looked like the corner of a canvas. Heart pounding, I pulled out a beautiful botanical painting Phil and I had missed. What a find!

But where were the journals?

The bracelet was replaceable. The diaries were not. I was missing a huge slice—the last three telling years—of Rachel's life.

This was insane. Her mind was gone. She was gone. Piecing her life together wasn't going to bring her back. But her latest journal might reveal why she had started using again. Why she took cocaine, a drug she never used, when she was newly in love and seemed happy. These questions gnawed at me. At home, I re-combed her room. Rifled through storage bins in our basement. I wondered if Josh had already jettisoned the journals. I pictured him in his white shirt and knee-gashed jeans tossing them, one by one, in the blue dumpster in the apartment parking lot.

I was beyond obsessed.

On November sixteenth, the day before Rachel's memorial service, I received an out-of-state call from an unknown number. Struggling to finish my eulogy, I did not have the time or emotional wherewithal to speak to anyone.

I don't know what compelled me to pick up.

It was Josh's mom, whom I had never met, calling to offer her condolences and ask if she could attend the memorial service. Apparently, she and Rachel had just been getting acquainted via email when Josh broke the tragic news. An attorney practicing in Virginia, she would book a morning flight to Rhode Island with a return flight in the afternoon. Before hanging up, she asked if I wanted her to forward Rachel's email correspondences.

I accepted, little knowing it was an answer to my prayer. Miraculously, in one of the emails, Rachel, herself, solved the enigma of the missing journals:

*Sent: Sat, Sep 1, 2012 2:00 pm*

*Subject: Re: Something you might consider*

*Sorry about the delayed reply . . . it's been kind of nuts for us with my health insurance drama, Josh trying to sign up for a course, an emergency vet trip, and me starting to waitress a few shifts for the first time in years (I'm actually on disability for my neuropathy). Writing used to be my passion. I have stacks of journals, many with poetry. Then about three years ago, I started fiddling with an old set of paints and found I couldn't put them down. I've been painting rather than journaling ever since. I'd love to send you one as a gift. I've included a link to an online album done rather shoddily, with a crappy camera, but it'd give you an idea ☺.*
*—Rachel*

I could finally exhale. At least the journals were not lost. Certain things about Rachel's final years I would never know. However, had she kept writing, my walls would not be graced with her paintings. I would not think of her multiple times a day as I passed this or that lovely canvas or watercolor. Years later, recalling how Rachel had painted feverishly in her final years, lavishly gifting her work to family and friends, I would wonder if it were deliberate—Rachel's way, as it were, of remaining with us.

# DIABULIMIA

I DON'T REMEMBER DECORATING that Christmas. I do recall displaying the two tri-fold memory boards. After the memorial service, I leaned them against the living room wall, meaning to return the photographs to their respective albums and boxes. Instead, I unfolded the boards. Maybe I liked the semblance of order, Rachel's short, chaotic life portrayed in perfect categories—birth, siblings, school, family trips, graduation, prom. The smiling faces, reminding me of sweeter days. In any case, I couldn't bring myself to break down the boards. So, I left them there, grateful no one said a word, even as days turned into months.

Sympathy cards replaced Christmas greetings that year. One envelope weighed more than the rest. As I opened it, a folded paper fell in my lap. It was a letter on heavy-gauge stationery from the Rhode Island Foundation, informing me that in Rachel's memory, and per the recommendation of her dear friend Amanda, a grant from the Ophelia Fund[1] had been awarded to Dr. Ann Goebel-Fabbri, a clinical psychologist at the Joslin Diabetes Center in Boston, Massachusetts, for her research on diabulimia.

Dia-what?

Rachel had met Amanda in the Partial Hospitalization Program for Eating Disorders[2] at Hasbro Children's Hospital at age sixteen. Their bond was instant and lasting.

Though warmed by Amanda's gesture, I wasn't sure how this research pertained to Rachel, who had diabetes and bulimia. Maybe diabulimia referred to people with both illnesses. Whatever it meant, it gave me chills. Merging the two words made it sound almost diabolical. I resolved to research it soon.

I drifted in a fog of grief through the holidays. Not smelling roasting turkey or pine trees, blind to colored lights, deaf to Christmas carols and New Year horns. As I floated, that word—diabulimia—bobbed in my subconscious until a disquieting thought emerged: What if Amanda knew something about Rachel that I did not? I rushed to my study, barely seated before opening a Google browser. My fingers flew over the keys as I typed "diabulimia," gasping when I received 77,800 hits.

I learned that diabulimia is an eating disorder (ED) unique to people with type 1 diabetes, primarily adolescent girls and young women, who purposely reduce or skip their insulin to lose weight. When they "binge" on forbidden foods without adequate insulin, their blood sugars soar, causing their bodies to "purge" excess sugar and calories through urination.[3]

I was stunned. I knew Rachel was under-dosing her insulin. She had told me in her early twenties, shortly after moving out; however, I foolishly thought she was the only one.

"I hardly ever take my short-acting insulin anymore," Rachel interjected into a casual conversation we were having one day when she came over for dinner.

I took her insulin manipulation as another twisted act of independence. Since moving into her own apartment, Rachel also told me she went braless and smoked indoors.

"How can you just stop taking insulin? What happens when you do?" I looked up from chopping baby cucumbers and a yellow pear for a spinach salad.

"I suppose my blood sugars run high," she said, avoiding my eyes while setting out dinner plates like she was dealing cards.

"Rachel, that's dangerous! I can't believe you'd do that! And what do you mean by you *suppose?*"

Head lowered, she began intently folding napkins, placing one beside each plate. "Well, I rarely check my blood sugars anymore."

"What? Then how do you know how much insulin to take?" My tone finally forced her to look up.

"I just guess." Her blond hair was pulled into a haphazard bun. Expertly outlined with bronze pencil, her blue eyes popped. She was a beautiful girl.

My heart started thumping. Abandoning my task, I walked toward her. "Rachel, that's crazy! You're asking for serious trouble! Blindness, kidney failure, amputation! This is nothing to fool around with."

"I don't care. If I took all the insulin they prescribed, I'd be a whale." She slammed down forks and knives at each place, sporadically clinking the plates.

"I don't believe it. Even if it were true, there are ways to control your weight without hurting yourself. You can exercise, cut back on sugar, or cut it out completely—"

Sighing profoundly, she said, "I've tried, over and over. It isn't that simple. I want to feel good in my skin *now.*" Her voice was calm, resolute. She held my stare. "I don't care what happens later."

"You say that now because you're young, but you will care when the time comes. When you find a man or a profession you really love, you'll want to be healthy. When you give birth, you'll want healthy eyes to see your newborns and healthy feet to run after your toddlers."

For a moment, her eyes were large and contemplative. Then she vigorously shook her head as if trying to rid her mind of the images my admonishments evoked. "No, Mom. You don't get it."

"I get it. I just don't agree. You're taking the easy way out. Compromising your future to feel good now."

Over the next year, we had similar talks. They always ended in quarrels and tears.

Suspecting that diabulimia, also known as "insulin restriction," had more than a little to do with my daughter's demise, I could not read the facts on my screen fast enough. I discovered that diabulimia affects eleven to thirty-nine percent of adolescent and young women with type 1 diabetes.[4] However, since the disorder is hidden, researchers believe that the percentage of females who practice it is much higher.[5]

My astonishment grew as I read story after story on the Internet of young females who also secretly skipped or stopped taking insulin altogether, thinking they, too, were the only ones. Though aware of the related health problems, all the women cared about was weight loss.[6]

Moving on to academic journals, I learned that as common as EDs are among the general population, people with diabetes are 2.4 times more likely to develop them than nondiabetics,[7] for numerous reasons. First, their strict diets require such extreme focus on food that eating-disordered thoughts and behaviors often follow.[8]

Rachel had to eat a prescribed number of meals and snacks containing a specific number of carbohydrates at specified times. I recalled her fixation on nutrition labels. She had never liked grocery shopping, but after her diagnosis, list in hand, she never missed market day. Pushing her own cart, she scoured the shelves for sugarless products and those with low carb counts. In any given aisle, I would find her, head down, studying the labels on soup cans, cookie packages, or frozen dinners. "The trick," she told me, "is finding the lowest values. The fewer the carbs, the more I can eat."

Weight gain related to insulin usage may be another reason young females with diabetes develop EDs. Prior to their diagnosis, most girls are hyperglycemic and, therefore, very thin, which pleases them;[9] however, once they start taking their prescribed insulin, they generally gain ten and a half pounds.[10,11] Rachel had made this connection after gaining ten pounds, yet multiple doctors had shot her down.[12]

"If insulin doesn't cause weight gain, why are so many diabetics fat?" Rachel pointedly asked our latest endocrinologist, a petite woman with diabetes herself, whose A-line denim dress could not conceal her own heaviness.

"There's no evidence to substantiate that," she snapped.

This was our fourth endocrinologist. The first two had relocated their practices to different states, while the third dropped Rachel for noncompliance. Until this gaffe, I had hoped my daughter would relate to this female doctor with diabetes and the relationship would last.

Excess weight distresses most preteen and teenage girls who tend to obsess over their looks, but especially those with type 1 diabetes, who often think poorly of themselves because of their illness.[13] In 1998, pop culture's fixation on the tall, thin female physique probably didn't help. Girls with diabetes who felt they didn't stack up secretly fought back, many discovering the "dirty little secret" about insulin. If taking their required dose resulted in extra weight, underdosing it did just the opposite—allowed them to shed pounds quickly and painlessly.

Though a convenient way to control weight, the effects of diabulimia can be devastating. First, diabulimics find that, like any ED, the behavior does not die easily. Habitual insulin restriction only gets worse; adolescent girls tend to deprive their bodies of more and more insulin as they grow into young adults.[14] Practiced over long periods, the behavior becomes ingrained, often defying treatment.[15]

Also disturbing were the many studies showing that people who restrict insulin are more likely to have poor control of their blood sugar,[16] resulting in serious diabetes-related health problems. Short-term complications include hyperglycemia, infections, hospitalizations, and ER visits, as well as regular episodes of diabetic ketoacidosis (DKA).[17]

DKA is a serious condition that all Rachel's endocrinologists had warned her to avoid. Whenever this subject arose, smiles vanished, brows creased, and doctors spoke with deepened tones as they explained the gravity of allowing one's blood sugars to remain elevated for sustained periods. This causes the body to burn fat for fuel, releasing toxins called "ketones" into the blood. "Rachel, you'll know you're experiencing DKA if you feel thirsty, dizzy, tired, and compelled to urinate," her doctors had explained. "If this happens, call me immediately. If you feel shortness of breath, sharp stomach pains, or you start to vomit, call nine-one-one."[18]

Equally alarming are the long-term health complications that can occur sooner than expected among people who restricted their insulin. High blood sugars over long periods can cause heart attack, infertility, retinopathy (retina disease, resulting in partial or total vision loss), neuropathy (nerve damage), and kidney damage, among other health problems.[19]

Most distressing is the premature death rate among diabulimic women, who tend to die thirteen years younger than non-diabulimics, according to a long-term study.[20]

And these were just the physical effects of diabulimia. The other dreadful dimension to this disorder I would discover mainly from reading Rachel's journals is its psychological effects—the horrible thoughts and feelings that assault young women who know they are deliberating destroying body organs through insulin omission.

As my knowledge grew, so did my anger. With so much at stake, why had not one diabetes clinician told me that my adolescent daughter was a prime candidate for diabulimia? This research wasn't new. Researchers had known since the 1980s, fifteen years before Rachel's diagnosis, that young females with diabetes were secretly shorting their insulin to lose weight, a practice that could cause severe, sometimes irreversible health problems.[21,22] I understood that it took time for practitioners to catch up with research. However, these studies concerned a fragile population, adolescent girls. Diabulimia would torture many girls for decades, shaving years off their lives. Shouldn't there have been a push to inform parents?

Drawn to the memory boards, I crouched before them. Studying the photographs, I noticed a startling progression. Rachel was all smiles in her childhood photos, posing with Ryan and Matt, but as an adolescent, she looked lost. Of the six photographs, she was not smiling in one. In her young adult photos, a brew of smiles and frowns, she looked tough. What had happened? And how much of it was related to diabulimia? Only her journals would tell.

April 1–November 8, 1999

# "This Journal
## Never Gets Me in Trouble"

Gently falling snow in early February garbs our yard in white, frosting fence posts and trees. Snow-dredged deck rails glitter in the morning sun. I watch dancing flakes, trying to take solace in this scene. But Rachel's absence echoes through my heart. Since her voice and laugh have ceased, the silence is ungodly.

As I brew coffee, her journals call from the dark storage cabinet in her room. They tug like an ocean tide. I long to start reading. I want to learn what happened to my daughter, and not just for me. No doubt, Rachel's adult diaries are a trove of information. Surely, her honest, articulate records on diabulimia will educate parents who have teenage daughters with diabetes, as well as young females grappling with this serious disorder right now.

But it's only been three months.

Mom's voice—maybe in a year—halts me.

I have not even started to heal. I cannot speak. I bob on a boat fifty yards from shore, separated from family, friends, even God—or so it feels. My prayers end in deep sobs. *You took back my baby girl!* If I read the journals too soon, I'll float farther out to sea.

I compromise with myself: I'll read the benign Everything Journals, the nine notebooks Rachel composed between ages fourteen and sixteen before she got into trouble. Written about her first love, I expect these to contain the melodramatic musings of a lovesick girl, which is fine. What I need most right now is to hear my daughter's voice without getting burned. My research will have to wait.

Kneeling before the storage cabinet, I locate Rachel's collection of adolescent journals and carry them downstairs to the living room. A steaming mug of Starbucks Sumatra awaits me on the coffee table where I lay the journals. I take a sip. Leafing through them and locating Everything Journals I, II, and III, I settle into the sofa.

I open the first black notebook, delighted but not surprised to see its pages edged with vivid flowers, artistic embellishments I will find throughout this set. Rachel decorated her hand-made notes the same way. On the front page, she'd printed the following in her careful hand:

*This is dedicated to Paul.*
*You gave me the motivation to sit down and write it*
*And I'm not going to hold anything back.*
*I'll probably hold my breath when I hand it to you.*

So Paul was the reason Rachel had started journaling again. She had kept a journal from the time she was eight but had lost interest for several years. It was after meeting Paul on a skiing trip she'd taken in January with her father and brothers at age fourteen that she had picked it back up. I take a sip of coffee, then turn the page.

### April 1, 1999

*I just got off the phone with you. This'll seem strange, but I feel worse now than I did before we spoke. I can't deal with the surface talking we do. I feel like I'm hiding so much from you, and that's why I can't talk to you in a relaxed way.*

*I wish you could know what I'm going through. It's like I'm creating this false impression that everything's okay, but it's not, and I don't want to be untruthful to you. Paul, I feel so disconnected from myself, and I can't explain how much that disturbs me. It's a battle within myself. Should I let you know what's going on? This is where I get messed up. If I tell you, you worry. If I don't tell you, I worry I'm drifting away from you. I want you to really under-stand, but CAN you? The answer to that question scares me because that's what determines how long we will last.*

### April 2, 1999—8:54 a.m. (FIRST PERIOD . . . history)

*This journal never gets me in trouble . . . the teachers always think I'm just taking notes on their classes. You're going to ♡ the letter I put in the mailbox for you this morning. I hope it lifts your mood some. I was thinking of how bad it must suck to be sent back to that restrictive boarding school. The only way I can help is to write you every day & send that tape to you.*

That little sneak. A smile tiptoes across my face. I shake my head. I can't believe Rachel brought this journal to school, openly writing to Paul under the guise of taking notes. My stars, she was gutsy!

### April 3, 1999

*I've listened to Wonderwall so many times last night and this morning. It seems like this is our song. So sad, but it relates so well. Maybe you're going to be the one that saves me. Maybe.*

*Songs are kind of like musical timelines. I mean, I could hear this song when I was 90 and still remember you. My mother always told me when I was young—"Rachel, you never forget your first love." I want to get over this confusion and be with you forever. I want you to be the one to help me through difficult times. I want to dance with you at my senior prom. I want to go to college with you. I want to marry you, build a home together, travel, and see beautiful places with you. I want to have children with you one day and later grow old with you. Maybe you're gonna be the one that saves me.*

I'd let the first Wonderwall reference slide. Now my brows rise at seeing these lyrics a second time in the same entry. I rise to refill my coffee. Save Rachel? Save her from what? Cupping my hot mug, I remind myself Rachel is fourteen. She's also overdramatic and in love for the first time. This probably means nothing.

### April 6, 1999

*I'm not sure, but I think I am in love with you. I just can't describe how I feel. No—no. I have to try. I feel totally motivated. I feel total joy, like I'm overflowing with happiness, like I want to share a piece of it with every person on the planet who feels despair. I want to tell them to have hope. I don't know why people say you fall in love. I feel completely high. Everything around me is beautiful. I feel alive. I feel like my heart is on fire for you. Because of our love, I feel like I am totally immune to anything bad. I love you so much. I wish I'd never said I love you before, wish so many people didn't throw the word around, so you could understand how fully I mean it. I have to tell you. Tell you I need you. Tell you I love you.*

My throat cramps at Rachel's description of love. I had not expected such strong feelings or powerful language from a fourteen-year-old girl. I was about to learn it was a mistake to underestimate adolescents. Not only were they capable of sophisticated thoughts and feelings, they were not afraid to act on them.

### April 9, 1999—3RD period

*I'm still cracking up! The funniest thing just happened. Me + Dee were out there walking to class, and it is so nice outside today—feels like summer. So I was like, c'mon—skip with me. So she sarcastically was like, "alright!" and tripped over these huge shoes she wears + fell in some mud. I was like, "Damn, Dee—skip class—not skip and fall."*

*Demetria is like a female Kramer from Seinfeld. She's the farthest thing from graceful, but I ♡ her just the same.*

*Hey—totally changing subjects—I was thinking about our first kiss. I need to explain why I was wearing sunglasses! See, bright lights give me really bad headaches, so I have to wear them to not be miserable. Sometimes I don't need them, but at the mountain—it was terrible. Anyway—there you go.*

### April 11, 1999—between 11:15–11:20, I think.

*I'm sitting up in my bed*
*writing by candlelight*
*I've got those pains in*
*my stomach again.*
*I wish I could hear your voice*
*to soothe them.*
*It's worse this time than it was before.*
*I could try to play your*
*voice over in my mind*
*to concentrate on it*
*and picture what you'd say*
*but the thought of doing that*
*makes me feel like crying.*
*My stomach kills*
*I think I'm going to take a shot*
*just a little*

*I mean, they'd never know*
*I don't have to tell them.*
*I am so tired of everybody*
*taking everything away from me.*
*I am taking this for myself.*
*It's times like this that I can't*
*hear His voice.*
*or yours, for that matter.*
*Good night, Paul.*

What is this? Setting down my mug, I remain on the edge of my seat, studying these lines. In this poem, penned by candlelight, Rachel confesses something to Paul that she both does and does not want him to understand. Why does her stomach kill? Why does she inject insulin without testing her blood—and why just a little? Whatever she's doing, she's hiding. A chill climbs my spine. Surely, she was not restricting her insulin—diabulimics took less, not more. Furthermore, Rachel had told me she had begun this dangerous practice in her early twenties. "I hardly take my NPH anymore," she had said after moving out. I read on, scanning page after page for more clues. Not finding any, I "pin" these strange lines, allowing the narrative of Rachel's first love to draw me back in.

### April 13, 1999—8:20 a.m.

*I fell asleep writing this last night. When I woke back up, it was two a.m. The moonlight was sifting through the blinds. I really don't feel like myself. You're so perfect for me, and I was thinking last night that it was hard for me to believe this isn't only a dream. These doubts are a part of me that I really want to change for only you. So . . . I've got my mind made up now. Tonight when you call, I'm going to tell you we're not going to talk until I've overcome this.*

*I'm sorry to say that this is an obstacle you really can't help me with. All I can ask is that you wait for me. That is so much to ask because I've already caused you such hurt. I just have to tell myself that by staying with you & jerking you around, I'm hurting you more than I would be by just explaining exactly what's up. I mean, either way, you're going to get hurt, and that's why I'm so hesitant. Aside from that, do you really even want to be aware of the bad parts . . . Ugh, I am not okay, Paul.*

**April 14, 1999—11:48 a.m. (Wednesday)**

Dear Paul,

I've made a decision. I'm going to keep writing to you even if you don't write back. I mean, for all I know, there's just some problem with the mail—not necessarily with you. I know it lifts your mood to get letters, so I'll do it for that reason too. I doubt you want me to stop. I'm so worried about you. For all I know, you could be in a hospital somewhere.

I won't stop writing. The day I stop writing you is the day I stop loving you, and I can't picture that happening. I want to keep you close to me, but it seems like you're pushing me away.

I'm losing sleep over this. What can I do? I pray for you all the time. I know that helps. Maybe I'll go check the mailbox after school & find a pile of letters from you. Who knows? It's in God's hands because I put it there. Because I know it's safest there.

I'm thinking about being baptized. I wasn't as a child—and I don't believe those count. It has to be my choice. I never told you my testimony. In fact, I've never told anyone. It's only between me + God. I'll tell you someday.

Well, love. It's midnight. I need to sleep so I can get up for church tomorrow. I love you.

Thank you for being there for me. I have a sure feeling we're going to go far. If you're up to it as much as I am. (Don't worry—I already know your response to that.) (And I love you for it.)

always,
Rachel


Hold me
I love your neck next to mine
listening to you breathe.
hands that always reach out to help me
holding them through mittens
on ski lifts that ended too soon

so many phone calls
till the early hours before dawn
when you were softest
I want you back again

**11:30 p.m.**

*I have to say . . . I am so disappointed in you. Are you not writing because you think you have nothing to say? You cannot possibly be aware of the damage you are doing.*

**May 1, 1999—11:44 p.m.**

*I come alive at night. During the day, I feel almost like I'm sleepwalking. So far, sleeping pills + you are the only things I have found that make me tired. You'd better not put me to sleep in Boston. Speaking of that, my dad forgot to call your mom. We can't be too mad at him—he's got ADD.*

**May 5, 1999**

*Dear Paul,*

*I'm in 3RD-period science. I just got back from the nurse's office for being low. I hate that. It's so embarrassing. I have to lean up against the wall to walk sometimes (this was one of them). And I always worry I'll fall down the stairs. But I don't want anyone walking me down there, like I'm helpless or something, you know? Sometimes I have to—other times someone nice will see me + bring me there.*

With a pang, I recall Rachel sharing similar incidents with me of nearly fainting at school for having failed to eat her snack at the proper time.

"Why wouldn't you eat your snack?" I asked, certain her teachers had all been informed of her diabetes diagnosis.

"The kids stare at me when I eat in class."

"Can't you do it quietly, eat things like a peanut butter sandwich or grapes and cheese?"

"I've tried. They hear the paper crackle, and they smell the peanut butter."

"Rachel, food is part of your medicine. I don't want you collapsing in the hall. Wouldn't that draw a lot more attention than eating your snack in class?"

She shrugged, her overcast expression suggesting it was problematic either way.

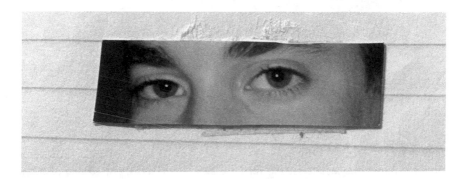

## May 8, 1999—12:19 a.m. (Thursday)

*after "quiz" phone call*

so . . . I take it you don't like ketchup??

and please, you actually mean to tell me that the thought of sex has never entered your mind? Give me a break.

## May 19, 1999

Dear Paul,

For some reason, I just can't let go and love you. This is probably the root of all my problems. I'm scared. Scared I'll be hurt. Afraid I'll become so attached to you that I won't be able to handle it if I lose you. I've been hurt a lot by this in the past. I don't want to talk about it, but just know that it was painful. I know what you'll say. You'll tell me you'd never leave me. You're right, you would never intentionally hurt me, but time changes things.

Let's go back to try to figure out where it all started. Those first few times at the mountain. Everything was perfect, no strings attached. I think it began with that first kiss. I felt nothing inside for you. I did when you held me on the lifts . . . but nothing when we kissed. I'm so sorry. I could see in your eyes that you probably did. When I got that first letter & you told me you loved me—that's when I knew I was in trouble. With the following letters, it only got worse. There was a slight pressure for me to return a feeling to you. I didn't realize this at first, but I do now. I was very afraid of letting you down. I figured that as time passed, my feelings would catch up to yours. I was wrong. Your feelings increased rapidly. Mine at a much slower pace. Still, I felt that pressure. When I saw you in Boston, I thought that would make it alright. I was wrong again.

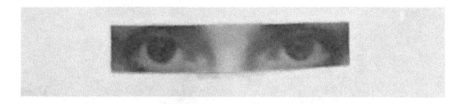

### May 28, 1999—12:23 p.m.

*So we come to the last page. My father took me out last night to buy another notebook. So I won't stop writing.*

*He can be an excellent father. He sure was last night. We got in the car. I felt numb. I had cried hysterically in front of him earlier. I saw the moon. I closed my eyes. He started playing music + it was that piano tape we were listening to on the way back from Boston. I cried when I thought I had nothing left to cry. Every single thing I saw or did reminded me of you.*

*He took me to Newport to walk around. All I could see was us walking around there. Dad was really sweet. He got me ice cream for dinner. That's a first, Paul. I'm wondering if we couldn't meet this summer. I had so many plans. For one thing, I was going to get tickets today for us to see Busta in concert on June 26. No, I'm not trying to bribe you. I just hope that I can see you this summer. Maybe by then, things will be better. We tried to progress things too fast during those first ski trips. We need to slow down. Why couldn't we just see each other for fun this summer—not for anything so heavy or serious? I suppose it all lies in me. Pray for me. I love you so much. I want to be able to let go + love you without worry. Who knows what might happen? So now I'm the one asking—will I ever see you again?*

My daughter's eyes stare at me from a cropped photo taped to the top of the page. It is like the photo of Paul's eyes on the previous page, only his eyes appear soft, guileless. Rachel's blue jewels hold back. They harbor too many secrets.

### May 30, 1999

*Memories, written as they come to me . . .*

**10:39,**
*one minute before our secret nightly call.*
*the rose lady*
*Ryan sliding down the mountain*
*hitting Matt with a snowball (where it counts!)*
*falling on each other in powdery snow when trying to hug*
*arm wrestling in the lodge*
*shivering in Boston*
*the moon—your promise to watch over me*
*Wonderwall*
*The pillow I made you*
*letters upon letters*
*soothing my stomach*
*first love*
*last love*

*Let's keep adding to that list.*

Heart throbbing, I close Rachel's third journal. I hardly know the girl inhabiting these books, who loved so fiercely and wrote so beautifully. And I had thought these adolescent journals would be mush. My cheeks burn at how wrong I was.

# "I HAVEN'T BEEN MYSELF IN A LONG TIME"

I AWAKE TO A heavy snowfall, the sky gray and unfriendly. Angry flakes slice the sky like spears while the howling wind whips snow-tufted bushes and tree branches. Except for the tire tracks of Phil's truck, our driveway is pure white. Perfect weather to cozy up and continue reading Rachel's journals. I pour a cup of coffee, grab a clementine and a handful of walnuts, and head to the living room. Locating Everything Journals IV, V, and VI, three weighty black volumes, I settle into the sofa, pulling an afghan over my lap. I will read these today and finish the last three tomorrow.

### July 18, 1999

So I say goodbye to my Love for another month. It's hard, and I feel heavy. I hate going through this.

I love his back. He loves my touch, and that works out well because I love to touch him. So I gave him a back rub. I held him for a change, and I sang to him. I laid my head in his lap. He gave me his shirt for a pillow; then he leaned down and kissed me.

"Would you dance with me if it started to rain?"

Ryan's sitting next to me. He's reading my words as I write them. He said, "Do you know you make germs when you kiss?"

### July 19, 1999

Well, it was a wicked funny movie. Not exactly romantic. So I can't understand why Paul would choose this time and place to make a move on me. Never mind the fact that I had 3 people sitting to the left of me. He really should've known better. That sort of disappoints me. Okay, it's not that I'm not ready for this. It's just that type of thing shouldn't be rushed. I know he was thinking, "Well, I'm not going to see her for another month. I should take my chance when I have it." That's just wrong. He should've waited for better circumstances. Paul always seems to want more and more. He kisses me so much it's not as special anymore. He says "I love you" so much it's losing meaning. Letters are identical. I hate the distance. Hate it, hate it, hate it. I can't hang on much longer. I want to be released. I need to feel free. I want to get back to myself. I'm happy solo. I don't want to lose Paul, though. I might never get him back. I also know that when we're together, I'd never think of leaving him. I'm holding the distance responsible for all these problems.

### August 3, 1999—8:32 p.m.

I'm in Florida with Dad and the boys, sitting in the bed of a hotel room that is identical to the one we stayed in while we were skiing, but no one seems to notice or care but me.

Called Mom a little while ago, mainly to see if I'd gotten a letter. That's six days without hearing from him.

Maybe it's because he thinks he has nothing to say, but I still want to hear from him. I feel ignored, pushed away, though that's probably not the case. He doesn't mean it, but it hurts.

It hurts to even think that the silence might hold some unspoken meaning. My fear? That he doesn't feel the same.

The only reason that this is increasingly worrying me is because I'm finding that I feel more and more for him every day.

Me
with my broken,
blue eyes.
Me
with my blond hair
around my shoulders
sheltering insecurities
Me
with my hesitant hands
working, writing, clenching,
they only fit with his

I love when summer trees shelter roads, like green roofs.
I love to hear children sing.
I have no control for ice cream.

*I love the color of wine, and the blue of Paul's eyes.*
*I love looking down on a golden city, as a plane takes off at night.*
*I love how people speak around a campfire.*
*I love the expansiveness of the sky.*
*I love to find the perfect words.*
*I like crisp hotel beds.*
*I have to stop and look when I see a waterfall.*
*I feel alive when I'm skiing down a mountain*
*so fast I could crash. I love that rush.*
*I love the first few tender notes of a really good song.*
*I love the brief fury of a thunderstorm.*
*I enjoy being awake when everyone else is asleep.*
*I love to be wrapped in the arms of someone who needs me.*
*I love summer nights with family.*
*I could eat Italian food every night.*
*I love to give presents I know people will love*
*& seeing that look on their face.*

My eyes sting, beginning to fill as Rachel's poetry conjures images of her. I can almost smell her shampoo. Hear her plucky laugh. The gray sky and howling wind don't help. I rise to wipe steady tears, the ache in my throat monstrous. Didn't I ask for this by opening her journals?

Subj: lots
Date: 8/24/99 11:44:51 AM Pacific Daylight Time
From: OGPaul
To: Rachbaby15

this is a long repetitive email--feel free to stop reading it at any time. there is a sentence at the bottom. i love you, i love you, i love you, i love you, i love you, i love you, i love you, i love you, i love you, i love you, i love you, i love you, i love you, i love you, i love you, i love you, i love you, i love you, i love you, i love you, i love you, i love you, i love you, i love you, i love you, i love you, i love you, i love you, i love you, i love you, i love you, i love you, i love you, i love you, i love you, i love you, i love you, i love you, i love you, i love you, i love you, i love you, i love you, i love you, i love you, i love you, i love you, i love you, i love you, i love you, i love you, i love you, i love you, i love you, i love you, i love you, i love you, i love you, i love you, i love you, i love you, i love you, i love you, i love you, i love you, i love you, i love you, i love you, i love you, i love you, i love you, i love you, i love you, i love you, i love you, i love you, i love you, i love you, i love you, i love you, i love you, i love you, i love you, i love you, i love you, i love you, i love you, i love you, i love you, i love you, i love you, i love you, i love you, i love you, i love you, i love you, i love you, i love you, i love you, i love you, i love you, i love you, i love you, i love you, i love you, i love you, i love you, i love you, i love you, i love you, i love you, i love you, i love you, i love you, i love you, i love you, i love you, i love you, i love you, i love you, i love you, i love you, i love you, i love you, i love you, i love you, i love you, i love you, i love you, i love you, i love you, i love you, i love you, i love you, i love you, i love you, i love you, i love you, i love you, i love you, i love you, i love you, i love you, i love you, i love you, i love you, i love you, i love you, i love you, i love you, i love you, i love you, i love you, i love you, i love you, i love you, i love you, i love you, i love you, i love you, i love you, i love you, i love you, i love you, i love you, i love you, i love you, i love you, i love you, i love you, i love you, i love you, i love you, i love you, i love you, i love you, i love you, i love you, i love you, i love you, i love you, i love you, i love you, i love you, i love you, i love you, i love you, i love you. I love you.

## August 29, 1999

I need to write tonight. Because I don't have anyone to talk to, and I don't know how to talk to anyone. Especially Paul. I don't know how to tell him. I don't know if he cares.

He's very unresponsive when it comes to real problems.

And then he always has to go.

Lately, whenever he has to go, I feel my heart drop about ten stories, and it was already low to begin with ☹.

He asked me tonight if I was his. The truth is, I'm not. . . . because I haven't been myself in a long time.

## September 15, 1999

I had to have bloodwork done. I don't know if u know, Paul, but I am so scared of bloodwork!! Anyway this bitch really REALLY hurt my damn arm. I couldn't *move it for about 2 hrs. The point is, you couldn't be there, but I had that stu-pid letter jacket and it really helped. I just held onto it real tight. I love wearing that jacket. That way, everybody who sees me, knows I am YOUR GIRL!!*

*Speaking of your jacket, today I was in the car with my mom and she said:*

*"You know, Rachel, I came into your room earlier this morning . . . and I saw you sleeping with Paul's jacket. It was just really sweet."*

*Then she said: "I never thought about it before, but I guess what you two have must be really hard."*

*Imagine that—I was really touched.*

The sight had moved me, the memory prompting more tears. Usually, Rachel's door was closed. That day it had been left wide open, revealing her sleeping soundly with Paul's maroon letter jacket wound around her, as if its cream-colored sleeves could replace his arms. Wiping my eyes, I continued reading:

### October 27, 1999—10:00 am

*So now he goes out with someone who is a restrictive bulimic. real nice. I ate something that was nine carbs this morning and I feel so guilty. I feel fat.*

Restrictive bulimic? I stop, pulse quickening. She cannot have meant that she was restricting insulin. I reread the line. Surely, she misused this term. Picked it up on the Internet or in some magazine. She did that—read things, incorporating new words into her vocabulary. I read faster now, flipping page after page, my heart nearly halting when I read this entry:

### November 8, 1999

*Shit, I have to go to the doctor's today. What if they find out? I need those doctors off my back—I want to deal with this myself. Something's going on behind my back. Dr. Abraham[23] must be warning the doctors because this appointment is before the scheduled three-month one. What the hell—what happened to patient-doctor confidentiality?*

*I know I don't know what I'm doing. My blood sugar is two-hundred-fifty all the time, and I'm tired. I want stability, but not at the price of getting overweight. I tried a different way of getting rid of the food yesterday. It didn't work. I don't know what I did wrong. I'm worried. I don't want anybody to find out because no one actually realizes how serious this has gotten, but it's working. I am losing weight. At the cost of my health, I am making progress. The fact is, and this is the bottom line, that if I'm overweight, even by a little bit, I am not happy or at peace. So, I'd rather do what has to be done, even if it's not good for my disease, to get to the desired weight.*

*These doctors don't get it. They don't see me. They see diabetes. That's all I am to them—the carrier of a disease. Well fuck that because I choose, and I am in control—not the diabetes. I will lie to them if I have to today. I just hope to God that I can pull it off.*

Dear God! When did this start? I glance at the date—November eighth, the day of our emergency endocrinology meeting. Rachel was fifteen. Gut roiling, I rifle through the journals on the coffee table. Finding her very first Everything Journal, I flip to that odd candlelight entry. Rereading it with enlightened eyes, I realize that her "stomach kills" because she had restricted no small amount of insulin. "I got those pains in my stomach again" suggests this was not her first time. The entry date confirms my sickening hunch that Rachel had started cutting back her insulin at fourteen, only months after her diabetes diagnosis.

She had guarded this secret for nine years!

Hand over mouth, I freeze. I should stop right now, close this book and return it to the cabinet with the other Everything Journals, but I cannot put it down. I continue inhaling pages like someone possessed, galloping through romantic entries to learn more about my daughter's illness. I read and read, into the night, Phil snoring softly beside me, and the entire next day; closing one book, I lift another. Sometimes words blur. Removing my glasses, I cry and cry.

With swollen eyes and a lead heart, I return Rachel's adolescent journals to the storage cabinet in her room where the other volumes wait in darkness. These were supposed to be the tame diaries, the ones that could not hurt me. How wrong I had been. About these journals. About everything.

*September 14, 1998—November 8, 1999*
*age fourteen*

# BROKEN

RACHEL AND I SAT side-by-side in an examination room, holding hands while awaiting the results of her blood test. The smell of rubbing alcohol hung in the air. I told her not to worry, but my heart pounded that September afternoon in 1998.

"I fell asleep in English class," Rachel had announced after returning from her first day of high school. Her uncombed dark blond hair hung around her drawn face, and she had circles under her eyes. She was very thin. Granted, she had been active that summer and may have even grown an inch or two. It wasn't until she confessed to drinking two cases of Capri Sun to quench her ungodly thirst that I knew something was wrong.

I immediately called her father. Though he had left four years earlier and our divorce had just been finalized, we still talked daily about our kids.

"Sounds like diabetes," he speculated.

Now, I waited for Doctor Newman, our pediatrician, to quell my fears. Instead, she returned to deliver the news that would change the course of Rachel's, indeed, both of our lives.

"It's diabetes," she said with a wry smile, seemingly pleased by the clean diagnosis.

Dr. Newman had been our kids' pediatrician for eight years since we had moved from Bristol to Middletown. She was fortyish with pale blue eyes, wire-rimmed glasses, and curly red hair she wore in a perpetual ponytail. She dressed in street clothes, her stethoscope draped over her shoulders like a shawl.

"What this means is that Rachel's pancreas stopped working," she explained. As she spoke, she obsessively adjusted her stethoscope. "Her blood sugars are over five hundred, which is dangerously high. A normal blood sugar value is eighty to one-hundred-twenty. Rachel will need to go straight to the hospital to have her sugars stabilized and learn how to manage her diabetes."

Tears streaked our faces as we tried to process this news.

"But how did this happen?" I asked. "How did Rachel get this disease?"

"Type 1 diabetes is genetic. The gene has to be passed down on both sides of your family."

I shuddered, thinking of the van that used to drive over the park grass at Mom's annual family reunions in Milton Junction, Wisconsin, stopping inches away from our picnic tables laden with homemade casseroles and desserts. My sisters, cousins, and I would watch the driver unload and squeakily unfold a wheelchair before carrying out Great Uncle Jack, who had lost half his left leg to diabetes.

"But why did it happen to me?" Rachel pressed, the vein on her brow distended, a sign she was distressed.

"I can't answer that," Dr. Newman said. "I can tell you that diabetes is manageable." She tugged on one, then the other, side of her scope. "It's not like cancer or other life-threatening diseases I diagnose in this office. Through insulin therapy and a proper diet, it can be controlled. Diabetics can live perfectly normal lives."

That's what I'd always heard. The people I knew with type 1 diabetes kept little insulin bottles with orange lids in their fridges and never talked about it. They were middle-aged men.

Rachel was a fourteen-year-old girl. Her experience would be very different.

✦   ✦   ✦

AT THE HOSPITAL ER, a nurse perfunctorily pricked Rachel's index finger. Rachel jumped, her eyes filling. I fought back tears. Swiftly and mechanically, the nurse drew up some insulin and plunged it into Rachel's arm, both our eyes spilling.

That evening, Rachel's dad and brothers visited. As we huddled around Rachel's hospital bed, they peppered her with questions, cracking jokes to make her laugh. After her long, intense day—starting high school in the morning, being diagnosed with diabetes in the afternoon, and hospitalized in the evening—it was nice to see her smile. Why hadn't I tried to cheer her?

The next morning, a middle-aged nurse named Polly conducted the parents' diabetes training. "Rule number one, always wash your hands," she said, scrubbing her hands in Rachel's sink. "Good hygiene curbs infections, which can raise blood sugars. So can illness, stress, and menstruation."

Polly taught us how to perform blood tests using a lancet, a tool with a retractable pin tip that pierced one's skin with a button click. She demonstrated using Rachel's index finger, which I noted was red and swollen from previous punctures. Rachel braced herself for the sharp prick.

Guiding Rachel's bleeding finger to the glucometer, Polly said, "You must cover the entire pad for a true reading, milking your finger if needed."

Head spinning, I looked away.

The glucometer beeped, displaying a neon green number that Polly charted. "When you get home, Rachel, you'll test your blood and record your values in a notebook several times a day. The doctor will need this data to adjust your insulin."

Rachel nodded with blank eyes. I wondered if she was listening as Polly explained the two types of insulin the doctor had ordered. Regular was short-acting, peaking in thirty minutes to cover Rachel's breakfast, and NPH was long-acting, kicking in to cover her snacks and lunch. These could be mixed together in one syringe. She would need shots in the morning and evening and more as time progressed.

Polly finally showed us how to draw up and inject insulin, a process that had more steps and caveats than I would have ever imagined. What if I drew up the wrong dose? Too much insulin could cause Rachel's sugars to plummet, resulting in a coma. Too little could cause her sugars to spike, resulting in serious future health problems.

After our training, Polly gave Rachel the television remote. I received a syringe, vials of Regular and NPH insulin, and an orange on which to practice. My confidence grew with each shot. Needing to know how it felt, I also tested my blood, wincing, as Rachel did, when the lancet bit my finger. The empty syringe that I plunged into my thigh also pinched, but the nurses promised that Rachel's skin would toughen up. She'd get used to shots.

That afternoon, with a nurse watching, I was allowed to test Rachel's blood and inject her insulin. I prayed to still my jittery heart. I did not want to hurt Rachel or, transparent as I was, to reveal my phobia of needles and blood. With a steady hand, I was able to perform these tasks quickly and gently, unlike some nurses who shot the needle like a dart.

On the third day, I was aiming the needle to give Rachel her morning shot when a nurse whisked in. Without saying a word, she took the syringe from me and gave it to Rachel, who held it like a cigarette.

"She's old enough to do this herself," she said.

Rachel and I glanced at each other, and then both swiveled to face her.

"Oh, I assure you, it's okay. I have patients much younger than Rachel who routinely test their blood and administer their own insulin." She fluffed Rachel's pillows. "And they do just fine. Diabetics must learn to manage their own disease, and self-care empowers them."

I was just getting used to giving shots, pleased this was one way I could help. Now this nurse wanted me to stop? Polly had implied that Rachel and I would co-manage her diabetes, take turns doing blood tests and shots. Was this nurse Polly's superior? She sure played the part. I should have asked questions. This was Rachel's health. But the nurse's gesture silenced me. By taking the needle from me and passing it to Rachel, hadn't she ceased all discussion, asserting in that simple act that this was the right and only way?

I would learn too late that self-care, the traditional model, was not the only nor the best method of diabetes care for adolescents. I would read over and over that chronic disease among teens is best managed by parent-adolescent partnerships. Parents' active involvement in blood tests, shots, and record-keeping keeps their teens' blood sugars on track.[24] Youths who manage their own diabetes often cheat on their diets and skip blood tests and shots, resulting in extreme highs and lows that lead to hospitalizations, among other negative consequences.[25]

Self-care pitted us against each other, I realized years later. At a time when Rachel needed me most, we were on opposite teams. She did the grunt work while I was the watchdog. She resented my monitoring her while I resented her breaking the rules.

More insidious, by not being directly involved in Rachel's diabetes care, I understood less and less. Like any skill, people improve with practice. Since I was not performing tests and shots, my knowledge plateaued while Rachel's grew. Pretty soon, she could deftly draw up insulin, whereas my unpracticed hands trembled the few times I had to give her insulin when she was sick. By reporting her fluctuating sugars to the doctor and adjusting her insulin accordingly for weeks after her hospitalization, Rachel became adept at altering her insulin dosages based on her glucometer values,[26] something I never learned how to do.

In short, I lost power while Rachel gained power.

Which turned out to be catastrophic in the hands of a fourteen-year-old girl.

With Rachel in charge, she trashed much of her training once she got home. She drew up the proper amounts of insulin—at least initially; I saw to that. Hygiene was another matter. She resented my reminders to wash her hands before testing or to wipe the injection site with alcohol. "I have to do this my way!" she'd snarl.

I would back down because she held the needle. Maybe she needed to tweak some rules to own her illness.

Hygiene wasn't the only rule Rachel tweaked. Her technique was also hard to observe. Shots were supposed to be quick, in and out. She'd poke around with the syringe, seeking a "spot that didn't hurt as much" before inching it in, a process that could take thirty minutes. She routinely missed the school bus.

"You're making it ten times worse by jabbing around like that," I told Rachel one day. "Just take the shot."

"How would you like to have to self-mutilate every time you eat?" In her fury, Rachel thrust the needle into her stomach and then yanked it out, folding in pain. "It isn't fair!" she said, flushing.

I wanted to hold her, but the rage in her eyes halted me. "You're right. It isn't fair, but fighting it only makes it worse. When you tense up, it takes longer and hurts more."

"How can I not tense up when I know that lancet is going to cut me? And some shots, like that one, burn like fire! I must've injected my muscle,"[27] she said, tears now falling. With one hand, she swiped them away while rubbing the swollen, red spot with the other.

I handed her a Kleenex, then hurried to get a cotton ball soaked with hydrogen peroxide.

Blotting the site with soaked cotton, I said, "I think it would be much easier to manage if you weren't so angry. Once you accept it—"

The vein on Rachel's brow bulged. Her blue eyes blazed. "Accept it? I will never, ever accept this god-awful disease!"

# First Love

Slamming car doors and voices followed by the thump of a closing trunk signaled the end of my quiet weekend. The kids were back from their ski trip with Perry in the Berkshire Mountains of Massachusetts in January of 1999. I stood in the foyer, that familiar ambivalence fluttering in my chest. I'd missed their sweet faces, voices, laughs—even their squabbles and gripes. When they were home, the house pulsed with life. However, in moments, my silence should shatter. Couches and counters would be strewn with their stuff. Food would vanish while dirty dishes and laundry piled up.

Matt burst through the door first, along with a frigid gust. Nearly six feet at twelve years old, he carted the kids' luggage, which he dumped on the floor, leaning his giant snowboard against the wall.

"Guess what, Mom, Rachel has a boyfriend," he announced with a wide grin, exposing several thousand dollars' worth of orthodontics.

Before I could answer, six-year-old Ryan entered, with a second arctic gust, dropping his stunted skis and Crayola backpack. He shed his blue knit cap, static electricity lifting his fine, white hair like a seeding dandelion. As I stooped to kiss his cold, plump cheek, he whispered, "I saw Rachel kiss Paul on the snow lift."

"Is that right?"

When the door opened a third time, I saw it in Rachel's shining eyes and dreamy new smile. She even walked differently, her shoulders held high.

Fourteen seemed young. I was sixteen when I started dating Randy, my first boyfriend.

Perry assured me that Paul was a nice boy who came from a good family. "He lives in New Jersey and goes to an all-boys school. How much trouble can they get into?"

I could think of plenty, but Rachel's smile muzzled me.

"You can call his mother, Lizzie, if you want," Perry said. "We're planning a second ski trip for March to get Rachel and Paul together."

That night, I flipped to the section on teenagers in a Christian parenting book I was reading to see if my qualms were justified. Surprisingly, the author claimed that dating could benefit teens, boosting their self-esteem during this difficult phase.

At first, it seemed true. If Rachel's diagnosis three months ago made her feel different and broken, Paul made her feel accepted and whole. She floated about the house, quieter now, her eyes often far away, that sweet smile spreading across her face at the strangest moments.

She still hedged me when I mentioned her diabetes, but she no longer carried on over finger sticks and shots. Now she performed these in her bedroom where she lived.

Passing her door, I'd hear the clattering of computer keys, which meant she was emailing or instant messaging Paul. Or I'd hear her chatting on the phone, her talk punctuated with self-conscious giggles. When it was quiet, she'd be hunched over her built-in desk doing schoolwork or sitting cross-legged on her bed journaling. During that period, if I poked my head in Rachel's room, she appeared put out. She'd look up from her diary with a what-can-I-do-for-you? expression. After a quick greeting or question, I backed out, closing the door, painfully aware that I was the last person she wanted to talk to.

If Rachel resented my intrusions on her space, I resented how little she helped me house clean. As an adjunct English instructor at Bristol Community College (BCC), I appreciated that Rachel watched her brothers when I taught night classes. However, I also wanted help with chores as I'd helped my mother when she started teaching grade school. Rachel had hours to devote to Paul but couldn't spare fifteen minutes to vacuum or pack the dishwasher.

"I have a lot on my mind, Mom. I don't always see what needs to be done."

That was the ultimate understatement, I would learn, but back then, I thought Rachel meant her romance. It was late February, and she was counting down the days before she would see her boyfriend of six weeks for the second time at Berkshire East.

"Get your head out of the clouds, Rachel. I'd appreciate some help around here."

She cocked her head. "That's so sexist, Mom. What about the boys?"

"Ryan helps with the groceries and laundry. Matt shovels snow—without being told."

She rolled her eyes. Nevertheless, for the next few days, I would walk into an uncluttered house with vacuum tracks on the carpets. I would think things were improving, but days later, the mess would return. We'd argue, she'd help for a while, then forget again.

One day Rachel ranted, "You've got your priorities all screwed up, Mom. All you care about is this house. Sometimes, your parenting really sucks!"

Usually, I did not tolerate disrespect, but Rachel was exploding over the smallest things. Attributing it to her diagnosis and/or teenage angst, I held my tongue. Following these outbursts, on my pillow, I would find the most precious apology notes.

Here is one:

*Dear Mom, I apologize for how I acted a few minutes ago. I was unbelievably overwhelmed and also furious with myself for not finishing my composition sooner. Unfortunately, you just happened to be in the wrong place at the really wrong time—when I couldn't bear that stressful feeling a moment longer. Oh, I just hate myself for this, what is happening to you, to me, and everybody. I hate the world being unfair to us. This is why I can't stand to see you buying me things. I don't want you to talk anymore about a winter coat for me. I can live without it. I'll just dress in layers or something. However, I also believe you should realize that certain things are a little more complicated when you're my age. That's all for now. Hope I haven't bored you to death, repeating myself.*

*So, so, so, so, sorry, Rachel.*

This was classic Rachel. Being empathetic, she felt everything deeply and always regretted hurting people. Unfortunately, she empathized less with herself.

While blood tests and insulin shots faded into the background of Rachel's life, food suddenly took center stage. Rachel had never overeaten, but now that food had to be meted out, each meal and snack containing only so many carbs, she wanted more of it. Sugar seduced her like never before. To her delight, we discovered sugar-free cake, candy, cookies, and ice cream. Still, we learned that even sugarless treats added up. Rachel gained ten pounds.

"Look at this stomach!" she moaned, grabbing a small fold around her waist. "I'm huge!"

"No, you're not. Your body's just changing. Every teenage girl gains a little weight when she turns into a young lady. I did, too."

"Yeah, it's real sexy," she said, stomping to her room.

When Rachel was younger, we talked about surface beauty, acknowledging how pretty women were noticed and favored. Beauty was potent, but it only went so far. An attractive but vacuous woman lost her allure the moment she opened her mouth, her charm fading with each cruel or vain remark. On the other hand, some plain women with pure hearts possessed a beautifying aura. Our neighbor, Catherine Nelson, was a case in point. When talking to her, one was too taken by her wise, witty words and the music of her frequent laughter, too busy marveling at her radiance to notice her weight, much less her handicap—she'd lost a leg to cancer.

But at fourteen, Rachel's views on beauty had changed. Now she was taking her cues from pop culture, buying into the notion that it was all about a thin, sexy body and pretty face.

Rachel vacillated between being silent and explosive. If I asked what was wrong, she did not want to talk about it.

She gained five more pounds. She now weighed one hundred thirty-five, fifteen pounds more than before her diagnosis. If this was unacceptable before she had a boyfriend, now it was catastrophic.

No guy wanted a fat girlfriend. This message had been drilled into Rachel since she was a child.

"Pretty," she would say, pointing to pictures of Cinderella or Rapunzel in the brightly illustrated story books we read. Not one princess had a double chin or wide hips. Slender and beautiful, they all got their prince.

As she grew, this idea was reinforced. Most leading ladies who fell in love in movies and on television were attractive and slender. The message was repeated at school, where hot boys walked hand-in-hand with the pretty, skinny girls.

"Look at the size of me!" Rachel's face registered sheer panic as she strained to zip up her jeans.

She began dieting, doing floor exercises, and running laps around our neighborhood.

Rachel's endocrinologist, Dr. Easel—Rachel called him Dr. Weasel—seemed unfazed by her weight concerns. He merely bumped up her insulin to cover her extra food consumption, which should have but did not lower her blood sugars.

Meanwhile, Rachel had taken matters into her own hands, engaging in two eating disorders. I would not discover her bulimia until she was sixteen and her diabulimia until roughly a decade later.

An insulin pump seemed like the ideal solution. I'd seen these advertised in magazines in Dr. Easel's waiting room. Apparently, they could be programmed to deliver a steady dose of insulin to regulate a person's blood sugars, eliminating shots.

Normally, Dr. Easel didn't acknowledge me. From our first visit, when he learned that Rachel was managing her diabetes, he spoke only to her. I remember trying to interject questions in an early visit when I couldn't follow their conversation, but Rachel had halted me with her hand, and they kept talking. No doubt, she was proud she spoke the doctor's language, but what was his excuse for ignoring me? I took it as self-care protocol, his attempt to empower the patient. Still, I resented how this model shut me out of my daughter's health care.

When I broached the prospect of an insulin pump, Dr. Easel finally regarded me. "Until Rachel learns how to manage her sugars," he said, frowning, "she is not a candidate for a pump."

Around that time, I started to notice gaps in Rachel's glucose log. She gave different excuses. She'd left her glucometer at school or had tested her blood but had been too tired to record her numbers. No big deal, she added, since the glucometer stored her readings. Sure enough, by the next day, she had filled them in, and I was relieved to note that some numbers were high. Had they all been healthy, I would have wondered if she had fabricated them.

Several days later, when I tapped on her door asking to see her log, she barked, "What am I—a child you need to check up on?"

Maybe this was overkill. Hadn't she proven that she was recording her sugars? After that, I did verbal checks, daily asking what her numbers were. Soon, I simply asked, "How are your sugars?" She would nod, occasionally mumbling, "They could be better." Convinced she was following protocol, I stopped asking altogether.

✦  ✦  ✦

RACHEL RETURNED FROM HER second ski trip jubilant. She showed me some blurry photos taken with an instant camera of her and Paul before a roaring fire in the ski lodge with gigantic smiles, stiffly holding hands. Days later, Rachel was holed up in her room again. If I asked how she was doing, she'd say with a dismissive wave of her hand, "I don't wanna talk about it."

"Well, I'm your mother, and I do want to talk about it!" I said one day several months later after she snubbed me once too often.

It was scorching for early June. Having crawled out of her hole, Rachel was journaling at the kitchen table. I had just taught a three-hour summer course and was annoyed that I was toting a briefcase instead of a beach bag;

wearing stockings and heels when I should have been digging my toes in the cool, wet sand at Second Beach; building sandcastles and body surfing with my kids. I stopped to face her.

"I love you, and I worry about you. Why won't you talk to me?"

"Because all you ever want to talk about is diabetes. It's like I'm not even a person anymore. I'm just a disease." The words tumbled out of her without a trace of attitude.

Dropping my briefcase, I sank into a chair beside her. Near tears, I said, "I am so sorry. I had no idea you felt that way! Can you please forgive me? I will try very hard to never make you feel that way again."

"I forgive you, Mom," she said easily, choking me up again.

It was a tender moment. I wanted it to last. She had broached her diabetes. Did that mean she wanted to talk? Did I dare draw her out? But if she meant what she said, I'd not only aggravate the offense but also break my promise.

Swallowing, I said, "You know, it isn't easy being a single mom. There's so much to do it makes me dizzy. I feel like if I stop for a second, everything will fall apart."

"You work too much, Mom," she scolded.

"I know, and I hate it."

I had just accepted a second summer course. The English Chair had called me in a panic when the instructor for an advanced literature course had backed out in the eleventh hour. I hoped it would improve my chances for a faculty position. Now, meeting Rachel's reproachful eyes, I regretted it. However, the course was only three weeks, and we desperately needed the cash. The $1,800 I would earn from these two courses was our only summer income. To supplement it, I was running a Bed and Breakfast in our home on weekends when I didn't have the kids. It was hit or miss. Some weekends I made $400, other weekends, zilch.

"How about I blow off work tomorrow, and we go to the beach?"

Her face brightened. "Are you serious? You'd do that?"

"Yup. If my life won't let up, I'll steal a day to spend with you kids."

I didn't tell her that one day equaled a week on the accelerated summer schedule. I'd have to do some fancy footwork to fit those three hours of instruction into the remaining classes.

But our beach day was worth it—the bright sun, the hot sand, the briny sea air. Gliding, crying gulls had circled overhead, landing inches from our picnic lunch. They stared with round yellow eyes. We tossed bread crusts and broken potato chips that they caught with their curved orange beaks. When our bites became too gritty, the kids plowed into the booming, foaming surf. I followed more gingerly, dipping one toe, the water so frigid that I doubled back to my chair. Rachel and Matt laughed at my cowardice while Ryan cried, "Come back, Mom!" until a wave flipped him over. Emerging from the surf, gurgling and laughing, his hair slick as a seal's, Ryan forgot about me. He rode the next wave with his siblings, their squeals the highlight of my summer.

# CASTING PEARLS

As I fastened the last clothespin, my top sheets took sail, billowing and snapping against the blue August sky. The late morning sun was blinding. In no time, the sheets would dry. I'd be sleeping alone tonight but in crisp sheets scented with the honeysuckle wafting over from Catherine Nelson's garden. Smiling, I picked up my laundry basket. Time to awaken fifteen-year-old Rachel. She would not want to miss one more minute of this gorgeous day.

She was supposed to be at Perry's but had opted not to go. Whereas Matt and Ryan stuck to an every-other-weekend visitation schedule, Rachel followed her whims. Sometimes, on my weekends, she stayed with her dad, possibly to have him to herself. Lately, she stayed put, mentioning her need for privacy. Though Perry's condo had two large bedrooms, he rented one out, crowding the kids into his bedroom.

On Saturday nights, I'd make a big bowl of salty popcorn, and we'd wash it down with icy diet ginger ale while watching ER. Sometimes, during commercials, I'd read compositions.

"Mom, you really need to get a life," Rachel commented that evening. "You sit here night after night, grading those stupid papers like an old lady. You should be out having fun."

I looked up from my clipboard, taken aback but also amused.

Smiling, I replied, "A man is supposed to sweeten your life, Rachel. The men I dated only added to my stress." I continued, more soberly, "I want someone with integrity who challenges me to be a better person. If I can't find that, I'd rather be single. It's better for me and better for us."

I'd come to that conclusion after a string of hapless relationships following my separation and divorce. Marcy introduced me to Richard, a lawyer, and entrepreneur. I met Harold, a novelist, at the Cape Cod Writers Conference; Markus, a high-end restaurant manager, at church. Brian, the only "bad boy" I dated, was an ex-student studying to be a social worker. I met Catherine's brother Todd over her fence. A photographer and recent divorcee with no kids, he lived in Connecticut.

All these relationships were brief and bumpy. If the men were not drinkers, they had problems communicating or were still pining for their exes. Not one knew what he wanted, least of all Todd, who broke my heart.

"Is that why you wouldn't let Todd in after he drove all that way?" She cocked her head. "I still say that was mean, Mom. What about forgiveness?" Rachel liked Todd's dry wit. She liked how I lit up when he called or came over.

That incident, eight months earlier, still stung. After breaking up with me over the phone and instantly regretting it, Todd had tried to call back, but I forbade the kids to answer the phone. It rang and rang. While I was praying with Ryan, tears leaking, Rachel secretly picked up the extension in her room.

Standing in the hall, hand over the receiver, she reported, "He's on his way, Mom, calling from his car phone!" In 1999, Todd and Richard, the lawyer I dated, were the only people we knew with car phones.

"Rachel, you were told not to pick up! Have you forgotten that you're phone grounded?" Rachel still had three days left of her one-week sentence after being caught talking with Paul way past her curfew.

"But he's driving from Connecticut!"

"Hang up right now!"

Mumbling something in the receiver, Rachel disconnected, reluctantly confessing, "He wants me to leave the slider unlocked so he can get in."

Rachel had dived into her romance with Paul. As she dated more, I worried that she would give too much too soon and get hurt. This might be a good object lesson.

"It's too late, Rachel. I gave him my best, and it wasn't good enough. If I feel this bad now, how am I going to feel if he does this again?"

"What about fighting for the man you love?"

I shook my head. "No. You have to hold something back, so you're not totally bankrupt."

I deadlocked both doors. "Don't you dare let him in."

Knowing that Rachel was a rebel and a romantic, trusting neither my daughter nor myself, I also locked the door to my bedroom. Sure enough, an hour later, I heard Tod's light footsteps on the stairs, my doorknob rattle, his soft curse, and louder descending footsteps.

How to explain that that room was my heart and more precious than any man?

"Forgiveness is one thing, Rachel. If I saw Todd at Mrs. Nelson's, I might wave or chat with him, but you don't return to a man who tosses you away like the morning paper. That's like throwing your pearls before swine. You have to know your worth and guard it with your life."

✦　✦　✦

BEING SINGLE HAD ITS drawbacks. Last Valentine's Day, while driving home from work, I watched florist trucks deliver flowers all over Aquidneck Island, knowing that my doorbell would not ring. I would not receive a long white box nor press my nose into velvety red blooms, inhaling their exotic perfume. It was Friday—Perry's weekend with the kids—and I was alone.

Then it struck me, with blinding clarity, that while I did not have romance, I hardly lacked love. I received it from friends, my mom and sisters, my precious kids, and my Lord. As this revelation washed over me, my self-pity drained. I thanked God for lavishing me with love and opening my eyes to see it. Doreen was one of those dear friends. She helped me survive my divorce: watched Ryan so I could work; made me laugh when I was down; bought me dinner when I was broke; showed up for the kids' birthdays and Christmas with colorfully wrapped boxes and shiny gift bags. When I got home, I called her. She leaped at my offer to watch Jordan so she and her husband could go out to dinner.

Gradually, I came to appreciate being single. It cleared space in my crowded mind. Gone were those nagging questions—what did he mean, why did he lie? Now, I could focus on what mattered: my kids and my work.

Then, one day toward the end of August, Marcy called me breathless.

"I've found you the perfect man."

Chuckling cynically, I asked, "What makes you think that?"

"Well, he's tall and dark, with a mustache—I know you go for that. He's a plumber, so he's got the mechanical requirement covered." Marcy knew I could not assemble a Cracker Jack toy. "And, like you, he's a traditionalist. You should hear this guy talk about his two girls—twelve and six, I think." Apparently, while Mystery Man installed Marcy's shower, they chatted at length.

"He's got kids? I'd rather date guys who don't to avoid that whole mixed family mess."

"You've got it backward. You need a man who has kids, so he knows how to parent yours."

"Look, Marcy, the truth is, I like being single. I feel good for the first time in ages. I don't want to sabotage that." She, Gerri, and Doreen knew better than anyone my pitiful dating history.

"I get it. There's just one problem." She paused, and I heard her take a sip, probably of chardonnay. It was nearly dinner, and she liked to have a glass while she cooked. When she lived next door, I used to walk across her fiancé's golf-course lawn and join her.

"I—um—sort of already told him you might be interested."

"Ughhhh, Marcy!"

"Just email him. That's all I ask. His name is Phil."

"Fine," I sighed.

I was washing windows when she called, having just booked last-minute Bed and Breakfast guests for the weekend. I had one day to clean, cut the lawn, and whip up something wonderful for breakfast. In the whirlwind of preparations, the paper on which I'd scrawled Phil's address disappeared.

All right, so I threw it out. Being single felt safe. What I failed to realize was that I was still destitute after five years. Nor was I aware, with the years racing by, that when Ryan turned eight in less than two years, per my divorce decree, I'd have to sell the house.

But God, who saw it all, and other dark storms gathering in the distance, knew what I needed. I think He used Marcy to get my attention.

"What do you mean you lost Phil's email address?" she ranted when she called back. "He's coming tomorrow to fix my garbage disposal. I told him you'd contact him. He's gonna think I blew him off!"

"Fine," I snapped. "Give it to me again."

That night, I wrote Phil a short, upbeat email introducing myself.

By the next morning, I had received a similar message from Phil—only it was devoid of punctuation. He misspelled the simplest words. I stared at the screen, a smile pulling at my lips. He still knew more about writing than I did about pipes.

We emailed for several weeks before graduating to phone calls. Though Phil seemed nice, our conversations lacked depth. I was trying to figure out how to gently extricate myself when he invited me to dinner. I guessed one date wouldn't hurt.

Phil asked me to make reservations for that Friday night, anywhere I liked. I opted for Melville Pub, a lovely though reasonably priced dockside restaurant only miles from my house.

"There's just one thing." He paused. "My truck's kinda beat up."

How humiliating to have to admit that on a first date. "You can drive my Corolla," I offered, "if you can handle a stick shift."

"Of cawse I can," he said with his New England dialect.

For our date, I wore a navy maxi skirt and a white knit top with mid-length sleeves, both from the Gap clearance rack. Rachel had just painted my toe-nails fuchsia; I stepped into black leather flip-flops to show them off. I pulled my long brown hair into a half-ponytail, slipping on pearl earrings. I lined my eyes to bring out the blue, lengthened my lashes, and gingerly applied mauve lipstick so as not to disturb a healing cold sore.

Not bad for ten minutes and twenty dollars.

As I was spritzing my wrists with the lemony notes of Chanel Cristalle, the doorbell rang.

Before answering it, I ducked into Rachel's room for the real test. She was sitting cross-legged on her bed journaling. Looking up, she gave me the once over and smiled.

"You look nice, Mom."

That was a relief because she could be ruthless. "Your shoes look like some-thing Grandma would wear," she said once. Another time, she likened my new kitchen valances to "frilly aprons." It was uncanny how her comments could taint items I had just loved; I couldn't return them fast enough. When she began dab-bling with different styles, I dished it right back. "Jeremiah Johnson!" I teased the first time she wore her jeans with rawhide laces on the side seams. "If Madonna is the look you're going for," I said, referring to the black 'pleather' pants she bought on eBay, "you nailed it." Henceforth, she only wore them on Halloween.

I opened the door, arrested by Phil's good looks. Handsome, tanned face. Kind brown eyes over which hung the sweetest, meekest brows.

"Hi. I'm Phil." He smiled, flashing straight teeth and dimples to match his cleft chin. Dressed in jeans and a crisp white, tucked-in T-shirt—surprising dinner attire, but it sure beat creased pants and tasseled shoes—he had quite a body.

Maybe this date wouldn't be so bad after all.

Wrong.

Phil talked about drag racing nearly the entire meal. As an ex-mechanic, he had worked in the pit for a professional race car driver who toured all over the country. Maybe he thought it was fascinating stuff. My only thrill was watching his handsome, animated face. Feigning interest, I fantasized vault-ing over the table and kissing him just to shut him up.

The next day, I emailed him, gently explaining that I thought we were too different to pursue the relationship. He immediately phoned asking for another chance. The guy was so dang sweet. Rolling my eyes, I agreed to go miniature golfing with our kids, though Rachel had opted to take a babysitting job.

That evening, I saw other attractive sides to Phil. As Marcy had predicted, he was good with kids. He assisted them with difficult shots, cheering when they drove the recalcitrant, dimpled ball into the hole. When Ryan, twirling his golf club like a baton, accidentally whacked Krissy's head, Phil didn't overreact. He checked her injury and, seeing it wasn't serious, said, "Stop crying now. It was an accident."

I was struck by how many people greeted Phil, both at Mickey's Miniature Golf and at the adjoining gift shop where he bought ice cream. While he passed out cones, Nikki became belligerent when he refused to buy her a hot pink hooded sweatshirt. Leaning down to meet her eyes, he said in a tone that wilted her haughtiness, "Don't you evah talk to me that way again, do you unduhstand?"

Next, he took us to his apartment on Oliver Street. He lived on the third floor of a three-family house that had formerly belonged to his grandparents and was now owned by his uncle.

"I grew up here," Phil explained as we ascended the creaky stairs, the heat intensifying with each step. "Grandma and Grandpa lived on the first floor, we lived on second, and a cousin lived up here," he said, unlocking and opening his door to a blast furnace.

"It's hot in here!" both girls groaned. Phil flicked on the light and two oscillating fans.

While the kids played Nintendo in the centrally located living room with slanted ceilings, he showed me around. In spite of its small size and modest furnishings, his apartment was spotless. The linoleum kitchen floor and cast iron sink gleamed, and there were vacuum tracks on the worn carpets. Later, while walking through his bedroom to access the only bathroom, I surreptitiously pressed my first two fingers into his mattress, noting to my satisfaction that it was firm.

Several nights later, I invited Phil over for lasagna. During dinner, he joked and chatted with the kids. Afterward, he took the boys outside to play baseball.

"What are you doing with that guy, Mom?" Rachel asked as soon as Phil gently closed the slider door behind them. "He's a mud fence, and his nose looks like a ball."

Her comment was so graphic and fresh that I almost laughed but caught myself. "Rachel, I'm surprised at you. You don't even know him," I scolded. Such harsh judgment was not like her. Was she jealous? After eight months, the glow of her own romance had dwindled. Paul wrote even less, and recently he'd gotten grounded and had to cancel a rendezvous.

"I don't want to, with his lame jokes."

"He has a good heart—and great parenting skills."

We watched Phil through the slider as he showed Ryan how to hold and swing a bat.

I was not going to let her sour my opinion of him. He was a person, for heaven's sake, not a pair of shoes.

"I'm going to give him a chance. As for his nose, I think it's adorable. It looks sort of like yours."

# WALKING OUT

LATE MORNING SUN STREAMED through open windows, flooding the kitchen with light. A brisk September breeze lifted lace curtain hems. Fall semester started in two weeks. With a notebook and pen, I sat down to write a syllabus for my literature class, shivering deliciously as sunshine warmed my shoulders like a wool shawl. Boys' shouts and laughs and the slap of a basketball drifted through the screen—Ryan, Matt, and their friends, out playing, determined to squeeze every last second out of their summer vacation.

Rachel entered the kitchen, rubbing her eyes. "I had another one of those dreams, Mom."

"Tell me about it," I said, looking up. These nightmares had become so frequent and so disturbing that I had recently found Rachel a reputable child psychiatrist.

She had started to pour Raisin Bran into a bowl, but now she froze, box in hand, her eyes large and contemplative.

"It was the creepiest thing. I was staring at myself in the mirror when I started to feel sick. I pulled up my shirt and looked at my stomach. My skin could be peeled up, only it didn't hurt. I rolled up my flesh like a shade. Inside was an infestation. Thousands of little bugs resembling ants crawled in and out of my intestines and lungs." Shaking flakes into her bowl, she asked, "What do you think that means, Mom?"

I liked to analyze dreams; Rachel and I both did. But what could I say to this? My arms had broken out in goosebumps. My mouth was agape. "I really don't know, Rae. I think you should ask Dr. Abraham."

Rachel met weekly with Dr. Abraham. I had hoped that during the forty-five-minute drive home from Providence, she might share portions of their sessions. I needed to know what was disturbing my daughter. The first week, she answered my questions in monosyllables; then she reclined her seat, turned on her Walkman, and fell asleep.

The next week, I tried again: "So, what did you and Dr. Abraham talk about today?"

"Oh, Mom, I've just been spilling my guts for an hour. I'm too wiped to talk right now."

"I understand, but at least tell me this: do you think he can help you?"

She paused, her face pensive. "He's intelligent. I'll give him that much."

Rachel met with Dr. Abraham for nine months, never missing an appointment. I took this as progress. However, she continued to guard the content of their sessions. As did Dr. Abraham the one time I spoke with him.

Shaking my hand, he offered the chair opposite his broad walnut desk. He was a petite man, with probing brown eyes and olive skin that stood out against his white lab coat.

"Rachel tells me you and your husband are divorced," he said, eyeing me directly.

"That's correct, since last year. But he actually left in ninety-four. We were separated for about five years."

He nodded, scratching notes on a legal pad without seeming to break eye contact.

"How would you describe the atmosphere of your home before the separation?"

"Well, it was fairly normal. There was no alcohol or drugs. No infidelity I know of. No abuse, physical or verbal, though sarcasm had become a way of life for us."

Dr. Abraham arched his brows. "So, why did you and your husband separate?"

"We're very different. I needed respect and communication. He needed sex, which was difficult for me without the other two pieces."

Nodding and writing rapidly now, he asked, "Did you try working out these issues through therapy?"

"We did, but not until ten years into the marriage." I sighed. "By then, the walls we'd built were impenetrable."

"How would you say Rachel relates to your ex-husband?"

Finally, a question about Rachel. "Very well. She loves her dad."

"So, if she chose to live with him, you'd be okay with that?"

I swallowed. "I didn't say that. Why? Have you and Rachel discussed this?"

"I'm afraid I can't answer that." Clicking his pen closed, he set it down. "But it's not uncommon in the context of separation or divorce for a fifteen-year-old to opt to live with the other parent or even bounce back and forth between them. It's perfectly within Rachel's legal right."

I walked back to the waiting room with my heart in my heels. I did not think living with Perry was in Rachel's best interest. He was far too lenient with her, not to mention his indiscretions with women. Hadn't I just caught Rachel and Matt snickering over some red silk panties they found in between Perry's couch cushions? Also concerning was Rachel's recent admission that her father often criticized overweight women they saw at the mall, making her feel uncomfortable.

After that meeting, I never heard from Dr. Abraham again. I resented this stranger having a peephole into my daughter's emotional life while I was shut out, but at least Rachel was talking. Hopefully, he could help her accept her diabetes and deal with whatever demons were fueling her dreams.

As I drove home from Providence that day, Rachel slept soundly beside me, her mouth slightly open, Alanis Morissette emanating from her Walkman. I noticed the trees bordering both sides of highway I-95 were already changing color, bursts of red and gold popping among the flocks of green, a sight that usually turned my head.

But my mind drifted back to my meeting with Dr. Abraham. His pointed questions about my marriage had unnerved me. No doubt, he was sizing up our dysfunction. Fortunately, there wasn't much to report. Why, then, this weight on my chest? The prospect of losing Rachel was part of it. There was also that article on divorce I'd read in the waiting room. It claimed that kids of non-feuding parents are crushed by divorce when the bomb drops out of nowhere. When openly hostile parents split up, their kids see it coming and at least gain peace. Our kids lost the ground beneath them and gained nothing.

I wondered how much of Rachel's distress was related to our divorce. I hated looking back. My mind had bolted most of those doors; nevertheless, I coaxed it down that dark corridor, and, surprisingly, the door to the day of Perry's departure swung open.

✦　✦　✦

IT WAS A SUNDAY afternoon, New Year's Day, 1994. Ryan was napping while Matt and Rachel played in their rooms. Grabbing a blanket and book, I curled up on my bed for a few stolen moments of solitude while steadily falling snow wrapped the world outside our four bedroom windows in pure white.

Suddenly, Perry walked in. He stopped at the foot of the bed.

"I want to try an experiment," he said without prelude.

"What's that?" I asked, closing my book. I might have felt less unnerved had he moved closer, sat on the bed.

He swallowed. "I have an opportunity to house sit for Tom Murgo for three months. It's a way to try this out without having to pay rent."

By "try this out," I surmised he meant a separation. Tom Murgo was the contractor who had built our house, with whom, until that moment, I'd always felt a warm connection.

My heart started pumping erratically. Ryan was only eighteen months old, Matthew seven, and Rachel nine. I'd only just started teaching at BCC four months earlier. I had no job security, no benefits.

"I don't think it's a good idea," I said, feigning composure. "As long as we stay together, God can still work this out."

But even as I spoke, a shadow darkened my heart. I'd been praying for our marriage to improve for twelve years. I had hoped that the new house would give us a fresh start. We did try, especially after Ryan was born. Months of marriage counseling taught us to curb our sarcasm, but I was painfully aware that we were still strangers occupying the same house.

Maybe it was time to part.

*Oh, but my kids!*

Panic must have flooded my face.

"I'm not saying it's permanent, Carolyn." Perry moved closer but remained standing. "Maybe some distance would do us good, you know, give us objectivity to sort things out."

"It's not like we haven't experienced separations. You take business trips all the time." My gut suddenly knew what this was about. "If you leave, I won't know who you've been with. I can't promise I'll take you back."

Perry left days later without paying the bills or telling the kids.

Night after night, we sat at the dinner table as if nothing were wrong. At first, the kids didn't notice. Perry's empty chair was nothing new between his business trips and evening construction work on his Providence rental. Then, eight days later, Rachel asked, "When's Dad coming home?"

I hesitated. They had a right to know. It was wrong to pretend.

"He's—uh—not. See—he's not sure he wants to be married to me anymore, so he's—left for a while."

Rachel and Matt seemed to deflate like punctured balloons. They stared at me, their eyes blinking while Ryan, grinning and oblivious, ate sweet potato fries with his pudgy fingers.

"Are you going to get a divorce?" Rachel asked, her voice wobbly. On her fair brow, the blue vein stood at attention.

"I don't know, honey. Listen, I know this is hard. What I want you kids to try to understand," I said, rotating between her and Matt's doleful eyes, "is that Dad didn't leave you. He left me. He still loves you very much. That will never change."

For the next week, Matt dragged his Jurassic Park sleeping bag into my room and slept on the carpet beside me.

Matt and Rachel hardly talked about their dad.

One day, I gave them paper and asked them to write or draw what they were feeling. They didn't write or draw much. But Rachel wrote in her journal:

*January 8, 1994*

*Mom and Dad are having a separation. Dad stays at Tom's house, and Mom stays here. Mom won't let Dad in. At Tom's house we can do whatever we want. Here Mom makes us follow rules. She won't let me bring the hermit crabs of Tom's into the house. Dad lets us have whatever we want at meals. Tom has two cats, fish + hermit crabs. Poor Dad. I'm on his side, you know. I have to face the truth, Mom and Dad are going to get a divorce.*
*Bye.*
*Rachel*

I signed Matt up for basketball, which he hated, followed by soccer, which he tolerated. I enrolled Rachel in an art class at the Newport Art Museum, hoping that while it developed her creativity, it would help her emote.

By spring, Matt was his flighty, smiling self. Rachel was still sullen, so I got her a duckling. My dad had bought me one at her age, and I had loved it. She would have preferred a puppy or kitten, but she had just been diagnosed with asthma and chronic allergies to pet dander and dust.

We drove out to a farm in Tiverton, following the owner to an old barn that was empty, except for some bales of sweet-smelling hay. Just inside the doorway was a chicken coop filled with peeping ducklings.

"Mom, look how cute they are!"

"Oh, my stars!" I exclaimed, stooping beside Rachel to get a better look. Rachel poked her finger through the chicken wire to touch one, causing the ducklings to hurtle en mass into a corner of the coop, peeping frantically, necks extended, tiny wings fluttering in distress.

"It's okay," the owner said. Opening the cage, he grabbed one, handing the duckling to Rachel. It stared at her with black bead eyes, peeping shrilly through its comical beak. Smiling widely, she stroked its gray and yellow down.

Rachel named her duckling "Herbie," after mine. She kept him in a box in the basement lined with soft, clean rags.

When he outgrew his box, we transferred him to a chicken wire cage Perry built on four-foot posts to protect him from animals at night. During the day, Herbie was either swimming in Ryan's wading pool or waddling behind Rachel. If she sat on the grass or steps, Herbie nested in her lap. Even after his peep turned into a quack and his down into greasy feathers, Rachel loved him.

Then one dusk, she found his cage empty. We had just returned from visiting Matt at Newport Hospital. Rachel darted to the backyard to check Herbie. Shrieking, she ran inside, swearing she'd latched the cage. We phoned neighbors, combed the neighborhood to no avail. Herbie was gone. Rachel

was hysterical, crying in her bed. I should have held her, talked to her. I'd been up all night. Matt had one of his nocturnal asthma attacks, appearing at my bedside like some child ghost, gasping for air; I had to rush him—all the kids—to the ER. Just wanting to halt her pain, I gave her half a sleeping pill.

The next day, we bought another duckling.

✦   ✦   ✦

WHEN PERRY'S EXPERIMENT ENDED in March, he asked to come home. I said no. Not, as it turned out, because he had slept around, but because for the first time in a long time, I felt whole. I no longer had to shut off my heart and my mind when he reached for me at night, fragment myself to keep my family intact.

I would not return to a sham. On the other hand, God could heal our marriage—hadn't he raised Lazarus from the dead? Reconciliation was the best outcome for our kids. I would not take him back, but neither would I file for divorce. I would watch and wait.

By June, I'd seen enough. Clutching a cashier's check for $1,500 in my trembling hand, I found myself parked by a Providence law firm. I was using cash I desperately needed to violate my marriage vow. Could I do this? *Should* I do this? I pondered my twelve-year marriage, so painful and lonely from the start, but the last few months had been the worst. In March, when I had agreed to take Perry in until he found housing, I saw condoms in his open shaving kit in our bathroom. Maybe it shouldn't have mattered, but it did. The kids blamed me when I kicked him out.

In May, he enrolled his Japanese girlfriend in the English as a Second Language (ESL) program at Salve Regina University where I was teaching. I begged him not to. What if she was placed in my advanced classes? What if I had to teach my husband's lover? On registration day, when I saw them walking toward me—him with a defiant smirk—I realized it was the same willowy woman with waist-length black hair who'd trespassed on a family video weeks earlier. One moment, I was watching Matthew blow out five birthday candles on his Thomas the Tank Engine cake. The next moment, there she was in a white lace bra, panties, and high heels serving Perry a candlelight dinner! He had borrowed our camcorder to film Matt's soccer game, or so he said.

Was this a careless error, like the time he taped a football game over video footage of my master's graduation ceremony? Or had he deliberately done this to hurt me?

Inhaling deeply, I opened the car door.

✦ ✦ ✦

AT THE END OF June, Mom moved in. She paid me two hundred dollars a month for rent. I ripped her first check in half. She wrote a second check in her perfect, slanted script.

"This is nothing, really. Besides, you're hardly in a financial position to refuse me."

I told her I was keeping the house. Our lawyers had worked out a deal for Perry to pay the mortgage, $1,255 per month, in lieu of child support.

Mom stopped transferring neatly folded clothes from suitcase to dresser to mentally calculate the numbers.

"That's only about fifteen thousand a year. How much does he make?"

"Sixty, maybe?"

Her jaw clenched. "So that's one-fourth of his income for you and three kids." She shook her head, her face reddening. "And you think that's a good deal?"

"He also has to pay two hundred a month in alimony for three years and keep me on his Blue Cross until he remarries. I'm responsible for everything else."

"And how much do you make teaching at BCC?"

"Five thousand four hundred a year, plus another nine hundred if I score a summer course." Seeing her alarm, I added, "But I've applied for a full time faculty position in the English Department."

Sighing and continuing to transfer clothes, she said, "It's nowhere near enough. You'll have to sell the house."

"And move into a crappy apartment or neighborhood with mean kids? Rachel and Matt have friends here, nice kids from good families. I have to keep things as stable as possible. I have to keep the house."

Mom nodded, but her jaw twitched.

I did not get the faculty position. There were three hundred applicants, and I did not make the third cut. It would have been ideal for a single mom—good pay, benefits, minimal hours, and summers off.

I continued to scour the want ads in The Providence Journal and The Newport Daily News. Even with a master's degree, there wasn't much for which I was qualified. I needed a Ph.D. to work at a university and a teaching certificate to work in public schools. Full-time writing jobs were not an option. It would have meant daycare for Ryan and house keys and summer camp for Rachel and Matt. So I kept looking and applying for teaching jobs with mothers' hours.

With a master's degree in reading, a teaching certificate, and twenty years of experience, Mom quickly found work at an inner-city school in Providence. She taught GED to disadvantaged mothers in the Head Start program, which included free preschool. On days I taught, Mom brought Ryan with her and plunked him in the inner-city preschool.

During dinner, under the warm table light, she told us stories about her day. Whereas I kept mundane incidents to myself, Mom dressed hers up with details and voices to draw us in.

Mom helped me potty train Ryan, who adored her. When he outgrew his crib, he slipped into her bed each morning, awakening her with his warm breath or a wisp of his angora hair. Mom shuttled the kids to doctors' appointments and birthday parties and supervised their homework. Now when Matt had an asthma attack in the wee hours, I could rush him to the ER without having to drag along Rachel and Ryan. On weekends, she brought us to yard sales, craft fairs, children's museums, the Newport Winter Festival, and Cape Cod cranberry bogs. Random words prompted Mom to sing silly songs that made the boys grin and Rachel groan, "There goes Grandma singing again!"

Mom stayed for two years before returning to Wisconsin to care for her ninety-five-year-old mother. We packed her Honda to the roof with the treasures she'd accumulated. After a weepy goodbye, I stood in the driveway, waving but feeling lost as I watched her gold car disappear.

✦  ✦  ✦

THE SUN HAD SLIPPED behind the trees, veiling I-195 in shadows. I studied Rachel, still sleeping in the passenger seat, her mouth now frowning. I felt like I had failed her. Failed all my kids. For five years, I kept them in our nice house in our new colonial neighborhood on my adjunct salary. I kept them clean, healthy, fed but was often too tired to talk, too busy to play.

When they lost their dad, they lost me, too.

We both walked out on our kids.

# SOS

I SAT ON THE living room sofa to fold clothes, crisp fall air floating through an open window. Our trees were pure gold, sunny leaves fluttering on branches, some twirling to the ground. I never heard Rachel enter. Suddenly, she was just standing there, her face solemn.

"I think I have an eating disorder, Mom."

It was fourteen months after her diabetes diagnosis and six weeks after she had started psychiatric therapy.

"Why do you think that?" I asked, continuing to fold clothes.

In 1999, EDs were getting more press. Celebrities like Princess Di, Calista Flockhart, and Paula Abdul were publicizing their struggles with bulimia and anorexia. Rachel also had an active imagination.

"My body perception's messed up."

"What do you mean by 'messed up'?" I stopped folding to study her face, a bath towel warming my lap.

"Well, kids at school tell me I don't look any different—I mean, no fatter—but I think I do." Her eyes flitted around the room before finally settling on me. "So maybe my body perception's distorted."

"I don't think so. You have gained a little weight since your diagnosis."

The look that leaped into her eyes quickened me to qualify myself.

"You're not overweight. What I mean is, you're seeing correctly. You're seeing what's actually there. So, no, I don't think you have a distorted body perception. I don't think you have an eating disorder."

I didn't think to probe deeper, to ask if she had other symptoms or concerns. I assumed she had told me everything. I had a lot to learn about teenage girls.[28]

A troubled look hung on Rachel's face.

"What's wrong? Aren't you relieved?"

"Not exactly," she said, exiting the room.

In my mind, an ED was so out of the realm of possibility that I never even considered researching it. Sure, Rachel struggled with eating and weight, but what teenage girl didn't? She already had one label that made her feel different. I did not want her saddled with another, so I tried to write her a reassuring letter. We had been communicating this way, through letters and notes, since she was five years old and had learned how to write phonetically.

*October 29, 1999*

*Dear Rachel,*

*Thanks for telling me about your ED—or what you think is one. I'm not sure whether it is or not. But I don't think so. Most teenage girls are obsessed with their body image. This can cause an ED, but in your case, I don't think it has.*

*You have gained weight since your diagnosis. I don't say this to criticize, merely to point out that you correctly see the extra pounds. Maybe kids say you look the same because the difference isn't that dramatic, or they don't want to hurt your feelings.*

*I remember being preoccupied with my weight at your age. If I gained a few pounds, I felt guilty about everything I ate. I tried to diet, and, like you, if I cheated with Cheetos or chocolate, I figured I might as well eat whatever I wanted for the rest of the day. If you talk to other females, you'll find this is not uncommon.*

*I understand your wanting to have a certain body type, Rachel. You're on the right track with exercise, and I can help by cooking and baking more low-carb foods. Just don't compromise your health for a thin body. Please don't play with this. The long-term complications are too devastating. You can't see that now because you're young; your current issues are too pressing for you to consider your future. However, time does pass.*

*If you take care of yourself now, you'll be healthier later. I want to help you however I can, but first, you must let me in. I've tried to respect your privacy because I know it's very important to you right now. But please know that I care deeply about your mind, heart, body—everything. Maybe it doesn't seem like it sometimes because I'm so busy, but it's true.*

*Love, Mom*

Reading this letter retrospectively was humbling. My motives were pure, but how little I knew about EDs when I offered this counsel. No wonder Rachel did not want to discuss it.

I now understand that though most American women are weight conscious, they are not dogged by thoughts of food and weight night and day, like Rachel was. Nor do they gorge themselves if they indulge in a few potato chips. (I might have stretched my own experience on this point to empathize with her.) That behavior reflects all-or-nothing thinking, the tendency to think and act in extremes, without considering any moderate alternatives, like enjoying a bowl of chips and then resealing the bag. Food fixation and all-or-nothing thinking are symptoms of disordered eating, as is excessive exercise, a purging technique that I had actually encouraged.

In short, I told my daughter that her behavior was normal when it was not. I implied that she did not have a problem when, in reality, she had a big one.

Having received little guidance from me, a week later, Rachel disclosed what must have been some disturbing ED-related information to Dr. Abraham, who reported it to the Pediatric Diabetes Clinic where Rachel was being treated. We were immediately summoned for an emergency meeting with her endocrinologist.

Dr. Siru got right to the point. "It's come to our attention," she said, rotating her grave brown eyes from me to Rachel, "that Rachel has been substantially cutting back on her insulin so she can diet without getting hypoglycemic." Looking directly at me, she added, "Her blood sugars have been in the two-hundred to three-hundred-range for several weeks."

My head spun to face Rachel, who flushed deeply.

"Mom, I weigh a hundred and forty-five pounds! I've got to diet and exercise to drop some of this weight!"

Though I'd told Rachel last week she looked fine, her waist and hips had filled out; even her chin looked chubbier. At five feet, six inches, her weight was technically normal, her body mass index spot on. Still, I knew it did not feel normal to her. Her shape was different than it had been before her diagnosis and, in her mind, probably even less like that idyllic stick figure she craved.

"I understand that, Rachel, but not at the risk of your health, never by hurting yourself!"

"I know, Mom, but I can't control myself. That's why I think I have an ED."

"And what do you think, Mom?" Dr. Siru asked, turning to me. "Do you think Rachel has an eating disorder?"

"Frankly, I don't. I think it's normal for teenage girls to obsess over their weight. And I've never seen Rachel engage in any other abnormal eating behavior."

Mind you, I had no inkling that insulin omission was a symptom of disordered eating, nor did the doctor enlighten me.

Rachel never made a peep.

After my uninformed two cents, the meeting ended. I felt relieved. Rachel had simply gotten off track. Reducing her insulin was not good protocol, but it was an isolated incident that we could correct; she by taking the prescribed dose, and I by monitoring her more closely.

No doubt, as an endocrinologist treating adolescents, this was not the first time Dr. Siru had encountered diabulimic behavior among this population. In her clinical notes that day, Dr. Siru recorded her suspicion that Rachel had a "likely eating disorder," evidenced by "preoccupation with weight and shape" and "insulin manipulation." Weeks later, she notified Dr. Neuman, Rachel's pediatrician. I did not discover this until fourteen years later when I requested Rachel's medical records. Why Dr. Siru did not share her suspicions or copy me on this letter, I do not know.

What is even more curious is why she did not test Rachel for an ED that both she and Rachel suspected.[29] If she had, those results might have been added to the heap of Rachel's other symptoms, resulting in an immediate diagnosis. When EDs are caught and treated early, outcomes are more positive. But when they're allowed to fester, they become intractable and difficult to treat. They become monsters.

Granted, EDs among adolescent girls are notoriously tough to diagnose, but that's because most girls conceal them. Rachel was screaming for help. Though she kept a tight lid on her insulin omission, the most dangerous aspect of her ED, she had reported her obsession with food and weight to not one but four adults. The last was her middle school English teacher, I learned years later while searching through her school papers.

When prompted to explore one thing in her life she would like to alter, Rachel wrote:

> If I could change one thing, I would want to be relieved of the obsession and anxiety of my eating disorder. I'm tired of not feeling peace. I'm tired of being exhausted. I'm sick of having my life taken over by food and the manner in which I consume it. I wish I didn't obsess over my weight. I want to change this feeling I have of hanging on by a thread. The anxiety drives me crazy.
>
> I would like to be healthy, but I'm killing my body slowly. I don't like the guilt I feel over that, but the guilt of eating and suffering the consequences is more than I can stand.

Though Rachel's teacher had marked her paper with a check plus in red ink, she did not comment on its disturbing content, most notably that Rachel was "hanging on by a thread" and "killing my body slowly." Nor did she report it. I don't believe that any human being, much less a teacher, would ignore a young girl's cry for help. I can only deduce that she missed it.

Rachel's teacher, doctor, and mother all missed the signs. If one of us had responded appropriately to her SOS, Rachel might have survived. Instead, she began her slow decline. Over the next nine months, as Rachel secretly continued to experiment with ever more risky purging techniques, she eventually birthed, as it were, twin monsters, diabulimia and bulimia.

# "Not doing too well today"

**November 12, 1999—11:52 p.m.**

I am dying. I feel it everywhere. I want so badly to have somebody hold me + honestly love me despite everything. I'm so scared. I wish I could stop. I went to an eating disorder specialist today. I hate how it makes me feel so heavy, like I'll never get through this. They did so many tests. They think I'm developing eurythmia[30] or something. They put all those little stickers + cords on me to check my heart rate. They took so much blood that I wanted to kick the fucking shit out of them.

I need people's help, but no one understands. Everyone's too wrapped up in their own shit.

I'm failing school. I'm depressed. I've found the old Celexa + I'm taking 40 ml. Maybe now I can sleep.

**December 18, 1999**

God, I feel like I'm going to explode. My blood sugar is at least four hundred, and it must have risen by now. My stomach kills. I'm going literally insane obsessing about food. Abraham wanted to put me on Zoloft, but there's no way in hell I'd take it. I couldn't look myself in the eyes if I did.

I'm tired and tired of being tired. It takes 2–3 hours to fall asleep; then, these dreams start. Nightmares, usually. I'm naked or being attacked. Defenseless and powerless, like the one with the animals. I wake up a lot in the middle of the night sweaty. On the weekends, I wake up so early and can't get back to sleep. I'm too exhausted to do schoolwork. Abraham calls it obsessional anxiety, and it doesn't sound like a misdiagnosis to me.

**January 24, 2000**

I'm so scared. I think I have ketoacidosis. I was reading about it in that book yesterday. Apparently, when your BS [blood sugar] is consistently high, your body's total acidity rises, and the condition is deadly. My BSs have been in the three hundreds, four hundreds . . . and yesterday I got so dizzy I almost passed out twice. Still feel dizzy and out of it. Can't concentrate on anything. I'm aware I'm hurting myself. What scares me is I don't care. I don't care if I'm hospitalized. I don't care about kidneys or retinas or amputation. All I care about is losing weight. It comes before everything, and it's ruling my life.

What kind of person bases their entire existence around food and their body? Sometimes this drives me so crazy I burst into tears and just want to end it. I swear I don't go two minutes without food crossing my mind. I starve myself and then binge. It happens every day. I could never tell anyone how serious this is because then they might try to stop me.

### February 14, 2000

I went to the Hasbro clinic on Valentine's Day. I'm sick of everybody pushing me the fuck around and telling me what to do with my body. I'd rather die than keep living like this—taking all this insulin and working so fucking hard but never getting results. I hate being physically weak. I hate having to go to the hospital if I cut my foot. I hate all my scrapes turning into scars. I hate being so susceptible to all the damn viruses that last forever. I hate not being able to see because the excess sugar is entering my retinas. I hate knowing that just because I have fucking diabetes, I have to slowly trash and kill my body in order to lose weight.[31]

### February 16, 2000

I was mean and bitchy to everyone all day. I was so tired that afternoon that I fell asleep instead of going to Matt's birthday party. When I woke up, no one was home. It was past Valentine's Day, so I ate the chocolates I was going to send Paul. I felt so sick. It wasn't only physical. I felt guilty. I wanted to throw up so bad, but I couldn't make it happen. I have no gag reflexes. Then I remembered the ipecac. It's meant for ingestion of poison. It makes you throw up. I put some in a glass and stood there. Tired of holding back, I just drank it. Then I waited. It takes fifteen minutes to go through your system, and it's some violent shit. I threw up four times. It was terrible.

So I'm bent over this toilet, and it occurs to me that I'm no longer rational about this. I don't have any control. Mom called the Poison Control Center. I kept crying, shaking. I recall purple, shaky hands. Red eyes. My God, they were so red. Feeling empty and limp. I made her promise not to tell anyone.

The next morning, I weighed one hundred thirty-nine pounds. It's sick the shit you have to go through to reach your goals.

## March 8, 2000

There's something up with insulin. Let's say I work out extremely hard. Even if I eat no carbs, I will not be able to lose any weight if I take sufficient insulin. It's not only in my head; the scale affirms this. Now, if I don't take the required amount of NPH or wait until very late to take it, something incredible happens. I get results. My stomach shrinks, and I lose those few pounds that never seem to want to leave.

## March 24, 2000

People think they get it, but no one has a damn clue, and I don't have a damn clue as to what I should do about it. Fuck, I'm pissed. I'm so fed up with this. It never leaves me alone. NEVER. I want to live, and I can't. I feel like I'm so trapped, and no one is willing or knows how to help. In the meantime, I'm dying, or at least that's what it physically and emotionally feels like. Pains streak through my body all the time. I'm constantly dizzy and faint. Keep having these awful dreams where Paul is indifferent towards me. My heart just falls to the ground. I cared about school last week, but now I just don't give a fuck. Nothing makes me happy or excited but food.

## April 3, 2000

I wish somebody truly understood. Sometimes I wish someone knew. I can't and don't know how to take this all on by myself. It's so overwhelming. I have no idea where to begin. I'd just rather push it all away, live on the surface.

## April 15, 2000

I've been having these thoughts lately of when I die. I don't think it's that far off. The doctors say every time I do this [restrict insulin], it's like Russian roulette. I guess that's because of the risk of going into cardiac arrest. I pray every night for God to take away my sins, let me go to heaven. I think one night, I'll go to bed and just never wake up. I see flashes of people at a church. Mom giving Paul all my journals. I love these people, but I can't just make this all go away. I love them, but I can't live normally anymore. I know in my right mind I should be saying, "Stop this now before it's too late." But it's not that simple, not all black and white.

## May 30, 2000

Today for the first time, I got myself to throw up—normally. This only worked because I put the back of a toothbrush down my throat. If you do it about three times, it'll come up by the fourth. I came home and ate six bowls of bran flakes, so I felt it had to be done. Shit—bran flakes. If I had waited a few days, I probably could have just shit it all out. I couldn't stay at the cookout either. I could see the food + and my soul just started grabbing for it. I didn't deserve to eat.

Everybody should leave me alone. I feel like shit. I don't deserve anything. I'm ugly inside and out.

I wish somebody really cared. I wish I had somebody to trust who lost sleep over me.

I'll do this again. It's not so bad—just not so thorough or quiet.

### June 9, 2000

Before, I was displaying the anorexic eating patterns—the control issue. Now I'm leaning towards bulimia—feeding the empty soul. When I came home from school today, I felt it. The inevitable onset of a binge. I was not at all hungry. Why did I suddenly crave food? I need to figure out the triggers so I can avoid this. I ate two pieces of bread and around three bowls of cereal, and I was sitting by the toilet on my knees for the second time today, watching the water in the bowl shake. The only explanation I have is Paul. I was writing to him when the urge to eat arrived. I doubt I can be with him. I don't think I can not be under pressure or not manipulate myself when he is in the picture.

Anyways, what I learned tonight is that I'm emotionally confused, but just because I bury my confusion by eating does not mean I deserve to stick a toothbrush down my throat and make myself vomit. So I made a mistake by eating. I was a confused wreck. Maybe I will learn from this and avoid the situation next time. What precious little I have left of myself I need to hold onto, embrace it, make it strong. I will develop a relationship with myself and learn to nurture her. Paul trips me up. I know I have more control when he is out of the picture. I think the next step is to tell him goodbye.

Shit, how can I do that?!? Shit.

### June 12, 2000

Today I was kneeling by the toilet again, and I thought, "Hell no. I just ate a lot because I was confused + upset, and there is no fucking way in hell I'll punish this confused girl for that." It was hard, but I left the bathroom. I knew I loved myself and didn't deserve that and went to read and write.

I'm proud of that. I weigh 139 pounds, and I do not feel deprived. This book, *Breaking Free from Compulsive Eating* by Geneen Roth, is a lifesaver.

### June 15, 2000

At the moment I do not want to eat, but yesterday I did. Going through old letters from Paul usually does it. Sometimes, if I get a new letter, I open the shoebox and compare it to one with the same date one year ago. That hurts unbelievably and always brings on the urge.

I have to get ahead of myself and prevent the binges. Not only that, but I want to be at peace, enjoy life fully. No one is going to take that from me. It is a vow I make to myself.

I don't give a damn how cheesy this sounds. Like Roth says, I love everyone when I love myself; therefore, I have to fall in love with myself.

### July 4, 2000

Something I want to get off my chest: I don't know if I have a very long time left. Due to the extremely decreased dosage of insulin, my heart literally hurts. God—it beats so fast. The only way to describe it is that it's strained. Oh, God, but please help; because I just can't bring myself to go back to the way it was—don't let me go yet, God, help me get better. I got this feeling it's just You and me because nobody else could understand.

I have to go to bed. My heart is beating too fast. I'll come back. I love you, Rachel. Not sharing you with anybody yet, babe. I love you—nobody else does like I do.

### July 5, 2000

Well, happy birthday to myself. Finally, I'm sixteen, though it feels like I should be seventeen.

I figure today's going to be a new start. I'm going to try again. I started on Celexa once more last night, and I will walk every night—three to five miles.

The insulin at some point also has to be regulated. I wonder if it's true what they say—that hyperglycemia eats up your organs. I know ketoacidosis is more dangerous—that's what I've heard, anyway. My heart beats so fast it scares me. My kidneys feel—I can't explain it—fragile, I guess, like I have to walk slowly over to the bathroom so they won't rupture. The worst is my brain. I think the damage has started. I see inanimate objects moving. Last night, I was running, and I was so jumpy because I saw spots in the street moving around and shit following me. God, this is so messed up. I really have to stop. I'm going to try.

I loved having Paul here these past two days to celebrate my birthday. Just wish I could talk certain things over with him—say them out loud to have a *reality check. He would think I was being a drama queen. That's not true—this is really scary, and I just want someone else to be worried + look out for me.*

*When he was in my room + we were talking about the eating disorder, I just couldn't stop crying because I was face to face with the source of my disorder! I have to tell him that he triggers me because I'm sexually attracted to him, and we also have to talk about self-control. That binge last night: she's upset. Feels forgotten. I have absolutely no other alternative than being my 100% true self around him, or this is all over.*

### July 6, 2000—10:52 p.m.

*I'm really sorry I talked to Paul. Obviously, I'm the only reliable support system. I am so mad. I let somebody in to help out + I feel worse. How lonely to be in love with someone who doesn't care.*

*I'm also mad that he puts me in a position where I have to feel like a damn slut just because I'm a normal teenager. Why didn't he take some of the blame when Mom caught us under the streetlight? I think I'm done.*

### July 7, 2000—1:18 a.m. (Friday)

*Not doing so good these last few days. I eat so much + am relieved because I don't have to deal with it—I just pee it out. The fact that I want to constantly eat tells me something is very wrong. This is classic; I eat like that because I feel empty. Why do I feel empty? Maybe because I'm killing her to have a beautiful body. It's funny, you know . . . sometimes I'll look in the mirror and see progress—I'll look good, skinnier. Then I get this overwhelming urge to eat, and nothing fills it up, the void, I mean. I don't get it. It's as if the lack of the struggle lost my personality. It is so much of who I am. Or maybe it's because I'm so immersed in beautifying my outside instead of my inside. God, I can't believe I wear a 3/4. And what's up with my eyes being so red? I hope that's not permanent nerve damage or some shit—I hope it's just a side effect of sleep deprivation. Speaking of which, I better go to sleep. Sometimes I'm scared to. Like Abraham said, it's Russian roulette. I'm afraid I won't wake up. Sometimes, I get scared that someone will be reading this after I'm dead. This is so fucking dramatic but realistic. I'd miss being alive, even though I don't enjoy it. This is my battle. To survive and save my soul, my personality, my body.*

August 1999–July 2000
age fifteen to sixteen

# OBLIVIOUS

IN THE MONTHS FOLLOWING our emergency endocrinology meeting, Rachel seemed to be back on track. She appeared to be counting carbs, and when I asked if her sugars were good, she usually nodded.

Granted, there was that ipecac episode on Matt's birthday in February of 2000. I had just returned from his party at Pizza Hut when Rachel met me at the door, confessing in a shaky voice that she'd overeaten and made herself vomit with syrup of ipecac. Her face was blotched and drawn. "It was horrible, absolutely horrible! I will never, ever do that again!" she vowed.

Certain that Rachel had learned her lesson, I forgot about it. After all, I'd seen no other evidence of disordered eating. I do recall Rachel's anxiety when we were low on milk. If we were down to even two-thirds of a gallon, she'd leave an urgent note or phone message, insisting I buy more when I thought I'd just bought milk the day before—or was it two days ago? Never certain, I chalked it up to growing kids and acquiesced, never dreaming that cereal was Rachel's major binge food.

I thought Rachel was improving, finally talking, not only with Dr. Abraham but now also with me, admitting that diabetes made her feel like "damaged goods," inquiring over and over why she had gotten it. As we talked, I thought we were chipping away at her illness, reducing it to a manageable size.

Then one day, she asked, "How would you feel about me getting a pancreas transplant?"

Realizing for the first time how desperate she was to be free of her disease, I had to consider her request. What if an operation did rid her of her nemesis? What if she could wake up and never have to worry about blood tests, shots, diets, or future complications? But then I pictured my adolescent daughter on an operating table. I shook my head. I could not endorse a risky surgery with no guarantee that her body would even accept the organ when diabetes could be safely treated with diet and insulin.

Though deflated, Rachel did not argue back.

Nor did she abandon her belief that surgery was her only hope.[32] That same month she covertly applied (but was not accepted) to participate in an islet transplant[33] trial at the Diabetes Institute for Immunology and Transplantation at the University of Minnesota.

With the same stealth that Rachel sought a pancreas transplant, she continued to practice her EDs. In the evenings, when she wasn't out running, she was in her room journaling or talking with Paul. After a year and a half, their romance had hit some bumps, but they were still together.

As for my romance with Phil, it kept getting sweeter. On weekends when we both had our kids, we took them to matinees or played board games. I made big dinners, sometimes with themes.

The kids were always wild. Matt and Nikki were close in age, respectively thirteen and twelve, so maybe their playful put-downs were flirtations. But Krissy and Ryan, both seven, seemed to be fierce rivals, determined to outshine the other by their mutual digs. Meanwhile, Matt and Nikki never missed a chance to bash their kid sibling for a cheap laugh. Gales of laughter followed jab after jab. When Rachel wasn't babysitting, she joined in, hooting at the dynamics while doling out her own insults. As the oldest, she felt everyone was fair game.

During one of these dinners, I eyed Phil, who was seated at the opposite head of the table, smiling and shaking his head, all dimples. "I can't do this," I mouthed, probably spooked by Doreen's recent remark: "You better think twice before taking on that Brady Bunch."

He got up, stooped beside me, and took my hand. Lacing his warm, calloused fingers through mine, he said, "I know it's nuts, but I can handle anything as long as it includes you."

THOUGH I'D BEEN PRIMED, it was still a punch to my gut when in March of 2000, Rachel went to live with her dad. Of course, she felt closer to him. He and Paul's mom, Lizzie, had coordinated a surprise Christmas reunion that involved Rachel traveling to New Jersey. Apparently, I was the only parent concerned about a fifteen-year-old girl taking a six-hour train ride alone. I eventually gave in—the romance had to run its course—but my initial misgivings must have driven a wedge between us.

Two months later, Perry dumped Rachel back on my doorstep, claiming it had not worked out. Rachel was jealous of Cam, his current girlfriend.

Who could blame Rachel? I'd met this curvaceous Vietnamese woman several weeks earlier while painting some rooms in Perry's new condo.

It had started as a joke. Laughing, Perry had offered me ten dollars an hour to paint his kitchen and living room. Also laughing, I countered with twenty dollars. Both laughing—but now mutually serious—we settled on fifteen dollars, and he handed me a key.

I was perched on a ladder in torn Levi's and a paint-splotched T-shirt, rolling white paint on the last stretch of the living room ceiling, when I heard keys rattle in the lock. I looked down to see Perry's grinning face, a petite woman with long, black hair rushing past him.

"C'mon down. I want you to meet Cam, but first she wants to freshen up."

Now, that was ironic. I was the one whose face was so stippled with paint that I'd startled myself in the bathroom mirror earlier. My hair was matted down by a red bandana. Yet she was freshening up.

I waited and waited, his leather couch squeaking as I crossed and uncrossed my legs until Cam finally sashayed in. I'd seen framed photos of her in his condo, but she was prettier in person: heart-shaped face, hair stylishly layered, a few bangs falling seductively over her arched brows and exotic eyes. Full red lips to match her stretchy red T-shirt that, though not low-cut, left little doubt as to the enormity of her breasts. "Cam must be proud of her rack," Rachel remarked one day, "because she shows cleavage in every outfit. When she leans over, the boys look away." Tight, flared jeans showcased more of Cam's curves. In wedge-heeled sandals, her blood-red toenails, tiny as a doll's, peeked out from her denim hems. As Perry introduced us, I crossed my arms over my insignificant chest, inching my size-nine sneakers under his coffee table.

Over the years, I would see Cam many times, but my reaction of pure awe never changed. She must have worn costly facial creams, primers, and foundations because her makeup was always flawless. Mine melted in an hour. I saw how she turned heads, and I coveted her power. Could I look that good if I exerted the effort? But my reveries ended there. That took inordinate time and resulted in bondage—too dear a price to pay.

I understood why Cam might not give Rachel the warm fuzzies.

"He completely dumped me for that—that—stunted Barbie Doll!" Rachel spat out the day she returned. Her hair was braided, drawing attention to the swollen vein on her troubled brow. Rachel's eyes blinked back tears. "I can't believe he would choose her over me—his own daughter!"

I wanted to phone and ream him out. Nevertheless, I restrained myself as I had done countless times in previous years, recalling Marcy's advice.

"Never ever openly bash Perry in front of your kids. Regardless of what he does, he's still their dad. Bad mouthing him will only hurt them."

"I'm sure it wasn't deliberate, Rachel. He has a different kind of a relationship with her."

"No doubt about that! It's obvious what he sees in her! But how do you think that makes me feel?" Her eyes were wild, outraged.

"I can see you feel very wronged."

"That's an understatement!" She exhaled a few short puffs. I thought that was the end of it, but then her lips trembled, and her face contorted. As sobs rocked her body, I embraced her, feeling her spasms like stakes through my heart.

There was no mention—not one word—of this abandonment in Rachel's journal. She treated it like her diabetes diagnosis and everything else that cut too deeply: by tucking it away.

# Bittersweet Sixteen

Paul's gigantic blue eyes jumped out at me first when Rachel introduced us. As I caught my breath, the rest of him followed: short, honey-brown hair, medium height, easy smile. He wore a wife-beater, long, baggy shorts, and skateboarding shoes. Oakley sunglasses perched on his head. I didn't expect the slight Southern drawl, but it certainly fit.

A sweet kid, Paul seemed mutually smitten with Rachel. From the moment he arrived on her birthday, July fifth, two thousand, until he left two days later, their hands were fused.

Paul detached himself long enough to show Matt some skateboard moves. He manipulated Matt's skateboard like a yo-yo, doing "ollies" and "kickflips" with ease. From the window, I observed Rachel watching him, her lips curled into a proud smile. Matt's mouth was agape. Even Ryan, Krissy, and Jordan, who were riding their bikes around the neighborhood, stopped to gawk as Paul whizzed by doing skateboarding stunts.

Rachel's sweet sixteen party was slated for July fourteenth, but since Paul couldn't attend, we celebrated it twice. As we sang "Happy Birthday," Rachel smiled self-consciously. Paul gave her a mood ring. After cake and ice cream, Rachel and Paul excused themselves to take a walk. I guess they deserved some space. The kids had trailed them all day as if Paul were a rockstar.

I watched the clock as I cleared dishes, not sure how much time to allow.

Shouldn't I know these things? After three years of parenting a teenage girl, shouldn't this be getting easier? Yet, I kept second-guessing myself. Was I giving Rachel too much privacy or not enough? Which issues should I enforce, and which should I ignore? My uneasiness reminded me of Rachel's birth when on discharge day, a nurse had handed me a human life, wrapped in pink flannel. As she bid me good luck, I thought, Is she nuts? I have absolutely no idea what I'm doing!

I gathered I was to stand back as Rachel toddled toward independence. Falling down was part of the process. Yet, wasn't I supposed to keep her safe—wasn't that my job, too? Rachel was impulsive. Brazen and curious, she took risks. How could I shield her from harm while letting her grow up? It seemed almost impossible.

After forty minutes, I set out to find the lovebirds. It was a balmy summer night, with a yellow moon and singing crickets. I hadn't walked far in the neighborhood when I spotted them under a streetlight in the strangest position: sitting spread eagle on the sidewalk, feet to feet, leaning way over to hold hands. Of course, they were dressed, but what a pose. How pathetic that in trying to find privacy, they had ended up so exposed.

On the one hand, wasn't their passion natural? At their age, hadn't I run through damp grass at dusk with Luke Conklin, craving shelter to kiss him? But that was in the '70s when for me, even French kissing was out of the question—I'd clenched my teeth to bar tongue. Kids today didn't stop at kissing. I don't recall what I said, only feeling the weight of their shame as they scrambled to their feet and shot off toward the house, holding hands.

On Sunday, Phil and I drove Paul to the train station. The teens whispered in the back seat, their fingers interlaced. Phil purchased Paul's ticket per Lizzie's request as Paul had run out of cash. As they kissed goodbye on the platform, I felt a pang, wishing I hadn't separated them so abruptly.

✦    ✦    ✦

Rᴀᴄʜᴇʟ's sᴡᴇᴇᴛ sɪxᴛᴇᴇɴ ʙɪʀᴛʜᴅᴀʏ party happened on the hottest day of summer. Thank God for air. How I had protested when my ex-mother-in-law had offered to pay for it. I told her the summers on Aquidneck Island were bearable. On scorchers, we hit the beach. "You'll need it for your B&B," Pattie insisted. She sent a check, and air conditioning was installed in the spring. That morning, while baking Rachel's birthday cake for the first time without sweating rivulets, I blessed Pattie, who had remained my friend long after her son left me.

The smell of chocolate cake taunted Rachel, Phil, and me as we strung aqua, lilac, and silver streamers around the kitchen. From the ceiling, we hung silver paper lanterns. Rachel's chatter accelerated as the room glittered and glowed. We dressed the deck off the kitchen with more streamers and string lights, tying sixteen different colored helium balloons around the perimeter. Without the slightest breeze, the balloons barely moved.

Rachel had refused birthday parties two years in a row. When she requested a sweet sixteen birthday party, I was all in.

Her handmade turquoise invitations promised:

*A Moonwalk*
*Tight sounds*
*Mad food to get fat from*
*My fabulous version of Truth or Dare*
*Water balloon fight (no, we are not too old)*
*And me—which is reason enough!!*

Rachel had one stipulation: "No siblings, real or potential. The last thing I need is drama from those clowns. I'll make an exception for Phil." She invited eight friends. I knew them all, except for a couple, or rather "an item," as she called them, who were "popular kids."

The Moonwalk was way out of my budget, but this birthday was special. To justify the expenditure, we celebrated Rachel's birthday later that year, using the bouncy house for Ryan's birthday party on July fifteenth. I bought the other party fare but drew the line at sixty dollars' worth of M&Ms: too much money—and sugar. Leftover cake and ice cream were problematic enough.

Over the last month, Rachel had become increasingly transparent about her food urges, especially sweets. She had struggled with overeating for two years, but there was a new urgency in her voice. "I think about food twenty-four-seven!" she confessed. "I never, ever get a break!" She admitted being unable to resist her impulses while babysitting for Carlene Barone, whose kitchen was stocked with every possible confection. When I refused to buy the M&Ms, Rachel bought them herself. The colorful candies clicked happily as she dumped bag after bag into a large yellow bowl.

That my daughter had a serious eating problem was suddenly so obvious. How had I not seen it sooner? I resolved to call Dr. Siru after these parties.

The guests were due at four. By three p.m., the pizza was ordered, the cooler stocked with soda and moved to the deck. Phil had even washed the windows in the kitchen and adjoining sunroom where the kids would likely congregate. Rachel had cleaned the entire house just in case her guests ventured upstairs. I smiled, noting the gleaming bathrooms and spotless floors, her fashion magazines fanned attractively across the oval coffee table in our living room.

Beauty and fashion magazines had begun to appear on our couches and end tables earlier that year. Rachel said they were outdated versions from Carlene Barone's beauty salon.

"You know, those magazines are really shallow," I remarked. "They make you think all that matters is your looks—making yourself beautiful to get a guy." Yet, I couldn't deny their allure. I'd never purchased a beauty magazine, yet in doctors' offices, I found myself reaching past *Time* and *Newsweek* for *Vogue* or *Elle,* mesmerized while flipping through them by the vibrant glossies of tall, flawless women, each more arresting than the last.

Rachel shrugged. "Oh, I don't read the articles. I just cut out pictures for the collages in my journals."

I didn't want to thwart Rachel's art. Still, I knew she was viewing myriad images of perfection she could never attain. She already struggled with her body image. We made a deal: She could keep her magazines if she also read *Brio,* a Christian magazine for teenage girls published by Focus on the Family that contained character-building articles, as well as girl talk and tips. I hoped *Brio* would, if not counteract, at least balance the negative effects of beauty magazines.

Approaching the spread of magazines that day, I was pleased to see *Brio* nestled among *Vogue, Cosmo, Marie Claire, Glamour,* and *Allure.* Hoping to highlight *Brio,* I increased the space between these magazines, but it still appeared lost, outnumbered, and outsized by these mega magazines.[34]

Rachel wore a silver crocheted off-the-shoulder shirt over her silver bikini top and white shorts. She had wanted to wear her newly bleached hair down, but as she was filling water balloons at the kitchen sink, it got in the way. She abruptly stopped, wound her long hair into a knot, and cinched it with a silver scrunchie that she bit off her wrist.

I was taken aback when Rachel had returned from Cam's salon platinum. A skilled colorist, Cam had been applying subtle highlights to Rachel's dark blond hair for over a year; however, this color screamed look at me, screamed cheap. But platinum hair was "in." Marcy and Doreen had both gravitated toward whiter highlights. I let it go.

At first, the party crawled. The kids sat on the deck, their talk tense as if they were trying way too hard to be cool. The "item" held hands, smiling but hardly contributing. The water balloon toss was anticlimactic. Even the moonwalk was deserted. The heat didn't help—the teens wiped their brows, popping soda after soda.

While I was leaning over to restock the cooler, I felt cold water droplets pelting my back. I looked up. Phil had dragged the garden hose over to the deck and had opened fire on the kids.

"What are you doing!" I yelled.

Damp streamers drooped. The floral paper tablecloth and napkins were buckling before we'd even sung Happy Birthday. I grabbed the M&Ms and chips while the kids, shrieking and laughing, scattered. Most charged into the backyard, only to be soaked. Rachel, on the other hand, pulled open the slider door and ducked into the kitchen with a few kids behind her.

"He's in for it now!" she vowed while frantically filling large kettles and bowls with tap water. She handed these to her guests, who were all lining up for ammo, drenched but alive, smiling. Sloshing water on the counter and floor, they exited out the slider and doubled back to ambush Phil. Each time he was soaked, he turned the nozzle on the guilty kid, only to be doused from behind.

When everyone was revived and dripping wet, Phil turned off the hose. Rachel and Kira splashed him one last time with simultaneous waves of water. He laughed and shook his head like a wet dog.

"I was trying to save your daughtah's pahty," he explained as we walked to the front of the house. I sat on the brick front steps smiling while Phil removed his wet sneakers, emptying the water. Next, he pulled off his socks and tank top, wringing them out and draping them over the white picket fence.

"Want a towel?" I laughed.

"Nah, this actually feels good." He sat beside me in his wet Levi's cutoffs. Closing his eyes, he tilted his head toward the sun. Water droplets glistened on his full, dark chest hairs.

"Do you ever feel like you have no idea how to raise your daughters?"

"All the time." He smiled.

"I know I'm supposed to monitor Rachel, but if I watch her too closely, she resents me. Still, I don't trust her. I feel like if I turn my back, she'll get into trouble." I sighed. "I can't seem to find that middle ground."

"You have to keep half an eye on her," Phil said, his eyes now open, one hand shielding the sun. "Let her go, but check up on her. That reminds me," he said, standing. "We need to visit the lovebirds." He held out his hand. "I think I saw them slip into the Moonwalk."

To carry out his operation discreetly, Phil went around the opposite side of the house. I followed him, stomach churning. I did not like busting teens. I think it was the discomfort—theirs and mine—that I shrank from. Phil was about to show me how it was done.

Entering the bouncy house, we saw that, sure enough, "the item" was entangled on the cushy floor, making out.

"Is this a private pahty?" Phil asked, smiling. There wasn't a shred of censure in his warm brown eyes and dimpled grin. The kids immediately pulled apart, laughing as they fought to right themselves on the unwieldy inflatable floor before clumsily exiting the bouncy house.

So that was all it took, a noncritical cliché?

Who was this guy who was teaching me how to relate to teens? Who cared enough about the success of a sixteen-year-old girl's birthday to risk her mother's wrath? I hadn't known Phil a year, yet in every new context, I saw more endearing traits that drew me to him.

As soon as we resumed our seats, we heard Rachel rounding up her friends for Truth or Dare. To escape the heat, she had opted to play this game in the air-conditioned sunroom, a luminous room in the front of the house, with two large windows and double French doors leading to the kitchen. This room could also be accessed from the foyer by a single French door.

From the front steps, Phil and I were completely hidden from the kids' view. We couldn't see them, but we could hear them even through the closed windows.

"Now it's your turn," Phil whispered. "We listen 'til it gets vulguh. Then you step in."

I nodded, hoping it wouldn't come to that. I did not want to make a scene.

The game began innocently enough. We heard kids read questions like, "What age was your first kiss?" "Have you ever cheated on your boyfriend or girlfriend?" "Who's the sexiest person here?" The kids' answers triggered groans or laughs from the group. The dares—smelling another's armpit, licking the floor, putting ice down one's shorts—also got quite a rise. I was starting to think this was a great teenage game until I heard some hapless kid read the question, "Have you ever given or received head?"

Jumping up, I burst through the front door. Opening the single French door, I said, "Rachel, may I talk to you for a minute?"

The smile slid off her face. "Uh, yeah." The kids' solemn eyes followed her out of the room.

"Phil and I heard that last question," I said, leading her into the living room and out of earshot.

"So, you guys were spying on me?"

I ignored her attempt to shift the blame.

"You kids were having such a good time. Why did it have to get dirty?"

"We always ask those kinds of questions during Truth or Dare."

"Not in this house you don't." Softening my tone, I added, "It's your birthday, Rae. I want you and your friends to have fun. I just want you to keep it clean."

Reddening, she nodded.

"The peetser's here!" Phil suddenly announced, managing to enter through the front door while balancing five large boxes. The smells of bread dough and pepperoni permeated the air. "There's soder and watah in the coolah," he added, motioning to the kids in the sunroom with his head.

Rachel brightened, joining the posse of hungry teens following Phil to the deck.

✦   ✦   ✦

AFTER THE PARTY, RACHEL and Kira, who was sleeping over, disappeared upstairs. Cleanup was easy, as Phil and I had been wiping spills and collecting trash all day. When we were finished, I lit a Citronella candle and carried it out to our patio table. Phil followed with two glasses of chilled chardonnay. The mild night air carried a note of smoke from a neighbor's firepit. Stars glistened in the sky like loose diamonds on black velvet. Smiling, we dropped into deck chairs. Rachel's party was a success, a sparkler during a dark stretch that was about to get even darker. For one full day, she enjoyed being a normal teenage girl. And, with a little help from Phil, I enjoyed being her mother. Maybe I could get better at this. At the end of that day, anything seemed possible.

July 18–August 27, 2000

# "I WILL BE BEAUTIFUL"

### July 18, 2000

*No matter how high or low I get, I'm going to make some changes. I am going to make her so internally beautiful that I'll walk around like I used to—like I have this deep, priceless treasure inside of me. The food isn't bothering me like it used to. I am so thankful for that. I mean, I still run to it, but I know it doesn't serve any purpose. I know I'm going to get the body I want. I believe I am capable. I'm going to become more spiritually aware. These are my goals. I'll slip up, as I always do, but I love her, so I won't be so angry. She'll make mistakes, but . . . I'd rather live with her as she grows.*

### July 19, 2000

*God, will You help me? Fill me up with you, not the desire for food. I can write about whatever I want, whenever I want. Babe, don't be afraid to write in here. Granted, there's a lot to sort out, but you'll never get well if you fail to even attempt. God, please, I am afraid to trust You. I'm afraid of being let down. I can't do this anymore, God. Please, please, please, please help me. Sometimes I get relieved at the thought that I will die one day. At least then, I will be at peace. I'm at the eating disorder clinic now. It helps to come here, even though a root canal seems more appealing. It's like these doctors keep me in check. Somebody knows, you know? I can't believe I'm 128 lbs. My belly is sticking so far out.*

### July 23, 2000

*Why do we feel empty sometimes? Like I have no company inside. It's very uncomfortable to feel my stomach so full; yet feel dead. Maybe I shouldn't run away from it. Maybe she just wants to be still and to listen. I hate that disconnected feeling.*

*Everything feels unfamiliar tonight. The road always feels so long.*

## July 26, 2000

I dyed my hair last night to cover my roots, and nobody likes it. I do, though. What happened to only caring about what I thought? Screw what Paul thinks. What gets me is that he liked how I looked before—maybe that's some subtle hint that he liked who I was before. I miss it too sometimes—just being myself—and stupid as it sounds, it's like I have to rebuild identity every time what I look like changes. But I like this hair color.

I'm definitely paying the price of thinness. Because of all the excess blood sugar in my system, I can't get over these illnesses. Bacteria feed on sugar, so no efforts my immune system makes are effective. I have conjunctivitis, a yeast infection, and what I think is a sinus infection.

## August 1, 2000

Sometimes I receive this creepy feeling like one day people will be reading the documentation of a girl dying to be thin. Maybe I should explain this.

Well, I love life.

I want to enjoy it to the fullest. I can't enjoy A DAMN THING when I am overweight or have overeaten. If I die doing this, know I died happy. I like my body. I like feeling sexy and dancing without having my stomach stick out. I love being able to eat crap and not paying for it. I love losing weight after I've worked for it. I love waking up and eating what I want. I can't express how incredible it feels to live normally for this period of time. It's so nice to take a break from being diabetic—nobody could understand how nice.

## August 7, 2000

They are forcing me to go to the hospital. I do not want to go. I want a normal summer, no matter how effective the partial hospitalization program may be. I want to work, visit Paul, and just be lazy. If you could only understand how sick I am of seeing that hospital and all those doctors.

When Paul called, I couldn't explain how bad I was feeling . . . I had a traumatic night, and FORGIVE ME if I wasn't immediately open to spilling my guts. Some people need to be eased and soothed. I'm not exactly relaxed about having to spend the next few weeks imprisoned in a hospital because my life is out of control—so when he said, "Whatever, I guess I'll talk to you, like, later <click>" . . . I burst into tears.

### August 10, 2000

*I'm at the hospital now. I feel so anxious. I'm tired, and I feel extremely strange to not be incessantly eating. But I feel safer here.*

*I have learned so much in the last ten hours. Heavy emotions—the ones I'd rather forget—trigger overeating. I want to keep a record of the emotions that make me crave certain foods to avoid bingeing. I think I like that food excites me. When the excitement dies down, I get scared—like there's nothing left. I feel myself getting vulnerable.*

I can't believe all the eating I've done here. There's really no supervision—it's not hard to binge.

The nurses said exercise was good for metabolizing blood sugar and let me walk laps around the ward. The walks proved to be a bad idea. There are four little kitchen-type stations on my floor that serve as holding compartments for food that comes up from the cafeteria at mealtimes, as well as snack bars for patients and visitors. Any time I want, I can put on Dad's huge green sweater and circle the ward, slip into one of the kitchen-rooms and hide whatever I can find in the long sleeves of the green sweater. I've swiped ice cream, crackers, even leftover food from other patients' trays; then, I head back to my room to eat it under the sheets.

They found the containers of ice cream. I wonder how many there were. I lied to one of the doctors—said it was my brother's. After eating the ice cream, I had to cover my tracks by taking extra insulin. I forgot I had left the stolen bottle of Humalog & a used needle in the drawer. I can only imagine what the nurse thought. Now I'm confined to my room.

## August 27, 2000

I will not become dependent upon this environment. Because then when I get back to the real world, I'll be vulnerable and scared—and that's not me.

I will keep myself strong, on the right path, and somehow figure this garbage out.

I will learn all I can from this program, including appetite stabilization, weight loss techniques, and better diabetes control.

I will accept the fact that the relationship w/ me and God comes first. Paul must take second place. I'll talk to him about this. If I feel empty being w/ myself and am reliant on him, something is wrong.

I will write down everything she says. I have to protect her future.

# August–September 2000
## age sixteen

# FALLING DOWN

RUSHING INTO RACHEL'S HOSPITAL room, I nearly tripped over a security guard stationed in front of her door, whose long, uniformed legs were stretched out like a barricade.

Startled, I excused myself.

The guard did not smile.

On August 10, 2000, Rachel had been admitted to the hospital and finally diagnosed with disordered eating and uncontrolled diabetes.

Shortly after Rachel's party, I had contacted her endocrinologist, recounting what Rachel had told me about her unrelenting food urges and binges. Dr. Siru already knew about Rachel's insulin manipulation, and by then, her A1c, the test that revealed her average blood sugars over several months, was off the chart, literally 15.1 when it should have been 6.4 or lower. The doctor made the diagnosis she should have made nine months earlier, placing Rachel in the Partial Hospitalization Program (PHP) for Eating Disorders at Hasbro Children's Hospital. However, doctors in the PHP quickly determined that Rachel needed a more intense level of care: hospitalization and suicide watch.

At the time, I thought the guard was a good touch. Treating Rachel like a criminal might teach her to take better care of herself.

I had forgotten that she had confessed her ED to multiple adults, myself included, who had neglected to help her.

Did she understand why she was being watched?

"I guess he's protecting me from myself," Rachel mumbled when I asked. She was propped up in bed journaling, her blue-print johnny exposing one frail shoulder.

During her hospitalization, Rachel continued her treatment at the PHP. Weekdays at 7:30, she rode the elevator to the top floor of the hospital to participate in individual and group therapy, supervised eating, nutrition counseling, and arts and crafts with the same five girls. That's where Rachel met Amanda, who was also blond and bulimic. Both girls loved to eat and laugh, unlike the reserved anorexic girls. Only now, at 3:30, when Amanda and the other girls went home, Rachel rode the elevator back down, walking the distance to her room.

That first week, Rachel received four flower arrangements, one from her brothers and me; two from the Barone family she babysat for, one from Carlene and Rich and another from their kids; and one from Paul. Now the perfume of roses and carnations mitigated the harsh smell of disinfectant that hung in her room. Rachel placed her beloved's basket of pink rosebuds, daisies, and baby's breath on her nightstand, relegating our blooms to her broad windowsill. Her face glowed every time she glanced at it.

Despite Paul's sweet gesture, his calls ended the next day. When Rachel tried to phone his school, he was unavailable. At his mother's house, the answering machine picked up. The flowers started to shrivel, shed petals, hang their heads. The odor of Lysol reclaimed the room. Yet, still no word from Paul. By the beginning of week two, I found his flowers in the trash. Three weeks would pass before Rachel understood his silence.

When Rachel was most upset, she ate. I would discover that being hospitalized for an ED did not stop her. Once the guard was removed, and the nurses relaxed, she conducted massive food heists, lifting leftovers from patients' abandoned trays and snacks from the nurses' station. The nurses never found out. Except for some empty ice cream cups discovered under Rachel's bed, the medical staff was blind to Rachel's bingeing. The guard had been a sham, merely posturing vigilance and protection.

At the end of week one, Rachel and I were summoned to a meeting with her medical team, which included an endocrinologist, a psychologist, an ED specialist, an RN, and a registered dietician. We met in a glassed-in, carpeted conference room not far from her room. Sitting around a vast conference table, the team took turns introducing themselves, each explaining his or her role in Rachel's recovery. We hadn't gotten far when one doctor began subtly chastising Rachel for not following protocol. His comment was so benign—he might have mentioned the ice cream—that I don't even recall it. However, Rachel leaped up from her chair, red-faced, the vein on her forehead bulging.

"Do you think 'cause you're a doctor you know something? I don't care how many degrees you have. You can't talk to me like that! You don't even know me! None of you people know me!"

Her electric eyes scanned the stunned faces around the table before she stormed out of the room. I watched her tirade as if from afar, realizing I didn't know her either. Excusing myself, I ran after her. By the time I caught up, she was halfway down the hall, her bleached braid swinging. I did not dare speak. Her rage gagged me.

Was this about Paul? I understood she was hurting, but what sixteen-year-old girl lambasts a roundtable of doctors?

Back in her room, Rachel climbed into bed. Her eyes darted to the broad window where cars raced down the interstate. Her face was still flushed, her expression murderous. Normally, I would have drawn her out; I was not one to hold back when something needed to be said. But I'd never seen her so enraged. What if words stirred her anger, aggravating her wound? Weren't onlookers warned not to touch injured bodies, lest they hurt them more? Better to wait for the paramedics.

Though Rachel's bingeing went unnoticed, this outburst did not. When coupled with some of Rachel's other behavior, her team suspected a personality disorder that they recorded in a cryptic note on her hospital report without informing me.

For that matter, I still didn't know about Rachel's diabulimia. Though her team was aware that Rachel had been restricting insulin since she was fourteen, not one doctor ever sat me down and plainly stated, "Your daughter is depriving her body of insulin to lose weight. She has a dual eating disorder: bulimia and diabulimia. Both are dangerous. Both are progressive. Both are mental illnesses. When combined with her diabetes, they can be deadly."

When Rachel was discharged on August twenty-seventh, I was no closer to understanding the scope of her disordered eating than I was before her hospitalization.

Despite the severity and longevity of Rachel's EDs, her team prescribed only five additional days of outpatient treatment in the PHP. Adding those days to the seventeen days that she participated in the PHP while hospitalized, Rachel received twenty days of therapy.

Twenty days to treat two eating disorders, with deeply ingrained thought patterns and habits Rachel had been practicing for two years. This meager treatment was inconceivable, especially given that untreated EDs intensify— and have the highest mortality rate of any mental illness.[33]

✦ ✦ ✦

SHORTLY AFTER RACHEL'S DISCHARGE, I received a call from Lizzy, Paul's mother, who demystified Paul's silence. Apparently, prior to her hospitalization, Rachel had mailed him several of her journals, which Lizzie intercepted and read.

"Please understand, I didn't read Rachel's diaries completely, just enough to get the gist of them." She paused. "I was only trying to protect my son."

I couldn't fault her for that. If some love-struck girl had mailed her journals to Matt, I might have done the same thing. Still, Lizzie's next comment took me aback.

"Your daughter is, well, complex—probably way too complex for Paul, what with her diabetes and now her eating disorder. Paul's young. He shouldn't have to deal with all these heavy issues. I want him to have fun. Your daughter's dragging him down."

While I was trying to recover from this vicarious slap of rejection, Lizzy continued.

"Look," she said in a let's-be-reasonable tone, "Rachel should focus on her health right now anyway, right?"

Right. And maybe you should have thought twice before nurturing a long-distance relationship between two fourteen-year-olds, I wanted to hiss.

Instead, I said: "Right. Goodbye." Click.

Rachel flushed deeply when I told her. Tears filled her incredulous eyes. "How could she? Those journals are mine!" Still, Rachel had enjoyed Lizzie's good graces for two years. The following day, she seemed ready to forgive all. "It's not over," she casually remarked. "Paul will work on Lizzie. He'll fight for us. We'll be laughing about this in a day or two."

But two weeks later, Lizzie transferred Paul to a co-ed boarding school, reporting to me in an email that Paul appeared happy and had his pick of girls. Of course, Rachel discovered it on our family computer.

Rachel desperately wanted to be known. I think she shared her journals with Paul to show him the facets of herself—the flashes of brilliance and creativity in her poetry and prose—that he missed in everyday conversations. She wanted to captivate him. That the journals precipitated their breakup, that her finest parts were boxed up and mailed back, was the ultimate rejection.

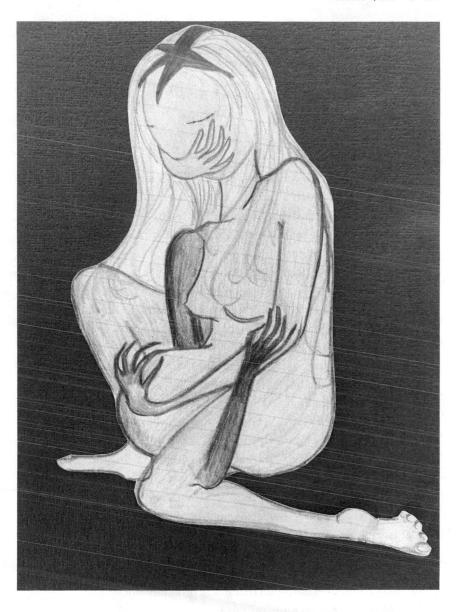

In this sketch I found tucked into an adolescent journal, Rachel captures her horrible quandary—her hands had turned against her, covering her mouth as she withheld insulin and harbored her "child self."

# Girl with Snarls

The Saturday after Rachel's discharge was a dreary stay-at-home day. Soft rain pattered on the roof. Ryan had slept over at Jordan's. After a breakfast of spinach and broccoli quiche, Matt retired to his room, the tedious melody from Zelda emanating from his Nintendo.

Rachel and I loitered at the table. She flipped through Glamour while I scanned her hospital report.

"What's suicidal ideation?" I asked, my pulse quickening.

Though I had read, "Rachel *denies* suicidal ideation at this time," even seeing my daughter's name in the same sentence as "suicide" was jarring.

"It just means suicidal thoughts," she said nonchalantly.

"You don't—"

"Of course not!" she snapped. "C'mon, Mom," she added, eyeing me directly. "You know me better than that."

I relaxed, even felt foolish. I'd never seen a hint of suicidal behavior in Rachel. In spite of her issues, she was usually upbeat. Wisecracks spouted from her, often followed by a chuckle at her own joke.

I would learn that my daughter was living a double life and getting darn good at lying about it.

There was another technical term in the psychological section of that report that I kept to myself—personality disorder deferred. I'd never heard of that term; however, it did not concern me—a personality referred to one's nature or disposition, and Rachel's was generally fine. Its "deferred" status made it sound even more benign. That her team had never mentioned a "personality disorder" confirmed that it was probably nothing.

I could not have been more mistaken.

Personality disorders (PDs) are serious, progressive mental illnesses. Surfacing in adolescence or young adulthood, PDs assault young people with a slew of distressing symptoms that disrupt nearly every aspect of their lives. There are good therapies for PDs. If caught and treated early, teens can live long, quality lives. Without help, though, youths can suffer for years, even decades, as their mental health deteriorates.[36]

Rachel's diagnosis was probably deferred because she was only sixteen. In 2000, doctors avoided diagnosing adolescent patients whose unruly teenage behavior might pass as PD symptoms.[37] Still, deferred diagnoses served as red flags, alerting doctors that certain patients had demonstrated enough PD behaviors to warrant being watched.[38]

Tragically, Rachel's team looked away. I would discover that her mental health at that time was already "serious," according to the GAF[39] score on her hospital report. However, she was not diagnosed with Personality Disorder NOS by Butler Psychiatric Hospital until eight years later, by which time, without medical care, twenty-four-year-old Rachel's GAF score had dropped to "severe."

Rachel's NOS designation meant "not otherwise specified." In other words, her PD did not match one of the twelve clinical PDs, listed in the bible of psychiatry, better known as the Diagnostic and Statistical Manual of Mental Disorders (DSM-IV-TR).[40]

From my vantage point—both what I observed and read in Rachel's eleven years of journaling—her symptoms bore a mirror-like resemblance to borderline personality disorder (BPD).

BPD or "Borderline" is a dangerous PD, marked by an unstable identity, emotions, and relationships, according to DSM-5.[41] Borderline commonly co-occurs with bulimia nervosa and substance abuse disorders, among other illnesses.[42] A person needs five symptoms to qualify as a clinical PD.[43] Between ages fourteen and twenty-eight, Rachel regularly grappled with seven of its nine symptoms. Identity disturbance, profound emptiness, fear of abandonment, turbulent relationships, fluctuating emotions, impulsivity, and self-harming behavior were common themes in her journals.

DSM-5's definition of identity disturbance is as vague as it is narrow: "[an] unstable self-image or sense of self." However, current studies,[44] along with Rachel's journals, suggest that this definition does not begin to convey people's suffering. A shaky identity makes it challenging for people to retain work, reach goals, or follow their politics and/or religion.[45] Rachel lost jobs, dropped out of college, and found it impossible to consistently practice her faith.

Most distressing to people with identity disturbance is their awareness of their fractured identities; some feel "fraudulent," like they're operating out of a "false self."[46] Rachel felt so psychologically split, so removed from her true self, that she began to refer to herself in her journals in dual terms, as both "she" and "I." The first time I read this, I paused. Who's this "she," some other girl? Then I realized it was Rachel. She was using two different pronouns to express her fragmented identity.

Certain Borderline symptoms Rachel hid from me. I was not aware of her intense emptiness, dizzying mood swings, and fear of abandonment until I read her diaries. Other symptoms, such as her impulsivity and turbulent relationships, I saw glimmers of as early as age fourteen, never dreaming they pointed to mental illness. After all, she was my eldest, and I took this as typical adolescent behavior. Nor did I know about her identity disturbance, the symptom that tormented her most, though she did send out one weak distress signal.

"I don't listen to my inner child like I ought to," Rachel announced one day at fifteen.

I looked up from the dishwasher I was packing, a plate in my hand. She had just entered the kitchen, wearing her pink backpack, comb tracks in her wet hair. It was Saturday, Perry's weekend with the kids, and she was waiting for him to pick her up, having opted out of Friday night to "get a break from my punk brothers."

Slipping the plate into a slot, I stood up to face her.

"What do you mean by inner child?"

"My true self, the part of me that's real."

I would learn that, true to Rachel's usage, "inner child" and "true self" meant the same thing: authentic personality. She was referring to the Rachel who spoke without a filter, as opposed to her phony social self, also called an ego or false self, according to Doctor Charles L. Whitfield, who wrote extensively on personality disorders and their link to substance abuse.[47]

"Have you talked to Doctor Abraham about this?"

She nodded but would not offer a crumb more.

"Well, why would you not listen to what's real?" I played along, trying to nudge her in the right direction. It wasn't the first time I had the disconcerting feeling that my adolescent daughter knew more about a subject than I did. "I would think that following something true would be smarter than following something false."

"You'd be surprised, Mom," was her grave reply.

Just then, we heard a sustained horn beep.

"It's Dad. I gotta bail." Slinging her backpack over her shoulder, she disappeared behind the slammed door.

At once, my mental to-do list started chanting: Grade papers, write lesson plans, apply for jobs, pay bills, call Mom. During those survival years, that list was a powerful force, drowning out Rachel's delicate plea for help.

I never followed up, never asked her why she didn't listen to her true self. Nor did she ever broach the subject again.

Except in her journals. To my astonishment, from fourteen on, these were brimming with her tremendous effort—and tragic inability—to nurture and follow her true self.

Rachel's failure to blossom into a healthy woman pained her because she knew she was no ordinary flower. Rachel possessed all the building blocks to succeed: Christian standards to cultivate a strong moral character; social skills; intelligence to pursue an education; even a relationship with herself, indicative of stable mental health. She was poised to make good friends, fall in love, find meaningful work, and live a long, successful life. At fourteen, that trajectory changed. Shortly after Rachel's diabetes diagnosis, as she was grappling with two budding EDs, Borderline joined her pack of disorders. At that time, she noticed a perplexing transformation in her personality as the real Rachel began to fade and a false self—Reckless Grace—took its place.

Apparently, this very real psychological wounding occurs when a person is made to feel inferior. Celebrated pediatrician and psychoanalyst Donald Winnicott blames the mother, believing that this happens in infancy under her watch. Abused or ignored by her own mother, she fails to fully validate her own child early in life. Feeling inadequate or nonexistent, the child retreats into her psyche, like a turtle into its shell.[48]

When a person's true self checks out, her false self steps in to control her life, stunting her development, according to Winnicott and Whitfield. Whitfield says a person with a dominant false self is naturally defensive. She denies feelings, distrusts, controls, and conforms to an extreme,[49] some of the very sentiments about which Rachel had begun journaling.

Initially, I scoffed at this. I may not have been the perfect mother, but I did not neglect Rachel during her infancy. I did not cling to my baby or use her to meet my own needs. Abuse was out of the question. This did not pertain to me. However, after I read about this mental wounding numerous times, even in current research, I had to take another long, hard look at Rachel's early years. My loveless marriage. My fog of depression. My drive to finish my master's degree. No doubt, I missed plenty.

A mother's "devotion" to her child for her first few years ensures good mental health, Winnicott claims.[50] Alice Miller, author of the best-seller *The Drama of the Gifted Child: The Search for the True Self,* calls it "rapt attention." A mother must be fully engaged in every facet of her child's development.[51]

Like most new mothers, for the first thirty-six months, I was enthralled by every sign of Rachel's growth: her first tenacious pull on my breast; the first time she rolled over or lifted herself on shaky arms; that first heart-melting smile of recognition; the musical notes of her first giggle; her first word, "ducky." I was riveted to Rachel's dimpled hands and downy hair. Until asthmatic Matt was born.

Next to her infant brother, Rachel suddenly looked huge. And whereas he was constantly coughing, wheezing, fidgeting, and crying, she was perfectly calm. With her toys and crayons, she could occupy herself for hours. And I let her.

Whitfield asserts that precious few mothers affirm every step in their child's development; therefore, most of us suffer some degree of mental wounding.[52] He further claims that other factors besides maternal influence reinforce the message that people are inadequate, including education, organized religion, politics, and the media.[53] Eminent psychiatrist and author James F. Masterson suggests that genes are also involved; some people will develop strong true selves while others will struggle.[54]

I'll never know the exact cause of Rachel's PD. What is clear from reading her journals is how much identity disturbance, a single Borderline symptom, distressed her.

Sitting beside my daughter on that lazy Saturday, the rain falling harder, streaking the windows like tears, Rachel looked like any other teenage girl. As she leafed through *Glamour,* occasionally stopping to clip a picture, I thought she had turned a corner. Her ED had been diagnosed, she had received intensive treatment, and had been referred to an ED specialist. I had no idea I was staring at someone who imagined an unkempt little girl who "never grew up" living within her. The girl, in a ratty nightgown with tangled and dirty hair, was Rachel's true self.

*September 8, 2000—July 7, 2001*

*I am a broken girl*

*I have broken blue eyes*
*fragile unsure hands*
*gripping for stability*
*grabbing like mad*
*for cold hands or things to hold*
*I am an empty girl.*

*She doesn't work like she used to.*

# "She has to survive"

**September 8, 2000—10:37 p.m.**

Everything inside of me is crying. I'm an undecipherable mess of emotions.
She's furious, depressed, frustrated, and dying.

**September 10, 2000**

And I lay down and felt it
running through winter's trees
standing at that window seat in the hospital
watching the freeway
wondering what it would take to fall
through that glass
the rage in my shaky arms
as I tried to escape from all the doctors in that room.
letting loose tides of profanity
on the bathroom floor
sobbing uncontrollably
the door open a crack
no privacy
she watches me in her white ignorance
why are their hands always at their
mouths?
oh God
let me fall through that window
and make such lovely colors
upon the pavement

**September 15, 2000**

I'm sitting in a bathroom. Do you know why? Because I am incapable of eating
like a normal human being. I can't now. I probably never will. No matter how

many times I tease my own mind into thinking I will one day be better, the reality is I see no possible way to do it short of a lobotomy.

I hate my body. I'm a disgusting gluttonous person. My thighs are big and disgusting, my stomach is huge, my upper arms are fat—nothing will ever be good enough. Because once I come within reach of this goal, I fuck it up. What's terrible is I have nowhere to go. The program barely helps and consumes all my time. If I tell my parents, they will send me back to the hospital. I'm too embarrassed to tell my friends. I can't even write because it's so redundant. I care, but I'm losing more strength every day. How long is this going to keep on going? I want it to end, but I will not commit suicide—ever.

I do not see an end to this road.
I see frequent periods of relief . . .
but I do not see myself cured.
I see myself inhaling
piles of food
Running miles and miles at night
I see anxiety consuming me.
I see this being a struggle every day
because I don't want to let go—
of the excitement food brings.

### September 20, 2000

I feel so anxious and unsettled today.

I still cannot believe Lizzie read my journals.

Paul's letter jacket is in a box ready to mail to him. Apparently, my journals are on their way back here. I realize I'm letting go of my last innocent tie to him. It's too late for anything anymore.

This is my book.
No, it is not just a book,
it is my heart, soul, mind
Written, arranged, and
made tangible.

Date: 09/20/2000 7:25:01 PM Eastern Daylight Time
From: Lizziemae42
To: Nouvelle18

*Hi, there. Paul had every intention of making good on his debt—he received two paychecks after he left for school (I received them for him). He will pay Phil back for the train ticket out of that. Sorry for the delay. The letter jacket got back to Paul—he mentioned wearing it the other day, though he did not mention that Rachel had returned it.*

*Paul is doing well at school—he's very happy, and very busy. If it has not already happened, I predict a falling off of contact with Rachel. While I was dropping him off at school, two girls came into the dorm room anxious to meet him. It was quite funny. He also seems to be hanging around with one girl in particular (no need to mention this to Rachel as I am unsure of the nature of the relationship). But he seems very happy when I talk to him. How is Rachel doing with her program?*

*Hope all is well.*
*Lizzie*
[Email from Lizzie to Carolyn, taped in Rachel's Journal]

### September 22, 2000

*Dear God, I know we haven't exactly been on the same page lately, but here it comes, that ice cream is in the freezer, and guess what?! I happen to want it! Please help, please draw me so close it doesn't even cross my mind. Draw me so close nothing can touch me. Raise me up from the dead, save me from my starving soul. Protect me from what is not Your will. If there is time and still some magic left, someday I want to be filled up.*

*I will feel full every day.*
*People will want my company.*
*I will go on road trips.*
*I will write a memoir.*
*I will raise children.*
*I will be with someone who knows how to love me.*
*I will pray every day.*
*I will remember my childhood.*
*I won't hesitate to sing in public.*
*I will enjoy every facet of every day I am given.*
*I am given so much.*
*There will be no abuse.*
*No aching stomachs*

no cries from the floor
no anxiety at food.

### September 25, 2000

I'll probably get my journals back today. That's good. I guess. What a dick. As if he forgot my address. Not worth it. Not worth it.

I am forced to restore what I did not steal. He stole my joy; there's nothing dramatic about that.

Last weekend Amanda + I met up in Providence. We got these really hot clothes—not revealing, just attention-grabbing and stylish. We got picked up by this college tennis team of ten guys who took us out to dinner. I was treated like gold by my date—his name was Matt. He didn't take advantage of anything. The point was I was treated so well I felt like I had to give myself away. He was cute, not fine, but confident, charming, and finally, someone who challenged my mind.

### September 26, 2000—11:00 a.m.

I lay myself upon the train tracks
She's inside me
hollowing out her Caverns
Running through the reddened trees
Ash upon the soles of her feet
No one will come near me
As I
possessed by every demon
Out stretch my arms upon the hospital window
and lean all the weight I do not have upon it

### September 30, 2000

I cannot forget the person I call my love, who puts school before me, turned his back on me, was given too much, doesn't fight for me, doesn't fight for us, shouldn't be taken seriously, doesn't see who I am, releases me, isn't concerned with my illness, has taken so much, pearls before swine.

I will remember this is who I call my love.

I dream of you
and your sunglasses

*and your arms*
*that do not want me.*
*All I can I think of is the incredible*
*amount I have consumed—the weight of it*
*yet solitude and loneliness*
*still surface like the coming tide*
*all I can think of is how abruptly*
*you left the last time I saw you*
*the train door anxious to shut*
*How you left*
*and never turned around.*
*I wonder if you knew then.*

> Subj: Re: (no subject)
> Date: 10/07/2000 11:42:30 PM Eastern Daylight Time
> From: Sipfromthisglass
> To: Rachbaby15
>
> um . . . ok . . . i myself would like to know what happens at school, but
> ok.. i see that you are very oblivious to everything around you. um . . . you
> always make things up in your head to believe what you want to believe. bye
> [Email from Paul, taped in Rachel's Journal]

### November 13, 2000

*I'm standing in the shower this morning, post-insulin, wondering why I'm down.*
*Then I remember my body. Funny how uncomfortable I am being thin. This*
*body reminds me of him. All I can think when I'm looking at myself is: he*
*would like this. I get this bound feeling, thinking fuck it, this was for him. I*
*don't know what type of body I want. I just know that I don't want to cheat*
*to get there. I think I just don't want to eat. No calorie counting, none of that*
*bullshit. I just don't even want to start, as once I do, progress and determina-*
*tion are gone. I'm stuck here, uncomfortable with this little waist.*

*The things I remember.*

*No one can take from me the times I have truly lived when I felt peace,*
*growth. Gardens inside of me. I knew I was special and wanted someone else*
*to notice.*

*But that isn't where anything begins. It begins in an old blue Honda trav-*
*eling hours upon hours to reach unfamiliar roads. The terrain gradually rises*
*to mountains and the purity of the snow. This is when we began to watch.*

I separated myself from the arguments of my two brothers and father, from the crowd of luggage . . . and looked out my window.

I remember the clean frozen air. The awareness we didn't have the money for this. My numb fingers in my gloves. I remember all the details, the frigid air in Princeton by the phones. This November chill is hauntingly familiar. There was always such cold air around Paul and me. At the mountains, in Boston, on the anthill, always the cold air. Remember the bus? Lips and ears so close, whispering as bricks in the wall crumble. Don't you miss who I became for you? I miss something to hold onto. My soul disappears with the landmarks out the window as she is scattered. Stepping gracefully onto the train platform, I am born. Stomach in knots. Palms sweaty. So excited! Why do you still wait there? My life is burning up now, can't you see? Heart all over the place, then the world pauses, and I'm alone.

I have so many terrible secrets inside me that I have to get out. I hate living. I hate coming back to these rooms, these mistakes. I hate mirrors, how pale I look in them. I push everybody away now. I can't stop eating. Fuck even trying because I will never be able to stop. It's like I can see my whole life on a plane stretched out before me. I hate being stuck in the middle of my different worlds, never knowing who I am.

### November 23, 2000

I walked three miles to buy that ice cream. When I finally got home, I devoured half of the container. When I leaned over the sink to throw it up, it was still cold. This is my life. I want all the food I see. My soul is already gone. She hates me, and so do I. I feel SO ANGRY AND POWERLESS. I gave up everything for him. I have nothing. No matter how hard I attempt to persuade myself otherwise, I know the truth.

I hate Paul, and I hate myself because I have no self, no identity anymore. Every day it feels like miners keep searching for diamonds inside me. They carve out my insides, but there is no treasure to be found. I'm raw, empty.

I feel your cold fingers on my back.
I see it now, what hurts the most.
I do not feel special unless you see me.
If you don't know me,
no one else matters.
If you don't crave me
I am worthless.

## November 24, 2000

*I saw snow today. It hurts to look at it. I remember the snow at the ski lodge, the infinitesimal diamonds glittering in it. Then there were the trains. I keep seeing myself in that yellow, sick train light. It's the cold, though, that races up your spine and chills you. Freezes your body and mind so you cannot focus on anything else. That is what this breakup feels like.*

*I miss who I am with Paul.*

## November 28, 2000

*Dad told me to think about my goals and write down what I really want out of life.*

*Of utmost importance to me is who I am. I want to find her and keep her without ever having Paul cross my mind. Eating is just too weak for me anymore. It's pathetic to live my life getting ready to be with Paul. I didn't even realize I was doing that. My focal points should be assisting others, God, and development of self.*

*Right now, I just want to concentrate on the undeniable fact that eating is addictive for me. It's hurting me. I need to help whoever I am underneath this eating. I will take insulin. I will take the anti-depressants. When the overwhelming urge to eat comes, I will sit with myself and see what's in there. I will.*

*I still do.*
*Still wonder where my mood ring fell when I threw it.*
*Still wonder where the train runs.*
*Still see your dewy eyelids shift as you fall asleep.*
*Still walk into stores*
*see things you'd like*
*I still wonder if I should get you a Christmas present*
*Still look at sexy underwear*
*Still wonder if I'll be thin enough to wear them for you*
*then I cast myself a hateful look.*
*This is what it comes down to*
*Today is when it starts*
*This is my body.*
*I am responsible*
*for making it last as long as possible.*

*This is my soul.*
*I am its only defense.*
*I am the bouncer to that club.*

### December 14, 2000

I think I'm becoming addicted to my pills. The appetite suppressants, the laxatives in particular. I thought I was just taking them temporarily, but now I must take three every day, five if I take them every other day. At least I'm not throwing up anymore, though I seem to alternate between bingeing + purging in several different ways. From fasting to not taking insulin, to laxatives, to vomiting, to severe exercise. Right now, I'm alternating between laxatives, fasting + not taking insulin. It hurts so incredibly much to know that none of my work, my attempts, the harm I did to my body was to make me happy. It was to look good for him. So now, when I sense my body losing weight, this anxiety comes over me like I'm only doing it for him. This scares + repels me.

I need strength, from me, friends, and God. I'm still going to travel. Where? I'll figure it out. Maybe to search for the love God made for me. I'm going to help anyone out that I can. I'm going to keep picking up those that fall because THIS MAY BE MY ONLY PURPOSE. I really wish Paul appreciated me enough to know what is slipping away. LET'S GET ONE THING STRAIGHT. Just because I slip from him does not mean who I am, my identity, slips away. Got it??

### February 5, 2001

I try to keep myself occupied to escape the loneliness. She sits, uneasy with me, at a loss for what to do with her hands. Sometimes I wonder what I write for. All these journals—what for? Who sees them except for me? Are they just garbage someone will read after I've died? Everything is locked up in here. Probably my reason for writing: I want to share the beauty of what I've learned, help people face their secrets.

### February 11, 2001

Today just hurts. All over, everywhere. Dad just brought in my insulin. I wish he had pushed to spend some time with me. I really want someone to talk to and listen to me. I don't care how pathetic it sounds. I want someone to at least be interested, to at least care. I remember how tight we were when I first lived with him. He listened to my troubles and then offered solutions. Sometimes they were audible answers, wise advice to dilemmas that may have made other parents cringe. Other times he just held me as I cried. I'd kill to go back to that time.

### February 14, 2001

I'm strong enough now. I feel she is with me. I feel her inside, waiting to be released from the dark into the light. I feel happier when I haven't eaten. I feel no conflict.

I am closer with God.

I have alternate things to do: journal, work on my collages, write poetry, run, lift weights, go online, help my friends, write my novel, get compliments from drooling guys, read the Bible and get to know God better, be more committed to youth group, help out Mom, look sexier in clothes, find the decent guys, get A's, go tanning, make ca$h, go to Boston, have a fake ID made, read, watch movies, look good in a bathing suit, etc.

Yes, missing Paul hurts. Still, I must keep living.

The eating must stop because it's deceptive to not be managing my blood sugars. I keep forgetting that all the sugar is running throughout all my veins, my organs, my heart, and brain.

I will die if I don't stop this.

She has to survive

For the preservation of the gardens

For the accomplishments I will make

For my family & friends

To have my book published

To really live

For my future husband God has for me

For the beautiful children I will have

For me.

# "Heal me, O Lord,
# the hope of the world"

Jeremiah 17:14–18

*"Heal me, O Lord, the hope of the world,*
*and I will be healed; save me*
*and I will be saved . . .*
*for you are the One I praise.*
*They keep saying to me,*
　　*'Where is the word of the Lord?'*
　　*Let it come to me now . . .*
*I have not ceased being your shepherd.*
*You know I have not desired your days of despair.*
*My word is open before you."*

Psalm 61:1–4

*"Hear my cry O God;*
　　*Hear my prayer*
　　*From the ends of the earth*
　*I call to you*
*I call as my heart grows faint*
*lead me to the rock that is higher than I*
*For you have been my refuge . . ."*

　　　I long to dwell + take refuge
　　　in the shelter of your wings.

Psalm 69:1–4

*"Save me, God*
　　*For the waters have come up to my neck.*
　　*I sink in the many depths,*
　　*where I have no foothold.*

*I have come into the deep waters*
        *the floods engulf me.*
*I am worn out calling for help,*
    *my throat is parched*
    *my eyes fail looking for my God . . .*
    *I am forced to restore what I did not steal."*

Please quiet my anger
my misdirected rage towards you
for I know you are right
in your disappointment in me
and I, too, inwardly weep with regret.
Instill in me a new heart, Oh God.
Let me feel the sunlight on my face
Let me know you are here

### February 16, 2001

I called Lance, that new hot guy, and his friend, Ken, the worst two I could have called. Got through to Ken. Had my work schedule not interfered, I probably would have traveled to Tiverton. Upon arriving, if circumstances were right, I might have had sex with him. I would have sold myself and God short. I'm a sellout. Instead of defending myself and my beliefs, I did the same stupid bullshit as I did with Paul. I manipulated who I truly am, and I left no facet of myself sacred. After the conversation, I binged and felt terribly void.

I could at this point say that I haven't learned shit, but that's not true. This taught me how unready I am for a relationship.

How I still need to guard myself.

How I need to listen to myself + God.

How I need to learn to not compromise my standards.

How I am selling myself short by being with the wrong guys and by not being who I really am:

-Christian

-pro-virginity!

-ill

-still in break-up

-intelligent

-easy-going

-relationship w/ self

-sensitive

-deep


Dear God, I must be the biggest disappointment to You. I am fraudulent, a liar, a thief, weak, unpure, foolish, vain, cruel, unfaithful, destructive, rageful, proud, stubborn, and blind.

God, I'm terribly drawn to sin and to worldly things. I associate it with fun, excitement. I am unwieldy. I give You permission to work on me. Although I may give up on myself, I do not cease to see You as my solution, my salvation. So please do not give up on me.

My qualities used to keep me motivated and hopeful. Now there is nothing precious or priceless about me. I'm just another carbon copy of the crowd, fixated on meaningless things.

I never knew I had all these hopes of getting back with Paul. I never knew I was still in love with him. It wears her out. He stole my world. I'm a stranger with no identity. I have no fingerprints. Whatever formerly radiated from me is gone.

I can't accept anything. I can't even accept that he's gone.

## February 18, 2001

My absolute favorite thing to do now is to come home to an empty house and go up to my room. I close the blinds but crack the windows. Then I strip down to underwear and bra so I feel bare.

I keep a little makeshift ashtray hidden on my windowsill with a book of matches. I sit in the dark, blowing smoke out the window, letting my head swim. I only smoke a third to a half of a cigarette. Then I lay down in bed, feeling the softness running about in my head as though the tornado of nicotine is consuming my rage. I lay on the pillow and hear my heartbeat through my arm. It calms my head . . . I feel peace for those few minutes.

Yesterday I smoked three times though I only had about one and a half cigarettes. It worked—I didn't binge. I ran and tried to get accustomed to my body. It was overwhelming . . . I felt so scared that if my physique was perfect, or nearly so, I would rush to preserve the moment and lose my virginity.

Sometimes I think, "If I just got sex over with," I'd have one less stressor. It might be more of a benefit than a loss, something to secretly savor and *document. That thought made me feel extremely secure, but times of relief are so rare; I feel like I have to burn up in being alive when they occur.*

*I have thinking and writing patterns now as if I'm trapped in my own bell-jar. My actions and my mind are both desensitized and indescribably convoluted. It makes me very sad to spend time with people I love. I feel like I'm going to die and will miss them. I want to leave an imprint on somebody; I want to leave parts of myself with someone.*

### March 1, 2001

*My eyes have been opened to other pleasures in life—bus rides to Providence, good talks with Dad, flirting with guys. I know I could enjoy my experiences without food. Eating, though, makes it ten times better because it tastes great and fills in any gaps of emptiness or sadness. So for a few minutes before the guilt sets in, all is well; it's elation.*

*I can hear God's voice, speaking in a tone that is audible yet quiet enough to let me go my own way, even if I should choose that tunnel descending into darkness. I feel him working. I pray I will begin to trust more. God will keep that demanding, implacable, upset little girl in her garden. She should be saved then be encouraged to grow into a woman.*

*But to die feels comforting, like an assurance of sleep and rest.*

*I am not a happy girl.*

*I am a flaring and dimming type of supernova. Blinking, sending out faint distress signals. Unfortunately, the human race seems to be sleeping. I don't know what or why or for who I do anything anymore. I never find a place with steady ground. Sometimes who I am is like sand in my own palms.*

*I can't see anything behind the eyes staring back in my reflection. I have been consumed. Just like the infestation of my body in that dream. And what about the dream Dad told me? Sure as hell gave me goosebumps. He said his job was to push people off a cliff. Only they knew it was coming. They seemed apathetic and didn't put up a fight as they fell to their deaths. They were all overweight.*

*That was me he was helping to push.*

*The things this[55] has made me do. Lie, steal, dishonor people, devastatingly hurt my body, and give up my beliefs.*

### April 27, 2001—2:08 a.m.

I feel detached from everything. It's as though I have been turned inside out. The wildness, the unwavering strength that used to be buried, is now my exterior. That sweet, vivid, vulnerable identity is somewhere deep inside, in fragments. She speaks to me now. I hear her voice cut through any attempts to placate her. When I was smoking the other day, it occurred to me that just as food dumps on her, silencing her with the masses of it . . . the dizzying smoke can envelop and quiet her.

### May 12, 2001

There is nothing to grasp
I blindly let myself be violated,
Never knowing how much I hate her.
I want to see her ended,
All the rage,
The seas of saltwater.
With no one here to fight,
I wage war against myself,
attack her frame,
throw her to rapists,
that stupid insatiable bitch
forever clamoring to kill me.
I cannot fight her.
She keeps my blood flowing.
Her tears and appetite
give me substance.

### July 5, 2001

It really hurt that my father totally disregarded my birthday. I mean, I can see if he didn't give me a gift. Life is hectic; there's not always time. Still, if he had cared, he might have put forth the effort to treat me special on this day. That just didn't fall on his list of priorities.

### July 7, 2001—2:51 a.m.

I suppose I should explain why I don't write in here as much. I have been feeling disconnected, so detached from whoever the hell I am that I don't even recognize my reflection in the mirror. I thought writing down my ideas might give me more substance, but that felt weak. And lately, my thoughts are not good. I don't like them trapped on paper.

Sin seems to fill me; I like the recklessness, the freedom, the wide-open space and fulfillment of it. I like what is considered bad. It's more to take in, more to occupy me.[56]

Both sides are pulling at me. Lance on one, Heaven on the other. Funny how I wait on the filthy, empty, broken side of the gate.

*August 2001—December 2002*
*age seventeen to eighteen*

# RAVENOUS

I LAY STRAINING TO hear the hum of an engine or the slam of a car door, signaling Rachel's return. All I heard were chirping crickets and Phil's rhythmic breathing. Moments earlier, we had laughed about how pathetic we were, turning in at ten p.m. on a Friday night, only two months after our June wedding in 2001. However, after a full workweek, we were bushed.

Rachel's curfew was ten p.m. The glowing green hands of my alarm clock now read ten twenty-five. She was never this late. Where was she? As the hour hand inched closer to the eleven, my irritation turned to concern. What if something was wrong? I gently shook Phil, who agreed we should get up and go look for her.

Rachel had been talking about Billiards, a new place in a Middletown strip mall where she said minors played foosball and pool. I had pictured a game room. When we arrived, we were met by a smorgasbord of fluorescent beer signs that nearly covered the storefront window. Somehow, Phil and I each located an empty space between these colorful incandescent signs to peer inside.

We spotted Rachel at the pool table, wearing a pale pink top designed to fall off one shoulder with tight, flared jeans. Smiling, she tucked her long, bleached hair behind an ear, flashing a large silver hoop, then leaned over to shoot the ball, laughing when she missed. Her onlookers, mostly men in their twenties holding beers, laughed, too.

We glanced at each other: time to enter. The dimly lit bar smelled of smoke and beer. Christina Aguilera was bellowing "Genie in a Bottle" from blaring speakers.

We walked directly to the pool table where Rachel's opponent had just shot the cue ball against his desired target with one loud click, driving it into a corner pocket with a conclusive thud. The group cheered, but Rachel sobered up when she saw Phil and me. Setting down her pool cue, she approached us.

"I want you to meet the owner," she shouted over Aguilera's chanting, steering us toward the bar. "He's a friend of mine. A really great guy."

At the polished pine bar, the smell of beer intensified. We shook hands with Vinnie, who was fiftyish with graying hair. He deftly mixed drinks and poured draft beers, limping from customers to cash register. Rachel had told me he wore a prosthetic leg, having lost a lower limb to diabetes complications. When there was a lull in customers, he limped back to us.

"I just want to assure you that we do not, under any circumstances, serve alcohol to minors here." Behind him was a stunning array of liquor, three shelves high. "In fact, we don't emphasize drinking here at all," he said while varying shades of amber liqueur in cut-glass decanters winked in the background. "The kids just have a good time. It's all about the fun." He smiled, whisker lines forming around his eyes.

"Thanks for the explanation, Vinnie," I shouted over the music. "It was very nice to meet you."

Outside, Rachel turned on me. "I can't believe you'd embarrass me like that in front of my friends! Coming after me like I'm a child!" She threw herself into the back of the Corolla, slamming the door so hard the ruby sedan shook.

I slammed my door, too, whirling around to face her. "You're a minor! That place is a bar! You made it sound like a 4H club!"

I should have asked more questions. At the time, my mind was churning with strange new emotions. Following our weekend honeymoon at a Newport bed and breakfast, Phil's eight-year-old daughter, Krissy, had moved in, her sister, Nikki, opting to live with their mom. Now we had four kids—five every other weekend when Nikki joined us—all clawing to find their place in our new family. Phil and I refereed daily quarrels and showdowns that wore on our new marriage, making me obsessively question my motives and loyalties.

"For God's sake, Mom, I wasn't drinking!" Her eyes grew in indignation.

"That's what you say, but how do I know? What's to stop one of your buddies from slipping you a drink?"

"There's a thing called trust!" she barked.

"Yes, there is. You really shattered it tonight, didn't you? You whitewashed that place, not to mention blowing off your curfew!" Mindful of Rachel's trials, I usually controlled my voice, but that night it felt good, almost cathartic, to shout.

"Mom, you've got that place all wrong!"

"I don't think so. I know a bar when I see one." I said, composing my tone, my throat slightly raw.

"It's not that way. All the minors do is listen to music, play pool. It's just a place for us to chill."

"Even if you weren't drinking, Rachel, I don't want you hanging around people who do, especially guys. They get ideas after a few drinks."

"Oh, pleeease!" Rolling her eyes, she waved a hand dismissively, her three silver bangles braking on her forearm, then tinkling back to her wrist.

"That's right, Rachel. Don't act so naïve."

I recalled my own baffling shift from the shadows to the spotlight: the stares and smiles from strange men and male neighbors who used to look right through me. Makeup, I quickly learned, could double that attention. What teenage girl, or grown woman, could resist that power? She would wield and relish it until—no less baffling—age cast her back into the shadows.

It was Rachel's moment to shine, but not by going to a bar and mixing with adult men.

"What about your curfew? You totally blew it off," I pressed.

"It's still summer vacation, Mom. School doesn't start for two weeks."

"Rachel, you just turned seventeen!"

"I'll be an adult in one year!"

"You still have no business being out alone past ten any day of the week! Bars are out of the question!" I was raising my voice again, aggravating my throat.

"Are you serious? Phil, will you please talk some sense into her?"

Sometimes, Phil took Rachel's side with a look or soft word if he thought I was being unreasonable.

"Sorry, Rae," he said, regarding her through the rearview mirror. "I'm with Mom on this one."

Phil had just stopped at a red light. The harsh light from a Shell station shone in Rachel's window. Even with her chin jutting in defiance, she was lovely. The whimsical clothes. The bleached hair that might have looked cheap had she worn heavy makeup; however, she applied foundation and blush with an artist's precision and restraint to create a whisper of color; the palest pink lipstick to downplay her pouting lips; the finest line of gray or bronze to highlight her large, blue eyes, the star of her face. She had that innocent look with a hint of sultriness that turned men's heads.

Rachel huffed, "I don't believe it! That was the one place I could go where I felt accepted. I could talk to Vinnie about my diabetes. He's the only one who gets it." Her eyes started to tear.

It was a shame that besides the arcade and the cinemas, there wasn't much in town for teens to do. Nearly every venue catered to adults and included alcohol.

I felt bad, especially when she brought diabetes into it. Talking to Vinnie probably did help. Seeing his prosthetic might even prompt her to take better care of herself. The friendship might be positive, but not in that context, and not at seventeen.

She had slumped against the door, her head resting against the window. "I can't wait till I turn eighteen! I'm so moving out! My bags will be packed the night before!"

"That's your prerogative," I said, reaching over to lock her door. "Until then, I expect you to follow our rules."

We drove home in silence. Tomorrow one would approach the other to patch things up, but right now, I felt like I had failed. Though I'd done my job, she was upset, and we were estranged.

These teenage years felt like a dark, endless maze. I was shamefully aware that I just wanted them over. I was biding my time until Rachel grew up and we could be friends. I saw us in that clearing—mother and daughter talking, shopping, laughing. Yet it seemed so far away. Most seventeen-year-olds were settling down as they pondered their futures, but Rachel was just taking flight. Whereas she'd spent the last two and a half years locked in her room, now she sought excitement —loud music, bright lights, merchandise, crowds, boys. She had only just started driver education, a year after her peers, previously bumming rides to Rocco's Pizza, where she waitressed part-time. College wasn't even on her radar. When I broached it, she replied, "If I go to college, it won't be till later. I need a break from the tyranny of teachers." When Rachel wasn't in school or working, she'd hop a bus to Providence Place mall or downtown Newport, informing me by a Post-it stuck to the fridge. Occasionally, she brought her friend Kira, but usually, she went alone.

I urged Rachel to seek out one or two girl friends with similar beliefs and interests. I told her I always had close friends. In high school, Linda and I dissected every possible topic while walking remote country roads. In college, Ellen and I shared several creaky apartments on Milwaukee's East side. When Todd dumped me, Gerri, my co-worker friend from BCC, said in her raspy voice, "You'll spend the weekend in Marion." Her welcoming hug, coupled with the smell of homemade beef barley, was a balm to my battered heart.

In every new phase or place, I made female friends who sweetened my life and saved me hundreds of times. I wanted Rachel to experience that same love, support, companionship—that same incomparable resource.

In grade school, she had girlfriends galore. Most came from military families that were stationed at the Newport Naval base for one year. When they moved, she lost friend after friend. In middle school, the girls were mean. The school nurse told me Rachel regularly ate lunch in her office. She did have one pal, gangly, goofy Dee, who used to show up after school, towering over Rachel, her perpetual smile flashing a mouthful of braces. Now that they were in high school, I never saw her. Rachel said Dee got a job, but I wonder if Rachel blew her off.

Rachel had always been rebellious, but now she possessed a daunting new moxie. What made her so wild? Was it her growing awareness of her attractiveness to men? Her painful breakup with Paul? Maybe it was being recently thrust into two mixed families. Perry and Cam had married nine months before Phil and me, moving two of Cam's four kids into the condo where Rachel spent alternating weekends. There were plenty of reasons for her bold new behavior.

In retrospect, I wonder if Rachel's unruliness was related to her borderline personality disorder. After three years without medical care, her journals revealed that her mental health had deteriorated, especially her identity disturbance. At fourteen, Rachel had cherished her true self. When she sensed that "precious," "priceless" girl slipping away, she fought to recover her "fingerprints" in entry after entry. However, at seventeen, in one poem, she expressed pure hatred for that "stupid, insatiable bitch," wanting "to see her ended." That alter-ego, her false self, Reckless Grace, had become more dominant, increasing Rachel's profound emptiness, another core Borderline symptom.

Apparently, identity disturbance and profound emptiness go hand in hand. Alice Miller suggests that people severed from their authentic selves—everything in them that pulses with life—naturally experience a deep, disturbing void.[57] This is not like the bouts of depression the rest of us might feel. According to Doctor Charles Whitfield, "No matter what [Borderlines] may experience, gnawing away in the background is always a feeling of emptiness, which aches and cries to be filled."[58] This keen void also produces restlessness. These individuals cannot sit still, Winnicott claims. Anxious and easily bored, they are driven to seek external experiences that make them feel briefly alive.[59] Rachel was no exception. At seventeen, she gravitated toward shiny, shallow things she hoped would fill her but never did. Her quest led her to increasingly sordid places and greater thrills that only multiplied her sorrows.

IT WAS CLOSE TO midnight when Phil and I got back into bed. In seconds, he was out. I nestled against him, my body rising and falling with his measured breaths. He smelled like Dial soap and faint Gray Flannel. Now that Rachel was home, I could finally relax. Eyes closing, I uttered a frequent but fervent prayer, *Thank you, dear God, for sending me this sweet, sweet man.*

# LANCE BLACK

RACHEL SAT AT THE kitchen table, scanning the Help Wanted ads in the Newport Daily News. She wore a chartreuse camisole with aqua crystal earrings that resembled mini chandeliers. Rachel liked colors that "clashed well." Having just started her junior year, she was determined to drive to school. She had gotten her license that summer, as well as a beat-up Ford Taurus from Perry. Now, she needed a real job for car insurance, gas, and constant repairs.

Within two weeks, Rachel secured a desk clerk position at Seaside Manor, a ritzy Newport hotel and restaurant where she booked rooms and events. Her favorite task, she told me, was greeting guests and showing them to their posh, water-view quarters. Though the youngest employee, Rachel charmed her co-workers with her quick wit, strong problem-solving skills, and impressive vocabulary. No one would have guessed how ill she was beneath her sunny veneer.

Rachel loved how the sleepy hotel bustled before weddings, when decorators festooned the castle-like foyer and ballroom with white lights and paper lanterns. Florists delivered potted plants and gargantuan flower arrangements that wafted fragrances of roses, orchids, and lilies to her desk. Once a party started, these blooms competed with the smells of costly perfumes and sumptuous foods. No two events were alike, yet all were lavish, money being no object for those who booked at the Manor.

Shortly after starting her new job, Rachel found a new romance. From the beginning, she knew Lance Black was a boy to avoid. Still, she was breathless that September afternoon when she described the new kid who had transferred from Tiverton High School to Middletown High School (MHS).

I had exciting news, too, I said, pointing to the insulin pump displayed on the kitchen counter. A $6,000 device, it had arrived that day via Special Delivery.

Six months earlier, we had found a promising new endocrinologist who had encouraged Rachel to consider trying one. A diabetic himself, Dr. D. used a pump. Rachel's last endocrinologist had shot this idea down due to Rachel's high blood sugars. Dr. D. said one of its purposes was to regulate patients' sugars by delivering a steady dose of insulin. Pulling his pump out of the pocket of his lab coat, Dr. D. showed us how to program it. He couldn't praise it enough. I was sold, but Rachel cringed.

"Have you ever seen the size of those pump needles, Mom?" Her eyes grew. "They're like freaking fangs, and they get injected directly into your stomach. You have to change them every three days." However, Dr. D. worked on Rachel for months using humor, tact, and kindness until she finally agreed to try it.

Rachel lifted the sleek silver pump, turning it over before pressing it squeakily back into its foam mold. Then, scrunching up her face as if in pain, she exclaimed, "Lance Black is so fine!"

I thought the pump merited a little more fuss. Still, I grinned. It was the first time in a year she'd mentioned another boy.

Though stationed at the kitchen table, Matt hadn't spoken yet. A high school freshman, he was bent over his books, a glass of milk, and a hill of Doritos on a paper towel beside him. Unlike Rachel, who would start assignments, even papers, the night before they were due, Matt would complete his first thing so he was free to play video games, skateboard, or hang out with friends. Having started this drill in junior high as an honor student, he was determined to continue on this academic track in high school.

"That kid's a pothead," Matt now announced, his head popping up like a jack-in-the-box.

Quick to deflect Matt's charge, Rachel muttered, "Like every other kid at MHS."

Ducking into the pantry, she emerged with a box of Raisin Bran. She showered flakes into a bowl. Matt did not disagree.

I crossed my arms. "Well, I hope that doesn't include you two."

"Weed is for losers," Matt scoffed without even looking up.

"Are you kidding me?" Rachel spoke as she soaked her cereal in skim milk. "Pot gives you the munchies. I stuff my face twenty-four-seven as it is. *Please.*"

"So, Matt, how do you know this kid smokes pot?" I glanced at the clock, grateful Krissy and Ryan, both fifth graders, wouldn't arrive for another twenty minutes.

Matt raised an eyebrow. "I've seen him smoking in the parking lot with the other stoners."

Rachel stood at the peninsula, impassively chewing her cereal. She did not defend her new crush.

I didn't want to douse her enthusiasm. Nor did I want her dating a boy taking drugs.

"Do you think it's a good idea to date someone who smokes pot, Rachel?"

Swallowing, she smirked, "Oh, Mom, I'm not serious about Lance Black. I'm just window shopping right now."

Two weeks later, Rachel was dating Lance Black.

✦   ✦   ✦

AT PUMP TRAINING, DR. D.'s nurse programmed Rachel's pump to deliver her prescribed dose of insulin. She explained how to modify the settings based on Rachel's fluctuating blood sugars and eating habits. I braced myself as she attempted to diagonally insert a needle that resembled a thumbtack into Rachel's abdomen. Rachel flinched; she cried. It took several tries. Tears sprang to my eyes. We left the office with Rachel's pump in place, her face pink and blotchy. She didn't speak all the way home.

When we had to replace the needle, it was like a replay of her initial duress performing finger sticks and insulin injections, only magnified because this needle was notably larger. Try as we might, we could not reinsert it without Rachel reddening and tearing up. Nor was she willing to have Dr. D.'s nurse reinstall it. She reverted to shots.

"The pump's not for everyone," Dr. D. replied when I called to inform him.

I tried to reason with Rachel, claiming that she'd get used to that needle; other pump users did. They ended up loving the pump's flexibility. I stressed the necessity of regulating her sugars to prevent complications, something she'd never consistently managed to do.

Then one day, she admitted it wasn't just about the daunting needle.

"I don't want a piece of machinery attached to my body," she confessed.

I hadn't considered how awkward that might be for a seventeen-year-old girl. Any time she pulled out the pump in public, it would herald her illness.

But her health was at stake!

"This is the age of technology, Rachel. People use beepers, Walkmans, even mobile phones. You think anyone's going to notice? It's under your clothes, for heaven's sake!"

"I will," she said with equanimity. "I don't want that device connected to me."

A week later, when Rachel strolled into the kitchen holding hands with tall, gorgeous Lance, everything clicked. They were a striking couple, she with her vivid blue eyes and long, platinum hair, and he with his cropped black hair, intense brown eyes, and brooding black brows. While she was chatty and witty, quick to chuckle at her own irreverent jokes, he was sober and reserved. When he did laugh, his face shone like the sun after a rainstorm.

Rachel and Lance clashed well.

✦    ✦    ✦

RACHEL DOWNPLAYED THE POT. In the boonies of Tiverton where he lived, there wasn't much to do. He didn't smoke all the time. He was trying to quit.

Lance rarely visited our house. Rachel said he felt uneasy around us, but this setup probably served them both. I had rules. His parents did not. So, Rachel drove to Lance's on her evenings off. After dinner, they retired to his room.

By the end of September, Rachel had moved back in with Perry and Cam to their lake house in Scituate. For father and daughter, it was a win-win: Perry got reduced child support. Rachel got carte blanche. Concerned, I called him to suggest that I keep Rachel when he took business trips.

"You talk like you think she's having sex. Don't you trust her?"

"I don't trust the intensity of either of their feelings. They may not be having sex now, but if you provide a cozy little context, they'll keep going further. Please stand with me on this," I pleaded. "Please tell her when you travel, she has to stay here."

"I'll talk to her, but I'm not sending her back to you when I travel. For God's sake, Carolyn, she's seventeen."

Weeks later, Perry called me hysterical: "I just walked in on Rachel and Lance having sex!"

I had been shopping with Gerri at the Bass Outlet. Swooning, I sat on a wide red-cushioned bench between the long shoe aisles. Seeing me blanch, Gerri abandoned her shoe search to sit beside me. She said her daughter was fifteen when she lost her virginity, which oddly consoled me. At the same time, my mother's heart keened at how easily girls jettisoned their innocence.

By the fall of 2001, one year after Perry took Rachel in, he dropped her on my doorstep once again. She had been caught snooping through Cam's closet more than once; only this time, she had worn and stained some clothes, charges Rachel did not deny. Phil and I welcomed her back, our only condition being that she honor a midnight curfew.

Rachel returned wearing silk skirts and dresses. In between school, work, and dating Lance, she somehow managed a full beauty regime—manicures, pedicures, tanning, hair appointments, not to mention shopping at Victoria's Secret and Express. She also shopped obsessively on eBay, often receiving multiple mailers a day containing makeup, jewelry, clothes, shoes.

Despite her extravagant beauty efforts, Rachel hardly seemed happy in her relationship. When it was new and exciting, she tolerated a lot; however, senior year, her discontent dribbled out. Lance did not support or compliment her. He rarely paid for dates. When Rachel had car trouble, she called Phil, knowing she couldn't count on her boyfriend. On holidays, Lance gave excuses, not gifts.

Meanwhile, Rachel didn't need an occasion to lavish Lance with concert tickets, sweatshirts, sneakers, jeans. Their second Christmas together, Rachel drove all over Rhode Island talking to breeders to find the perfect purebred puppy for Lance. She settled on a frisky terrier for $600. On Christmas morning, I held the warm, wriggling pup while she strung a shiny green jingle bell through a red satin ribbon, tying it around its neck.

"Lance loved the puppy. Named him Bullet," she told me that evening.

I imagined the luminous smile that broke over his stormy brow.

"What did he get you?" I almost hated to ask.

Avoiding my eyes, she stammered, "He's broke right now, but as soon as he finds work, he's going to buy me some Uggs."

"Why do you stay with him?" I asked her when she aired her gripes with me.

"I stay because he needs me. I'm not going to dump him like Dad dumped me."

"Rachel, your father loves you, even if he doesn't always show it. You know, he didn't have the easiest upbringing, being the oldest of seven kids with alcoholic parents."

Imagining her grandparents' neglect, Rachel's eyes softened.

"Your loyalty to Lance is very noble," I continued, "but a healthy relationship is reciprocal. Give and take. In your relationship, you give, and Lance takes." My eyes bore into hers. "You deserve someone who adores you. Do you think he's better than you?"

"Of course not," she snorted.

"Are you sure?"

Rachel blinked several times before retreating into her room as if the question were beneath her.

✦　　✦　　✦

ON JUNE 16, 2002, Rachel was radiant in her white cap and gown. She wore her bleached hair long. I held my breath as she click-clacked across the stage in strappy white, precariously spiked sandals, her toenails painted red. Smiling widely, she accepted her diploma to loud applause. She appeared to be pleased with her achievement. I would learn that she was pleased to be alive.

After the ceremony, Phil and I wound our way through the throng of giddy parents and graduates under the vast tent to find Rachel. When I embraced her, she whispered, "Have you seen Lance? He said he'd come." A year older than Rachel, Lance had graduated the year before. Pulling away, she scanned the crowd, adding under her breath, "He sure as hell better have brought flowers, but I'll bet he didn't."

I shook my head, praying the yutz would at least show up. After hugging Rachel, Phil took photographs of her. Rachel flashed the same dazzling smile, but in between shots, her eyes searched for Lance. Suddenly, he was standing beside me, in a black shirt and khakis, holding a bouquet of mixed flowers, sporting a rare, almost bashful smile.

Six months later, to my surprise, Rachel registered at the Community College of Rhode Island to study nursing. Though I had expected psychology or art, nursing was a challenging, reputable career. I could have done cartwheels.

*September 6, 2001–July 7, 2004*

# "She looks like deception to me"

### September 6, 2001

no matter how enraged I am
at what was stolen
I smother the cries
with sleeping stones
covering my detestable frame
and exhale
just slowly enough
that I am not crushed
I cannot make myself fight
If my will is in chains
Mere survival
is all I have.
To walk that wire
and let all else fall.
It's not so bad now.
The sleeping stones
are as heavy as the ocean
It's not so bad now.
when every facet is numb.
and death is the only variable
But the sleeping stones are heavy
There is nothing else to feel
save the sacrifice of a taut body
and my eyelids will close.
and the stones will settle.

### September 14, 2001

I'm busy and thoroughly enjoying it. I worked at the Yacht Club this morning, and now I'm at Seaside, with seven hours to go.

*It was wet, cold, and gray at the Yacht Club today and even windier on the ocean, where Mom and I served at a men's luncheon. Her fears were most likely confirmed when she saw me eating chocolate chip cookies and coconut bars. There's something exciting about eating food not meant for you . . . especially where there is a large quantity and a lot of choices. I still smell like the smoke from the fireplace there. I adore that smell . . . it reminds me of the bonfires Phil made in New Hampshire, even more of the cabin on the water in Cape Cod where Auntie Dolores and Uncle Dale brought us. I remember Ryan's clothes drying in front of that fire when he followed the Canadian geese straight into the ocean. He was probably one or two.*

*The best thing about working at the Yacht Club is the aerobic activity. The constant walking compensates for the food I ingest. Whereas here at Seaside, I'm just sitting on my expanding ass.*

### October 1, 2001

*The other night when I called Lance, I'm certain he was still high. I would never stay with him if he was like that on any regular basis. I can't stand it. Nonreceptive, monotonous, and a complete waste of my time. If I left, I don't think I would miss him. Then I think of random moments like whispering into his ear while lying on my blanket at the beach in Tiverton. Or when we were at that Labor Day cookout, and we snuck away so I could smoke. I was standing by the trees, trying to feel the few rays of sunlight filtering through the branches. I turned and caught Lance looking at me.*

*Lance doesn't know me. He doesn't have the capacity to. He does not know what is inside himself; he has no motivation to find what is inside of me. He doesn't feel anything when I am in pain. I'm beginning to think that he only thinks he loves me because of what we've done. Apparently, something reaches him during sex.*

*There, I said it. Now let's hope no one reads this.*

*When I thought I felt almost ready to leave him, this lonely, wandering feeling hit me. Yet last night, when I knew I had to give him up, I felt calmed, like I didn't need to eat. Sometimes I think if I took him out of the picture, I wouldn't want to binge as much.*

*I wonder if I'm still inside myself. The dirty little girl, I mean. It's a little frightening to wonder how much would come out if I willed myself to write several times a day. If I did, would I feel less anxious? More peaceful? Would I know* myself once more? Or for the first time? Would others see me? I want to be preserved in people's memories. Namely, in the memory of someone who loves me.

### November 5, 2001

I hate this job. I mean, I really hate it. It's tedious. It's nerve-wracking. Seaside stores so much food I feel at the mercy of my urges. I've consumed over 4,000 calories today. That's enough to make anyone sick.

There must be some reason as to why things settle when I am with Lance. Maybe he fills a void that food usually fills. I guess if I ever really wanted to binge, I would tell him. I'd probably get no response, which would break me up. Still, I would tell him, if only to hear myself ask for help.

### November 13, 2001

They put a new padlock on the walk-in freezer. The other smaller refrigerators have locks, but I know which keys access them. I'm sure if I wanted to, I could find the key for the new padlock too, but I'd rather not. Besides, if I took more than a small amount, they would know it was me.

### November 14, 2001

Last night I dreamt I was looking down from a mountain top onto a small section of the world. Everywhere was breathtakingly beautiful and ornate, save for what I recognized as Newport. I could see the harbor as though looking through a telescope. The sea was red and churning, almost boiling with a storm. Then I was in an old hotel. I went into a room and found someone. I think we had sex against my will. Or maybe it was Lance, and it wasn't against my will. I remember that Lance and I took a drive down a lonely road along the coast. When I got back, my father accused me of having sex, and I denied it. His expression turned from violently angry to sad, but he forced a weak smile. This was the face of God as I break my promises. He's frustrated with me but sadder that I'm falling away.

I woke up and asked for forgiveness. I felt such relief and such love exchanged that I was able to cry. Partly from gratitude and partly from despair because I knew I wouldn't leave Lance. Still, those few minutes with God were such resuscitation. He gave me glimpses of what a life of freedom could feel like. I felt held.

Again, relief and love when I received my period the next day.

### November 16, 2001

*I went to Lance's last night. I feel excited, more free. It was good to just lay with him. We needed that. It was good to have the opportunity to cry. I wonder how well he listened to me. I wonder how well any of it was absorbed. He told me he loved me. I didn't answer back; I wanted to let it sit with me for a little while, because I didn't know how true it was. This was after we had made love if that's what you want to call it.*

*When we talked, he told me about the drugs, and his back got hot. He said, "There were a lot of things that I did. Worse things than you probably know about."*

*And he told me. Acid. Mushrooms. Speed. Ecstasy. Cocaine.*

*Even writing it, I can't believe it. He's so young. So lonely and young. He said the saddest, most hopeless thing I've ever heard: "I don't think I'll ever be what I could have been. It's too late."*

*I was so hungry when I left his house, but by the time I got home, the hunger had gone.*

### March 10, 2002

*It feels like there's this separate entity, this horrible girl living inside of me. Her body rises up inside mine, and she scrapes at my insides. She's in a rage, furious and crying. She's just wild, miserable. I hate to have her there. At this point, the only way out that I know of is to eat something. Sometimes when I'm doing this, it feels like my hands are mechanical, like I'm not the one making them bring the food to my mouth. I don't even taste. I feel like I could consume everything in the world and still feel empty. The only thing that would stop me would be the size of my stomach because it couldn't hold anymore.*

### March 13, 2002

*I couldn't stay away.*

*I got out at noon and drove up to Lance's after a maintenance stop at Mom's. I wore a black shirt and those scribbled pants. I put on lotion to mask the smell of cigarettes. As I walked up to his house, I kept my mind preoccupied by talking to myself about irrelevant things. The red door was open. I pulled the handle of the glass one and stepped inside.*

*Lance's hair was wet from the shower. I love men in gray t-shirts. So welcoming, so approachable. We didn't know how to act around each other. Still, I walked straight to his room and sat down on his bed. We talked about nothing:*

Where to go. How clean his room was. How his game system was still humming. I touched him first. On the shoulder.

We kept talking about nothing, and at some point, he laid down. I studied his body language with complete attention.

Who touched the other's hand first? I don't know, but we re-discovered each other. He stroked my hand, periodically holding tighter to it. His face was rather blank with an intermittent clenching of eyelids. He let me rub my hand around his face. He let his eyes close, and he let me run my fingers in his dark hair. We didn't speak, but the conversation of hands filled the room. I closed my eyes as I ran the back of my hand down his face. We ventured further. We lay side-by-side, and he held me very close. I told him I miss him. I miss us. Our palms moved along each other's backs and arms, hips, and neck.

He was excited. I was comforted. It was beautiful.

### April 9, 2002

I can't stop crying. The release is needed, and I imagine how nice it would be to lay against Lance in the back seat of my car and just cry until the ocean dried up. To just let the fishbowl tip, the contents crash out and have whatever is in there floundering about finally escape.

Lance asks what's wrong, and I know I can't explain it to him. Still, I want him to understand the reality of my death. So I tell him about my recent dream:

My mouth is sealed. Strangely, there is no need to breathe. The dirt presses against my eyelids. I can feel my cold blue arms suspended in the soil. I am dead, but the dim light within me yearns to leave the ground.

"But it's a dream," he says. "Just a dream. That's all."

I want to tell him that it's not. That it's more, that I can foresee it happening, but these frail excuses never strike air.

### May 23, 2002

I feel foolish. I skip school to have him come over. Even though I have my period, we have sex. The sex has improved. I admit I feel guilty if I don't focus on him or if I have a better orgasm than he does. Then we go out to lunch, and I pay. Then he's off to Ken's, and I return to an empty house.

Why does this make me feel used? I feel abandoned when he goes. I wonder if I love him more than he loves me. When I look at my painted eyes in the rearview mirror, I don't like her. She looks like deception to me.

I went to his house yesterday, I don't recall why, but I just ached to have his full attention. When I lay with him, I cried because he was depressed, and I love him, yet I failed to reach him. He thinks I cry all the time. God, if he only knew I want to just let oceans run.

## July 4, 2002

One disappointment after another. Kira not only cancels our 4th of July plans but my birthday plans as well. Glen, one of the new managers at work, and I leave to go to a bar to celebrate my birthday tomorrow, but it's closed.

I wish I had a father like Glen. He's crazy about his daughter Jessica. He must know every little thing about her. Tonight he was talking about her teeth—how she hadn't fully grown into them yet because there were still little spaces in between them. I almost wish he wouldn't talk or try to do nice things for me. It only makes me realize how inattentive my father is to me. And it will never change.

Time is a funny thing. There are certain stretches where if you don't remain close, you risk being estranged forever. It still hurts. I remember how we used to talk, how he would come to me, and I could go to him. I think he genuinely cared. I remember us talking in the apartment when he was lonely, and I was the only one he had. I remember trying to cook for him on holidays. If Dad paid a quarter of the attention to me that Glen pays to his daughter, maybe I could get that pancreas transplant.

Last night Dad was talking to Cam and her two kids, and he didn't know I could hear him.

They were sitting in the living room, and he started telling them about diabetes. About all the maintenance he assumes I do. "She has to test her blood four times a day and take shots accordingly. Yet, no matter what she does, each day, her cells get a little more damaged. There's nothing she can do."

Amputation. Blindness. The words just tore through me, broke my heart as I heard my death sentence.

I'll never come close to healing.

Oh Dad, if you only knew I'd be lucky to live to see twenty. If you only cared enough to help me get that operation.

I just fell crying.

I think deep down he loves me. He's just too busy to really love me.

I told Glen today what I heard Dad talking about, and I cried on the drive home. I can feel it closing in, like high tide.

*There's no real time.*

*I wonder if God will really save me.*

*I thought about swerving into an oncoming car, and the thought comforted me for a second.*

*When I got out of the shower, I was looking in the mirror at my naked body. It's horrible—fat in this overweight childlike way. Even as I examined it, the urge to eat was oppressive, so I ate pasta with my hands and smoked Menthol into my lungs. Then I was quiet. Because I don't think anyone can hear you cry when you hold your hand over your mouth.*

### August 31, 2002—2:25 a.m.

*It may have taken me too long, but I've decided to start journaling again. Every day I write is one more day accounted for, to reflect, to touch the glass and know that there is someone behind it.*

*Mornings are horrible. There's nothing planned, and even if I had plans, they would fall through.*

*Lance and I drank for the first time in a while at Damien's. Sometimes I enjoy myself very much while drinking. The lack of inhibition is, without any argument, a beautiful thing. I say anything I please. Secrets emerge. I don't care how far my stomach sticks out, and I'll eat without caring who sees. Boundaries blur. I like that.*

*But this morning, I'm waiting by the toilet at six a.m., certain I'm going to throw up. Whenever this happens, I get so scared. It's violent when I vomit. I will promise anything to get out of it. Nothing comes up. I walk slowly back to bed, feeling that faint, racing heartbeat. Pain shoots underneath my breasts. It feels like holes where something has eaten through my tissue.*

*I try not to fall too hard into bed. Sometimes my body feels so frail I think it will fall to pieces.*

### September 10, 2002

*I eat too much at work because I have access to every key to every lock in the building, and I'm left alone at night. Sometimes it's only me and one or two guests. I eat until I feel I might cry, then I take more food—fruit, cereal, bread, cookies—and put it in my trunk. To have what I have is to constantly worry about the future, to prepare for it. Bingeing is a very costly endeavor.*[60]

### October 12, 2002

*I dreamed last night I was at a party. I hid behind the enormous trunk of an old tree, watching you, but you found my eyes anyway and got into your car. You punched the gas pedal to the floor, and I thought you were going to try and hit me. Instead, you stopped, got out, and walked in my direction. I don't remember how I felt about it, but you pushed me against that tree and raped me. Nobody saw.*

*Suddenly I felt sick. I pulled up my shirt and looked at my stomach. I grabbed hold of my own skin and peeled it upwards, just like another shirt. And just like always—an infestation. Thousands of little bugs resembling ants crawled in and out of my intestines and lungs.*

*No matter how often I have this dream, I wake up terrified and drenched in sweat.*

### October 24, 2002—9:07 p.m.

*How can I leave Lance when I have felt what he feels? Just as no one knew how I suffered when I was young, just as no one broke through that silence, just as I was alone, scared, hoping that someone would understand and stay . . . He needs that from me. How can I deny him that?*

*I love Lance. I do. He's my world. So why is he so blind? Why doesn't he understand why I cry?*

*He hasn't asked if I've taken my shots in over two weeks. Sometimes I could spit at his parents for the negligent manner in which they raised him. For the fact that this is acceptable behavior to him. People should not have to constantly fend for themselves. Everyone needs to be held up from time to time.*

*I fell asleep in Lance's room when we got home. I dreamt that two girls were fighting violently. They had brown hair, but I think one of them was me. We had swords, and the other girl cut me badly and kicked me on the ground. I was bleeding; I could feel the pain and stress. Then she kicked me down an endless flight of stairs. I just kept rolling down, being thrown into steps, bleeding. She was close behind, ready for me to hit bottom so that she could cut me again. For some reason, during the dream, I felt that this other girl represented me. That it was me versus myself.*

### November 27, 2002—2:15 a.m.

*These last, what, four or five years are hard to describe. I remember carrying around more water bottles than textbooks in my backpack. I remember wanting* to cry while I waited for teachers to dismiss me to the bathroom, I needed to pee so badly.

I remember how tired the hospital felt. The squeaky, disinfected floors. The color schemes of forced hope. When it rained, droplets would get caught in the window screen. The gold from the streetlight would hit the raindrops, making them look like the hot oil that dripped on Grandma Pattie's lamp. The hanging lamp had a gold figure of a Grecian woman standing in a garden; clear filaments in the stand carried jewel drops of oil up and down. I really like that lamp, I had told her. Oh really? I'll leave it to you in my will, she had said.

The first morning home my mother made me get up early for the a.m. shot before the visiting nurse came. The nurse sat in Mom's chair at the kitchen table, her equipment spread out. Soft morning light filtered through the window. She wore a typical white nurse's uniform, save for the obsolete hat. Her dark hair was still damp from the shower. She commented on the Mason jar of wildflowers. Then she started in about measurements and restrictions. The way she emphasized portion size and adhering to your meal plan, I just wanted to say, "Fuck you." She talked with my mother about the same garbage we learned in the hospital. My mother's eyes were wide and nervous as an eight-year-old, listening as though she were hearing it for the first time. Bullshit. Complete bullshit. I stood behind the peninsula counter, nodding as if I were listening. I moved the toaster in front of me so they couldn't see me putting more grapes into my measuring cup. It was then I took back a fraction of control.

And then there was the blood-testing. It took me a good while to get used to that. I just couldn't dive into self-mutilation. It took me fifteen or twenty minutes sometimes to do a fingerstick. I would just shake, waiting for that "click," the gun's trigger. I would sweat. I would cry.

I remember one night how bright I thought it would be to eat one of Mom's chocolate chip cookies while performing this test. It would distract me. After all, I'm hurting myself. Don't I deserve compensation? A reward?

### December 10, 2002—5:42 p.m.

In the past week, I registered with CCRI for spring courses, bought a new car for a fair price, and found purebred puppies for half the price.

I have found I am a very adaptable creature. When I have less money and even less opportunity to spend it, I eat less, make lunches at home, try to drink water instead of soda. Buying cigarettes induces guilt, but I have no trouble smoking as many as I want. I really felt guilty when I bought a pair of five-dollar underwear, but they were so damn cute. Speaking of five-dollar purchases, since when is a box of generic tampons five dollars?!

I can feel Lance's stress about money too. I haven't really thought about what he might be getting me for Christmas. What I'm so excited about, so looking forward to, is giving him the puppy.

I want to go to the Dartmouth Mall before I see him and put it in a cage there, with a sign next to it that says "Reserved." I will drag him in there to look and play with it. Then I'll say, "Who is this reserved for?" And the person working there will say, "Lance Black." I hope they will let me do that.

### January 1, 2003—(but after midnight)

I'm falling deeply in love with Lance. It's a dangerous sort of state. I can't be with him enough.

I used to think he held onto me just a little too much. As in a display of dependency, not love. Now, too many minutes in his presence without being touched makes me quiver with insecurity.

I love this man.

I love the way he holds his arms without any self-consciousness. I love the intensity of his eyes. Since I've begun to feel this way about Lance, I feel ugly. I feel he does not appreciate me, and I know my looks are going. Not enough sleep, too much sugar, sun, and bleach. I'm getting dull, fading. I don't make myself exciting anymore.

### April 24, 2003—12:20 a.m.

Today while walking down the massive ramp of the CCRI campus, carrying a Diet Coke and a plastic-wrapped sandwich on a Styrofoam plate balanced on top of it, I knew everyone was watching me. Nobody leaves campus with a meal. Nobody walks five rows back to their car with the hassle of carrying that load.

Look at her stomach. She probably isn't even taking classes here; she just wants the food.

Oh, they were looking all right. I tried to walk lightly, gracefully. My car was so far away.

I couldn't believe what a massive deal I was making out of this. Nevertheless, the spotlight was on me: the fat pig hauling food to her car. I tried holding it another way, the cup in one hand, the plate in the other. This alleviated it a little bit. Everything appeared less stacked.

A week or so ago, at Lance's, I was watching TV while he buffed the spray paint off of his truck. There was a program on MTV about eating disorders, and TV cameras followed a young bulimic girl around. Seven to ten years. That's what the documentary said, seven to ten years to get over an eating disorder. So long. Yet, I am not surprised.

### July 6, 2003—2:24 a.m.

Something in me is starting to go crazy again, like a wild animal. I see the lines, imperfections, deposits in my skin, the pale expanse of my thighs, the dirty little secret about my stomach.[61] I feel myself aging ten months a day. I can barely drive at night anymore. Taking shots in the evening is enough to drive me mad. It feels like fingers tickling, teasing my neck, poised to grab, strangle. I think I have been telling myself that it's only so many more of those shots I will have to take, only so many more nights of it. I realized tonight I will never have a night when I won't have to think about this. I'll do it till I die. I can't deliver myself.

# "Why can't I just give up on him?"

**September 23, 2003**

I met Jim when I was completely drunk. I was at the bar, already talking to someone when my eyes opened up on him. He was alone. He went outside, and I followed. I sat on the curb, under the harsh yellow streetlight, smoking, head down. We talked a little bit about regrets. I liked whatever lonely thing was happening with his eyes. Had I not been smoking, I wanted a window in which to kiss him. We went back inside, I in search of the ladies' room.

He had to have been following me. The moment I stepped inside to collect my drunken self, he appeared. Hands on my waist, mouth on my neck, and I kept telling him to leave.

"Just let me kiss you," he said. I suppose I wanted to, with my inhibitions floating in alcohol, but I will not kiss after smoking.

He probably thought I was misbehaving.

I suppose I shouldn't have let this even begin.

**October 1, 2003**

I saw Lance on Monday against my better judgment. We smiled at each other from across the table. I had three glasses of wine in the restaurant and a bottle waiting for me in my car.

And into the night we went, only a little tipsy. We went to a couples' house, Wanda, a friend from work, also a bulimic, and her boyfriend. They were twice our age but welcoming.

I stood out, not meaning to; I just wanted to wear my new silk skirt before storing it for next summer.

At his house, we just held each other, fitting perfectly. I told him I didn't know if I was ready. We started to kiss, and it wrapped me up. I don't remember which clothes came off first. It must have been the silk skirt.

It was great. Both times around. Afterward, though, as we held each other, again, something was missing. I break a little, wondering if he felt that too.

## November 2, 2003

*Why does it make me so upset that nobody called? Why can't I forget it? When I said, "Nobody called," I meant Lance or Jim. Now, I really didn't expect Lance to call me. I would be an absolute fool to think, even for a moment, that he would actually worry about me. And God, if that doesn't still hurt.*

*Every man in my life, every one, has been unreliable.*

*I held Jim to a higher standard, hence, my disappointment + sensitivity.*

*I went through Lance's and my scrapbook tonight. So much time & weight with him. The only thing that hit me was that we looked cute. I hope Mom isn't right about our relationship being superficial.*

*I have also just about had it with these diabetes issues. I will call RI hospital tomorrow about the transplant. I must be ketoacidic because my levels will not drop. Plus, I'm getting chunky. I have a good mind to skip that Lantus injection tonight.*

## November 25, 2003

*I drove to Lance's house tonight after Dad and the boys left for Tennessee. I tuned into a radio station playing only Christmas carols, even though it's not Thanksgiving yet. I was reminded of how great Christmas was last year—how consumed I was in keeping the puppy a secret. I recalled being so overcome by the sheer joy in the giving of that present that I didn't even think about what I was getting.*

*I had forgotten how uncomfortable it was eating dinner with Lance's family. Barbara alleviated this a little bit by talking on the phone at the table. Roger glared at her. I am always embarrassed eating in front of Lance's folks. If the dish is at the far end of the table, I'll rarely ask to have it passed to me. At one point, without any prompting, Barbara passed me the dish of chicken. I had only had one leg; that was what everyone started out with.*

*"How did you know I wanted that?" I asked, and she just shrugged.*

*Then Lance proceeded to eat a chocolate bar in front of me, that bastard.*

*Afterward, we went to his room, and I had a sneezing, runny-nose fit. The thought of needing—being overdue for—a Lantus shot put me over the edge, and I started to cry. I'm sick of being sick, to begin with. Having a cold + my period on top of diabetes is just no fucking fair.*

*And I thought, "Well if I were with Jim, he'd probably fish around in my purse for the insulin bottle + needle and then draw it up." He remarked a few days ago about being willing to do that.*

*Anyway, Lance did not offer to draw up the needle, nor did he ask any questions while I cried in his bed. He stroked my cheek, then my arm. It hurt how superficial everything was.*

*The truth about Lance is that he's self-centered, unmotivated, unappreciative, short-fused, completely lacking in empathy, immature, and uncompassionate.*

*He doesn't ask me about my diabetes or my eating problems.*

*He doesn't ask to read a paper when my professor tells me it's excellent.*

*He doesn't kiss me like he used to.*

*He doesn't reach for my hand or put his arm around me like before. We don't make love anymore, and we don't even hold each other after sex.*

### December 6, 2003

*How warm God feels to me. Distant but warm. Welcoming. Like whatever wrongs I've done don't matter anymore. He just wants me there. The only thing it could be equated with is a fight with your lover. After a while, you don't care what he said. You just terribly want him with you. It feels like a warm night in winter, where I could close my eyes and be God's daughter. Then I think about Lance. The lost cause with the dark eyes. And I no longer have any compass. I wonder what I'm doing, if any of me is even left anymore. If I'm just trying to leave him, so I feel appreciated by him.*

### December 11, 2003

*I'm finding everything I see unattractive, undesirable. Worthless. I wish I could find solace in just crawling into my bed, but those dreams are still there. Just this week, I have dreamed that Lance killed Ken and forced me to help cover up the murder, that I was homeless, searching about a rainy New York City for shelter, and just last night that I was badly injured. Instead of accepting Lance's ride to the hospital, I chose to lay on the ground with Paul while our two dogs jumped around us playfully.*

*I cried on the way to work today. Our love is like this dwindling flame. I don't want to take him to the holiday party, and I don't want to exchange gifts with him and feel all that emptiness on Christmas day. What Mom used to say keeps coming back to me, about how I was going to end up with somebody who is just crazy about me. Lance is not crazy about me. I feel like I'm turning into Barbara, trapped in this dead, empty relationship. Why am I afraid to leave? Because he has been the only one for the last two years. He's mine. When Mom said that she thought I needed him just as badly as he needed me, maybe she was right.*

*I'm so lonely. Why? For years I've thought I was destined to die young from diabetes. Now that I'm taking care of it, now that there's the possibility of a transplant . . . what now? Now I'm going to be a nurse? Do I even want that? Sure, I said I did, but that was to placate people who asked about my future. What was I supposed to say? "No, I don't plan on doing anything but eating sugar and dying of ketoacidosis in a few years."*

*I've fixed my health, my relationship with my dad, and I am moving toward an actual future. Despite this whirlwind of positive change, I'm not happy. I don't have any friends, any confidants, any love. I wish Lance could be here. I wish he could have changed. I didn't expect it. I just wanted it. I just wanted to pour my love over him, wrap him in it, but feel it back and feel safe. He can't give me that, though. He's in the same place, probably worse off than the first night I invited him to my house. I didn't do him any good, and look at all I lost.*

## January 15, 2004

*I almost called you tonight. What would I have said? Just want to hear your voice, tell you I'm having a hell of a time?*

*It's 11:20. You're probably driving home, close to the Fish Road exit. I picture your truck going off the road. I worry about drugs + you driving drunk.*

*I want to tell you to come home to me. That I need you to hold me. That I am aching, I miss you so much. You broke my heart even though I was the one who let go.*

## January 19, 2004—1:02 a.m.

*When I was about to step into the shower this morning, and the phone rang, I knew it was you. I ran into the kitchen naked to answer it. Everyone was at church. It hurts my feelings when you talk about sex withdrawal. Of course, I miss that too, but it's not foremost in my mind. I wish you would tell me something else you missed. Maybe that's it.*

*Tonight, you slept with Amber, didn't you? This is why you aren't calling now; you aren't sure you'd be able to trust yourself talking to me. You might slip & tell me.*

*The only nice thing today was the shower I just took. I almost had to cry at the water. It felt like mercy, just being touched. That it would fall all over, rinsing me like forgiving fingertips. I thought, I don't even deserve this.*

## March 12, 2004

It terrifies me that he's fallen into drugs again, and I don't know what to do.

What if these are the final days, the final chances? I hate that only now he tells me things I waited years to hear. I don't want it because I know if I reach out and grab it, it'll just dissolve in my hands.

## March 13, 2004

I made myself throw up tonight. This wasn't some little "rid yourself of the ice cream" episode. I ate pizza, peanuts, a sliver of bread, and low-carb ice cream, and I cleared the dishes from the sink and relieved myself of the afore-mentioned. Afterward, when I felt cleansed and back on track, I was already thinking how painless and rewarding it was and what a great solution I should do more.

Tonight Matt and I were talking about sleeping with people. I told him I slept with Chris. He proceeded to ignore me for the remainder of the evening, obviously disappointed and disgusted. That makes two of us.

Chris. That fucker has something of mine, something I can't get back. There's not a damn thing I can do about it. He doesn't know he has it. It was left somewhere in his dirty bed, on his muddy floor. I lost something that will always haunt in the background, especially for Lance. Chris doesn't care, but I do. I laid the pearls out, and in his drunken apathy, he trampled them. I am still surprised. Are my pearls worth that little? I must think so if I gave them so quickly. I had tried to say no. I said no over and over and over. Then I thought, maybe he will see my worth if we exchange this thing. I can't for the life of me comprehend how he missed it.

I'm going to have to tell Lance. I really should have told him before I slept with him again. We had vowed that if we were going to continue being intimate, we were supposed to inform the other if we were seeing someone else. I drove up to Lance's after church today. At one point, I almost chickened out. He'll turn me away, I thought. I could barely meet my own eyes in the glass of his front door.

We fell into bed just to warm up, to wrap legs around legs, and let our feet play around together. Bullet dove in the middle and laid on his back, totally in the way and obnoxious. I wanted to kiss. I had to get that in, just in case he never let me do it again. When things started to get a little feverish, it was time to come clean. As I started to talk, I watched his body stiffen. When I got to the part where Chris and I decided to go to Narragansett because we weren't tired, I paused. "That's it?" he said. I said no. Finally, he said, "So you're not seeing him, you're just sleeping with him?"

"I did once," I said.

I thought I saw Lance's body jerk; otherwise, he didn't move or speak. I wasn't even sure he was blinking.

"Say something," I demanded. "Are you angry, sad, disgusted?"

I assured him the sex was empty, and there was no love. What I didn't say was that it may have been the single most violating thing I've done to myself. Though all I wanted from Chris was to be held, I went into it knowing I would feel used and ugly afterward, and that's exactly what happened. Chris didn't love one thing about me.

Lance said he couldn't be in the house anymore. He hugged me before he left. That wonderful angel. There was my grace.

### March 16, 2004

Yesterday Lance drove me to the eye doctor where I got a prescription for glasses. They dilated my pupils for the exam, and Lance said it looked like I'd been eating mushrooms. We made love twice at his house after his parents had gone out to dinner. He said he couldn't do this anymore if I was going to be with other people. I don't know if he meant sexually or relationship-wise, or both. Then we started on some wine and stopped his truck at the Park-n-Ride to smoke pot. Afterward, we went to a restaurant (Chinese buffet—what else?), and I gorged myself. I told Lance I'd made myself throw up for the last three nights in a row. He didn't say anything. I'd told him once before on the phone, saying it was more healthy for my diabetes than taking too little insulin. He said he just couldn't picture me actually doing it—throwing up.

I wanted to make myself vomit last night, but I lacked the coordination and focus. So I skipped Lantus and peed + guzzled water all night long.

I feel like I will never be able to stop eating, and the anxiety and emptiness are beginning to overwhelm. Once I vomit, no food is appealing; the seas are calmed, but it would be easy for this to get out of hand.

### April 6, 2004

Why me? Why me? I'm tired of being a pincushion. I know it was unrealistic to think I'd get the transplant and be pulled out of this abyss, but now I'm dropped back in, only lower because there's nothing to look forward to. No transplant. Not a solitary thing to be hopeful about.

I told God He was awful. I said it repeatedly, meaning it more and more every time until it concreted into blasphemy.

"God, you're awful. Awful, awful, awful."

### April 18, 2004

My love is smoking heroin. I haven't really dwelled upon it much; if I did, I might morph into a panicked mother, lecturing, interrogating, getting nowhere. He seems to think it's no big deal. I just wrap my arms around myself and picture him in dingy, cramped apartments in Fall River. I envision shady characters with tattoos and sinister smiles. These are the types of people I would dismiss. This is my love.

But I cannot say anything. I got up this Sunday morning, barely able to move from muscular fatigue, and hobbled off to the kitchen after everyone else had left for church. Then I ate ice cream, two bowls of cereal, a small slice of cake, and threw it up in the sink while the disposal was running. What am I supposed to say when my addictions are just as destructive, just as filthy?

### April 22, 2004

Last night Lance was sitting uncomfortably at the table while Phil and the kids piled in to eat dinner. I could feel every raised voice, every unnecessary comment fraying his nerves. Finally, I motioned for him to join me on the couch, but I thought, "Why can't he like my family?" I always pictured "the one" to like my family; for God's sake, they're not that terrible.

### April 29, 2004

Today I found myself crossing the line into territory where the b/p[62] is overtaking me. It started when that shaky, directionless, paralyzing anxiety hit me, and I realized I wasn't thinking about eating food and having it calm me down. I was thinking that once I threw up, I would feel calm. I didn't want to eat. I just wanted to throw up.

### May 10, 2004

I went out driving with Lance and we smoked pot. Three drags, to be precise, and I'm high out of my mind. Hungry, we pull into Burger King. We buy a Chicken Caesar Salad to split, a Kids Meal for me, and a Chicken Value Meal for him. We sit in the parking lot and eat. I throw my bun out the window like a Frisbee and find it hysterical. I think we should get movie theater popcorn and tell him so.

Then I tell him we need mud pies and he agrees. Stop & Shop, after all, is just across the street. He drives over. "Don't forget croutons," I call out the window.

While I'm waiting, I finish the fast food and then move on to the chocolate cake I have stashed in the back seat. It's fantastic. That's what gets me about pot. I'm actually able to enjoy eating because I'm not so anxious. So I eat half the bloody cake while Lance is no doubt meandering around the store searching for fucking croutons.

The people in the cars around me load their groceries into their trunks or back seats. I decide to throw up in a plastic bag. No big deal. There are plenty of napkins to clean up with. People are used to a particularly foul smell associated with vomit. This is because they only encounter sickness vomit, which consists of older digested food. When you throw up right after eating the odor is not offensive. It pretty much smells like the food you've just been ingesting. I actually find the smell, though slightly tainted, comforting at this point. I puke and puke, not giving a flying fuck if anyone sees me. But when I spot Lance coming through the door I quickly knot the bag.

Smiling, he gets in.

Shit! I forgot milk, he says.

Bingo! Want me to go in and get you some? Huh? Huh?

Yeah, he says.

No prob-lem-o, buddy.

I go into the bathroom, puke again, wander around looking for Swiss Cake rolls to replace the ones I binged on. Can't find them. Get popcorn instead. The yellow, buttery kind. The cashier is kind to me. I know I look like hell. I saw myself in a store mirror: red eyes, bloated jowls, shaky fingers.

Lance looks at me closely this time when I get in with his 2% milk. Decides not to eat his pies. We drive home in silence while I munch guiltily on the popcorn. At his house I puke again. My allergies are ruthless. I say I must go home. He doesn't protest.

In the car, I polish off the cake while swigging Diet Coke, then pull into a parking lot next to the police station. Puke into another plastic bag and briefly visualize a curious cop wondering what the black car is doing parked at a closed business. I imagine telling him I've done nothing wrong. I'm just throwing up. But if he drug tested me, I'd fail. I finish up, hastily. Dump a bottle of water over my sticky fingers, throw the bulging bag by the side of the building. What a precious thing for some unfortunate employee to have to clean up in the morning. I drive home, head pounding, throat swollen, eyes sore and itchy, *comforted by the fact that Hey, I've eaten. And I'm neither hungry nor bloated and, therefore, quite pleased.*

### June 4, 2004

*Lance and I sat in the car for a long time after the movie. He told me he hadn't felt the same way about me for the last few months since I told him about Chris. We decided to take a break. Actually, he decided. Afterward, I didn't binge once that day. I had a very productive work out and could have danced.*

### June 12, 2004

*Tonight I told Stan that if I couldn't kiss him before the night was over, I would never speak to him again. He's a sous-chef at Seaside. Divorced with no kids, or so I heard. We drove to Castle Hill in my car. We kissed and kissed. I thanked him for being slow with me. He told me that every part of my body was beautiful even though he hasn't seen it. Imagine if he truly did think that. He said he could see it when the lights from the kitchen shone through my dress. I should have appreciated the comment, but all I could imagine was the curve of my inner thighs, and the image was far from erotic to me.*

### June 17, 2004

*With Mom and Phil safely tucked away at a B&B in Cape Cod, and Ryan at Dad's, Matt and I filled the bathtub with beer and bought tons of junk food. Matt invited friends, and Stan came. We cranked Tom Petty and Dave Matthews.*

*After everyone left, Stan and I were on the deck, listening to The Eagles and smoking. Stan said he was going to bed, which, of course, meant my bed. I went too and told him to close his eyes so I could change. I put on the purple slip—the one I haven't worn in a long time.*

*In bed, his body felt as smooth as mine. I missed the roughness of Lance's skin. He kissed me, and his hair fell a little on my face. I've never had anyone's hair fall into my face. It looked darker in the dim light, almost Lance's color. I moved away from him, and he asked me why. I told him I was thinking of someone else, but my words were careless, thanks to the wine.*

*Stan got up and stiffly began to dress. I pulled the blankets around my stomach and asked him what he was doing. He was bent over putting his socks on and didn't respond. I started to cry. Then he said something like, "I just got out of a situation where she was thinking about someone else. I don't need* that." I told him that was not what I had meant. I just had not learned how to detach sex from the other things it was tangled up in: trust, love, security . . .

He said gently, "That's how it's supposed to be."

He didn't leave after all.

Stan is twelve or thirteen years older than me. It's just plain fact: a person numbs up with time, and he's had many more than I have. I don't know to what degree I can safely do this. I haven't been hurt quite enough yet.

### June 24, 2004

The beach is utopian-esque today. There are varying colorful beach umbrellas, shrieking children chasing the gulls. There are sandcastles yet to be trampled, white cellulite-ridden grandmothers keeping a watchful eye on the undertow. I am in the dunes, and I think my shins are on the verge of burning, but what the hell are you going to do? They're shins, for God's sake. Yesterday, Lance came to Seaside to pick up the concert tickets and give me the money for them. He parked right next to Stan's truck, which I kept nervously glancing at like it was surveillance equipment.

### July 7, 2004

What Stan did last night was sobering. He called late, as usual, said he had just woken up. I told him we had to do something in civilization and to call later if he wanted to go out. He never called. Granted, over the last few days, we had spent a lot of time together in his room, always in his room. I don't get it. Maybe he's a homebody. Maybe he's broke. Maybe I really am just a booty call.

Then, I think, don't I have my own selfish reasons for this? Boredom is one of them; that need to stay occupied is still as rampant as it ever was. I need to be seen now, remembered like this because it will not last. At least Stan talks. Yesterday morning, he was talking at length about fishing and surfing and scuba-diving in different places he's been in the Caribbean.

When he didn't call, I almost called him. I'm glad I stood my ground, but it was my birthday, and I really wanted to see him.

July 2004
age twenty

# DOVES MAKE FEEBLE MOTHERS

I KNEW RACHEL WAS dating two men. There was Lance, whom she couldn't seem to live with or without. Then, she started seeing Stan, who was older, emotionally removed, and from what I gathered, no prize either. Still, she frequented his weathered house on the sea. Lance always drew her back; then he'd disappoint her, and she'd return to Stan. This went on and on, despite my subtle and not-so-subtle objections.

"Why do you bother with either of them?" I asked one day. My question hung in the air like a bad smell. "Has either guy helped you grow as a person—or helped you in any practical way?" She knew I meant carrying groceries, pumping gas, paying for dates—the things you'd expect a boyfriend to do, but hers never did.

Rachel looked right through me, her blue eyes miles away.

"I didn't think so. For God's sake, Rachel, dump them both!"

Tuning back into me, her eyes looked tired, defeated.

"I wish you'd find some female friends." I softly added, "Even just one you could hang out with and talk to. It would help you so much."

"I know, Mom, you keep saying. I just don't have time."

"If you dumped those two losers, you would!"

PHIL PLUNKED A ZIPLOC baggie stuffed with what looked like basil on my legal pad. I had been at my desk for hours, writing lesson plans for my new job, teaching English as a second language to international navy captains at the Naval War College. My pen froze.

*Oh, no! Now, Rachel's smoking pot?*

"I found it stashed inside Matt's snowboard cover," Phil said matter-of-factly.

"Matt? Are you kidding me?" Matt hated pot and scorned people who smoked it. "How did you know he was smoking?"

"Red eyes, mainly. He also comes home smelling like cologne and heads to his room. That's not like Matt. He usually hangs out with us or at least says hi."

Last week, Matt had returned giddy after going out with his friends. Face flushed, my gangly sixteen-year-old son had waltzed me around the kitchen while I laughed, savoring the moment. Now, I realized he had been stoned.

Phil had probably known for a while but was waiting until he found hard evidence. Of course, he would have seen the signs. Phil was the guy in high school who lit joints at rock concerts and sent them down the row. I was the girl who passed the tiny blunt with the glowing tip—how did they smoke those things without singeing their lips?—to the next kid without taking a hit.

We flushed Matt's marijuana. When cornered, he confessed but refused to quit. He said pot helped him relax; he had more fun and related better to people while smoking. He shot down every argument—it was illegal, there-fore, immoral; bad for his asthma; he'd get lazy; he'd get hooked. His only concession was vowing never to drive under the influence.

Phil continued to raid Matt's room and car and jettison his stash. Once, he found a haul the size of a small bush. Too large to flush, I decided to take it to the dump. As we carried it out with other garbage via the deck, Matt followed us, irate.

"You guys can't just trash my weed! I paid a lot of bank for that! You have to pay me back!"

We shook our heads.

Matt stalked back inside, slamming the screen slider door so hard Phil jumped. He had just repaired it for the third time that summer.

Rachel, sitting on the deck steps impassively smoking, finally piped up. "You know, it's a shame to waste perfectly good pot. You two should smoke some."

She was dead serious.

✦   ✦   ✦

AGITATED, I DROVE THE short distance to the transfer station. The glorious blue ocean emerged at the end of Greene Lane like a faithful friend. Except for a few trees, one got a clear shot of the scintillating water all the way to the dump and to the Newport Naval Base beyond it. Normally, it had a calming effect, its beauty and grandeur dwarfing my problems. Today I just sighed.

What was wrong with my kids?

When I was in high school in the 70s, I didn't need pot or alcohol to have fun. At our parties, the camaraderie and music—Jethro Tull or Supertramp blasting from someone's portable eight-track player—was enough. Beer flowed like the Milwaukee River. Of course, most kids didn't know when to quit; their voices became slurred, and soon some girl was boo-hooing over some drama while the guys, red-faced and grunting, were hunched over a table arm-wrestling or gunning their engines to drag race. That was my cue to go. Though I'd arrived with my boyfriend Randy, I often left with Linda and Ellen.

Seduced by the Jesus Movement,[63] we had become Born-again believers the year before. At fifteen, Linda, Ellen, and I were not looking for religion. We never expected a Jesus freak to attend St. Rita's teen retreat. Nevertheless, there Louie was. Flannel shirt, torn jeans, auburn ringlets, probing brown eyes, asking us point-blank, "Are you saved?"

We shrugged our shoulders. We didn't drink, smoke, or steal. We'd never think of killing someone. Sure, we cussed, but we hardly deserved Hell. Hell was for killers and rapists.

"Next to God's holiness, we're all sinners headed for Hell," Louie said matter-of-factly. "A just God requires a punishment for sin." He was our age, with peach fuzz and a bobbing Adam's apple, yet he spoke with authority, leafing through his worn Bible to point out passages.

Linda, Ellen, and I swallowed in unison. In all our years of Catholic church and catechism, we'd never heard this. Just when I felt doomed, Louie smiled. "But Jesus paid the price. He died in your place." As often as I'd stared at Jesus' torqued body hanging on the giant crucifix at church, I'd never understood why He had to die. Now a faint light flicked on. "Salvation is a free gift," Louie continued, his smile expanding. "You just have to take it."

That evening, during a break, I spied Louie praying in a dark room, his smiling face and uplifted hands lit by a single candle. Overcome with longing, I accepted God's gift.

After my conversion, high school felt less hostile. My identity was no longer based on how I looked or who I knew but on Whom I served. I'd never belonged to the popular crowd, but suddenly it didn't matter; I was part of something larger and more real that removed the sting of their cliques.

Granted, it got tougher when I started dating Randy—one look from him and my legs turned to butter. But I learned that God's rules were not intended to spoil my fun but to protect me. I saw this when girls who slept around got pregnant and faced impossible decisions; or when the principal announced over the crackling loudspeaker that another student was critically injured or killed while driving drunk or high.

My faith kept me safe and propelled me forward. I wanted this peace and protection, this same productive path for Rachel and Matt. I thought they did, too.

But now, three years later, Matt was smoking pot, and Rachel was sleeping with two different men. Meanwhile, my church friends' kids took mission trips to Africa and received college scholarships.

Where had I gone wrong? I wondered as I pulled into the town dump, gravel crackling under the tires of my Corolla. Was it my divorce? The thriving young adults at church came from stable homes. I had read in Doctor Mary Pipher's *New York Times* bestseller, *Reviving Ophelia: Saving the Selves of Adolescent Girls,* that when parents back out of their marriages, kids naturally rebel. They reason that if mom and dad break the rules, they can, too, and single parenting, with its ungodly workload, allows kids every opportunity to get away with it.[64] Didn't I know it. I sprinted from task to task.

That day, as I pondered my kids' misbehavior, engine idling, I barely noticed the line of cars ahead of me. Sea air wafted in my windows. Surely, my dismal work history played a part. With three young kids, I could not work full time, could not stomach leaving them in daycare and summer camp. I settled for low-paying teaching jobs that consumed my time but never led to anything permanent. I was forever, if not writing class plans and grading essays, searching the Internet for better opportunities. No wonder I had missed the signs.

Digging deeper, I considered my upbringing. "Children should be seen and not heard," Mom often chirped. Did she want us to fade into the brown paneling? It sure felt like it.

An intellectual, Mom had started college before she met and married Dad at age twenty. She loved to read and chat with friends. She did not like cooking or managing a house. At four p.m. each afternoon, panic would seize her face as she realized the house was trashed, she had no prospects for dinner, and Dad was due home at five p.m. An hour of mayhem followed as she barked at us to pick up toys, scrub bathroom sinks and toilets, dust furniture, and shake out rugs. While the vacuum roared, she rifled through the pantry and fridge to make a meal. In between opening cans and sautéing onions, she'd check our work. If we were slacking, she jerked the toilet brush or dust mop out of our hands to demonstrate how it was done.

Mom gave my Sicilian father four daughters in eight years, but she hated being "stuck in the sticks with no car, no money, and four god-darn brats."

Mom slapped us at the slightest provocation. When she was really mad, she charged after us with a red fly swatter. One day, when she was thrashing me with the fly swatter, her blue eyes crazed, I dove into my open closet, burrowing deeper and deeper until I was in a far corner. Unable to reach me, she walked away.

Mom taught us a few things. How to save a buck by going to garage sales and buying clothes on clearance. Showing kindness to the disabled and indigent. But she imparted so little about the nuts and bolts of life or even our developing bodies. At eleven, I'd never been taught to apply deodorant under my arms. Instead, Mom said, "Someone in this car has body odor, I'm not going to say who."

Dad was a parts technician in the Air National Guard. He spent his free time working in the yard or wood shop. Dad stressed the importance of respect ad nauseam. We were to respect laws, our parents, and all adults. But I had no clue what he meant. One day he was lecturing me for something at dinner, striking the air for effect with a butter knife that had margarine stuck to it, which I found hilarious. After straining to hold a straight face as long as was humanly possible, a smile slipped out, followed by a snicker. His free hand slapped my mouth, giving me a lip-throbbing lesson in respect I never forgot.

Dad was also big on modesty, another idea he never explained. God forbid if Anna or I, at ages seven and six, forgot to pull our window shades before dressing. The day he found us naked on the front lawn, he was livid. Having just shared a bubble bath, feeling clean and giddy, we had wrapped ourselves in the rainbow afghan our Aunt Mary had crocheted. We skipped outside, giggling and twirling around on the grass. When Mr. Kreuger saw us, he smiled. But Dad's eyes smoldered. Pulling the afghan tightly around our shoulders, he ordered us inside. "Get dressed and stay in your room for the rest of the day!" He raised his hand as if to whale us. "And if you ever do that again!"

Their parenting improved, especially after the Jesus movement wafted through the Catholic church—St. Rita's called it the "Charismatic movement"—in 1977. As Mom and Dad joined Bible studies and prayer groups, God began to transform them. Mom shed her selfish nature like an old snakeskin. Her voice lost its edge. The smile she reserved for guests and Dad she now wore daily. She suddenly gave wise advice. She even began to embrace us. If her hugs felt stiff, it was because her mother had never given her a crumb of affection. Whereas I had feared Mom as a child, she became my best friend, the first person I called if I was elated or distraught.

Dad's transformation was no less dramatic; however, in 1980, when he was diagnosed with brain cancer, he had another reason to seek truth: he wanted to ascertain his final destination. Dad's pride slowly ebbed. He learned to apologize and cry, unlike my former dad, who would not tolerate tears the day of his operation when we learned he was going to die. Mom had warned us not to cry, but when I saw Dad's sad brown eyes and bandaged head, I broke down. He pushed me from his bedside.

My new dad and I wept freely. He allowed me to feed and bathe him before dying at fifty-two.

Inching my car forward, I sighed. I had rejoiced over my parents' transformation. Dad felt peace even as cancer nibbled his vitality, and I had a mother for the first time. But it was too late to reap their wisdom—by then, I was a college student living on my own. I had absorbed their early parenting. Though I had made a concerted effort not to repeat their errors, who knew what I passed on to my kids?

As I approached the vast trash receptacles, flies circled around my windows. I batted them away. No doubt, all these things contributed to my kids' misbehavior, I concluded that day, the most damning factor never even occurring to me until years later. In her journals, Rachel made several references to my "childlikeness." Each time, I cringed. I viewed myself as mature, tenacious, strong. Hadn't I remained in my dismal marriage for twelve years? Chiseled away at a master's degree while diapering infants and managing a house? Paid the bills on my paltry income after Perry left?

I would come to understand that Rachel did not mean weakness of character, but naivete. She was pointing out my ignorance of popular culture. I was not totally blind. I knew that EDs were rising, teens were having sex earlier, and drugs were easier to attain. However, I lacked those nitty-gritty details that made these risks real and urgent; for example, I did not know that EDs were serious mental illnesses that intensified without care; what adolescents were doing sexually; or where they were getting alcohol and drugs. To educate myself, I read a book on parenting teens, as well as attended a lecture on adolescence at Rachel's middle school. However, neither resource yielded a scrap of cultural data. I should have dug deeper. I kept meaning to research the pop culture's effect on teens, but more pressing issues always arose. Eventually, I released this duty into the vortex with the other vital tasks I could not tackle as a single working mother. In my gut, I believed my kids would be fine. Having grown up in a Christian home, they had been taught morals and values that were reinforced in church and youth group. They were probably not going to fall for these temptations any more than I had.

I hadn't realized how radically the times had changed. In the 1970s, during my adolescence, sex and substances were merely implied in music and the media; however, in the 1990s and early 2000s, these ideas were in my young teens' faces. Once, Rachel and Matt compared stories of their physical education teachers fitting condoms on cucumbers to demonstrate safe sex. Another day, I heard Rachel sweetly singing with Alanis Morissette about "going down on someone in a cinema." In 1999, when we got a home computer and Internet, even with parental controls, my teens had access to plenty of raunchy information. They were living in what Pipher calls a trashy, dangerous, highly sexualized culture.[65] This is how American adolescents grow up, by moving away from their parents and embracing the broader culture.[66] Though this "junk culture" clashed with everything Rachel and Matt had been taught, they gravitated toward it like flies to trash. Experimenting with drugs and sex made Matt and Rachel feel like adults.

To help them make this daunting transition, my teens needed a savvy mom who understood the rules and risks of their world. Someone who could help them process the new ideas and experiences flooding into their awareness and offer practical advice without judging or reacting.[67]

At fourteen, Rachel learned that I was not that mom.

"A hot kid on the bus just asked me to give him head," she announced one day after school.

Gasping, I asked, "Rachel, do you know what that means?"

She nodded, smiling dreamily.

I told her the boy's comment was not nice. It was sexual, disrespectful, and totally inappropriate. Couldn't she see that? At age nine, when an eleven-year-old neighbor boy started patting her rear, she reported it to me. Now she told me girls in junior high did that for their boyfriends.

The information flattened me. In my day, eighth grade boys revealed their feelings through a friend or in an awkward note. Now they were requesting oral sex? As a parent of an adolescent girl in 1999, I should have known that. As a Christian, I was supposed to be aware of what was going on, "as wise as a serpent but as innocent as a dove."[68] How could I teach, protect, and guide my kids if I didn't investigate the darkest corners?

Had I been informed, rather than expressing shock and outrage, I might have asked Rachel some pointed questions. We might have had a productive talk about teenage sexuality. Instead, she skipped off with stars in her eyes. I came off as old-fashioned and ignorant, certainly not someone Rachel could trust with her secrets, as she confessed to me at age twenty.

[Letter from Rachel, dated April 4, 2005]

*There were (and still are) times I felt like I couldn't approach you with a lot of things happening to me because I liked worldly things you were either naïve of or shocked by or worried too much over or just plain didn't understand. And I wasn't ready or willing to stop things, like my diabetes denial, drug experimentation, sex, the ED, drinking.*

*I just didn't feel a connection to you—I felt like we were so different. You were obedient; I was rebellious. You were eloquent; I was crass. You wanted me to control my diabetes—that was when I started to deliberately avoid you. I didn't want to think about having diabetes. I was happier to be in denial. I know I pushed you away, but I don't think that's going to be the case anymore. I think you + me are going to become a lot closer than we ever were.*

My hands would tremble as I read her letter. First a stab—a sickening pang that I had failed her. Left her alone to grapple with such onerous things. Then a rush—warm and deep—when in the next breath she forgave me.

Despite Rachel's sweet pardon, certain mindsets and habits had cemented. My misguided parenting and her ingrained behaviors would run their course.

Swatting away flies, I tossed the mass of marijuana into the dumpster along with the other trash. I felt like a weight had been lifted. Granted, Matt's drug problem remained, but at least we were aware and were handling it the best we could. Still that naïve mother, I had no inkling what trouble lay ahead, especially for Rachel.

## July 8–October 10, 2004

*I can't do this forever.*
*I go to bed feeling tired and old,*
*and it occurs to me*
*that life could rush on like this,*
*exercising and dieting,*
*and I will have missed everything.*

# "There is vomit on my shirt."

## July 8, 2004

I look down.

There is vomit on my shirt.

Nothing a little water won't take out.

It didn't start out this way, oh no. I never used to do this at work.

At one point, I envisioned myself sitting down with Heather, explaining why I didn't want to work night shifts. She'd be sitting at her desk, me in the side chair. I'd tell her I don't like to be here alone when it is quiet. Too much time, I'd say. I eat and eat. You see, I'm a bulimic.

She would fidget, stiffen slightly.

"Well, do you . . . do it here?"

"Oh no. I would never even think of it." Which would have been true at the time this hypothetical conversation would have taken place.

The first time I did it at work, I felt I needed to be over a sink with running water, so I could keep the toothbrush that went down my throat wet and also to continuously rinse out my mouth. I did it in the back kitchen and clogged the sink, which was such a nauseating hassle that I didn't attempt it again for months.

Then one night, for one reason or another, it had to be done.

I suppose I could have just used a toilet, like everyone else, but instead, I used the wastebasket in the handicap stall, armed with an extra liner. In place of a toothbrush, I used a large pen I kept hidden on a ledge. I pulled out the extra liner, tied it up, and buried it under paper towels when I was done. This method worked for a while. Now it goes directly into the toilet, thanks to a tube of lip gloss, the most effective device I've used so far. My eyes water, but if anyone calls me on it, I say I just took a very painful injection of insulin in the bathroom. That's what I told Heather when she asked, though I couldn't meet her eyes when I said it. If I had my way, I would probably do this at every meal. Because I do like to eat, and I love how vomiting makes the urge to eat go away.

*Things I thought I would never do I now engage in without a second thought. I will do it when everyone is home if I feel I have half the chance of getting away with it. I watch people's patterns. Mom going upstairs to use the computer always guarantees she'll be out of the way for a while. Matt going out for a long drive. Losing Krissy and/or Ryan is as simple as telling them to walk the dog. I even did it at Stan's house early the other morning after eating a big, pretty, blueberry pancake with syrup I found in his fridge. I used his toothbrush. Disgusting? Yes, but I can't dwell on it. It is what the fuck it is. I rarely argue with it anymore.*

## July 9, 2004

*I can't stop. I find myself having to devote blocks of time for it. Especially the two rounds before bed. Without exception, those must be accommodated. Coming home at three a.m.? Too bad, I'll be up till five, no matter how tired or how much I dread doing it. The worst part is, before, I wasn't even hungry, but I did it anyway to get it out of my system before sleeping. Now, I just want to eat. I can't find a way to discipline myself. I can't even identify what the triggers are anymore. I have even skipped two shots. Which, of course, leaves me groggy and lackadaisical in the morning.*

*Just as I got off work, Stan called, which did light me up though I accused him of making yet another booty call.*

*At Stan's, I tried to focus on the sex. I want to be free there, but I know I am not. I'm too aware now that I do not belong anywhere. I'm not sure what needs he barely manages to meet for me aside from preoccupation. He's not nervous about being naked around me anymore. I suppose this could be a cool thing if I, too, had fallen into that comfortable place, but I haven't. I think of Lance undressing and how beautiful I found it. His childishness, his ridiculously handsome smile.*

*Lance and I still talk. It hurts lately. I want to spill my love for him, but I bite my lip. The other day I managed to say, "You know you're still my favorite, right?" And do you know what he said? "Thank you." As in thank you, I needed to hear that.*

*I wish he would attempt to work things out.*

## July 15, 2004

*Last night Lance, Ryan, and I went to see Spider-Man 2. I thought it would be okay for Lance to go. The situation is safer with Ryan present.*

So we had our tickets, and before we went in, Lance said he had to use the bathroom. Ryan and I waited in the theater, watching the previews. An odd amount of time had not really passed, but I suddenly knew. I walked back to the men's room and lingered by the door. Then I walked in and saw his feet. Sideways. I listened to him snort heroin, over the toilet paper dispenser I assume, and I walked out. All I could think was how someone else could have seen my feet, and how they would have been backward, facing the toilet bowl, but it would have been the same.

### July 20, 2004

I drove to Lance's house, and then we went to the beach. We listened to a quiet CD, talked a little, mainly toying with the physical boundaries that have been raised the last month. He held my hands, touched my hair, said he wasn't used to holding back. He said he was incredibly lonely not being in a relationship with someone.

He didn't look the same. His face was hollowed out, and when I said it was time for me to go, he covered his eyes with his hand. Then, after a moment, he said, "Well, I guess this can't last forever."

"We can stay a little longer," I told him. Our faces were together, and he was bringing his lips close, but I didn't want him to kiss me. Kissing is lethal, I have decided. Kissing usually says more than sex. You get something out of sex. Kissing you engage in solely because you are being intimate with someone you love.

We drove back to his house. Frustrated. In the driveway, we were giving unsatisfying hugs goodbye. There was more to say, more to clear up, but I was too tired and confused to talk. Bullet heard us and began to bark. I had to pee so badly, and I asked if I could use his bathroom. He said, of course.

Bullet was ballistic by the time we got to the door. He's turned into a little chunker. Lost all definition to his stomach. He is rotund.

I sat on the floor in Lance's room, playing with Bullet. Lance was walking around, a bit nervous. Probably of the mess. I asked if I could sleep there. It was three or four in the morning, only a little while until he'd get up for work. The talking, the sitting, the weight of the whole situation had thoroughly exhausted me,

I got into bed. When he climbed in under the covers, we immediately curled up together.

It was not wrong. It was the puzzle pieces reunited, fitting.

We had sex, and it took a long, long time, which surprised me. He had to start getting ready for work as soon as it was done.

We were walking out to our cars, and he kissed me goodbye and said, "I love you," in this fleeting, sincere way. I could get used to hearing these words every morning. Then again, they wouldn't carry the weight they did that morning. He meant it. I could see it in the way his eyes locked on mine. He told me later that he needed to say it but didn't want to say it immediately after having sex.

### July 25, 2004

I ate half a package of sugar-free vanilla wafers, eggs with two pieces of toast, and sugarless chocolate for breakfast. At the tail end, I heard Matt's alarm going off. It was 11:30 am, so I went to the upstairs bathroom to get rid of it. I've found that laying a few pieces of toilet paper into the bowl as you would lay noodles into a lasagna pan minimizes the splash back.

The other day when Lance and I were hanging out, he was beside himself with fatigue. I told him to nap in my bed. Meanwhile I left to buy a vanilla and raspberry swirl sundae that I ate with my fingers. Then I broke into a package of Almond Joys. While driving and eating I decided I might as well go all out. I went to McDonald's, eyeing the clock, nervous as hell he'd wake up and call me and want me to rush back. In line at the drive thru, I ordered two double cheeseburgers and a medium fry. I pulled into a parking spot and ate it hardly tasting the food. Enjoy it! Enjoy it! I kept telling myself, trying to electrify the binge so I could get it out of my system for the few remaining hours in the day.

After finishing, I wrapped up the trash and went in. Their bathrooms have only two stalls, and one was occupied, so I paced while waiting for them to get the fuck out. I could hear them just standing there, breathing, like they were waiting for me to leave. I wanted to blurt out, "Are you a bulimic, too? Because we can just get this over with together!" Finally, I bent down and looked under the stall. I saw two children. One was sitting on the toilet, clearly constipated, the other playing with a plastic water jar. I suppose I could have just gone into the other stall and done it, but I didn't want to. Not in front of them. Little kids shouldn't be subjected to such evils.

### July 28, 2004

I've always heard that eating disorders are related to control, but I've never stopped to consider whether my demons are control related. It makes sense I would have developed an ED at the time of my diabetes diagnosis. Suddenly, I had a chronic illness and wasn't allowed to eat like everyone else. Naturally I rebelled. Now that I think about it, every recently diagnosed diabetic teenage girl would be at risk of an ED because all the ingredients are there. How unfair.

*To me, the fact that I am a diabetic is an emptiness, a void that desperately needs filling. Because my diabetes cannot be fixed—there is not a fucking thing I can do about it—I am driven to control something else. The natural solution would be to accept this disease. I keep running, though, because I know if I were to stop, I would become just as obsessed with trying to manage it as I am at trying to bury it. As a diabetic, I would obsess over everything I put in my mouth even more than I do as a bulimic. I would want to take care of myself yet always fall short. I cannot take care of my diabetes and be the right weight—not as a diabetic—unless I starve myself. I'm convinced that diabetes, and the means by which patients must manage it, promotes weight gain. Is blood too low? Eat food. Is blood too high? Take insulin, which is a growth hormone and will eventually result in craving more food. It's a ridiculous, ridiculous cycle. (No one tells you to lower a hyperglycemic reaction with exercise.) If I take insulin, I gain weight. If I ignore it, I am encouraging an eating disorder. I can't see how there could possibly be any middle ground.*

*You know what?*

*I'd rather have the ED. Give it to me any day. Over being fat? Absolutely. If this is the best middle ground there is—to take care of it somewhat and throw up what I've eaten that I shouldn't have—then I guess I haven't done too bad. Sure, it's exhausting. Everything is. I'm not getting skinnier, but I'm not getting fatter.*[69]

*Or am I? I really need to buy a scale.*

### August 2, 2004

*I did it seven times yesterday. Last night, after closing the day with it, I sat on the front steps in the humidity, watching the deeper shades of blue creep into the sky, and I thought, "I have done nothing the last week. I am in a terrible place, and things seemed to be better off before I was spending time with Lance."*

*On Saturday night, we smoked pot. I don't remember where we were going, but we had already had dinner. I ate more than I felt was acceptable, so I threw up in the bathroom while he went to make a phone call. He never suspected.*

*Afterward, we went to Lee's Market in Westport, a yuppie grocery store, as Lance put it. Whatever. Yuppies like low carb, and so do I. So we bought some overpriced crap. The greatest part was the anticipation. Endless possibilities behind the freezer case glass. I knew Lance was watching me, that bastard. Didn't he understand that I could eat this if it wasn't going to stay in my system?*

*What can you do instead of bingeing and purging, the doctors in the hospitalization program had asked me. There's only a small interval when you can* do something else. I recall saying I've used journaling as a preventative method. Then I had a great idea: Maybe I could make a journal to help Lance with his drug problem. It could be formatted to ask questions—what is your mood today? What did you do because of it? What could you have done instead?

I told him my idea. He said no. Shot it down without a fragment of a second thought. Knowing how opposed he was to trying anything to better himself disgusted me. I was so repelled I didn't want to have sex with him anymore. It was literally making me angry, doing these things to him. I felt degraded, stupid, and used. These were not the types of things I wanted to do to someone who is such a lost cause. When I stopped towards the end, he asked what was wrong. I said I had to go, that I would not allow myself to feel bad. He threw his head back onto his pillow, tantrum-style.

I went into the kitchen to get my nectarine out of the fridge and the sixth ice cream cone out of the freezer. He walked out of his room, struggling to pull a shirt over his head. I shifted the ice cream into my left hand. We walked outside to the driveway. He told me after much hesitation and apologizing that he's not motivated to try anything new because he doesn't think we have a future any-more. He said he couldn't stop visualizing me with other people. Namely Chris.

Mosquitoes were landing on my arms and fingers. I wanted out of there. I was working first shift in the morning, and I wanted to binge before bedtime. There was so much he could have said, and yet he just opened and closed his mouth like a fish, unable to speak. Finally, he shook his head as though he'd exerted a tremendous amount of effort and said forget it.

I told him I loved him, but I would continue to leave if he stayed the way he was. He said he knew I meant to help, but when I got up and left, it only made it worse, and by "it," I knew he meant the drug use. Well, the mosquitoes were getting vicious, so I told him I needed to go, I needed to write, as a preventative measure, and if I didn't get home to do it, I'd be forced to eat out of my mind. This was, of course, a lie. I knew I was going to binge to get the shit over and done with so I could get to bed. Instead, we went for a drive.

In the car, he said at least twice that he was thirsty, so we stopped at a Stop & Shop. When he said he had to go to the bathroom, I thought that was odd. I knew after a few minutes what he was doing. I moved on to another section of the supermarket where I could keep an eye on the bathrooms. I kept looking over and thinking if he comes out now, it means he probably didn't do it. Every time I looked up, he wasn't walking out. Every minute he didn't appear, I could no longer say there was no chance he was doing it unless someone was beating the shit out of him in there. Even constipation doesn't take that long.

*What really got me was the fact that I needed to be doing my shit, extricating my demons so I could get to bed at a reasonable hour, and I wasn't because he told me that when I left, he was more prone to using. So I didn't leave, and now here he was snorting heroin in the bathroom.*

*When he came out, I pretended I didn't know. I didn't even know what to say.*

*While I was searching for yeast infection treatments, one of his biddies called, inviting him to smoke pot. When he got off the phone, I asked, "Why do you need to go? You just did it."*

*He said he hadn't.*

*"Yes, you did," I said.*

*"When?" he asked.*

*"Just now in the bathroom."*

*He looked me dead in the eye and said he had not.*

*"Please, Lance, you were in there forever."*

*He mumbled something noncommittal, and I grabbed his arm to leave the store. We ended up only buying the medication for me, cucumbers, and some nasty cheese. By the time we got back to his house, I'd still had no food to speak of and was so beside myself with irritation that I didn't even want to hug him goodbye. I sped off and drove back to Burger King (directly across from the f-ing Stop & Shop). I ordered a double cheeseburger and a large fries. The lady at the drive-thru asked if I wanted ketchup, and I said, yes, lots. I got my order and was already stuffing fries into my mouth as I pulled away. When I approached the exit to get back on the highway, I realized the bitch hadn't given me ketchup. All fucking day I had been waiting for that binge, and this bitch ASKS me if I want ketchup and then doesn't put one fucking packet into the bag. I am ineffably pissed, convinced it is ruined, convinced the binge will satiate nothing. I eat it anyhow (she didn't even put ketchup on the burger), and I swear if I saw her on the street, I'd clock her.*

### August 9, 2004

*Tonight I had the worst gas of my entire adult life. I was outside, after a particularly spicy chain of flatulence, watching a little skunk lurk around. I heard footsteps behind me. I figured it would be Stan. It was. He asked me what I was doing, and I pointed to the skunk. We started to throw things at it, which didn't seem to bother it. Instead, the skunk took them in his mouth and carried them back to wherever he called home.*

*Stan said he had been going to get a soda but didn't want to walk down to the machine now for fear of getting sprayed. He asked me to do it and* was touching me, flirting. I told him he had to stop. At first, he searched my face, smiling, and then he said, okay, could he trade me something for the keys to the snack fridge. I figured he wanted to trade me a kiss. Now I had just eaten this (orgasmically good) dinner, so between the bloating, gas, and urge to vomit, I wasn't in the most romantic mood. Instead, I wanted to haul ass to the bathroom. He started to touch the edge of my skirt. I told him he shouldn't. It wasn't fair to his girlfriend, and it wasn't fair to me. He got quiet, and I asked him what was wrong. He said I was right; it wasn't fair. Then he told me that his girlfriend was leaving for Spain for four months. Though he knew he needed to support her, he felt he had given up a lot for no good reason.

"I lost you," he said.

I got quiet. Noting my arms were crossed defensively, I made the effort to uncross them. I liked his attention. I also knew I would be wasting my time and energy if I gave it another shot, so I said, "Even before that, you made me feel like I wasn't worth much." His expression fell between hurt and shock.

"I'm sorry. Is that a terrible thing to say?"

"No," he said. "That's the way you feel." Then, "You didn't like my company?"

I hesitated only because the question seemed irrelevant. "Of course I did," I said.

"But I didn't make you feel special?"

"No, not really."

### August 14, 2004

I didn't want to go to Dad's house for his birthday, so Lance and I went to the mall. I'd gotten a hundred-dollar gift card to Express from somewhere, and I was anxious to blow it. Lance went to get a haircut, and I found myself in a dressing room surrounded by piles of overpriced gorgeous clothes. I also discovered, to my shock and pleasure, that I wore a size 2 instead of a 4 or 6. I couldn't believe it. Strangely enough, while the numbers have shrunk, I see no physical difference. Probably because my stomach still appears so bloody distended.

### August 16, 2004

Lance confessed to being on heroin since February. I had to drag it out of him, but he said it began when I told him about having slept with Chris. He cannot bear to talk about it. He just cries, and there isn't a damn thing I can do because it's my fault. Though he assured me it wasn't the case, I reveled in my blame. I tried to tell myself this was sick, unhealthy, but bearing the responsibility felt more satisfying.

## August 17, 2004

I made myself run today. After about two miles, I looked down at the green grass next to the road and thought how nice it would be to lay there and forget about everything. I will work and work and work for this, and to what avail? At what point will I be able to stop and say, the work I have done is good, now I can allow myself to rest. Never. Because then I will be responsible for maintaining it. Once in a checkout line, while buying copious amounts of shit-food, I fantasized the cashier saying, "How do you eat like this and stay so thin?" And I imagined replying, "Nobody should be jealous of me. I'm a fucking bulimic."

Lance doesn't think this is an addiction. Of course, vomiting is not an addiction, but my bloody drive to eat sure is. After working ten to seven yesterday, I drove to the mall and shopped until ten. I'd eaten scanty amounts of nothing all day. As I was leaving the mall, the urge to eat reared its head, but I didn't feel the need to go to a drive-thru. I'd dropped over a hundred and fifty dollars on clothes. A seventy-dollar cashmere shirt? Shopping is a binge in itself.

## August 18, 2004

Stan called me back to the office. He said he needed help with something. He moved in for a hug and backed me into a filing cabinet. He said, "I hear rumors you're back with your boyfriend." Am I back with Lance? Lance would say, has said, "You tell me."

I simply say, "Stan, he's going through heroin withdrawal." I did not say I will support Lance to the bitter end.

Lance came to Seaside last night. He stood at the front desk staring at me. I was in the middle of a binge. I felt bloated and ashamed when he caught me. Luckily he was stoned. I don't know if he noticed when I went to the bathroom twice. Twice because halfway through the first round, I flushed my gagging tool down the toilet.

I think about what it would be like to have somebody who knew my secret. Somebody who loved me and knew and cared and worried. I remember the night I told Jim, and he let me hug him for as long as I wanted. Which was a long time. It was ridiculously humid that night. The moon was huge and so low you could pull it off the sky and use it as a plate. Clouds raced past, leaving smoky trails, but curiously, there was little wind. He held me and sighed. Said he was sorry. I think he said it pained him to think I thought I was anything less than beautiful. I remember the word "pained." I more vividly remember thinking I could get so needy in arms like his.

Stan doesn't know. I suspect if he did, he would have no clue how to help. God knows, every time I hug him, though, I feel like I need it more and more. I feel greedy at the touch of someone. I feel like maybe I will involuntarily whisper it to him, and he will hold on tighter for everyone to see. It will be simple, and it will somehow be enough.

I must stop lying to myself. It will never be enough.

## August 19, 2004

Last night, Lance and I met at the Park-n-Ride to go to dinner. Only about an hour before, I'd "extricated my demons" with a package of two-dollar sugarless wafers. We went to Pub 99, and I ordered a Caesar salad with chicken and did not decline croutons or bread. Nor the popcorn that was set between us. I ate that first, against my better judgment. Popcorn should be last, but I couldn't wait. I knew I was going to vomit, so why wait. After I ate, quickly, even dipping the bread into the extra dressing I had to ask for, because lo and behold, someone in their kitchen knew the meaning of "light on the dressing," it needed to be done. Did Lance suspect? He had already said he was paying for dinner. Tough shit, I thought. I headed to the restroom while visions of the Seinfeld episode played in my head. The one where George is dating a bulimic, and he yells at her for throwing up the food he paid for.

The bathroom had only two stalls and no music playing, though the lighting was soothing. Fortunately, no one was in there, and it was quick and easy. Except for the fact that I was hungry, and I didn't want to get rid of everything, just the popcorn at the bottom, but try as I might, I could not get those nasty kernels up.

When I left the stall, the circles under my eyes were exaggerated, and my face was undeniably puffy. I smoked a cigarette, pissed as a hornet the popcorn was still there. I briefly thought about going back to get rid of it, but I was still hungry, so I returned to the table. Lance's food was already in a takeout container. He stared at me for a moment too long, and I knew that he knew.

"Are you ready to go?" he asked.

"You already paid?"

"Yeah, you were in there for 15 minutes."

"I was outside smoking for most of the time," I shot back.

On our way out, Lance gave me a tight hug, and to my surprise, I held on in borderline desperation.

## August 20, 2004

I wonder if my father's warning is a blessing or a curse. "Don't you see, Rachel? Rob's on his best behavior right now, but it won't last." He's referring to his unreliable handyman who never stops looking at me.

I like Rob and don't want to hear this.

"Leave me alone," I say, but Dad won't let it go.

"If he can't keep a promise to a paying customer, he'll be blowing you off next."

Lance doesn't like Rob either. I've told him, as nicely as I know how, he's hardly in a position to tell me I can't have male friends.

"Yeah, I'm sure that's all he wants."

## August 21, 2004

On our third "date," we went to Rob's place. I like it there because it's impossible to binge. The walls are paper-thin. And his fridge is bare. Rob smelled of alcohol. I told him to get the fire roaring.

I'd already decided I'd likely sleep there. I hadn't considered where it might lead. He made pasta for himself while I shaved my legs in his bathroom sink. I was pensive and smoking. There's a school of thought that bulimics can be promiscuous. The logic being they are prone to taking what's not allowed, like at the onset of a binge. Their drives are strong, and they give in. Personally, I confuse a sex drive with being ready or acceptable for sex. As in, my looks are all right, and my body is decent enough to be remembered favorably.

That night when he came at me in bed, I was surprised. Not so much at his move as at my reaction. I felt like I was being attacked by his evil-looking mouth and experienced hands. I watched, as if through a window, unable to enjoy myself or even be present. Somehow I managed to say, "Rob, I'm not ready." He immediately let me go and curled up at my back. "Are you okay?" he asked.

I think I shook my head. I got up. Naked. That was okay. He could look. I put on my underwear and his T-shirt and went into the living room to smoke and think.

I was sitting on the sofa looking at my legs, which felt pale and big. When he came in, I felt this even more. He is so thin it almost breaks my heart. His lean body makes me miss a bigger, warmer, safer one. He really is quite strong, and he knows it, but there is nothing sexy about this man with few clothes on. It's like looking at a woman, a lovely, possibly ill woman with that self-assured and yet vulnerable beauty. This is how I should look, I think. "How can I take from you when I don't even compare?"

We sat on the couch talking. I don't recall the beautiful things he said, but I do remember him saying he was afraid of me running away. I think I might have eased his fears. But between Dad's warning and my revelation, I dumped Rob anyway.

## August 22, 2004

Today is awfully gray, dismal. Clouds cast a pall on everything, and I think about the canceled wedding, resulting in my night off. I go in the back to see Stan, but BJ informs me that Stan has taken the day off. Once I've finished my shift, I drive past the beaches, scanning the surfers to see if I can spot him. I don't see him, so I settle on Surfer's Second to watch for him. There is a hurricane off the coast which accounts for the shitty weather, but the surfers gathered here are in their glory. I watch the speckles of them bobbing up and down in the water. Gracefully catching a wave and zigzagging about only to be tossed back into the water. I watch a young girl in a red T-shirt haphazardly running about the foam on the beach, chasing a traumatized sandpiper. She has such energy, it is enviable. I try to call Stan twice. No answer.

Lance and I meet up later. He is in the heaves of withdrawal, stretched out on his bed, complaining of terrible aches. I look at him. He is painfully skinny. Skinnier than me. He looks weak. I try rubbing his shoulders and thighs. He can barely move and decides he needs pot in order to dull the pain. I am in the kitchen then, trying to fix him something to eat. Says he hasn't eaten in almost two days. He is at my back as I am staring into the pantry in a vain search for croutons. He asks, "Do you mind if I go pick up some food?" I stand there for a long time. Even though he's probably using this as an excuse to score heroin, I want him to go, but only if it's for at least fifteen or twenty minutes so I can binge in peace. "How long will it take?" I ask hesitantly. "Ten minutes," he says. More time spent staring at the shelves. I see chocolate, cereal. This could get ugly. "If you leave me here," I say, "I will have to eat." He says, "No big deal. I won't go."

## August 23, 2004

Stan flirts with me in a way I dislike because it is juvenile. He's thirty-two; he should be giving me bedroom eyes, not biting a banana while staring intently at me or searching my pockets for a lighter when my pants have no pockets. He is just looking for an excuse to touch me. Yet I need the attention. I want this man who will assuredly disappoint me.

*I have a fantasy. It consists of my being painfully skinny, so skinny that my sickness is visible to others. I come into work. I faint in the back kitchen, whether of starvation or low blood sugar . . . I don't really care. Either way, my body will crumple, helpless. They will then notice how weak and graceful and helpless I have become. Stan will carry me into the back, lay me down, and give me something to eat. Honey, maybe.*

Samantha Walters, my new shrink, said an ED is just someone making a dramatic incident; someone, obviously intelligent, who must remain preoccupied with a number of things, must remain at the center of the universe. What if this is so? I gotta say, I buy it. She said, You looked so angry when I asked you about diabetes. So angry? Me? Very clever lady, I think.

### September 4, 2004

While I was drying my hair after showering, Mom told me Stan had called. He wanted us to meet up. Though tired, I agreed to go because I was clean and ready. Mom did not look pleased. I had told her Stan was a deadbeat. Mixed messages, Rae, she said.

The anesthetized feeling began to creep in at the beginning of his driveway.

I enter without knocking. I can smell that he has showered, can feel the rising steam. He steps out from the bathroom, brushing his teeth, his waist wrapped in a blue towel. Uncomfortable, I fixate on the fish tank, which has turned a polluted, murky green. He pours us red wine.

We watch TV, and I get tipsy on my empty stomach. He pulls me down next to him while lying behind me. What happens next is a blur. Hands on the small of my back, lips on my neck. At one point, I pull away, and he starts kissing my right hip. I turn around to see how it looks. It looks small, feminine, so I do not ask him to stop. I decide, though, that I don't want this badly enough to go through with it. I think of something meaningful to say, a good reason that will haunt him for days. When I do this, I want to think only of you and nobody else, I say. Standing up, I add, I really should get going.

Somehow, I am coerced into having a cigarette on the deck. He is pure youth, talking about when he was a boy, skipping school to go surfing in the dead of November. I watch, careful with questions, not wanting to disrupt the miracle unfolding before me: A man talking, talking passionately to me. I listen, enthralled. It twinges within me that he has never questioned me like this, but for the moment, I am so overtaken by his rush of words, fucking words, that I don't care. I study him. Is he talking so freely because he respects me for stopping it before it went too far? His responses to my questions convey a belief in my sincere interest in his life, and can you not help but like anyone who shows an interest in your history? He seems riveted to me, and I am enraptured. I am being seduced for the very first time.

### September 7, 2004

Last night was a hazy, black trance of an evening. I began to binge repeatedly after Heather ended her shift, eating pretty much anything in sight. To make matters worse, I had left both lip glosses at home, so I didn't know what to use. I tried a few writing utensils, which tore up my throat. At one point, I thought I saw blood and didn't care. Again and again and again. I just couldn't seem to get enough up. So I thought I'd eat again, softer food this time, even when I didn't want to. Might as well, I figured, if I plan on throwing up again to completely get rid of any remnants. I used a tampon. It was better than the pen or the Wite-Out container.

Just when I thought I was satisfied, the urge would arise yet again. Finally, at home, I sit on the front steps smoking a cigarette, wanting it again. And I think, What is it, sweetheart? What is it you need? Obviously, it is not food. And I have an image of me, maybe eight years old, crying, standing, holding her arms out, anticipating help, though there is none. The world is emptying! she says. I try to talk to her. Well, yes, it is. Allow yourself to feel the void. Be strong. Lance is gone, but he was never there for you anyway. Let yourself hurt over this: it's all right.

But the world still feels empty, and I start to think that maybe being with him wasn't so bad. There was at least the sensation that someone was alongside me, a partner, and therefore I was validated. Alone, it is as though there is no one who sees me. I feel as though I am not even existing.

I go upstairs and read some of the Christian book Mom gave me.[70] It talks about purpose. One piece stands out: that we cannot reject any part of ourselves because God made it, and He knows what is best. He created our bodies a certain way for a specific purpose. This comforts me for a moment until a voice inside pipes up, "Your body could be so much better."

### September 9, 2004

Yesterday Mom and I were at the table drinking coffee, and she told me my weight looked "just right," and my arms looked "very toned." It really does kill me how I am ingesting much less food than she is, exercising twice as much *if not more, and yet she is smaller than me. I have this ingrained belief that a daughter should be smaller than her mother. I wonder if she could fit into my pants or if they would hang off of her. I am not jealous of her. Just fascinated by her metabolism. Why didn't I inherit this? I suppose I am lucky. If she were not so skinny, she might be watching me more closely. I think that she con-sidered it an embarrassment when I was overweight like I had "let myself go," so to speak. Eating little, eating healthy is the lifestyle she embraces. One's life should not revolve around food. I agree with this but am unable to engage in it. When I pull into a drive-thru, I marvel that this is legal. I feel like I might as well be buying cocaine. Yet, these people will hand me whatever I want, no questions asked. I can't even believe it. I order a large fries and multiple cheeseburgers. Salty, crispy fries. Red meat. I am helpless.*

### September 21, 2004

*Driving back from the mall, anxiety struck. I was nearing the exit for Fish Road when I got the urge to call Lance and have him meet me at the Park-n-Ride for an hour-long hug. Then I reminded myself how I would undoubtedly feel were I still with him, and the familiar weight began to accumulate molecule by molecule upon my shoulders. The silence. The joylessness. The pressure. The neglect. I called Stan instead, deciding that his arms would suffice. He was not home, so I left a message and headed to the gym. The gym scale said I weighed 128. Three pounds away from my goal. I put everything I had into the weight room and went home feeling pleased. Matt and Nikki were on the deck smoking weed. Stan called at 10:39 while I was eating bowl after bowl of Raisin Bran.*

*Fucking 10:39. When will I escape that time? I must see it five times a week.*

*I told him I had to work first shift, so I might drive out but doubted I'd be able to sleep there.*

*"I'd really like you to stay the night," he said. I was sold at the sincerity in his tone.*

*Matt and Nikki were stoned silly and made no objections when I instructed them to tell Mom and Phil I'd be sleeping at the hotel, should they ask. In a moment of relief that I was wanted somewhere, I told Matt this wasn't anything new. I'd never once slept at the hotel. Every time I said I was there, I was actually at Stan's. Matt shot me a sickened look. "I don't want to know things like that," he said.*

## October 9, 2004

So I spent the weekend with Mom in New Hampshire for a couple reasons.

One, I would have had nothing special to say about a Friday off if I didn't.

Two, I used to force myself to do what scared me, and these days, riddled with neurosis, everything scares me.

So I thought, how bad can a commitment to one weekend possibly be?

It can be bad.

We really didn't do much. My favorite part of the trip was curling my exhausted body up on the loveseat and watching TV after I had relieved myself in the bathroom. There was a gas fireplace. I'm always chilled afterwards and the warmth felt merciful.

When Mom went into the bedroom, I ate again. Raisin Bran is a beautiful thing. It's so damn good, and no one ever thinks you're eating something explicitly shitty. Then I discovered there was a garbage disposal in the sink. Mind you, this was after having puked into a plastic bag next to the sink with the water running, as the bathroom was a little too within earshot of the bedroom.

The trip was overwhelming. She wanted me to go with her to get a movie, but I convinced her to go alone. She wanted us to try the hot tub, but I cited dismay about getting into a bathing suit. Bingeing was all I could think about. I must have been a disappointing travel companion. It felt more like a test of survival than a vacation. Too many eyes in too limited a space. Even when I went outside in search of a nice bush to barf behind, every fucking tourist in New England must have been out for an evening stroll.

## October 10, 2004

I was eating a salad in the back when he came to say good night. It was the very first thing I had eaten that day with the intention of keeping. When he saw me, I was inexplicably embarrassed.

"Are you coming over tonight?" he wanted to know.

I was holding my sides. "No. I don't think so."

He asked if everything was all right, and I believe I said something along the lines of having seen better days. When I failed to elaborate, he took off.

I went back to my salad at a vicious rate. Then paused. I had been eating this. Now I was bingeing. It's all in the pace and the taste buds' involvement.

There had been three pans of lasagna served as an employee meal. By the time the coast was clear, it was stone cold, but I plated it up for myself anyway.

There was also a very promising-looking chocolate cake. I also grabbed a croissant. If you're going to do Italian, better have some bread.

I tasted nothing. Enjoyed nothing. He called right before I was about to inhale dessert.

"What's up?" he asked. I could tell by his tone he had already tried to reach me, and I hadn't picked up. I love how he never leaves a message.

"I don't want to talk about it," I said. When he asked why not, I told him he wouldn't understand, and so there was no point. He badgered me about it for a good fifteen minutes. Maybe more. Back and forth. He asked if I was happy, and I said no. He asked if it had to do with him, and I thought about it, pictured those nights awake in his bed when I should have been blissfully asleep. "It plays into everything," I answered. He asked if it was about Lance. Finally, after not getting any sort of explanation, he said he wouldn't sleep until he was told. Figures I'd be a sucker for anything encouraging insomnia.

"At least tell me what it's about," he said.

"It has to do with my having diabetes." Before I knew it, I blurted out, "I have a monstrous eating disorder. Can I go now?"

"Please come over here when you get out? Please?" His voice was kind.

"I'll try," I said.

"I'll be waiting," he said.

I changed into my black gym pants because I had just confessed to having an eating disorder, and I had to look the part.

The lights were on in the living room, but he was not sprawled out on the couch. I was stunned that he actually expected me to walk up the stairs. I went up. Asshole.

I opened the door quietly and found him sleeping with the television on. I began to close the door, somewhat relieved and somewhat hurt. "Wait, wait," he said. "Come here, lay down. Let me hold you."

He kissed me near my eyes. Many times. Said nothing.

"Why did you ask me to come over?" I asked.

"Because you were upset. I hadn't seen you in a while, and I miss you." At some point, he also said that he doesn't really know how to approach "this," but knew when I was ready to talk about it, I would.

Fat chance, I thought. It is quicksand, and I'm past my neck in it.

*September to December*
*age twenty*

# WEIGHTY MATTERS

RACHEL ROTATED BEFORE MY full-length mirror to assess her new charcoal dress pants. Purchased on eBay, the Express tags were still attached—size zero, with a thirty-four inseam. Except for the ridiculous length—inches of fabric draped on the floor—the pants fit perfectly.

"I'll hem them for you," I said. "They're really nice."

"Try 'em on," she said, unzipping them. She tossed them on the bed where I sat grading papers.

It wasn't the first time Rachel had bid me to try on her clothes. As she had lost weight over the preceding year, she bought lots of business attire in increasingly smaller sizes. When the pieces didn't suit or fit her, she offered them to me. Usually, they were too tight or trendy, not appropriate for a forty-something college instructor, but I appreciated her generosity. That time, though, her motives might have been different.

"There's no way they'll fit," I said, fingering the charcoal fabric. I wore a size two or four, depending on the brand.

"You can never find dress pants long enough. Just try 'em," she said, wriggling into and zipping her size-zero flared jeans.

I desperately needed dress pants, especially in charcoal. Those inseams would have been ideal, but I shook my head.

"Never in a million years."

"What do you have to lose? Different brands fit differently. Try 'em," she urged.

I guessed it couldn't hurt. Maybe they were mislabeled, a two marked as a zero; it happened on eBay. Or maybe the spandex in the pants would give them just enough stretch to fit. I was already mentally assembling outfits as I pulled them on, but they braked on my hips. There was no zipping those pants; both sides of the zipper were stretched taut, exposing a triangle of my flesh.

Rachel was strangely quiet, staring as I peeled them off and handed them back.

✦　✦　✦

As Rachel's ED became more manic, so did her workouts. She weight-lifted daily, increasing her weights and repetitions. On alternating days, she ran five miles. Not knowing that it was a purging technique, I approved of her strenuous exercise. Since she couldn't control her eating, I viewed it as a healthy solution—a way to burn calories while boosting her mood. Since her latest breakup with Lance, she'd been so blue.

Though tiny, Rachel's body had muscle tone; her biceps and thighs appeared cut, strong. Her skin glowed from frequent tanning. By looking at her, no one would have ever guessed she was severely ill.

Tragically, as her ED peaked, the compliments poured in. Rachel casually mentioned co-workers and boyfriends commenting on her thinness. Though I, too, thought she looked good, I hesitated to tell her. Rachel was already hyper-focused on her looks. To acknowledge her thinness or anything about her appearance only reinforced the cultural message that a female's appearance was number one. To counter that influence, I tried to compliment only her inner qualities—her kindness, intelligence, creativity, wit.

But one September morning in 2004, while we were drinking coffee, wanting to cheer Rachel up, I admired her muscle tone. Had I known how insidious weight-related comments are to people with EDs, I would have resisted the impulse. However, I had no idea that both positive and negative remarks triggered their disorders. Praising Rachel's thinness sent the message that her unorthodox methods were paying off. Pointing out weight gain, even when intended positively,[71] signaled that she was slacking and needed to step up her game. I would learn that nothing good comes from commenting on the weight or shape of someone with an ED.

Possibly because it was so unexpected, Rachel recorded my compliment in her journal. Years later, when I encountered that September 9th entry, I cringed. Still, the entry was eye-opening, some of her other observations helping me understand her ED and my part in it. For instance, she was indignant at having to work harder than I for a slender body. I never thought we were competing. I now know that rivalry is common among people with EDs, who compulsively compare themselves with each other, longing to be the thinnest and the sickest in the group. They even compete with themselves, for example, to achieve a smaller pant size or lower weight.[72]

Rachel did appear to exercise more and eat less than I did. My modest workout consisted of jogging two miles every other day. Moreover, while I ate three decent meals daily, at that time, Rachel subsisted mainly on salads.

As for her secret binges, she wrongly assumed that those calories were being regurgitated.[73]

Rachel also presumed that daughters should be thinner than their mothers, a perception she shared with me. I was about to name several mother-daughter pairs we knew who defied that stereotype when I realized those daughters were much larger than their moms. Not wanting to suggest that was how I viewed her, I told her we simply had different eating habits and body types. My height—I'm 5′9″, two inches taller than Rachel—only made me appear thinner, which was not always attractive; in some photos, I looked gaunt. Moreover, even in modest heels, I towered over most women and some men. Her height, I insisted, was ideal; she was tall enough to look good, yet she could still wear stylish heels.

Rachel's belief that I was ashamed of her weight was just plain false. Her weight fluctuated a lot, depending largely, I now understand, on whether or not she was taking care of herself. Her ideal weight for her frame was probably one hundred thirty three. When she was properly dosing her insulin and not bingeing and purging, she tended to weigh about ten pounds more. At those times, when she bemoaned feeling "uncomfortable in my skin," I commiserated with her, not because I thought she looked big but because I knew from my college years when my weight had fluctuated how uncomfortable she felt. I never thought she looked like she had "let herself go"; that was all in her head.

If there was one thing in Rachel's journal entry that hit a raw nerve, it was her insight that my thinness blinded me to her EDs.

"How much do you weigh?" I had asked after admiring her muscle tone.

"One twenty nine," she said, maintaining eye contact.

I assessed her weights based on mine, concluding with relief that since I was taller and had been perfectly healthy at that weight or even less, she should be fine at one twenty nine.

But it was a faulty comparison.

I did not have an ED.

No—my problem was pure ignorance. I lacked the most fundamental facts about Rachel's bulimia. Unaware of its progressive nature, I did not know that by then she was bingeing and purging multiple times a day; nor that she'd whittled her insulin dose to nearly nothing. I didn't see these things, even with her skeleton sitting in front of me.

My illusion was about to shatter.

✦   ✦   ✦

ONE SATURDAY MORNING, TWO months later, I overheard Rachel speaking on the phone. Wearing her white fleece robe, she was pacing, frowning, practically whispering to guard her conversation.

"Rachel, what's wrong?" I asked after she had hung up. Entering the kitchen, she headed straight for the coffee maker. She did not respond or even look up as she poured herself a mug of coffee.

"Really—what is it? Tell me. Tell me the truth."

"You can't handle the truth," she said as she added half-n-half and sweetener into her mug.

This had become Rachel's mantra in recent years. She said it as she breezed by me, often with a dismissive hand wave. If I pressed her for information, she would only go so far. I had accepted there were certain things she did not want me to know, things I wouldn't approve of. However, this time, she wasn't being flippant. Something about her—a slump in her shoulders—was seriously off.

"Try me," I retorted.

She studied my face as if to gauge whether unloading her burden was worth whatever repercussions would follow. Suddenly, her eyes filled.

"Lance is addicted to heroin, and I don't know how to help him!" Tears fell.

"Oh, no!" I gasped. "Let's talk." I motioned to the living room, coffee in hand.

Sitting on the hardwood floor, Rachel spilled the whole sordid affair.

I had slid down on the floor beside her. Now, I gently asked, "Don't you see an alarming trend? He keeps taking harder and harder drugs."

"Don't you think I know that?" she said, fresh tears filling her eyes. "That's my problem. I love him, and he's messed up!" She broke down again, her face contorting, her shoulders shaking. "But so am I, Mom!" she managed to blurt out. "I'm a raging bulimic!"

# CHRISTMAS TAT

I LISTENED TO SOFT Christmas music, Frank Sinatra and Nat King Cole while mashing red potatoes for dinner, the smell of a roasting chicken permeating the kitchen. Outside, snow gently fell. I felt my shoulders relax for the first time in weeks since Perry and I had started frantically searching for a treatment facility for Rachel's bulimia.

The search was more involved than I had anticipated. I had to wade through copious data on countless websites; learn about different types of treatment facilities and levels of care; call and email facilities for specific information; compare and contrast facilities; learn about the daunting role of insurance coverage while interfacing with Perry every step of the way.

Christmas, with its time-consuming traditions and tasks, would slow down my search, delaying Rachel's urgent need for treatment.

What if we sat this Christmas out?

Phil said it wasn't fair to the kids, especially Rachel, who needed normalcy more than ever this year. He was right, of course, but who was he kidding? A child at heart, Phil loved every facet of Christmas, from blinking lights and iced cookies to holiday parties and heavy snowfalls. He couldn't wait to watch *A Charlie Brown Christmas* and *Rudolph the Red-Nosed Reindeer*.

We compromised.

We would simplify shopping by not buying for each other, getting gift cards for relatives, and letting the kids shop for themselves. The week before Christmas, we would pile them into the van, give them each one hundred dollars, and turn them loose at Wrentham Premium Outlets. Phil's girls liked the idea. My three pissed and moaned about losing the surprise and not having gifts to open on Christmas. Still, we executed our plan. I passed out presents during the fifty-minute drive—fleece hats and scarves to keep the kids warm as they walked the massive outdoor outlet. Joyous music was piped outdoors. It was so cold we saw breath wreaths when we spoke. As we shopped, huge snowflakes started to fall. While driving home, the kids chattered and laughed, their bags crackling.

Phil also released me from baking cookies and sending cards. But decorating was non-negotiable; when it came to the tree and lights, he wouldn't budge.

Now, as I set the table, colored lights danced around me. I caught the blue radiance of the manger scene, the blinking tree lights, the soft glow of our brass window candles. I felt a pulse of pure joy. It only grew as I peered through the sunroom windows at the snow-tufted maple tree. Lit with primary-colored bulbs—Charlie Brown lights, I called them—their magical luminance cast a purplish hue on the snow, redolent of Wisconsin winters. Suddenly, the wind bawled. The snow had picked up, pelting the windows with those giant lacy flakes that collected in the corners, making me feel so cozy indoors. Just when I thought my joy had peaked, Vince Guaraldi started hammering out the happy notes of "Linus and Lucy."

Then I heard the front door slam, followed by the sound of stomping boots. I felt an icy chill snake its way into the kitchen.

Rachel dropped her bag on the table. Shrugging off her maroon faux sheepskin coat, she draped it over a chair. Despite the cold, she wore a cropped aqua T-shirt, low-slung jeans, and tan Uggs, the toes darkened with water stains. When Lance didn't deliver the Uggs he'd promised, Rachel bought her own. She was supposed to remove them at the door but never did, insisting she was barefoot and the ceramic tiles were freezing cold. Her hair was pulled in a half-ponytail, exposing the large turquoise teardrop earrings I'd recently given her.

"I want those," she had said with an impish grin the first time I wore them. I had almost bought her an identical pair—they were in my hand—but matching earrings weren't unique; she wouldn't have worn them. Rolling my eyes, I removed them, the stones smooth and heavy in my palm. Rachel had started this jewelry ritual by giving me her first gift from Lance, lovely, rectangular mother-of-pearl and sterling earrings that she said were too conservative.

"I can't. He'll be hurt," I said.

She pressed the white box in my hand. "He needs to learn what I like."

Rachel labored to find people the perfect gifts and wanted people to reciprocate. After getting a string of disappointing presents from her brothers and noting that I'd received plenty of duds from them and Phil, she hatched a plan to upgrade both our future gifts. Before birthdays or Christmas, we would slip each other our wish lists; then, I would help the boys shop for her and vice versa.

"I got a tattoo today," Rachel announced. "Wanna see it?"

My shoulders seized, holiday cheer draining from my chest like a slit tire. Don't react. She's twenty years old.

Rachel stopped before our wall-sized mirror Phil had scavenged from a plumbing job at a Newport mansion. With her back to the glass, she unzipped her jeans. Thumbs in waistband, she worked them down far enough to clear a square gauze bandage on her lower back.

Though I walked over to watch, I still hadn't spoken.

"It was sort of a Christmas gift to myself," she said to gap the silence. "God knows I won't get anything decent from Lance—if that schmuck gives me anything at all." Twisting to watch herself slowly peel off the bandage, she winced as she removed the last stubborn stretch of surgical tape.

As the bandage fell to the floor, I saw the words Vivid Reckless Grace, centered and stacked in a not uncomely cursive blue font. The modest-sized words were inflamed.

There was that term again: Reckless Grace.

Suddenly, the tattoo was no longer the issue.

When Rachel was fourteen, I had recoiled when she had chosen Reckless-Grace84 as her screen name. Was she proud of her recklessness? At the time, I had seen inklings of risky behavior I had brought to her attention—tossing used insulin needles in the regular trash rather than in sturdy bleach bottles as she had been taught; not wearing her seat belt; jogging at night on busy Greene Lane without reflective clothing; giving our phone number to boys she'd met on the Internet.

At that time, I had wanted to question the meaning of "Reckless Grace," but we had just quarreled about her foul mouth and neglecting to test her blood. I was probably overanalyzing this. Adolescents tried on new roles. Weeks earlier, she was using the screen name vividxraes01, and she had recently changed the spelling of her name to "Rachael." Let it go, I thought.

But Rachel's recklessness did not fade with adolescence. As a young adult, a single functioning headlight did not deter her from driving the long distance on dark country roads to Lance's house, nor did broken windshield wipers stop her from driving in the rain or snow. She thought nothing of walking alone at night even after I told her one of my best friends had been raped at knifepoint while hitchhiking solo.[74]

Rachel's recklessness baffled me. Why wouldn't she take precautions? I always locked my car doors while driving through sketchy neighborhoods and never picked up hitchhikers. In college, when rapes started multiplying on campus, I still closed the library most nights, but now I asked male friends to walk me to my dorm. No matter how maddening it was to wait for my escort at the library entrance when I was tired and, frankly, wanted to enjoy the starry night alone, I would not take that risk.

What was wrong with my daughter?

Now that she was twenty, I finally asked.

"Why would you tattoo 'reckless' on your body?"

Shifting her eyes from the mirror to me, Rachel replied, "I like this quality of mine." Next to the turquoise earrings, her unflinching eyes looked aquamarine.

As she freed her thumbs from her jeans, Grace was swallowed up in denim, leaving Vivid and Reckless visible just above her waistband.

"Are you sure about that? Do you know what it means?"

"It means wild and adventurous."

I didn't want to burst her bubble, that aura surrounding people with fresh tattoos, who seemed as pleased with their tolerance to needles as of their new body art. As a writer and artist, she would have obsessed over the words and design. And had probably paid plenty for it.

Was I provoked because she hadn't consulted me? Though an adult, Rachel lived with me. She knew what I thought of tattoos: they looked tough. However, their popularity among young people had recently taken off. Rachel's stepsister, Nikki, had gotten two elaborate tattoos without Phil's permission, and Lance sported a weeping Jesus on his right shoulder.

"I don't think 'reckless' means adventurous," I responded in a neutral tone. "I think it connotes impulsivity and risk-taking, dangerous behavior, which is hardly something I'd flaunt. I could be wrong," I added, reaching for our faded blue Webster's dictionary we kept handy to settle such semantic disputes. I thumbed through the Rs until I found it: "'Reckless, marked by a lack of caution; not showing proper concern for the possible bad results of your actions.'" Closing the dictionary, I looked up.

"Yeah, I know it means that, too," she said, more sheepishly now, her eyes swirling the room. "I want that part of my life behind me. I really do," she added, forcing her eyes to meet mine. "That's why I had it tattooed on my back. Vivid is my gifts. Reckless is me screwing up. Grace is God giving me another chance."

It was a powerful statement, the tattoo's placement on Rachel's lower back supporting her story. I wanted to believe her. However, her quick admission that she liked her recklessness raised my suspicions. Rachel was a rebel. She defied her parents, the law, even God. Sometimes, I questioned the authenticity of her faith. Believers were supposed to grow, but she seemed to be regressing. I considered drawing her out, dissecting the tattoo's words together to tease out its meaning, but I didn't want to be conned. Rachel, I was starting to realize, sometimes told a runny version of the truth.

"And you want to stop this pattern—right?"

She nodded.[75]

"Did it hurt much?" I asked, wincing.

"Like a bastard," she smirked.

December 18, 2004

# "Vivid. Reckless. Grace."

**December 18, 2004**

Vivid. Reckless. Grace. You think you are vivid. Sure, you have some of the elements. There's surface beauty. There's wit, passion, and undeniable empathy, but you want more. This is where recklessness comes in. You seize opportunities. Do regrettable things to freeze them in men's memories. You hurt your body to make yourself thin. You will not win. So, you fall to your knees. Empty, drained, you have sold yourself. Then there is grace. Which comes from God and has nothing to do with you. You do not deserve it. Not by any means. In this cycle, grace makes you vivid, whole again. The cycle need not continue. It can stop once it turns full circle. As long as you do not forget where your own footsteps have led you.

This is why I had it tattooed on me. Not in plain view where I am constantly reminded of it. No. On my back because I want it behind me. I will not run from it, only carry it as part of my history.

December 20, 2004–January 9, 2005
*age twenty*

# HEROIN 101

JUST DAYS BEFORE CHRISTMAS, we narrowed our search down to two ED treatment facilities that met our criteria, Remuda Ranch in Wickenburg, Arizona, and Canopy Cove in Tallahassee, Florida.

Both were faith-based with high success rates that respectively offered in-patient and residential care. Both had homey settings with small group sizes where I thought Rachel would thrive. Credentialed, multidisciplinary teams in both places offered customized treatment using the Recovery Model, which I liked. Both centers accepted patients with diabetes and were in sunny climates that Rachel would love.

My only concern was their short duration—one month for Canopy Cove and two months for Remuda Ranch. I was leaning toward longer programs, reasoning that a long-term ED warranted extensive treatment. However, when I had mentioned twelve or even six-month programs, Rachel and Perry protested.

"Mom, I'm not leaving for that long." Rachel's eyes were electric, her jaw set. "Do you have any clue how hard it is to leave for even one month?"

"You can't expect her to drop out of her life for several months," Perry agreed. "It's not realistic. One or two months, tops. It's my insurance, so I decide."

We quickly determined that Remuda Ranch, with its superior success rate, tighter surveillance, and longer, more intensive level of treatment, was the right fit for Rachel. Adamant about attending a faith-based facility, Rachel liked that Remuda had a chapel, Bible studies, and Christian staff.

However, Remuda wanted their $124K up front, a policy they enforced because they couldn't always count on insurance reimbursement. Though Perry and I would split the cost, who could afford even half? Friends who had sent their anorexic daughter to Remuda had taken out a second mortgage on their home, which was not an option for Perry or me.

Perry spent hours on the phone negotiating with Blue Cross. At the same time, he implored the Remuda billing director to take Rachel, trusting Blue

Cross would pay. Neither Blue Cross nor Remuda would budge. This put Canopy Cove back on the table, being the more affordable facility.

Meanwhile, Rachel had her own crisis: Lance had started *shooting* heroin. Since she had told me about his addiction, she railed at his stupidity. "No one gets off heroin," she continually seethed. Now, she was shocked anew.

"I've heard it's a better high, instant euphoria, they say, but shooting makes it even harder to quit." Her face folded in pain. "Now he's never gonna kick! Why would he do this to us?"

Because he's a drug addict, I wanted to scream. However, pointing this out in the past had gotten Perry and me nowhere. She already knew this, and our reminders infuriated her.

Rachel leaped at the chance to help Lance detox when his mother, Barbara, enlisted her help. It would take a few days, but Rachel would return before Christmas. This was an emergency; of course, she should help. Though I'd never met Barbara, I called to console her. She vented at length about Lance's drug history. I hung up, feeling like my problems were pebbles next to hers.

Though not Lance's first detox, I gathered it was the most urgent. Shooting heroin put him at risk of contracting HIV and hepatitis C—not to mention death from overdose. Due to his physical dependence on the drug, he would experience severe withdrawal symptoms.

I imagined Barbara and Rachel taking turns at Lance's bedside, sponging his brow, cleaning his vomit, changing his sweaty clothes and sheets. It would be a grueling ordeal for everyone, but then Lance would be clean, drug-free. Their efforts would pay off.

✦　　✦　　✦

WHILE RACHEL HELPED LANCE detox, our financing battle raged on. Blue Cross would not guarantee reimbursement, nor would Remuda waive their policy. Then one day, their billing director softened. She agreed to accept twenty percent, $24,800, up front and chase Blue Cross for the $98,000 balance; however, we had to sign a promissory note.

The three-page note in Perry's hand flapped in the frigid January wind. I opened my front door, wondering if it felt strange for him to ring the bell and stand on the brick steps of his former home. His mind appeared elsewhere. He entered, and we stood at the peninsula in the kitchen.

"I can't sign this," he said, holding up the wrinkled contract. "I could lose my house. Besides, they only need one signature." He handed it to me.

I accepted the note, knowing I could lose my house, too. But losing Rachel scared me more.

That evening, with Phil's nod, I signed the note.

On January 5th, I told Rachel we were sending her to Remuda Ranch. I thought she would be pleased to be moving forward.

"I'm not ready," she said, brushing by me. I followed her into her room.

"It's time, Rachel. We finally squared away the finances. They can take you this week."

A shadow fell over her face. "This is happening too fast."

I could see she was shutting down. I should have pulled back, but if we didn't take the bed, someone else would. Her recovery would be further delayed.

"You asked for this, remember? You told me your life was out of control."

Her eyes were cold blue marbles. "I'm not going."

I felt my cheeks burn. "Oh, yes, you are!"

"I'm an adult."

"You're not acting like one."

"Still, I am one, so you can't force me!"

She was right. Because she was over eighteen, unless I got a court order, no matter how disturbed she was, she could keep calling the shots to her own detriment. It was a frustrating, infuriating, and ultimately fatal wall I would bang into again and again for the next eight years.

I played the only card I had: "Oh, yes, I can. You either go to Remuda or move out."

Glaring, she said, "I'll get back to you on that."

"Fine, but either way, pack your bags."

Two days later, we fought again after Rachel refused to request time off work for treatment. When I threatened to get a court order, she unleashed a string of obscenities, and my hand reflexively slapped her face. Shaking, I went upstairs to my room to collect myself. Meanwhile, she made a call. When I picked up the extension, she said, "Get off the phone, you obnoxious, impervious bitch!" She had meant to say "imperious." How dare she call me arrogant and controlling for trying to help her! I flew back downstairs, prepared to slap her again. This time, she blocked my hand. Her eyes meant business. I dropped my hand, lashing her with words instead.

The next day, Rachel told me Barbara was taking her in.

I dialed Barbara, certain she would renege once she heard the facts: Rachel had a dangerous ED for which she had been hospitalized that could be life-threatening when combined with her diabetes.

I expected her to share my alarm, to assure me she would help safeguard my child—all the sentiments I had expressed to her weeks earlier. Except for some exclamatory sounds, Barbara was silent.

"This has been going on for years, Barbara!"

"Hmmmmmm."

"I need to get Rachel into treatment right away—surely you can understand this."

Silence.

"Barbara, please tell me you will not take her in."

"I can't do that," she finally said. "Rachel helped Lance detox. I owe her."

Our efforts to help Rachel screeched to a halt when she moved out on January ninth.

December 17, 2004–February 9, 2005

# "There are drug addicts in my cinema"

## December 17, 2004

He shot it. God Almighty. He shot his heroin.

I had watched Trainspotting with Stan, and he told me Lance was probably going to try "shooting," had he not already. Hell, after watching that film, I'd be tempted to. Despite what addicts' lives became, I couldn't help but wonder how good something like that felt and how bad life had to be to resort to it.

So I call him, and I'm trying to exude all the love I have for him, and I ask: Did you do it? And he tells me not to play that game with him. I swear I will keep it a secret. That's when he told him he had done it. So here I am, talking to myself, or to paper, whichever is more pathetic or pointless, and I'm picturing him with his arm outstretched. His vein raised. A needle. How good it must have felt. How bad it must be now.

My fault. All my fault.

I kept it to myself for a while, and then I told my mom. Some secrets I can never keep. I wish I could, but I don't trust my own judgment with enormously complex shit like this. I figure by running my mouth, I will get a better sense of how to handle the situation.

## December 19, 2004

It's my day off. Mom just asked if I seriously want my own place. I really do not want to move out, not that I wouldn't love having my own place with big windows and my own fridge. But I know if I lived alone, I'd isolate like a bastard. The ED would get worse. I imagine myself bent over a sink (wouldn't sign a lease on a place without a garbage disposal) without having to worry about anyone walking in. This is not a comforting thought. God knows what level it could escalate to.

Then Lance and I go to Ruby's. My dinner, that I am paying for, turns into a binge. I throw up in the bathroom. Two plates of salad with low-fat ranch dressing and a cheeseburger with fries. I notice, as I step into the last stall, that this is the third time I've thrown up in this particular bathroom. It's disheartening.

*We rent a movie. Lance is irritable. He tells me first, that he knows I will leave him again and then, that he wants "us." I want Lance to go on antidepressants.*

*He does not want to try them and cites this reason: He knows he will not stay on them.*

*I do not understand how someone could claim to want me, want what we had so badly, and yet be unwilling to try anything different to give us a better chance of making it.*

### December 20, 2004

*Heroin withdrawal week was interesting. I did a lot of babysitting at Lance's. Barbara wasn't inclined to sleep in his room, and someone had to keep watch. He had intimated, and I had speculated, that getting drugs hand-delivered through his bedroom window wasn't out of the question. He was an addict, and I couldn't sleep for a myriad of reasons, but mostly because he had to be watched. I slept about three hours in the four days I was there.*

*I brought a lot of shit over to Lance's house the first night, anticipating being there a long time. There was an electricity in the air. Nobody seemed to take it incredibly seriously though until I told Barbara he'd been injecting. Shame on that family for not jumping to action when he'd been snorting it. Still, I might not have spilled if Lance hadn't lied to me.*

*I knew he'd been doing it with Amber and that they had slept together. I knew the risk of AIDS, and God knows what other STDs that bitch was toting, was great. Lance said she'd shown him her papers, and as of a month ago, she was clean. I gave Lance sleeping pills to numb the pain. He opened them up and snorted the white powder through a straw. He said they got into his system quicker that way. After a few, mixed with C pins,[76] he got drowsy as hell. At one point, I asked him a question, and he sat up in bed, eyes squinting, voice soft from exhaustion, and said with the gentlest voice to me, "What, baby?" I bent down, and before I thought about what was happening, I started to kiss him. It was only supposed to be one kiss. But it turned into the most electrical thing I'd experienced that day. Frantic and passionate, HIV did not cross my mind. This was my man, my love. If he has it, I'll take it, too.*

*Afterward, and forgive me, because my memory gets a little cloudy here, he began to talk again about how much he wanted it, the drugs. He was like a little boy. "It'll be the last one. Just this last one." Begging and pleading. I started to refer to the last bag as the "Precious" from Lord of the Rings.*

I had him write out a list of things he had lost or was losing as a result of the addiction. Self-respect, reputation, strength, money, respect from family, sexual performance. I was third on the list. Then, I wrote out another headline on the notebook paper: *Things I Could Get by Giving it Up*. I just rewrote the same list as above. He still refused to flush it. He said, "Just let me do it. If you watch me, I'll be too disgusted with myself to ever touch it again."

At this point, I said, "You want me to take it?"

"You?" he asked. "The whole thing?"

I wasn't so sure about that. I was willing to do it. I want to know, even to this day, what everything is like for Lance. It kills me that Amber shared this thing with him, that she and he were alone in it, lost and running away from the world to ascend briefly to heaven together. I was very jealous.

"Can't shooting heroin kill you even the first time?" I asked, and he said yes. I think he said, though it was terribly unconvincing, he couldn't do that to me.

The idea had come to me suddenly, so I hadn't gotten over the initial fright of actually doing it. We were still deliberating when he decided to take a shower. Naked, he lingered by the doorway. I was sitting on the side of the bed, looking down at my stomach. I knew what he was thinking. He thought I was going to search through his shit for the "Precious" and confiscate it. "Lance," I said. "I'm not going to go through your stuff." I wanted him to hand it over willingly.

He had the eyes of a little, untrusting boy, and his nudity contributed to the image. "You promise?" he asked, spine slouched. I told him I would never do that.

He lingered but finally went in the shower.

I noticed after a little while that there was no fluctuation in the sound of water running. I didn't hear the water slapping about the way it would if his body were in there.

I got suspicious. I tried the door. Locked. I immediately searched for something to pick the lock with. I tried a sewing needle and a bobby pin, and when neither worked, I knocked. He opened the door.

"Why is the door locked?"

"I fixed it yesterday," he said. He stared at me, those eyes never wavering.

"You never lock the door."

"You're being paranoid, baby," he said.

I mumbled an apology.

Later I found the empty needle (an insulin needle, how precious) in the cat litter bag. I pressed on the plunger and was startled to see scarlet come out. Lance admitted he had gone into the shower with a needle curled up under his toes.

*Being there was hard. My routine was broken up. We felt helpless. Lance refused therapy, rehab, even visiting the doctor to get a prescription for a pain-killer. He stayed up tossing and turning, moaning and crying. He never vomited this time. He complained constantly of his back aching and being cold. I liked focusing my attention on nursing him. I put blankets in the dryer to warm him. I ran a hot bath to try and stabilize his body temperature. I put candles in there and gave him tea to relax. I rented films and bought food he liked. I cleaned his room and changed his sheets he had sweated through the night before. I made him lunch, rubbed his muscles, kissed his forehead. I bought him a sweatshirt to warm him, put his clean clothes in the dryer to warm them, too. The poor thing was so out of it, I don't even think he realized. He never said thank you.*

*Lance kept snorting my sleeping pills, whining about the pain, and refusing treatment. He had promised if he were to vomit, he would go to a hospital. He even made a "contract" to this effect on a little green sticky note, so none of us could understand why he wasn't getting sick. I started to think if he had done it in the shower and straight-faced lied to me, what was to keep him from doing it again?*

*While working second shift, I was vacillating between going to Stan's for a little reprieve or going straight to Lance's. Only I told Lance I was thinking about laying down in a room at the hotel for an hour or two before making the trek. He kept asking for specifics: "When would you be here? How long will you lay down?" I assumed he wanted me there because I distracted him from his cravings.*

*When Stan turned out to be a no-show, I called Lance and told him plans had changed; I was heading up. That was what he had instructed me to do—call. Only this time, he hesitated. He said he was talking to his mom and asked me to call back later.*

*Then I realized. Recognized. I called his mom and told her she shouldn't take her eyes off him. I suspected Amber was going to pass drugs through his window.*

*By the time I got to his house, I was so hateful and fuming that I wanted to scream. I marched in there with my black boots on. Lance was lying in bed. I was pretty sure Barbara had cleared out. I saw my belly from his mirror and wished I was wearing something loose. The weight was too much.*

*I asked him why he wasn't getting ill if he was off it like he said he was. He asked me what I was getting at. I said I thought Amber was bringing him shit through the window.*

*"Yeah, and like she's got the money to do that," he said.*

I was pissed. Tired and frozen with rage. It just came out. "All she would have to do is suck somebody off."

Lance told me to get out. I said I wasn't going anywhere. Then everything became a blur. I was so tired and so directionless that I just stood there for quite a while, staring at him. "What do you want?" he asked, and I don't recall what I said because I did not know what I wanted.

Eventually, Barbara came and set up quilts on the floor. It looked so good, so inviting, though I wasn't able to get any sleep. The floor was hard and smelled of dog urine.

Lance tossed and turned, groaned, and made lots of what seemed like extraneous noise. I wished he would shut the fuck up and let me sleep. Or invite me up to his bed so I would know I was forgiven. It felt like hours had passed. I wanted to tell him I loved him and was acting this way because it was my fault. Hadn't he started using heroin when I told him I had slept with Chris? Now it was my responsibility to make it right again.

More tossing, more moaning.

Did it really hurt that much, or was he trying to make me feel worse?

Finally, finally, he said. "Will you please just come here?"

And I slowly went to him and fell asleep at the edge of his bed.

### December 23, 2004

I'm back home with Mom and Phil.

I miss Lance. God almighty, do I miss him. When we last talked, he had slipped and used. He was using that soft voice he acquires, telling me secrets without realizing what he has said: "I can't stop thinking about your body. I keep playing scenes of us over and over in my head."

I replay certain scenes, too. That incredible kiss after he had taken that sleeping pill. I think we're both stuck on the memory of that kiss.

### December 24, 2004

I woke up twice today. Once at six, to eat, and now at noon. I can't get moving, and I can't find any direction. I am so cold I just want to crawl back into bed and sleep. Responsibilities, obligations loom. I could resist going to the gym and tanning, but then I'd feel like shit for being fat and pale.

I went to Lance's last night. I missed him. On the way up, I knew I was running away from the will of God and heading directly for disaster. When will I learn to trust those instincts? When will I grow up?

Lance thanked me over and over again for coming. He was different. It was as though a page had been turned. He was genuinely glad to have me there. He told me I was beautiful more than once. I felt funny touching his body. It was small and pale and weak, and I had the distinct feeling I was taking advantage of a twelve-year-old boy.

Lance couldn't maintain an erection when we made love. He was embarrassed and crying so I tried to be gentle. "You don't have any idea why this is happening to you?" He shook his head.

We were sitting at the edge of the bed holding hands when it popped out; I honestly never even thought before I said it: "You know, Lance, I would forgive you immediately if you told me you had slipped up. It would take a lot longer for me to forgive you if you were lying."

His head made its way to his hands. I thought about other signs: no money, those marks on his arm, throwing up two mornings ago, and now this erection thing.

I crawled onto his lap, ready for him to drop the bomb.

He said he only does it when we fight. He said it makes him feel like somebody else is with him. He said he didn't want to tell me because now I was going to leave. He said what a piece of shit he was, what a loser, a junkie. Terrible, damning words. I didn't know what to say. At one point, he actually told me I didn't deserve this, and he would understand if I did leave. I don't think he really expected me to, though. How on Earth could I?

I told Lance we were going to have to get some home drug testing kits. I told him I was sorry, but I couldn't trust his word right now. That also made him cry, but it made me want to cry, too. I told him if he was still positive after six to seven days, I would tell his mom. It never fails to amaze me how I can find the steps to getting his life back in order, but when it comes to my own life, I don't have a clue.

## December 27, 2004

Today was my only night off for the rest of the week. I wanted to do something fun, but Lance sat on the bed, dead-eyed.

He had gotten a few calls, all of which I partially eavesdropped on. His "friends" only called for one reason. One of the people who called was Ken. He had been out at sea for three and a half weeks straight. Now, he wanted drugs.

I started bothering Lance about how he should apply for a job somewhere. I threw the want-ads in his face.

"Why does a phone call from Ken cause this?" he asked.

"Because it's pathetic that Ken has a brand new car, and you can't afford to buy yourself a coffee. Because he's a little shit, and you're a hard worker. Because he's the prick, but he's not the one acting like it."

Lance sat on the bed for a long time. "I just don't know why I'm so fucked up," he said.

The only thing he cares about is getting high, and it's getting increasingly challenging to be around him. Who says I don't want to get high too?

We headed out for an aimless drive. Lance lit up a joint. Now Lance knows pot makes me eat. He knows I don't like it. He asks me to do it anyway because it's not as fun to do it alone, I guess. I said no at first, then joined him. I can't possibly feel any worse, I thought.

The rest of the day was a series of binges.

### December 31, 2004

I picture Lance and me in this big, airy house in the country. Aged hardwood floors and curtains spilling into the room from the breeze. The only furniture in our bedroom is a big brass bed.

I want more than anything for Lance to be the one. The possibility that he is not, that I have wasted so much time, heart, energy, would render me a fool unworthy of forgiveness. So instead, I let these images in. Us on a bed in the peace of the country. We have babies somewhere. The quiet black-haired boy with the blue eyes. The joyful blonde girl with the deep brown ones. They are playing on our wooden floor. We need nothing. These images are so vivid they hurt. I think, if I can only get him and me out of here. Out to the country. We would be okay.

### January 4, 2005

I used heroin for the first time on January 2nd. I was so scared when Lance gave it to me. Very, very frightened. I didn't try it only to see what it was like for him. I tried it to see what it was like to not want to eat. The heroin made me extremely sexual. Very uninhibited and driven, shall we say.

Lance must have known how badly I wanted to take a bag of heroin home. He gave me one hidden in a pack of gum. He told me to swallow it if I got pulled over. "This is serious," he reminded me. "Do not get caught with that shit."

Now Lance is fumbling with veins in the dark. We are parked at the movie theatre.

Though I am fairly used to the sight of needles, I am taken aback by the violence in this. The blood that comes out of his arm is such a dark red, almost black like tar. He leans over and sucks it up. He pokes around like I used to, in search of the right spot. There are expletives, streaks of red, paraphernalia covering the seat of his truck. Water, syringe, Q-tips, bags. He moves systematically, like a professional. I am supposed to be watching for cars. Police cars that is.

Lance finally finds a vein. Meanwhile, I open a blue slip of paper and empty out its mud-colored contents. How many flowers do you think it takes to make one of these? I ask. I know I ask far too many questions. I take a rolled-up dollar bill—the last dollar Lance has to his name. I snort it into my left nostril. Much like leaning over a sink. It burns my nose and makes me want to move immediately to the next thing because, God, a cigarette would be nice right about now. I snort and snort to feel it in the back of my throat. It tastes like a mixture of metal and blood when it falls.

Heroin is a pretty word, I have decided. Graceful.

I don't feel much of anything, but soon I will. At the very least, I will feel relaxed, alive. Then I remember this is how it started. You cannot tame a monster. There is a reason certain terms bring about nothing but trepidation and frowns. I block those thoughts right now. I deserve to feel good. I have felt like shit, absolute anxiety-ridden shit for six years.

As we enter the theater, the metal blood is making its way down my throat, bitter and poisonous and apprehensively welcome. Lance and I are all love and patience. We get our tickets, and I watch the manager turn a quick corner on the ball of his foot. I picture him making a frantic phone call to the authorities. "There are drug addicts in my cinema! Get here immediately!"

We get a large popcorn, and I tell Lance to answer "yes" when the girl behind the counter asks if we want butter. We pour lots of salt onto it too. Lance thinks this is funny; We walk in snorting with laughter. I think it's making us obvious. I go into the ladies' room. Heroin makes it unbelievably challenging to urinate. I look at myself in the mirror. Vega pants, Juicy Couture hooded sweatshirt, Vivid hat, ballet flats. I certainly don't look like a drug addict.

By the time we get into the movie, I am fairly high. I am warm and eating too much popcorn.

I go home and begin to have a low-grade anxiety attack. I am very physically hungry. I want to eat what I want to eat, and it's not salad. I stomp around a bit, desperate. I would rather be a drug addict than a bulimic. So I dump a bag of heroin on the counter and suck it up with a straw. When it hits me, I feel the urge to eat slowly dim till it is just a quiet hum.

### January 5, 2005

Lance and I are wearing our rings again.

We were going around one of those sharp turns, and I told him I was excited to have a baby. He was holding my hand and squeezed it when I said this. He wouldn't want a girl, he says. That stings the smallest amount, but maybe he's right. Girls are just far too much trouble, too aware for their own good.

This morning my mother said it deeply disturbed her to see me going back to spending so much time with him. I told her I thought I was still in love with him. I like the ignorance of being in love. It covers reality like a pristine blanket of snow.

### January 6, 2005

I was making real progress, I thought, using dope to escape food. But even with heroin, life still felt like a wasteland. Nothing but anxiety, burdens, nausea, and dread.

There were two bad nights in a row. During the first, Lance and I watched the DVD from Remuda Ranch. It's in the desert and looks more like a ritzy house than a rehab. Then he wanted to have sex, which entirely wasted my high.

The next night was far worse. I hadn't had a decent meal in a while, and it was time to brave a restaurant. I went to the gym in anticipation, enduring a particularly torturous workout.

We decided to get high beforehand. We went to a gas station, where he pulled out his bags and needles. I hate watching him do this. When he gets the needle in the vein, he just lets it fucking hang in there. Sometimes his veins swell up because he misses them, or maybe they're starting to collapse. I was already feeling nauseous and didn't want to snort the heroin. He suggested that I shoot it, but that thought made me want to puke my guts out. I'm no stranger to needles, but I don't understand how someone can willingly subject themselves to anything intravenous. So he dumped a bag onto the CD, and I begrudgingly snorted it. I hate how it tastes like blood and metal and creeps down the back of your throat.

I went into the store to buy a lollipop. When I got back, Lance was still fucking around with his needles, and I was still nauseous. Still, I did a second bag *on the way there. As we entered the restaurant, I was so queasy I would gladly have thrown up. All the food at the buffet looked, smelled, and tasted like shit. Lance watched me with a wary eye and kept asking if I was okay. I don't know if I was relieved or disappointed. I wanted to eat and felt I had earned it, but all I could stomach was broth and a little white rice. I was relieved as hell to get out of there, but I had also wanted to prove to myself that I could eat like a normal person in a restaurant, and it did not happen.*

*In the car, I put my hooded sweatshirt and flats back on and leaned against the car door and cried and cried. I felt as though I would never be normal. Life without bingeing is indeed a wasteland. Not that running from it or repressing it or burying it under two-hundred dollars worth of food is any better. But Jesus, there is just nothing there.*

*So here I was, suffering through my shit, strengthened by the thought that Lance was suffering too. Then I realized he wasn't giving up anything. He wasn't high all the time, but he wasn't weaning either, just staying high on as little as possible. So I felt betrayed, and I got angry. I was also mad because the heroin wasn't working like it used to. It wasn't making me feel euphoric or relieved, just nauseous, which was not the answer to a damn thing. I ate almost half a loaf of bread when I got home. I thought, fuck it. No one's on my side, and I lose every battle. So I fucking binged.*

### January 7, 2005

*Noticing the stunted loaf of bread, Mother dearest makes a comment that she knows last night didn't go well, and I say, "No. It sure didn't."*

*She asks why, and I tell her it's because it felt like no one was on my side, namely Lance for not fighting as hard as me, but also her for kicking me out. She gets defensive and asks if I'm going to cooperate with rehab at Remuda or have an attitude. I tell her an attitude.*

*It escalates into a huge fight, complete with obscenities and me threatening to kick her ass. I know I'm pretty strong. I was just dying to try it out on her. She called Lance a deadbeat. She called me sick and said, "That's the eating disorder talking," and said I was "just a bulimic." Stupid, careless, hurtful shit. Nobody should mess with me when I haven't been sedating myself with food. I am one mean motherfucker.*

*She told me I had better tell Heather I wouldn't be around for too much longer. When I told her I wouldn't go, she said I had till Monday to get out of the house. I told her I'd do my best. She said she'd subpoena my doctor if I* refused to go. Something was said about a power of attorney or some bullshit. Kiss my non-existent ass.

I called up Lance, and I kept hearing the phone upstairs click on and off. I knew Mom was listening, so I said, "Stop listening to my phone calls, you obnoxious, impervious, bitch!" While I was more concerned with whether or not I had used the word *impervious* correctly (I hadn't), she was hauling ass down the stairs, and we really got into it. At one point, I inadvertently spit in her face because I was screaming at her so directly.

I just don't know what to do. I'm afraid to pray about it. I know I'm miserable. I know I need some kind of help. I suspect going to a Christian treatment center might be God's will, and it's terrifying.

### January 11, 2005

Who'd have thought I'd enjoy myself living at Lance's house? Sure, the threat of overstaying my welcome looms, but I'm liking it. For one, I have gone almost two days without bingeing. I know this is partly because I have been suppressing my urges and irritability with the heroin. I don't care. It's a break not to worry. A relief not to expend all that energy purging.

Sure, I may be trading one addiction for another, but I'd rather do anything to rid myself of this one. Anything. Bring on the withdrawal.

I think I'm putting too much pressure on Lance. I want more than anything for him to get a job. I know I'm a bit overbearing. I'm simply adjusting to new surroundings and new circumstances. So of course, I'm trying to exert some control. I am also starting to see old signs that make my heart drop: his impatience, his unwillingness to cheerfully do the things I want him to do (like go to the gym or grocery store). It really bums me out that he doesn't like my brothers. I always envisioned the guy I end up with embracing my brothers because this would point to him being a good father.

I keep trying to build Lance up by telling him how much I believe in him. His response is, "I'm a loser. I'm worthless." I sense that he's lost respect for me because I continue to have hope for him.

### January 22, 2005

On Wednesday, the shit hit the fan.

Lance owed me his check. To my astonishment, Barbara had paid for the first brick. When it was gone, she'd said, he'd have to go to rehab. That was the deal. I had to portion it out, so Lance didn't overdose. Now he wants to buy another brick. I told him that wasn't fair and started packing my things in plastic bags. I asked him which was more important. He said, "You know you are." But then he went down to his basement and called his dealer. His mom finally caught on and forced him to call SSTAR.[77]

He approached me in tears and asked me to stay. I told him I couldn't. At the same time, I was regretting packing my belongings that I knew I would be unpacking in no time.

Lance lied when he said his dealer was out. In actuality, the dealer had told Lance to wait one or two hours, and if he did, he'd give Lance an extra bundle.

Barbara and I decided it would be a good idea to get Lance some medication because the appointment with SSTAR was five days away. Lance agreed to go to the emergency room, but only if I was staying. For good. I really wanted my shit packed up and to be en route to a buffet to binge out of my mind. Instead, I just kept shoving my hand into a box of Cheez-Its while I watched him.

I felt like I could see the whole future laid out. This would be a recurring issue, over and over and over again. He'd never recover. This would age me. He wasn't mine any longer.

We went to the hospital. On the way, I asked if he was hungry, and he shrugged.

Once we got onto West Main Road, I asked if he wanted to go to a buffet, and he said no.

"Then, turn into Burger King because I need to binge."

"That's not fair," he said.

I told him I hadn't done it in a few days, and I no longer had a choice.

He waited in the parking lot while I went in and ordered two burgers and a large fries, all the while knowing it wouldn't be sufficient, but unable to request anything more from the cashier.

I ate it in the car, fearing the smell would send him into unparalleled nausea. By the time we got to the ER, the food was almost gone, and I wasn't the least bit full. I was counting on vending machines. Lance approached the front desk to say why he was there. I stayed a step away.

"I used to be addicted to heroin," he said, "but I have an appointment at SSTAR . . ."

Used to be?? While inhaling the last of my fries and probably looking frightful from my nerves, I stepped closer and explained that we were worried about the withdrawal being painful. They sat us in the waiting room, where I fished around for change for the vending machine. When Lance was taken into triage,

*I bought Twix bars and Fresca and desperately stuffed my face. He returned in minutes. Meanwhile, I went into the bathroom and relieved myself. The chocolate stayed attached to the pit of my stomach. Dirty rotten shit.*

*When Lance was finally admitted, the room he was assigned to looked like a storage area. It was very small, nothing but a bed, a chair, and a trash can. The back of the room had one of those metal doors that lifts, the type a truck backs into to make large deliveries. They made him get into a johnny. I hadn't realized how thin he had gotten.*

*The doctor was quick, concise, decent, and not much else. He gave Lance two medications: one for anxiety and one for blood pressure. Lance took one right there. I let him drive, but halfway home, he started swerving all over the place. I told him to pull over and let me drive. He didn't object. Five minutes later, he was snoring. I kept the music low and stuffed my face with Gardetto's.*

*Back at the house, Lance crawled into bed without bothering to remove his jeans or hooded sweatshirt. His parents turned in, and I sat down at their kitchen table with a disappointing bowl of Raisin Bran and a Country Living magazine.*

*I'm getting increasingly worried about us.*

### January 28, 2005

*When Lance is high, he is so loving. He has every quality I had hoped for from him. He holds me, he asks about me, he listens to me, he talks to me.*

*Last night, he was listing, one by one, the things that made him love me.*

*I didn't even want to listen.*

*It's like a cruel trick. Here it finally is, and only because he's on the most deadly drug on the planet. In a few days, he will swear it off, and then what? Then it is back to lowered eyes and lowered hands and lowered expectations. I'd almost prefer the fantasy to continue. With heroin, our love is perfect. The voices and noise fade away, replaced by warmth.*

*I sit beside him on the bed. He is recycling his little cottons to pull infinitesimal remaining amounts of heroin out. I am talking aloud because it seems as though he is listening.*

*I tell him I don't want to eat. Then I correct myself. I do want to eat. I want to binge. I tell him I had wandered out to the kitchen and ate my leftovers from our dinner. Then I opened a package of cookies and ate four of them, and I wanted to keep going. I don't want dope, I say. I can't remember why. Because the taste might make me vomit?*

*He is quiet. Then he says, "So you want to shoot it."*

*I exhale. No, I do not.*

*He continues his task of extracting. I lose focus and say aloud, "God, I can't believe you are a heroin addict." He has set down his cottons and lifted his needle. It is in the air, but only for a moment, long enough for me to visualize him putting it down, taking me into his arms, and begging forgiveness. Instead, he plunges it into his arm.*

*I say something to the effect of, "I can't believe you would inject me. It's dangerous; it's not keeping me safe. It's not something you'd do to someone you love. How could you do it?"*

*He says quite genuinely and softly, "I'd inject you because I'd probably end up getting more drugs."*

### February 3, 2005

*The last month has been pathetic. There is nothing that I am proud of to write about. Take an honest look at your life, my shrink said. What would you say to someone you admired who asked what you've been doing for the last few years? This scenario makes me uncomfortable. What would I do? Probably flash some lame smile and think, "I'm skinny. What more do you want?"*

### February 9, 2005

*We woke up late. One-thirty, to be exact. This frustrated me because it made it impossible to get errands done before the weekend. It also left no time to eat. Bingeing chanted in my ears like chattering, greedy teeth.*

*Lance wanted to fax in his pay stubs to the SSTAR offices. I said I would, and as we sorted them out, I asked if he would cook my chicken so I would have something to eat at work. I felt like my mother: all high hopes that someone I loved would thankfully embrace a chore that would make life easier for me. He shrugged "yes" but never did it.*

*I asked Lance for the money he owed me, and he set a few twenty-dollar bills in my purse. I counted them. A hundred. At the very least, eighty-five dollars short for the four bags he had promised to pay for. "Oh no," I said. "You told me you'd pay for Dan's stuff."*

*He let out an exasperated sound. "Fine!" he said, rummaging through his bedside table drawer. "Take all my money!" And he threw a lot of small bills at me.*

*"I just want to make sure you don't have enough money to buy more from Davenport."*

Looking away, Lance shushed me.

"I'm done. I'm going home," I said, tossing the money away from me.

"Why?" he asked.

I turned around to face him and said without anger, only disappointment, "Because you're a fucking asshole."

He closed his door. Fuck him. I am not going to bow to these little fits.

On my way home, I drove down Ridge Road. Winds from the sea tossed the snow about, coating the trunks and branches of trees. They looked magnificent, a quintessential winter wonderland. Snow-covered limbs on both sides touched each other. I smiled as I passed through the tunnel they made and caught myself saying, "Thank you! Beautiful work!"

This day is His.

# February–March 2005
## age twenty

# INTERFERENCE

RACHEL RETURNED ON FEBRUARY 12, roughly a month later, announcing she was ready to go to Remuda. Sitting at the kitchen table, her face grave, she said the detox was a joke.

"He's in love with heroin, Mom. All he cares about is getting high." Rachel paused, as if calculating how much to tell, then plunged forward. "His mom actually bought him a brick of heroin if he agreed to go to rehab—can you believe it? She called it his 'last hurrah.'"

I shook my head. "Are you sure about that, Rachel?"

She nodded, her face sober. "Barbara gave him a hundred and fifty bucks to buy it. But she didn't want to get her hands dirty, oh no, that was my job. I had to dole it out."

I gasped, picturing Rachel in that situation. Was this how Barbara repaid her? I thought of Rachel's natural curiosity, her recklessness. Though she had railed against heroin, I had to ask.

"Did you try it?"

She hesitated, her eyes locked on mine. Then, exhaling deeply and looking down, she said, "I did—but I hated it." Grimacing, she added, "It tastes terrible, and I didn't feel anything."

"How many times did you try it?" I calmly inquired, though my heart was pounding out of my chest. No one gets off heroin, she had said.

"A few times, but I only took it to stop thinking about food, and you know what?" She finally looked up. "It did help. For a few bloody hours, I got relief."

"That's insane, Rachel! You don't beat one monster with an even bigger monster! You're asking for disaster! What were you thinking?"

"I'm not addicted to heroin," she snapped. "I came back, didn't I? I told you this because I don't want that life." She leaned forward, her grave face credible. "Don't worry, Mom. Food is my drug."

"Are you seeing now that Lance is not good for you?" My eyes bore into hers. "Even what Barbara did was unconscionable. Are you seeing this needs to end?"

She nodded, her face suddenly pained, her eyes welling. "Do you know he would have injected me—he admitted that—just to get more dope?"

My heart started charging again. "What do you mean? Why would he get more by injecting you?"

"Because I'd get hooked, and I'm more resourceful than he is." Tears slid down her cheeks. "Who would do that to someone they love?"

Who would love someone who did that? I shook my head, hot tears filling my eyes as I imagined all the pain my young daughter had experienced. And I didn't know a fraction of it.

✦   ✦   ✦

I TRIED TO PROCESS the information I'd just heard from the receptionist at Remuda Ranch: "We're booked solid. March thirty-first is the first available bed."

When I had called last month, they had an immediate opening. We were ready to put Rachel on a plane the next day. Now we had to wait *seven weeks*.

I reserved the bed, but I had seen how fast Rachel could renege.

In the interim, we sent her to an intensive three-week Partial Hospitalization Program (PHP) for Eating Disorders at Butler Hospital that ran weekdays. I would have preferred a seven-week program that included weekends. Rachel liked the schedule, which allowed her to rehabilitate by day while continuing to work nights. She said it gave her life structure and helped curb her binges.

The Butler PHP helped Rachel in another significant way. Though a secular program, it offered an elective "spiritual course," led by a gifted chaplain, who brought Rachel back to her faith. Rachel dropped Lance, stopped arguing and cussing. Whereas she had waffled about rehab, now she seemed more willing to go. I still held my breath. A lot could happen in four weeks. I would not exhale until she boarded the plane.

The spiritual course might have given Rachel a head start in her recovery had she surrendered to God, but that required blind trust. That stopped her cold.

Surrendering, as Rachel well knew, is a vital step in the recovery process at most faith-based programs. It requires individuals to give up control of their lives to a Higher Power that will guide them on a safe path. People with serious addictions are what AA co-founder Bob Wilson calls a "rare breed" who are incapable of controlling their impulses. If left to their own devices, they will certainly self-destruct.[78]

Resistance is not uncommon, Wilson claims. Most addicted individuals, himself included, do not want to relinquish control of their lives. It feels weak, and they resent having to do it. However, even the most reluctant addicts will capitulate once they have exhausted their resources and know in their gut that it's surrender or perish.[79]

Once addicts take that step, they are often astonished with the results. "What seemed at first a flimsy reed, has proved to be the loving and powerful hand of God. A new life has been given to us . . . 'a design for living' that really works."[80] With God governing them, they are no longer driven by their selfish whims. As they follow His will, their lives are vastly improved, infused with new meaning and purpose.[81]

Rachel had surrendered to God as a teen but had swerved off His path. For years, she sought happiness in external sources by chasing an ideal body and romantic love. Far from satisfying her, these vain pursuits only backfired. Her quest for thinness lured her into the dark world of bulimia and diabulimia. Her quest for love led her to men with no capacity to give it.

While Rachel waited out those four weeks, she tried to surrender again. In her journal, prayers and reflective entries on what she was learning replaced entries about lovers and drugs. But how she struggled to trust God. It seemed like there were multiple forces working against her, immovable barriers, thwarting her surrender.

Distrust was one barrier. She trusted neither her doctors nor her parents. "I'm all I have," she used to say, hugging her shoulders and rocking herself.

Her words hurt. Perry and I may not have been model parents, but she spoke as if we hadn't offered a crumb of love or support. As she became more self-destructive, I would think, She's the least trustworthy of all.

Rachel also struggled to trust God. She may have been dubious because her faith was new. She had never cultivated a long-term relationship with God, never requested His help and seen Him deliver over and over, like that rare friend. On the other hand, she was intimately acquainted with her EDs. Having practiced bulimia and diabulimia for six years, she could count on them to control her weight, calm her nerves, and kill her pain. Her EDs hardly kept her safe; they made her do horrible things, according to her journals. Still, in her twisted world, they worked, and, therefore, she trusted them.[82]

Rachel's independence was another obstacle. On the one hand, it was a good thing. Lack of a companion never stopped her plans. At fifteen, she was pleased to ride Amtrak or the city bus alone. Rachel's independence made her bold, strong. However, in the world of recovery, autonomy was her foe. She had three major addictions that she could not beat alone. As she was beginning to realize, her EDs and drug addiction could be a lifetime battle. She needed a group like AA or Overeaters Anonymous for accountability and support. She also needed God to strengthen and guide her. This was a proven route to recovery, the only logical solution given her beliefs. However, having to rely on people and God continued to gall her.

Fear also thwarted Rachel's surrender. She had many phobias, but two posed serious blockades. One was obesity. With God in charge, she knew she would have to stop practicing her EDs. She also dreaded losing her personality—or what she thought was her personality but was, actually, Reckless Grace, her dominant false self.

Apparently, it's not uncommon for people with severe personality disorders to make this mistake. Whitfield claims that when we follow our false selves for long periods, as Rachel had, "we lose awareness of our true self to such an extent that we . . . lose contact with who we really are. Gradually, we begin to think we are that false self."[83]

Obstacles notwithstanding, Rachel had good reason to surrender. During those weeks, she glimpsed not only her futile existence, spent beautifying herself, but also her self-destructiveness. She reached that vital juncture where she knew giving God the reins not only made sense but would also save her life.

Still, Rachel clutched those reins. She could not relinquish them, even to a God whom she was finding more and more capable and faithful. Nor could she fathom why she wouldn't choose health over illness, purpose over vanity, life over death when this decision should have been a "no brainer."

I would learn from Whitfield that the intense symptoms of an advanced personality disorder can interfere with a person's recovery from another illness.[84] And I would wonder if identity disturbance was not the greatest barrier to Rachel's surrender to God and, ultimately, her recovery from her EDs. According to Whitfield, people with this Borderline symptom have trouble relating, not only to themselves and others but also to their higher power.[85] Surrender requires openness and trust, which people who lead with their false self seem unable to muster. Defensive by nature, the false self is "unusually fearful, distrusting and destructive," so inclined, "to withdraw and be in control . . . it *cannot surrender*" [emphasis mine].[86] In fact, "our True Self is the only part of us that can connect to God."[87]

There was only one problem. The real Rachel was a child with snarled hair who didn't have much say.

February 12–March 30, 2005

# "Help me to trust in You"

**February 12, 2005**

I am eyeing the box of tourniquets. They are against the wall, on top of a box of latex gloves. Funny, I think. Never at Lance's appointments would you see them out in the open. Just like at my appointments, they have the special scales where the numbers are facing away from you.

I close my eyes while the nurse draws blood from my right arm for metabolic and STD tests. I am thinking about how Lance's eyes would light up if I managed to lift one of those tourniquets.

Valentine's Day is Monday. I know I won't get anything. It's not like I've ever been spoiled in the past by having flowers delivered or anything. Why am I already anticipating the let-down this holiday will bring?

Maybe because I have done the math.

I gave Lance two hundred and fifty dollars. Money I owed.

After seventy dollars to pay debts to friends, he had a hundred and eighty. An entire brick would cost only one-fifty, leaving thirty dollars. Even if he filled his gas tank, he'd have ten dollars left to spend on me.

I asked for a pair of underwear.

Tonight Lance told me that getting a brick through someone else is a hundred and eighty. Therefore, he didn't even have enough gas to drive one way to pick up my exhausted ass from work so we could see each other.

"Why don't I deserve to get a card?" I asked. He said he felt the relationship wasn't going well.

I wish I could go out to dinner with him. I would wear that red dress.

**March 4, 2005**

This place is safe. I'm in Butler Hospital. When I walk down our corridor, I'm reminded where I am by the plastic sign on the wall that reads, "Psychiatric Program." But it's friendly here. Structured.

I binged twice on my "off" day from the program.

It was humbling. I didn't slow to ask myself for God's help, His peace, and I knew it. I was consciously aware that I wasn't giving Him a chance because I wanted what I wanted. At first, I tried to distract myself from the actual bingeing itself with eBay, but it got to the point where the urge, the voice, was like a badgering child in a store: "Buy me this! Buy me that! When can I have it? When? When? When?" And finally, I got so fed up I gave in: "You want it? Fine! Have this shit! Just shut the fuck up!" After two salads, there were four blueberry muffins, three bowls of Frosted Flakes with blueberries, one bowl of Raisin Bran, two croissants, Cheetos, Peanut M&M's, a Snickers bar, and finally, into a painfully distended stomach, a Nestle Crunch caramel bar. It numbed me. I didn't even enjoy the act like I used to, but I did it anyway.

I couldn't even walk upright to the bathroom. I leaned forward. I looked at my stomach in the mirror: pushed out, like a damn sphere. I decided I would not burden myself with looking at my eyes. The liner in the trash can was secure, so I leaned over and barfed directly into it. It was situated between the two main sinks, so if anyone had walked in, they would have seen me, but I did not care. The pressure was so painful, I would have hurled on a public bus were there no other option. It felt like such a relief, especially those initial few rounds. I smelled that delicate decay.

Getting the remnants out is taxing because you're tired; it's tempting to talk yourself out of finishing the job, but pausing is a bad idea. Better to clench your lower abdominal muscles and keep going. Sometimes I have to punch myself in the stomach to upset it, but first, I wad up paper towels and place them in my underwear. The pressure I have to exert to rid myself of the last of it is so great that I involuntarily pee my pants every time, even if I have just gone to the bathroom. I've heard of girls exerting so much pressure, they break the blood vessels in their eyes, and their eyes look like they're bleeding.

I have just found out that they are discharging me today.

I think about the things this place has given me, and I'm glad. And frustrated there is nothing further.

When they asked why I thought I'd binged on my off day, I told them there has been too much on my plate.

I miss Lance. The marriage, the children with the blue and brown eyes.

I know the relationship is unhealthy. I love him like that because I hope for someone to love me like that. It is not very realistic to remain loyal to a selfish heroin addict. No one expects you to. Not even him.

**10:40 p.m.**

Dear Lord,

It has been eighteen hours, and I have not yet fallen, thanks to you. Thank you for giving me the focus to write, to organize things. I will fill out the paperwork for Remuda Ranch, and if it is your will, I will drop everything and go.

Thank you for allowing me the opportunity to go to the gym today. It helped; it relieved a lot of stress. Thank you for reminding me to eat some bread and milk and make a rounded dinner. It made me feel less deprived.

Lance has called twice tonight. He sounded funny, but I'm not sure if he's using or not. I understand that while I try to draw closer to you, I will be under spiritual attack. Help me to know that you have someone wonderful for me who will treat me very well.

Please let me hear your voice. Keep me in constant connection with you, always talking. Guide me. Keep me safe. Help me to trust you. I know I'm asking an awful lot, but I want you. I have nothing else. I know there is a lot more fighting to do. I know the demons want me back.

Amen.

## March 5, 2005

I woke up at seven-thirty a.m. out of habit. I ate an apple with peanut butter and thought about bingeing. My mentality was: Everyone's asleep. Better do it now and get it out of your system because if you want to do it later, everyone will be awake.

Trouble was, I had wandered downstairs to pee and had neglected to put pants on. Once I start eating, all the blood rushes to my stomach, and I get cold. If I was going to binge, I would have to go upstairs to get some pants.

In the end, I managed to just climb back up the stairs while saying no. Every part of me wanted to be down there, but I didn't want it badly enough. So I did it the hard way: I ignored the voices and went back to bed.

I could never tell you how that's done. It's a tremendous thing to walk away from.

I re-awoke at eleven. Mom and Phil had their legs entwined on their bed. I was sweaty. Soaked. Lately, I sweat more than can possibly be normal. I figure it's either my body readjusting to normal glucose levels or having consumed too much balsamic vinegar. I love the stuff. I must have at least two and a half cups daily on my salads.

When I got downstairs, the need was like a tidal wave sucking me in.

"Where are those Oreos?" I suspected my mother of hiding them. I found them in the second place I looked. They tasted so terribly good. The prayer was brief because I wanted this. Badly.

"Lord, I'm going to do it. If You want to intervene, You better send them down here right now." My hands were still on the package of cookies while I was muttering this poor excuse of a prayer, and at the same time, I heard Phil on the stairs. Mother fucker.

Definitely not happy at the answering of this particular prayer, I proceeded to have a slight panic attack. I smoked outside and then put some coffee on. Mom and Phil were sitting at the kitchen table, and I knew they wouldn't be moving anytime soon because of God being awesome like that (note the harmless sarcasm here).

"What's the matter?" Mom asked. She had poured herself a bowl of Raisin Bran.

I couldn't breathe; my chest felt tight. I decided the more of this bullshit I keep secret, the higher my chances of relapse. So I started talking.

"It's that you're eating the exact food I was going to binge on before you came down here."

Eyebrows raised, she stopped midchew. "If this is bothering you, I can toss it. I don't even like the stuff."

"I'm fine," I lied.

Mom got up and dumped it in the garbage disposal. I wanted to run after it.

The desire to do it this morning was so strong it was ridiculous, and there was no trigger I could see. I went back outside. Even though there was still snow on the ground, it was nice in the sun. While I was sitting out there, mad, I asked God, "Why did the urge come out of nowhere? It doesn't seem fair."

The answer was immediate: "Because you have to learn this success is not yours. You have to breathe me all day. I had to do this because you were starting to think you were okay alone, and you're not. You need Me."

## March 6, 2005

I'm too tired to pray at night. I'm still not trusting him to provide for me. I'm not breathing him. I need to be broken. There's a lot more pride, rebellion, and stubbornness in me than I realized. I guess I thought He'd help me back on my feet, and I do the rest. Not so. I have to surrender complete control. He's going to probably have to repeatedly illustrate to me that I'm truly helpless, that this is no short-term exchange; it's a life decision.

I was driving down Thames Street this morning, thinking I had time to stop at Sig's and buy binge food. 1590AM was on, and the speaker was talking about trials and Paul's thorn in the flesh. I know this was not by accident. I drove past the convenience store. It was hard work. I think maybe He's trying to show me my heart is proud but that I am also strong.

### March 8, 2005

I called Lance yesterday. "Can I pick up my things now?" I asked. He said sure. So I drove up, feeling energized yet detached. I turned into his driveway, and it didn't seem as long as it had before. To my surprise and slight disappointment, no one was home.

I let myself in and took their house keys off my keychain. I greeted Bullet and then packed up my clothes. Lance had put aside a lot of mementos from me: birthday cards, photos, movie ticket stubs, his ring. Among them was the little Pakistani case he had sworn he never took. It had held my last three bags of heroin. When I had accused him, he had said he would never lie to me.

"But I watched you," I said. "You lied to your mother for a straight hour."

"I love you," he said simply. "I don't love my mother."

But there it was.

Barbara drove up as I was leaving. I told her I loved her and gave her a hug. She told me I could call her to see what was going on. "But I understand if you just want to wash your hands of it," she said. "Sometimes I wish I could."

When I got home, I was nervous and angry. I ate, then went into the bathroom to pee. When I came out, Phil asked me if I had behaved myself in the bathroom. What the fuck?

"Did you see me eat a lot?" I snapped.

"No, but just because I didn't see it doesn't mean it didn't happen."

Well, douchebag, I wanted to say, it takes more than twenty-five seconds to barf in the toilet. Instead, I said coldly, "No, and I don't want you asking me questions like that. It's really inappropriate."

When I woke up this morning drenched again in my own sweat, I was low. I drank some juice but continued to shake. I used hypoglycemia as an excuse to binge. Though my blood sugar stabilized after the first bowl of cereal, my rebellious heart kept eating.

*Sometimes I wish I could just get electro-shock therapy. When will I let go of my aimless life and trade it for one with purpose? You would think it was a no-brainer, but demons whisper in my ears: "Don't you miss the old way? Don't you miss Lance? Shouldn't you be helping him? Isn't that what Jesus would do? Don't you know that the good things you feel now are false? Don't you know God just wants control over you? You will get fat. You will get clumsy. He will not care because He thinks it's vanity and foolishness, but it's important to you, isn't it, Rachel?"*

*I feel their serpentine tongues almost flick my ears as they hiss their tempting lies. Surely some things they say must be true; I will probably get weightier.*

*It's so much to process: the break-up, the spiritual battle, the blood sugar, the weight gain. So much easier to bury underneath a mound of masticated food.*

### March 9, 2005

*Dad calls at nine-thirty in the morning while I am at work. He asks if I'm ready for treatment. Caught off guard, I hesitate, then say, "I guess so."*

*With all the obstacles, I never expected anything to materialize anytime soon. Now faced with the "75%" chance that it is indeed going to happen "within the next few days," I'm scared. What if they will not let me exercise? What if I gain a lot of weight? What if they don't have balsamic vinegar?*

*I want more time.*

*I had to get drunk to make the lunches last night. I watched "The Magdalene Sisters" while I painted my toes red with Mom's polish. The buzz let itself in like floodwater under a door, and I broke down and called Lance when there was nothing else to occupy me and because I needed a good cry. We talked too much about too many resentments. He told me he had never been hurt by anyone the way he'd been hurt by me. That was why he always took me back.*

*I wanted to tell him what a slob, what a negligent, lazy, reckless person he had become. Instead, I apologized. I told him I couldn't imagine being dumped by him; it would be more than I could stand. He will never know that every time I dumped him (eight times, he says), my love for him never stopped. I made myself do it because I was repeatedly disappointed.*

*I let myself cry over him late into the night. I let myself mentally go through him from head to toe. The curve of his jaw. The hair at the nape of his neck, overgrown, enough to grab fingers full. The space between his eyebrows and above his nose. His soft, warm, living mouth. His hips, his legs, his back, and* the warmth of his skin. In between tears, I told God I was sorry. Sorry I loved Lance more than Him.

### March 13, 2005

Mom heard me on the phone with Lance. I admitted we still talk, but it's nothing like it was before. He knows it, and I know it.

Wanda had said he'd find some way of getting dope. Though I couldn't possibly imagine how, experience has taught me to trust her. Lance called to tell me he and Ken took forty dollars, mostly in one's, and fucked Bobby over for a brick again. Now someone wants to hurt Lance. It turns out Bobby's brother, Ramon, had somehow gotten ahold of Lance's landline and was repeatedly calling him, demanding a hundred and eighty dollars by the end of the night or "he'd get hurt." I was picturing Barbara's house being broken into and vandalized, which caused me further alarm. What if they hurt Bullet? I told Lance my concern, but he had done close to three bags and didn't seem to care. Instead, he asked, all weepy voiced, for the address to where I'd be staying. I am a sucker for his concern, even though it's only when he's under the influence.

Mom approached me after I got off the phone. She and I slid down on the wood floor in the living room, both wearing robes, and I told her about it. Lance's heroin habit, the dealers that are after him. Her spindly fingers clutched a coffee mug, and her eyes had that look of the naive little girl who's terrified of the evil in the world. I hate that; it makes me think of the work, the effort involved in talking to her about everything in my life right now. I would have to remove her from the situation, sit her in my lap, and tell her not to be afraid.

She told me we are to have a family meeting this morning about ED treatment centers. We met Dad at Atlanta Bread in Middletown. We sat next to a window where the snow was falling in big, fat, gentle flakes. I got a large coffee and listened to them tell me things I'd already heard. One, were I to go away, they would not allow me back into their homes before I completed the program, and they would make sure Barbara didn't take me back in. Two, they asked me point-blank what I wanted to do: continue battling to go to Canopy or drop everything and try for Remuda. Canopy wants thirty days; Remuda a minimum of sixty. Canopy leaves you unsupervised at night; Remuda won't allow you to flush the toilet after using it. Three, I had to anticipate the possibility of losing my job if treatment took longer, which I guess is almost always the case.

Looking outside the window at the falling snow, I felt like my parents and I were at the center of a snow globe someone had shaken. There was a certain calm, but it felt like a timer had been set—peaceful for the moment, but when the snow settled in this little globe, Hell would swallow me up again.

Still, they were waiting for an answer. Remuda was longer, harder, but they had Christian staff, Bible studies, chapel every day.

I chose Remuda Ranch.

### March 28, 2005

There was a wedding reception last night. I'd dressed myself in black: black T-shirt, black skirt, black boots, and put on the types of undergarments that wouldn't prevent me from pouncing on some unwitting wedding guest. I wanted someone to witness me. There is a groomsman here who looks too much like Lance. Tall, dark, brown eyes. Such intriguing eyes. He didn't bring a date. I have been picturing what it might be like to kiss him since we talked this afternoon. I have imagined what we might say after dues were paid; after we had sex.

It started innocently enough. The groomsman said he had broken the sleigh bed in his room and asked if there was anything I could do. His name was Jack. He had told me he lived on Long Island. I went up to his room, and we knelt down to inspect the bed. When we stood up, I locked eyes with him. He didn't turn away. "I only came up here for you," I blurted. "I can see something in you—you're very alive. It's hard to resist."

"You're obviously hot . . ." he said.

"Don't underestimate yourself. You have a ridiculous amount of allure." And then I kissed him without closing my eyes.

I sped home. I had told him I would return. I knew I shouldn't, that I would feel like shit about myself if I slept with this boy I hardly knew. But I'm infatuated, and I don't give a damn. I got home, lay down on my bed, and took my insulin. I didn't even feel it. I took a hot shower so I wouldn't smell like an ashtray, grabbed my bucket of lettuce for breakfast, and got back in the car. I had left a note saying I was sleeping at the hotel because I was scheduled for an early shift. Hey, nine a.m. is early for me.

I opened the three shades on the east side of his room, trading the lamplight for the yellow streetlight. I told him I'd been waiting hours for this. He was an incredible kisser. It was nice to have someone's face so close. I couldn't get over his eyes—they seemed so alert, taking in my every move.

At one point, I reached over for a bottle of water. He said, "My God, do you have an incredible ass." Other things he said made me bite my tongue. Or gulp. "The types of girls that usually go for me are, um, big girls. I mean, big."

But I blocked it out.

## March 29, 2005

I listened to Audioslave to drown out my conscience. I was leaving for Arizona in a matter of hours. Yet I was headed on a secret last-minute road trip to Long Island. Driving in pouring rain to see a boy that I hoped wanted to know me, wanted my company. He had sent me yellow roses that morning at work, swinging my uncertainty in this direction. Mom would have never agreed. I told her I was sleeping at Wanda's. Wanda was driving me to the airport. That much was true.

His apartment was a mess. Did he not care that I was coming?

I wanted dim lights, a full-length mirror, and lots of talking.

This is what I got.

He interpreted me rolling on my belly as wanting a particular sexual position. It really hurt. I told him it hurt, and he asked if he should stop, but I said no. He kept going, even though I was stiffening and flinching in pain. I felt used. I examined myself in his bathroom. The bleeding was minimal.

Afterward, he talked about his dirty past offenses, daring me to ask him anything I liked. I liked his candor. But I anticipated reciprocity, and it never came. He did not ask about my life or what my thoughts were. He did not soothe my nerves about going to Arizona. He did not even show that much concern that I hurt after having sex or got severely burned on the radiator in his bathroom.

I thought going there was spontaneous and cool. But all I did was cast my pearls before swine. I gave away something precious to someone who stomped on it. I realized this while I was throwing up in a small bathroom in a gas station after bingeing on the way home.

## March 30, 2005

I forgive myself for the times that I subjected myself to these acts, aware that they would never turn out as I had hoped. I forgive myself for putting men's wants before my needs. I forgive myself for hating my body, for being disgusted with it, putting drugs into it, exercising it to the point of exhaustion, being negligent to its dietary needs, denying it insulin, resenting it for being defective, for forcing painful amounts of food into it, for sticking objects down my throat to void it of those foods, for telling it to be silent when it wanted something. For never accepting it no matter how much time and effort I had invested. I vow to take care of her. I will put God first, her second, family third, friends fourth. I will never put Lance's needs before mine should they jeopardize my health.

I leave for Remuda Ranch tomorrow, so let's get one thing straight. I am mine. These walls are mine. This skin, this brain, is all I have. I have compromised myself before, but not this time. Not with this.

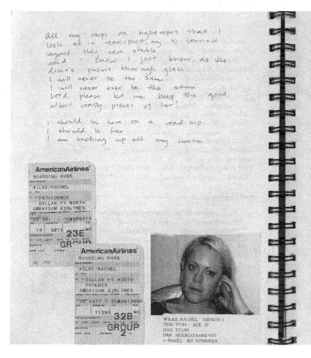

# PART III

March 31–May 6, 2005
February 12–March 30, 2005

*I know, I just know,*
*as the desert passes through glass*
*I will never be the same.*
*I will never be the same.*

# "MY EATING DISORDER IS NOT MY FRIEND"

## March 31, 2005

I am flying over New York City. I cried a lot on the plane. At one point, I slammed my head into an overhead compartment and cried more.

I am listening to music and looking down at the pear Jack bought me, rotting in the plastic bag of food at my feet.

His socks are packed in my suitcase.

But why?

Am I in this much need of distraction?

There will not be any more Jacks.

"We don't give up," Jack said.

We shall see.

The ride to the airport was stressful because Wanda and I were running late. I tried to soak up my songs, but she wouldn't shut up because she'd been drinking. She gave me red wine in a Diet Coke bottle, along with a lot of crap I didn't have the strength to carry: books, food, flowers, magazines. Even a stuffed rabbit with a dream catcher attached. She sounded nervous, like a piece of her was going to Arizona. I was exhausted, having slept for one hour and maybe four hours the night before.

I shake from uncertainty and fear. In a few hours, I will be in Arizona, where I will leave the world and comforts I have known. The Lord will not fail me. Sure, I'll fuck up, but this time, I'm getting her. I'm in love with her, with the idea of her. Happy.

## April 1, 2005

At the airport, an overweight, graying woman is waiting for me with my name printed on a sign. I thought she was going to make me sit in a wheelchair, but it's just a contraption she uses to carry luggage. She smiles when I walk up. Tells me her name is Wilma and that she sold Tupperware for twenty years before working for Remuda. Wilma's voice echoes in the parking garage. She lets me smoke while she loads my suitcases into a pristine, white van.

*And then we're off. Driving through such strange terrain. I don't know what I was expecting. Roadrunners being chased by coyotes?? The cacti are odd to see. At first, they look phallic. Then obscene, like a middle finger sticking up out of the ground. Then after a while, the way they are positioned on the mountains, they look like headstones.*

*This former Tupperware lady is literally driving me away from my past, my history. It's riddled with mistakes, but it is still beautiful, still mine! Why do I cling to the melancholy and try to tell myself it was all so fun, so enjoyable. It wasn't ever in those actual spaces. It was hard and heartbreaking, but that history is still mine. These veins of recklessness are mine.*

### April 2, 2005

*Dear Lord,*

*I suppose I have put this off long enough. I'm sorry for that. I know you know that by remaining here, I'm showing a huge display of trust and submission. I love you, and I don't want to keep distancing myself from you. It's just so hard to let go of my past. When I look back at it, in the fashion of a movie trailer, it seems like such a beautiful, fun, bittersweet life; then something says, "Come on, don't you want more of that? By getting closer to God, you'll never have that sinful, naughty fun."*

*But why wait for the world to deliver me yet another man I will bank a few sweet memories with and ultimately be disappointed in? The kind of man capable of the type of relationship I crave would have to have an incredible desire to know both You and me.*

*I deserve no less.*

*Help me to let go and trust that You will give me so much more than I have experienced. I am young. I know You will. I am just scared. Right now, the past is all I have.*

### April 3, 2005

*Remuda is such an oxymoron. So peaceful and vicious at the same time. The scenery and the people are so gentle; the battles in my brain, the fucked-up pieces of my past, are so violent. While I know it is inevitable, I just can't say goodbye quite yet.*

*Dear Lord, I am so frustrated with what I've learned: they want me to gain ten pounds. My muscle weight is going to deteriorate, causing me to go up 3–4 pant sizes. I know You know how uncomfortable I am with this.*

I know You know I'm aching to use this as an excuse to leave.

But, what do I know except how to keep myself comfortable in an eating disorder?

Maybe You want me to be eating high-calorie foods so I don't feel diabetically deprived, and the urges to binge will subside. Maybe at ten pounds heavier, I would stabilize and be normal. I will trust You. I will put it in Your hands.

In my heart, I do not want to leave Remuda; I want to do the work here to heal and receive the peace You have waiting for me. It helps so much more to obey You, to talk about You as a solution with these girls rather than to complain and question the rules with them in secret.

Thank you for being with me and for the overwhelming peace I've felt despite my fears.

Your daughter,

Rachel

### April 4, 2005

My room is small. Bed, nightstand, rainbow-braided rug. The first time I stood at the single window, the view of the clay landscape and purple mountains beyond it nearly took my breath away. Another good thing: I have no roommates, so I've been able to secretly do sit-ups and floor exercises.

I'm still worried about gaining ten pounds. When they gave me a snack of peanuts this morning, I put a few in my pocket. Just enough to feel like I had fought it some. Now I don't know how to focus until I get them into a garbage can.

I like the size I am. It's not ideal—ideal would be five pounds less or losing the little tire around my waist—but I could learn to live with this if it stayed this way, but they are telling me it cannot.

Dear Father, forgive me, for I have sure sinned. I haven't been as thankful as I ought to be for your many blessings. Instead, I focused on the bad cards dealt: a broken home, few friends, diabetes, an eating disorder, brokenheartedness. I have abused my body—your home, your temple, yet another gift you have given me. I have damaged it, working towards an unattainable ideal.

### April 5, 2005

Today, I was wearing my lime green skirt, illegally basking in the sun, when it billowed like a sail. I probably flashed half of the "cowboys" on this dude ranch. There's this ideal ratio of heat to breeze here. The air feels like brushing by soft, warm sheets on the line. The cushions on the patio furniture heat up in the sun, and they feel like heating pads. I'm sure the anorexic girls appreciate it; they constantly complain of the cold.

### April 6, 2005

I do not want to be here anymore. These people are asking for too much, too fast. Giving up bulimia, embracing God, accepting and regulating diabetes, gaining weight, giving up exercising, giving up my whole life. I'm strong, but I'm just one person.

Dear Father,
My fingers are loosening.
I give it all:
the boy sent as a stumbling block
my ED
my anger and resentment at being diabetic
my pride
my recklessness
my future

### April 7, 2005

They moved me into another room yesterday. I saw myself in a full mirror for the first time in a week and a half. There are mirrors in the lodge, but they're primarily for face painting and are only from the chest up. I was paler. I had lost definition in my stomach and hips. Maybe in my triceps and thighs too. I panicked and asked a staff member to take me out for a cigarette to talk. She said she wasn't allowed. I can't believe I had to have a demonstrative breakdown to justify smoking outside of the designated breaks.

### April 8, 2005

God's strength is sufficient for my weakness. I have a responsibility to the little girl who lives in me. The more I surrender my will, the more I feel His peace in and around me. I like the personality being revealed as I draw closer to Him; I do not feel diminished or less wild.

I am realizing that my eating disorder is not my friend. It is not a comfort but a counterfeit. Bulimia causes me to deceive and compromise myself. It distances me from her and God.

## April 11, 2005

Everything started colliding when I called home yesterday. I was tasked to phone three friends or family members and ask what changes they had seen in me and what they feared if I kept practicing my ED. Mom pointed out my preoccupation with food (storing leftovers) and having to eat the right thing (I shop for groceries daily). I think she mentioned my caretaker syndrome surrounding Lance, which made me put my recovery on the back burner.

I could picture her in the kitchen.

I could see where the Raisin Bran was, and I wanted it.

I shut down, too overwhelmed.

At the end of the day, I sat on the hill, smoking. I wanted only to be with Lance. In his truck, near a lake, high on heroin, letting summer swell in through the windows. Safe on drugs, instead of dealing with all the responsibility that comes with recovering.

"I'm sorry," I whispered, "but I love Lance more than I love You."

## April 12, 2005

When I first got here, I felt a profound sense of relief, joy, and peace. Now, where is Rachel?

She's fighting the nutritionist, who wants her to gain ten pounds. She's refusing God. When the other girls bow their heads to pray for help during the course of the meal, she thinks about stealing food off their plates.

At lunch yesterday, I ate a tuna sandwich, a salad, milk, a frozen yogurt, and a resource cookie. It was by far the biggest meal I've had here. It felt like a half-assed binge. "Okay," I thought. "Hand me about four more of that same meal and now we're talking." Instead, we walked to our nutritional portions class. We entered a small building and sat around a table that had real food on it. Chicken, pasta, fruit, rice, a jar of peanut butter. I thought I was going to die. I have never wanted to binge so badly in my life. Here sat these girls, learning what a serving size of peanut butter was, literally spreading the shit onto a real piece of bread in front of my face. I thought about just grabbing it, taking a big bite, and laughing like it was funny. It was horror.

I do think it's alright to binge and get rid of it occasionally when my stress flares. So I'm growing more and more impatient to do it. It's hard to summon up reasons why it's a bad idea. I can't remember the abuse anymore. Forcing *myself to gorge when I really didn't want to. The red eyes, punching myself in the stomach to extract every remnant. Depriving myself of sleep to make time for it. The nursing of it.*

*I have not found a coping mechanism quite as effective. I know God is, but trusting God means taking the power out of my own hands, which I still don't like.*

*There are two reasons I hesitate to relinquish control. One, I'm proud and want to do it myself. Then I could prove I don't need God or anyone; I am entirely in control and self-sufficient. Two, I don't trust these professionals that are telling me I need to gain weight. I don't give a rat's ass about their scientific formula that says eating disordered women are less vulnerable and impulsive once they reach a certain weight.*

*At the same time, I know God has only the best intentions for me. I know it is a lie that my coping mechanisms are okay, that they are what keeps me Rachel. Lies. The truth is, I've never even gotten to be her yet. She's been inhibited her whole life. Buried under food, weight, struggles, burdens.*

*Lord, please help me to cease fighting you. In my foolish head and with my wicked heart, I think that you will take away my personality. Please help me see that what I consider my personality is really anxiety, vanity, pride, insecurity, repression, and anger.*

*We went to chapel tonight, and the speaker told us she had looked up the Christian meaning of each of our names and written it on a card. She said, "God says He will call us each by name," and as she called out our names, each girl waited in anticipation, not only for the attention but also for the meaning of her name and a life-affirming, personalized verse. Mine said, "Innocent Lamb." I'm always the first to laugh if the joke is good. Once I started laughing (I'm the best they got for a "bad girl" stereotype here), everyone who remotely knew me joined in. Below is the card:*

RACHEL
"Innocent Lamb"
"Keep me from willful sins that they may
not rule over me. Then I will be blame-
less, innocent of great transgression.
May the words of my mouth the
meditation of my heart be pleasing
in your sight, O Lord." Psalm 19:13,14

### April 14, 2005

Last night, I caught sight of myself in a dark window and slowed down. I looked good. I looked pretty, and my body was fine. I was surprised at first. I thought: "I've been feeling so overwhelmed about gaining weight, but I actually look like this?!" And then I figured the mirror—the window—was deceptive. My body image is so out of whack I couldn't tell. I feel huge—my stomach, my thighs, my triceps. Raising my gaze to a mirror is a scary, tempting act. I almost wish there were none here.

### April 15, 2005

Grandma sent me a pretty pink and blue prayer shawl from some lady in her church. I pull it over my head to block the sunlight when I'm trying to nap. On chilly nights I drape it over my legs while watching house-approved videos with the girls. I feel protected, knowing a little old lady who'd never even met me was praying for me while knitting it.

It's crazy how comforting these things can be. I hung up the photo of Grandma, me, and Auntie Dolores on my wall by my bed. I wear the opal ring from Mom every day. It reminds me of her. I wish I had brought something from Matt and Ryan, like sweatshirts. It's like the time I was in Hasbro: I literally <u>lived</u> in Dad's forest green sweater, just because it was his. That is how it is with the opal ring. It ties me to Mom.

### April 16, 2005

Last night, I just had to try it. I had eaten carrot sticks and two packets of peanut butter for a p.m. snack. I didn't feel bloated. I just missed it a little, so I went into the bathroom with my lip gloss and threw up. There wasn't much. It smelled because it had already been partially digested. The worst part was that it numbed me. I remember that from binges back home. Now that I was anesthetized, I wouldn't be able to pinpoint whatever had been bothering me. I realized this as I stood up from the toilet. As long as I binge and purge, I'll never get to the bottom of whatever is gnawing at me.

Penny and I spoke a lot yesterday about my relationships with Lance and Dad. I know I can't see Lance for a long time. It would be too easy to fall back into using if he's still using. Penny and I both decided I should tell him upfront. Penny wondered if I was drawn to men like Lance because Dad had sent me the message that I was not worth much. I can't be sure yet. I would never have accused Dad of anything remotely like that until he married Cam. I must write further about how I may have felt like I had to play the caretaker, daddy's little girl, or act more like an adult while living there.

Penny also tasked me to have a conversation with my inner child and try to translate her tantrums to find out what she needs. How do I do that? Do I listen to music from that period after my diabetes diagnosis? Do I try to picture her? I have done everything in my power to keep her quiet. How do I put a spotlight on something I have denied for so long?

### April 17, 2005

Yesterday I rode a horse for the first time. He both whizzed and took a dump along our trail ride. He also tried to eat everything in sight—shrubs, flowers, leaves. They gave me a little whip to smack him in case he tried to eat a cactus. I said aloud, "Jake, buddy. I can't binge here, so neither can you. Stop eating everything!"

### April 18, 2005

We just had group therapy. It opened with a feelings check-in. Most of us seem pretty lost when it comes to identifying our emotions.

Danae is pale, small, and frail, yet she projects this counterfeit strength. "I'm fine," she said. Because she is scheduled to leave soon, we "attacked" her unwillingness to embrace the program. Your eyes are focused on going home, we said. She said she's doing her absolute best. By fixating on her discharge date? Foolishly telling herself she needs to get back and mother her son when she is not addressing her problems? I began to rock in place. I wanted to slap her, shake her for her stubbornness, pride, and, especially, her lies to herself! I was infuriated with her and sad at the inevitable outcome: She will not succeed. She cannot.

Then I realized something: sitting two seats away from her was me—that stubborn, blind, convinced-of-her-own-lies me. I just wanted to scream.

### April 26, 2005

I was still burping up dinner though I had eaten it two hours before. No one was watching me. Unsupervised, I am a threat to myself. I walked into the dark. Secluded in the shadows, I went behind a building at the end of one of the cliffs and, using my lip gloss, vomited the food that had long since been digested. I didn't even try to cover it up.

I felt bad afterward like everyone knew. They could see I was acting strange. They could see my red eyes. Smell the vomit. Pocketing the lip gloss, I went to the laundry room to wash my hands. I felt criminal like I had failed to take care of myself. The little girl cried, "Why are you doing this to me?"

All I can tell her is to hold on. Growth is uncomfortable. There are steps forward and back.

I did a ropes course today with Penny. I was brought to two totem poles, given a safety harness, and asked to choose which one I wanted to jump off by attempting to grab onto a trapeze bar of sorts. One totem pole had a platform; the other did not. I knew the platform would make it easier to get a running start, and I immediately wanted the harder way. I chose the pole with no platform and felt proud for doing so.

I climbed up the pole, surprised the height didn't scare me. Jumping did. The bar was ten feet away. I had no idea how I was to jump across to reach it without a running start. Penny told me I ought to assign a word to the bar, have it symbolize something. I believe I said submission and trust in God; then, I made myself jump. I missed. I climbed up again and missed. Penny gently suggested some other approaches. By the third time, I wondered if I should try again with the new suggestion or humbly climb down and try it from the pole with the platform.

I searched my heart, and I felt I would be missing out were I not to try one last time. So I jumped.

I almost made it.

Penny shouted from below, "You were so close!"

I didn't say anything. I gathered myself and walked towards the second pole. The easier pole. I felt defeated. I knew with the help of the platform, I would catch the bar, but I felt weak needing it. I climbed up the second pole. My shoulders hung. Should I have tried the first pole another time?

"Now, what do you want to attach to the second bar?" Penny asked.

I didn't even care. I don't even remember what word I attached to it, maybe something to the effect of knowing I needed help to overcome the eating disorder.

I used that platform to get a running start, and I jumped.

And I caught it the first time. My first thought was to hold on for exercise, to strengthen my arms. Then I thought, "No, this is God, and I need to hold on for dear life." And so I hung there, crying until I let go and slid to the ground, relieved and at peace with my accomplishment.

Sometimes, accepting help seems to be the only way.

Why is it so hard?

## April 28, 2005

I am in a foul, foul mood. I'm tired of it here. I'm tired of the girls, of the eyes, of the rules, of food, of church, of scheduled programming. I'm tired of being tired. I'm tired of low blood sugars at 4 in the morning and being forced to eat over 100 carbohydrates a meal. I'm tired of thinking about my bills back home, not keeping in touch with anyone, the circles under my eyes, and worrying and knowing that the odds are stacked against me.

It started at chapel when I was told the thing I knew to be true. Though the speaker's high-pitched voice made me want to lean my head back and scream profanity, she was right. "I gave the struggle to God," she said, "but I find myself constantly snatching it back."

I know. I know. How many times will I have to have my face slammed in the dust before I finally get it? Resilient my ass. I could stand on that pole, the one with no support, for as many years or decades as my stubbornness wants, but I know better.

There is another, better choice through God, and I do not want to make it.

## May 1, 2005

I've stalled long enough. Time to contact my inner child, but how to go about this? I've always sympathized with her but have considered her beyond help.

All she ever does is cry and throw tantrums and claw around. Like that little French girl in the psychology books who was raised in a cage, never loved, never taught to speak, never nurtured. Now I must have a conversation with her? Apologies could never even begin to reconcile the damage, could they?

I can picture her. She looks like I did at maybe seven or eight years old. Her hair is almost always in a state of disarray and darker, but that might be dirt. Her face is streaked with dirty tears. She is wearing a grimy jumper-type dress. I can see her knees just below the hem. Her fists are clenched.

She is in a small place with not much room above her head. This place is in my stomach. She claws at the walls. Scratches and screams for attention. That is how it usually is, and I put a lot of effort into quieting her. When food pours into my stomach, it rises to her ankles. More food is consumed—cold cereal, chunks of bread—and she's covered to her thighs. I guzzle soda. I eat sweets. "Isn't this what you wanted?" I say in a mocking voice until she is swimming in it.

She is never pleased, only silenced.

And then I vomit, and I suppose she is stunned. She finally sits down. She is wet, and her breathing is labored. She trembles, surprised she is still alive. Her body is in shock, and my brain is numb. She always behaves for a few hours following the ordeal.

Why would she ever want to talk to me?

I have not abused her, well, not much, in almost thirty days.

She is still. Expectant. Waiting. Her hair is cleaner. Her eyes are clearer. She is looking right at me, curious. I know the extent of her wrath, and I suppose she knows mine. I am afraid of her, and she is afraid of me.

R: Rachel, can you hear me?

r: yes.

R: I guess I'm sorry for what I've put you through. The bulimia. Will you forgive me?

r: i dont even know. all you care about is keeping me quiet.

R: I also care about keeping you peaceful.

r: yes. it is peaceful now but it is lonely. why wont you talk to me?

R: You're powerful. You dictate what I do. How I react.

r: i dont know what you mean. i am locked up in here.

R: If I let you out, you'd wreak havoc.

r: you dont know anything about me. i need so many things!

R: Well, what can I give you?

r: I need you to listen. take care of me. dont you want me? if you dont love me who will?

R: God?

r: you should love me too.

R: Probably, but I obviously don't know what's best for me. Because look what I've done to you.

## May 2005
### age twenty

# TEASPOON OF THERAPY

THE SUN WAS HIGH in the postcard-blue sky when Phil, Matt, and I arrived at a tall but modest cedar-post entrance that read *Remuda Ranch*. Pulling in, we passed a strand of towering pine trees on a lawn of struggling grass. We followed a long, paved drive flanked on both sides by a white corral fence. Gradually, the grass gave way to a terrain of endless clay. We passed colonies of cacti, and not much else until an upscale western house with a red-tile roof finally came into view. We would learn that the campus was small, the buildings dispersed. Parking beside it, we opened our car doors to an oven blast of heat.

It wasn't the first time the Arizona heat had assaulted us; exiting the Phoenix airport had felt like stepping into a sauna. Phil's dad and stepmom, who lived in Prescott, met us there, lending us a car to drive to Wickenburg for Family Week.

Family Week was a vital part of the program at Remuda Ranch. Rachel had invited Phil, Matt, and me, along with Perry and Cam, but thought it might be too intense for twelve-year-old Ryan, so I arranged for Doreen to watch him. For a small fee, Remuda offered food—families and patients dined together—and lovely accommodations on their one-hundred-and-fifty-acre ranch.

Flushed and sweaty, Phil and Matt had wanted to stop at our room, but I insisted we see Rachel first. We entered the building for directions, grateful for the air-conditioning. Soft worship music was playing in what could have passed for a sunny family room with Native American décor had there not been a small, glassed-in nurses' station tucked into the corner. I recognized this room, where, upon her arrival, Rachel said two nurses had greeted her by name, requesting hugs. She declined, but they persisted all the next day until she finally relented. "I thought it would be awkward and lame, but it felt really good," she admitted.

We found Rachel in another western-style house where she was staying with nine other girls. Large, domed windows drenched the common area with light, illuminating cushy leather couches, big-screen TV, Navajo rug, and a wall mirror where a pretty girl was applying mascara. Attractive girls in summer dresses and chic sandals whisked in and out of this room. I stopped one, whose green eyes grew when I identified myself as Rachel's mom. "Wait here. I'll get her," she said, vanishing. In seconds, Rachel flew into my arms.

After hugging Matt and Phil, Rachel took my hand. "Come out on the patio. I want you to meet the girls." We followed her through double French doors to a spacious flagstone patio with elegant outdoor furniture. Again, I was struck by the girls' common beauty. Except for two child-like anorectics, they looked more like fashion models than patients, with flawless makeup and hair, their bright summer skirts billowing, their perfect pedicures, a palette of pinks and reds, glinting in the sun as they introduced their parents to each other. *This disorder is cultural—its fixation on female perfection has made our daughters ill,* was my first thought, followed by, *I must look like something a desert rat dragged in.* Noting the other made-up moms in their chic summer clothes, I regretted not freshening up. Hoping I hadn't shamed Rachel, I resolved to take pains with my appearance for the rest of the week. With a pang, I realized that this beauty trap was real. Some women were just dug in deeper than others.

Six weeks into the program, Rachel seemed to be doing much better. Those initial weeks, she had repeatedly threatened to leave. First, when she was ordered to gain ten pounds. Fortunately, Remuda encouraged open communications, which I found refreshing after feeling excluded from Rachel's health care. Her nutritionist immediately called to explain that patients who are underweight, or even marginal, are more likely to binge. Weight gain reduces those urges. She promised to stabilize Rachel's weight once she gained the ten pounds, a small price to pay. Rachel begrudgingly agreed, for her physical and mental health.

Days later, when Rachel was relocated to a room with "high-risk patients," cutters and anorectics attached to feeding tubes, she was ready to depart again. "They placed me there because of my defect," she said. Since Rachel had been denying her diabetes for six years, she was severely hyperglycemic. Now nurses were regularly testing her blood and dosing her insulin, a cruel reminder of her incurable disease.

Diabetes was one of two wounds Rachel wrote about repeatedly in her decade of journaling. She had to accept it to heal; working through it was vital to her recovery. At the same time, it complicated her treatment. Whereas the other girls could focus on their EDs during private and group therapy, Rachel had to toggle between diabetes and her EDs. While all patients faced weight gain from their mandated meal plans, only Rachel gained weight from a secondary source, insulin.[88] The injustice infuriated her.

I was relieved when two other patients with diabetes were shortly admitted into the program, whereupon Rachel was relocated to a room with "normal" girls. In a shoebox marked Remuda, I would find dozens of notes from these girls, praising Rachel for listening to their stories, offering wise advice, and making them laugh through their tears.

✦ ✦ ✦

RACHEL'S OTHER WOUND WAS her father's abandonment, which she hoped to resolve during the Truth in Love session on the final day of the program. In this safe forum, she would finally confront him. She wanted her father back.

Rachel had heard from graduating patients that the Truth in Love was tough. Therefore, to get a head start, she and her father attempted to untangle some of their issues in letters prior to the event.

They agreed that Perry had overstepped his parental bounds when she was fifteen. "I leaned on you too much for emotional support when I was lonely, and I regret doing so," Perry admitted in his first letter. Rachel "sometimes questioned the personal things," her father said but believed that reciprocity was required to get his ear: "You let me spill my guts; I ought to let you spill yours. That was how I looked at it. I loved having access to someone with advice, and I didn't want to jeopardize it in any way. Moreover, I was a kid. I didn't know how to say, 'Dad, restrain yourself. This is enmeshment.'"[89]

Rachel explained why she was crushed months later when he met and married Cam: "I didn't expect the marriage to solidify as fast as it did. Combined with it feeling rash, my dad, who was once too close, was now almost gone. . . . I resented Cam. I had been the only girl in the house, and suddenly, there she was, and I paled in comparison in every way. She had beautiful hair and eyes, she was petite, her body was perfect, and she had natural grace. I was tall and clumsy and flat chested and overweight."

Perry asserted that Cam had suffered, too. She'd left her two older children in Albany with her ex-husband and was trying to adapt, not only to a new marriage but also to a mixed family, the reason he "spent every waking hour trying to pacify her."

Rachel questioned why Cam forbade her to see her father alone. Perry explained that his new wife viewed exclusive outings as "divisive" and "dishonoring to her." She wanted "a full union with everyone." His solution—to see Rachel when Cam visited Albany—made Rachel feel "like I was the last priority in the world . . . I got the crumbs." She withdrew because she "decided that it would be more painful to just get little doses of you."

Perry finally apologized: "I am truly sorry I was not able to be there for you as much as you needed me to while I was in the midst of my early marital difficulties." After waiting five years for this moment, Rachel might have needed a little more fanfare, a few more tender words. Instead, he rescinded this terse apology, asserting in his next letter, "In a sense, you walked away from us, and I really never left you at all. . . ."

Rachel called me distraught, not only over her father's curt apology but also her hunch that he cared more about unifying his mixed family than in addressing her ED, a charge she addressed in her next letter: "Family Week is not about reconciling you and Cam and me. It's about the fact that your daughter is severely eating disordered . . . I don't want to be selfish, but I need to know that my recovery from this monster of a disorder is first and foremost on our minds."

When Rachel thought the situation could not get worse, Perry announced that he and Cam would have to skip the last two days of Family Week.

"That means he'll miss the Truth in Love session on Friday!" Rachel wailed through the receiver. "I'll *never* get a real apology out of him!"

"Have a little faith, Rae. God can change his heart," I said, but my gut churned. What could be so pressing that after flying cross-country for an event that was vital to his daughter's health, he would miss nearly half of it?

Now that we were in Arizona, in this ED setting, I hoped Perry might come around. But the next morning at breakfast, Rachel appeared glum.

"Dad won't reconsider." She was pouring coffee from a fancy stainless urn. After filling her white mug, she depressed the lever to fill mine. Matt and Phil were already in the buffet line, the mingled smells of bacon, home fries, and eggs wafting our way. "Apparently, Cam has some commitment she must get back for on Friday," she continued. "I'm just supposed to suck it up. *Again.*"

"I'll talk to him."

Confronting Perry was the last thing I wanted to do. Though I had cherished our closeness while researching treatment facilities, it did not last. We had stopped talking weeks later when he accused me of turning Rachel against him. In truth, I was trying to help them reconcile. Seeing how much she needed her father, I explained why she refused his calls when he upset her. He only heard criticism.

After breakfast, I caught Perry alone. I tried to keep my tone light. "It would mean a lot to Rae if you stayed for the whole program."

His voice was flat. "I've told her three days is all I have."

"The Truth in Love session on Friday is supposed to be pretty intense—the climax of the whole week, and possibly the whole program. That's when the secrets are spilled and, from what I've heard, some amazing healing takes place."

Brows raised, he said, "Is that so? I didn't know that."

I nodded. "I've actually read about it in two different books on EDs. It's a big deal, Perry. Listen, we're only talking two days."

"I'll change my plans. It was just a client's hair appointment anyway."

I smiled, relieved for Rachel, but, really, a hair appointment?

The days rushed by as we learned about eating disorders, participated in art therapy, attended chapel, and watched rodeos. After dinner, Matt, Phil, and I toured the ranch, grit from the open, clay terrain somehow entering our mouths. We marveled at fiery sunsets and diverse cacti, with their bouquet of stunning blooms and wildly dissimilar arms. Matt noted that even their needles ranged from hairs to spikes. Ryan would have loved the reptiles that scuttled or slithered across our path; like Matt, he would have moved in closer while I jumped back. It was a shame Rachel couldn't join us, but her therapy continued during Family Week. However, if she behaved, she would earn a two-day pass, and we planned to visit the Grand Canyon.

Far too soon, Perry, Cam, Matt, Phil, and I were sitting in a circle with Rachel and Penny in the center of a quiet room. The light that poured through the windows hours earlier had waned. We were the last family to do the Truth in Love exercise. The five families who had gone before us now sat around the perimeter. Drained by their emotional interactions, some lounged on the carpeted floor, a daughter's head against her father's shoulder, mothers and daughters holding hands. After sniffling through their sad stories, I felt spent before we even started.

In the first step, Rachel had to explain why she thought she had developed an ED. At Penny's nod, she began.

"I got diabetes at fourteen. It made me feel broken." Rachel averted her eyes. "I started cheating on my diet, pretending I wasn't diabetic to feel normal again." Her blue eyes swept the crowd, then dropped again. "I got fat, so I made myself throw up. It got worse and worse. Now I'm a *raging* bulimic," she blurted.

Next, each of us had to tell Rachel how her admission made us feel.

"I'm afraid of losing my daughter," Perry said, his voice cracking with emotion.

"Worried sick," I said. "I've been so consumed with Rachel's issues that I've neglected my other kids."

"I'm mad," Matt said, crossing his arms. "She does lots of things for the hell of it and doesn't care who she hurts."

His reaction surprised me. The look that flashed across Rachel's face suggested that she hadn't expected it either.

"Worried . . . we don't want to lose you, Rae," Phil said, speaking directly to her.

"It make me sad," Cam said in her Vietnamese accent.

Next, beginning with Rachel, we had to ask forgiveness for our offenses.

She turned first to Matt. "I'm really sorry for being such a shitty role model. I know you've seen me do some bad things. With God's help, I want to recover so I can be a better big sister to you."

Smiling, Matt rose to hug her.

Next, she apologized to Phil. "At first, I thought you weren't good enough for my mom. I was wrong. You've been good to her—and me. You've actually been more like a *father* than a stepfather."

As Phil hugged her, I got a lump in my throat, recalling the day she'd likened him to a "mud fence." She'd grown up a lot, even through this.

To Cam, she said, "I blamed you for stealing my dad. I was mad at him, and I took it out on you, and that was wrong."

Cam smiled.

Rachel apologized to Perry for "routinely blowing off family holidays and birthdays." He embraced and forgave her.

Finally, she turned to me. "Mom, I love you, and I'm sorry . . ." She paused to take a deep breath. "I've lied to you a lot during this."

I nodded, aware that lies and secrets were a big part of EDs, but she wasn't finished.

"I threw up in the kitchen sink, every day, in fact, as often as five times a day."

I'm sure my face mirrored shock, possibly horror, as I pictured vomit in the sink where I washed my hands and lettuce. Still, I reached over, embraced, and forgave her.

Once the shock passed, my heart felt heavy. *How could a mother miss her daughter vomiting in the kitchen sink multiple times a day for several years?* If someone had told me this, I would not have believed it. I would have asked, as I asked myself then, How could you not have heard it, how could you not have smelled it, how could you not have known?

I missed Matt's and Phil's confessions. By the time I tuned in, Perry was apologizing for ignoring Rachel after he met Cam. Eyes tearing but wary, she rose to hug him.

If Cam expressed any remorse, she did not admit her part in the abandonment: she had put her own needs before those of an adolescent girl.

When it was my turn, I looked into Rachel's eyes, mine already filling, the pain in my throat immense. "I'm so sorry for not playing with you more when you were a child . . ." Swallowing, I continued. "Not coloring pictures, catching fireflies, and making snow angels with you." I recalled always having something more pressing to do—cooking, housework, graduate studies. In the end, none of those things mattered. My face was a wet mess. As I paused to blow my nose and wipe my eyes, I vaguely noticed others doing the same.

"I forgive you, Mom," she said, prompting a fresh wave of tears.

Pushing through my pain, I continued. "I'm also sorry for not talking to you more when you were a teen. I should have tried harder to find out what you were thinking and feeling. I gave up too easily when you pushed me away. I should have forced you to open your door." Even as she hugged me, my heart ached for my loss.

I tried to compose myself for the final, most difficult phase called "Offenses," when Rachel would confront family members who had wronged her. I knew it was mainly about her dad. She'd been anticipating this moment for years. After breezing through some minor gripes she had with us, Rachel squared her shoulders and turned to Perry.

"I know you were lonely, Dad," she said, her voice calm. "I understood your wanting to remarry, but when you met Cam, I felt like you dumped me. I felt discarded, left alone, like—like a baby in a back alley." She paused, swallowing, her lips suddenly trembling, her eyes filling, causing a chain reaction around the room. Accepting a Kleenex from Penny, she wiped her eyes and continued, her face flushed, her voice shaking. "You were the only person I could really talk to. When you left, it was like losing my best friend, my *only friend*." Her tears spilled again, falling down her face. "I felt so alone. I was only fifteen, Dad! I still needed you!" The vein on Rachel's brow bulged.

Sobbing too hard to respond, Perry had removed his glasses and was holding them with one hand, his broad shoulders shaking as he cried unashamedly. In twelve years of marriage, I had never seen him this broken. I was weeping, too. Cam draped one arm around him, but her face remained strangely stoic.

"I'm sorry, so sorry!" Perry finally managed through his spasms.

WORSHIP MUSIC WAS PLAYING as I entered the quaint white chapel that evening. Ignoring Cam and Perry, who were seated in the back, I slipped into a middle pew, beside Phil, Matt, and Rachel, who alternated sitting with them and us. A weight pressed on my chest. I had just come from an eight-hour session on forgiveness, yet I was fuming. Mad at Cam for not apologizing to Rachel. Angry at Perry for always putting his wife before his daughter. Furious with them both for nearly missing this day, causing Rachel undue stress *for a hair appointment!*

Yet, how many times a day, in large and small ways, did I fail? How flagrantly had I failed Rachel alone? If God forgave me, how could I harbor these grudges against them? It was only hurting me, robbing my peace.

I walked to the back and stooped beside them.

"I want to apologize to you both for my cold attitude. I know I haven't been very kind."

Perry's eyes widened. "Well, thank you. Apology accepted."

Cam just stared with a funny half-smile.

"HOW ARE YOU DOING?" I asked Rachel after chapel, linking my arm through hers. We were walking back to her room, a few steps behind the others. The night air was warm, so unlike chilly summer nights in New England. The black sky glistened with stars.

"I don't know. I can't believe it's going to be over in *two weeks*." She turned to face me. "Mom, I don't know if I can do this."

My pulse quickened. "What do you mean?"

"It's just so much to . . . process."

"Don't get ahead of yourself, Rae. You'll get overwhelmed. You covered a lot of ground today. Give yourself credit." Rachel looked unconvinced. "Listen, getting out of here for a couple of days will be good for you. You'll come back from the Grand Canyon totally refreshed."

Rachel stopped. "About that, Mom. I think I'm going to have to pass." The Grand Canyon was four hours away. She had been ambivalent about "being cooped up in a car" after being "jailed in a rehab." Now, she told me Perry wanted time with her and Matt this weekend.

I was disappointed. The kids might never get this chance again. Still, I understood that Rachel needed to share her time. I told her I didn't mind touring Wickenburg and going to Target as long as we were together. However, days later, when I gazed into the gorgeous gaping canyon, flanked by Phil and my in-laws, my heart sank at what Rachel and Matt had missed.

Ten days before Rachel's discharge, I began to receive panicky phone calls from her, echoing her reservations about leaving. It was time to think about the Remuda Life Program (RLP). Penny had suggested extended care to ease Rachel's transition home. Though Perry and I were both financially tapped after splitting Remuda's 25K down payment, we agreed to three weeks. On paper, the program sounded lovely. Rachel would live in a house on the grounds with four housemates. She would continue to see her therapist and attend groups, and the housemates would monitor each others' eating.

Had Rachel made some serious strides at Remuda, RLP might have helped; however, she was nowhere near ready for this lower level of care. Her journal would reveal that she had not even begun to resolve the core issues driving her EDs when she was discharged. Whereas a two-month program might have rehabilitated some girls, for example, those with a single ED and no co-occurring disorders, it was absurdly inadequate for Rachel, considering not only the fact that she had two protracted EDs, bulimia and diabulimia, but also that her treatment had been complicated by diabetes and a personality disorder. Less than a month later, she would confirm, with a remote look in her eyes, "I wasn't ready. I left Remuda way too soon."[90]

May 11–June 14, 2005

# "Waged in a War No One Wins"

**May 11, 2005**

My dad sighs a lot. My mother looks like a frail little girl. I am drained and frustrated. I am helplessly grateful to Cam for understanding my love for Lance, and despite Dad's emotional breakdown, I am relieved. I needed him to genuinely feel, if even for a moment, the grief and the guilt.

These are my confessions: my phone, the Sweet and Low, the diet soda, water loading before getting weighed, keeping contraband, trying to get out of the rodeo, not swallowing but saving the medication, drinking lots of coffee. These little things shouldn't drive me crazy, but little sins graduate into bigger ones.

I have been blessed with this family. I have been blessed by the opportunity to cry over Lance. Lance may have begun as a lustful experiment, but when my dad was absent, I looked to Lance. My dad questioned his role in my choice of men. It's true. All of them were desperate projects, like the ramshackle houses Dad buys and repairs.

We all agreed that I need to be single to work on my recovery. My parents asked me what life would be like without a man. I said it felt overwhelming. Life was too fleeting, and I felt too much to keep to myself. I had to find someone to love. They told me to find myself first, to not allow my identity to get wrapped up in a man's perception of me. What a waste. What a world of funhouse mirrors. I really need to scream, SCREAM to myself, not to date. I must take some time for myself to ensure the roots make their way deeper into the soil. It is foolish and terribly reckless to sacrifice my recovery for the frail hope that I may be the medium through which Lance is saved.

I still gravitate towards the "projects." I can't stand in the shadow of someone more "together" or aware than I am. Matt recently asked me, why not just go for a regular good guy? I had no good answer. The very idea of such a guy made me want to walk in the other direction. I thought, "I'm not ready, not yet worthy."

Bull. I am worth having a man who can lead by example.

## May 13, 2005

Today was the first day I was allowed to leave several bites on my plate. I didn't think I could do it, but I did. For the first time in seven years, I left a bite of my sandwich, and in doing so, lunch was more than just food. There was conversation and enjoyment. I've never had that before. Yet it felt within reach. I could almost touch it: eating when physically hungry, stopping when satisfied, and having no emotional attachment whatsoever to food. Imagine having that even once in a while.

## May 17, 2005

I will be discharged in fourteen days. I am absolutely terrified. I can't keep up. Everything here is ridiculously rushed. I am not being given the time to process everything that has occurred over the past week.

My father apologized for abandoning me.

My guilt and indecision ruined a visit with my family.

I have no idea how to grieve the fact that I am diabetic.

Lance was high last night, and I cried into the phone and told him I would wait for him.

I have not prayed. I cannot hold it together. I'm tired. I'm petrified. No one knows me.

Dear God, it is finally quiet now. My hands shake, and I am not thinking about You. I am thinking of everything but you. So when did it stop?

Target.

In the aisles, I was eyeing razors, laxatives, chocolate, diet pills. How to buy them, where to hide them.

Little sins do get bigger. They are like bulimia. Never satisfied.

Lord, I can't do this alone. I need so many types of support. To think I can manage this myself is asinine. So is the thought of jeopardizing my progress over the concept of Lance.

Or the concept of Jack.

Or the concept of a thin body.

Not a damn thing is worth it.

## May 18, 2005

So what rock will I leave in the desert? I had been thinking "self-will." Now I contemplate "reckless" because what I did when I drove up to New York to have sex with Jack, someone I barely knew, was not the kind of recklessness I am proud of. That is not why I had this word tattooed on my back.

## May 19, 2005

The therapist said calmly, "You're on a stage, and everyone can see that you are wearing a mask—it's not really you. You're not doing a good job of playing this game." Tsaili, the girl he spoke to, was quiet. I would have told him to shut the fuck up or punched him, but he didn't ask me to play.

I've been on a stage my whole life. I thought passersby would watch for a while, maybe become intrigued with me. No one did, not for very long. If they looked twice, I trembled. How long could I make them see me in the way I wished to be seen?

But Lance saw the truth. He saw my compulsions. He saw my rage. He saw my tears. He saw the vomit on my clothes. I laid it all before him: beauty and filth, strength and weakness, hope and despair.

He witnessed, and he was indifferent.

See me, see me, I silently wished, but he didn't seek to know me. Occasionally I would snap out of it and say, "He doesn't appreciate you! You're casting your pearls before swine again!" And I would leave him while feeling broken, broken, broken, wondering why my love did not love me. Believing I should go back and give him whatever I had left.

## May 24, 2005

With my discharge looming, I have begun aftercare work—lining up doctors and support groups to help me once I'm out. I found out about Butler support group and told Heather what I needed in terms of scheduling. Now I'm sitting here nervous that I basically confessed I am incapable of working weeknight shifts because I would binge out of my mind. Heather's probably driving home right now thinking, "Rachel is not the most stable employee right now. What have I just agreed to?"

I need to calm down. My motives are pure; I'm not trying to avoid boring second shifts. Those slow, unstructured weeknights are a major stumbling block. If I want to recover, I simply must work day shifts right now.

The voices are trying to suck me back in. "You idiot!" they say. "You've just given yourself away. Now your boss and co-workers will be watching you twenty-four hours a day!"

## May 27, 2005

Going to the Remuda Life Program (RLP) is the wiser path to take. I need to drop roots, I told Mom and Dad, but now I just want to eat. I'm beginning to seriously wonder if I really do need to be eating like a horse to be satisfied enough to not crave a binge. Because the urges faded with the weight gain supplements, and since those have been discontinued, I want to eat. Then again, I was stressed about going home. I can't tell if my cravings are emotional or physical. Now that I know I'm going to RLP, the urges have lessened but are still there. I just feel like I need to get bingeing out of my system. What if Mom is right? "What if you like it, Rae? Then one time will be like that initial drink for an alcoholic."

I don't know.

I miss eating until I'm satisfied.

But if I eat one morsel too much, I feel like I've entirely screwed up.

I need to learn to be more forgiving with myself.

Drop the either-or-thinking.

I miss home. I miss the sun. I miss my car. I miss Matt. I'm missing his prom, Grandma's visit. Micah's wedding. Yes, I can see with alarming clarity how easy it would be without any accountability to slip back into my old life. That is the biggest reason I'd benefit from RLP. Two weeks seems meager, but I must surrender as much as possible, befriend everyone I possibly can, challenge myself, embrace change, and dismiss the past. Because it's beginning to not feel like home or identity any longer.

## June 3, 2005

Dear Body,

I know I've put you through some shit and neglected you beyond belief. I'll never deny that. I've risked your health, nearly killed you. I've exhausted you during exercise, tortured you with laxatives, stuffed you with obscene amounts of food, and repeatedly forced you to vomit. Made your eyes red, your throat sore, your face swollen, your system dehydrated and unbalanced. Subjected you to painful, compromising sexual acts.

I've hated every solitary part of you. Your breasts never grew. You catch diseases easily. You have ugly moles and skin conditions. Your thighs have stretch marks. Your butt has cellulite. You store fat at your stomach—that really pisses me off. I've worked so hard to manipulate you; still, you rebel and stay fat despite my labor. Is this some fucked up power struggle?

*You're broken and defective—always needing a doctor's visit, glucose test, shot, or food. Why should I be the one out of a hundred to get diabetes? I'm too infuriated and resentful over the diagnosis to even grieve. Diabetes has cost me so much. Time, peace of mind, my ability to have healthy kids. I feel I've paid my dues. Like a virus, it should be over, but it never will be.*

*I mourn my life before diabetes.*

*I miss health.*

*What better way to pay you back for your deficiencies than through an ED? It let me regain some control by denying the disease.*

*And still you won. You still hold me hostage. I'm still fat. Still broken. Still entrapped by your interminable diabetic needs.*

*I detest you.*

*You are a leech. Criminal. Scum.*

### June 4, 2005

Too much time has elapsed. I'm at RLP with one week to go. I naively thought this morning, as everyone else headed off to volunteer, that I could stay alone in the house. Almost immediately after Megan, Erin, and Charmaine left, I headed for the pantry.

It's hard to remember what happens in those spaces. If my brain were a television screen, it would be static, the snowy, humming screen. I felt guilt, and no matter how earnestly I tried to tell myself to look and register what I was doing, I saw only static.

The first bowl of cereal was good. The three afterward, the ice cream, the Rice Krispy treats, the chips, the peanut butter, were not. I watched TV, trying in vain to distract the guilt. The food wasn't good. I wonder if I could learn to have just one bowl of cereal and take insulin for it because after that first bowl, eating was a chore. Plus, I couldn't look myself in the eyes.

### June 6, 2005

Dear Rachel,

This is your body. I got your letter. You began reasonably enough until you started listing my "shortcomings."

Do you honestly think I chose your DNA? Do you seriously think I wanted you to be diabetic? It takes a ridiculous toll on me!

Rachel, you almost killed me. You totally ignored what I needed to survive: I cannot function without insulin. You put me in a position where my organs were threatened and could have been permanently destroyed.

You punished me for being broken. Trust me, I'm very sorry that the pancreas doesn't work. I'd love to manufacture insulin like I used to. We were so much healthier and peaceful then. But I'm not liable for genetics, Rachel. That's God's domain.

We're supposed to be a team, not enemies. I need you to respect me so I can continue to do the things you love: see, write, run, sunbathe at the beach, make love to your husband, have babies someday. You must do your part. Eat as best as you can—I need carbs so I can minimize your food urges. I need you to deliver me insulin. Our eyes are damaged. <u>Please</u> let the damage end there. I'm not invincible. I cannot continue to serve you if I'm under attack by you and the ED. I beg you to keep it at bay. I know you can't do it alone, so call on the Lord. Forget your useless pride—this is life and death, Rachel. I want to take you through this precious life in optimal health. But we must work together, find out what is effective, and stick with it.

I miss health more than you do—you took it for granted. I don't want life to revolve around diabetes or an ED, either. I still love and serve you, Rachel. I just need you to take care of this one thing: give me enough insulin, so all our parts can function.

I miss freedom, too. However, I register what you've apparently overlooked: the "freedom" you're dabbling in by denying your illness is better described as an illusion. I scream for your attention because if you do not stop your behaviors now, you'll be debilitated or die.

Sincerely,
Your Body

### June 8, 2005

I smell like salmon. My fingers are shaking. Did I act appropriately? Did I sufficiently challenge myself?

We just had our first restaurant challenge at the Olive Garden. I deliberately ordered an entree with no starch—salmon—instead of my beloved chicken parmesan, so I could have breadsticks as my two carbs. I don't know if I really even like pasta. I think I must have eaten a bit too much because I feel bloated. I got Diet Coke, but Nicole OK'd it. I got Erin coffee for her birthday. I ate two servings of salad, and after the after-dinner mint (chocolate), I tried a caper (tasted like something found on the bottom of a dock) and an olive (even worse).

*I can't leave here. Please. Not yet. I need all the help I can get.*

### June 13, 2005

*I've never been so disappointed to leave a place in my life. It wasn't just the program. It was the women, the girls I fought the battle alongside. I've never had friends before, and leaving them behind was heartbreaking.*

*God, there is so much to reflect on, so much to process, and home seems the least healthy environment in which to do it. I want these Remuda people around me. I want the stupid rules and the supervision. I want the concern, the understanding. I want the church, the prayer.*

*I am still struggling to understand exactly what happened on Friday night.*

*I felt an urge, probably level one or two, so I had Megan, Erin, and Geeta pray for me outside on the slab rocks. I thought I'd be okay. I thought that was what God had wanted, for me to humbly reach out and request help. So with gritted teeth, I asked. Still, later I was found bingeing by a mental health technician. I told her I was done and took two units of insulin in front of her.*

*"How do you know how much to take?" she asked.*

*"I just sort of guess."*

*When she left, I had the gall to continue eating. As luck would have it, she came back and found me puking in the kitchen sink.*

### June 14, 2005

*Dear Lord,*

*The plane is landing. I don't want to be here. I am terrified to walk back into haunted grounds. Lord, it just landed. Please, please. You must know that I am not ready. You must. Did you just give up on me? Not that I would blame you, considering the way I behaved. I doubt the likelihood of my starting a new life. I doubt it very, very much. I'd rather die than go back to the way it was before.*

*It's raining here. I haven't seen rain in three months.*

*Lord, help me to know, really know, that you are in control of everything, down to every trivial detail. I don't want to forget what I learned.*

*If taking off in a plane feels like excitement, eagerness, falling in love, then landing feels like every force of gravity is against it, like determination, avoidance, dread. It's the sensation of trying to stop while traveling at hundreds of miles per hour.*

*June 14–23, 2005*
age twenty

# FREE FALL

Rachel loved string lights. For her homecoming from Remuda Ranch on June 14, Phil wrapped pastel orb lights around our twelve-foot pine out front. When he plugged it in, the boughs looked polka-dotted.

To our gambrel roof, he nailed my twelve-by-three-foot banner—red duct tape letters on clear, heavy-gauge plastic—that read, *WELCOME HOME, RAE! WE LOVE YOU!*

"Looks like someone splurged on decorations," Rachel remarked, finding me in the kitchen. Her smile was huge. Phil had picked her up from the airport while I finished the party preparations.

I hugged her tightly, thrilled not only because she was home but also because she had graduated. We'd grown closer through our calls and letters. Now that she had gotten help, I was giddy with the prospect of getting my daughter back.

"C'mon outside," I said, hating to break our embrace. "Everyone's waiting on the deck."

Rachel hugged her brothers, stepsisters, and Doreen's son, Jordan, Ryan's other half.

"For God's sake, Jordan, you grew another three inches while I was gone!"

Jordan smiled, flashing a network of braces. Though not even twelve, he was six feet tall and had a good two inches on thirteen-year-old Ryan, who stood beside him, squirming at that fact. Both boys towered over Phil's pretty, petite daughters, Krissy and Nikki.

"Jordan's almost as tall as Matt!" Krissy's dark eyes darted around for Matt to prove her point, but he had ducked inside.

Rachel smiled as she took in the scene. Colored lights tacked around the handrail of the deck, patio table laden with her favorite foods. Eggplant parmesan, sautéed portabello mushrooms and bok choy, organic greens with balsamic vinaigrette, watermelon wedges. Soy-soaked chicken sizzling on the grill. Except for the pumpkin, chocolate chip Bundt cake, I had tried to keep the fare low-carb.

"I'm glad you didn't skimp on the soda," she said, fishing a frosty Fresca out of a large yellow tub. "It was torture not having this elixir in there!" Popping it, she took a swig, burping happily. She kissed the can. "I missed this and my beloved music *so much!*"

"Quit makin' out with your soda!" Jordan joked, triggering giggles from the girls.

"We missed you, too, Rae," Phil teased, glancing up from the grill as he turned chicken, unperturbed by sporadic bursts of smoke and flame.

As if on cue, Matt appeared, toting his portable CD player. "What's a *pahty* without music?" he grinned, never missing a chance to mock Phil's dialect.

Blue striped boxers peeked out of the waistband of Matt's khaki shorts as he leaned over to plug his CD player into an exterior outlet. In moments, we heard the inimitable strumming prelude to Tom Petty's *Free Fallin'*.

"Tommy-boy! Oh, yes!" Rachel said, her smile expanding. Eyes closing in bliss, she sashayed toward Ryan. "Dance with me, Rye-guy."

Matt cranked the volume.

Laughing nervously—half braces, half gums—Ryan acquiesced. We chuckled, watching him stumble over his large, bare feet.

Rachel wore low-slung jeans and a fitted lilac T-shirt. Her mandated weight appeared so evenly distributed on her frame that I hardly noticed it. At the moment, it didn't matter. She looked free, the words she sang along with Tom Petty.

✦　　✦　　✦

"CHECK OUT THE SIZE of my stomach! I look like I'm ready to give birth on your rug!"

After the party, Rachel had tried on some of her pre-rehab clothes. Now she examined her distended abdomen before my full-length mirror. She frequently poked out her belly, often chuckling as she did. This time, panic twisted her features. The vein on her brow appeared.

"You've just eaten and drunk how many sodas? It's probably mostly gas."

"Even so, no one else looks nine months pregnant!"

Not wanting Rachel to feel powerless, I said, "It's nothing some sit-ups won't fix." Remuda might not have sanctioned this remark. On the other hand, ignoring a stomach that was staring at both of us hardly seemed honest or helpful.

Remuda had prescribed a strict aftercare plan that they treated like a contract. With the help of their counselors, prior to discharge, patients had to select an aftercare team that included a therapist specializing in EDs, a registered dietician with whom they would meet weekly, a doctor, and, in Rachel's case, an endocrinologist. Bi-weekly participation in two support groups was also required, ideally an ED group, like Anorexics and Bulimics Anonymous, and a twelve-step meeting, like AA or Narcotics Anonymous. Rachel also had to agree to correctly dose her insulin and to avoid contact with Lance. She made her calls and signed her contract. We should have known that even a contract signed with blood would not have kept her away from Lance.

Rachel's first Sunday home, she attended a new congregation in Newport with a charismatic young pastor.

"How did you like New Beginnings, Rae?" I asked when she entered the kitchen after church. I was foraging through the fridge for leftovers to make a stir fry for lunch.

"It was fine," she said, reaching for a Fresca. "Till I saw a man who looked like Lance and a woman who had a body I could only dream of. Must've been his wife." She popped the can and drank while I transferred ingredients to the counter—clumps of broccoli, a limp carrot, a rolling onion, and containers of last night's chicken and rice.

"Sorry, Rae," I winced. "That must have really hurt, but you don't know what perfect man God has for you. You just need to be patient. You need to get better first."

"I know one thing. Lance'll never be that guy, and I'll never be that girl."

That incident may have triggered Rachel's relapse, but looking back, there were many contributing factors.

For one thing, she had not been following her aftercare plan. Not only had she canceled her appointment with her dietician ("What a complete waste of my time"), she had yet to attend an ED or AA group. When I reminded her, she claimed she still had jet lag or the time or location of that day's meeting was inconvenient.

Though Rachel had met with her new therapist, she had returned sullen, confirming my hunch that this woman might not work out. In 2005, finding a local therapist who specialized in EDs was challenging enough. Rachel's insistence that the person be a believer made it nearly impossible. We settled for a Christian counselor who, while not an ED expert, claimed she had studied EDs and treated clients with bulimia. The partnership was short-lived.

In days, Rachel induced vomiting. I did not handle it well. I'd just had words with thirteen-year-old Krissy, whom I'd reminded for the third time that week to clean the bathroom she shared with Ryan, a chore they rotated. Krissy was *not* overworked. Still, I felt like the wicked stepmother, Krissy's wounded brown eyes still sharp in my mind when Rachel passed me on the stairs, evading my eyes.

"Have you had any incidents?" I asked.

"I just purged," she admitted, looking up.

I froze. Should I hug her? But wouldn't that reward the behavior? Rachel hardly looked fazed, much less remorseful. I told her to clean the toilet, which seemed like a fitting consequence that would lighten Krissy's load—and my lingering guilt.

Looking back, I realize it could not have been a colder, more inappropriate response. After that incident, I don't think Rachel ever admitted to purging again. When I asked how she was doing, she would respond with a lukewarm, "Okay." I didn't commend her because I wasn't convinced she was telling the truth—though who could blame her after my callous reaction when she did? I would learn that Rachel craved verbal affirmations during this vulnerable time. She needed me to notice her struggles and cheer her on, praising her sacrifices but also applauding her efforts when she failed. Understanding neither the magnitude of her battle nor what she needed from me, I let her down.

Except for Phil, we all fell short in showing Rachel affection, another thing she coveted. Had I known how starved she was for touch, I would have embraced her more, prompting her brothers to do the same. Phil did not have to be told. Naturally affectionate, he encompassed Rachel in frequent bear hugs that lit her face. Her exuberance should have tipped me off how desperately she needed human contact. Maybe I thought Phil's hugs would suffice. As if someone so broken could ever receive too much love.

When Rachel's primary support system failed her, her external support systems might have sustained her had she given them a chance. However, after one or two AA and ED meetings, with a wave of her hand, she dismissed these as being "totally unhelpful and lame." Though important throughout one's recovery, support groups are vital in the early days and weeks when addicts are most at risk. In testimony after testimony that I read, recovering alcoholics emphasized that their sobriety was directly related to their degree of group involvement. Those who attended meetings multiple times, if not every day of the week, reported the fewest, if any, relapses.[91]

The church was another viable support system that Rachel dismissed. Pleased with her spiritual progress at Remuda, I urged her to keep growing in her faith. Join a Bible study where she could meet people her age. Get involved with outreach. Nothing dwarfed one's problems like helping with the Prison Ministry or Soup Kitchen.

But Rachel was not like *those people,* she said. She did not want to hang out with Christians any more than she did with people recovering from alcohol or EDs.

However, she did want to see Lance.

"You promised you wouldn't. You said you needed to take care of yourself right now, remember?"

Rachel eyed me directly, her tone calm but firm. "I'm not saying I want to get back with him. I just don't see how one visit can hurt. I have a *history* with him—we've been together for *four years.*"

In twelve days, Rachel was turning twenty-one. If I forbade her, she'd run to him.

"*Please, please, please* think about this. Think of how many times he hurt you during those four years. *You* did the work. *You* paid the bills. *You* supported him, but he *never* reciprocated."

Rachel blinked as I spoke as if each indisputable fact were a slap to her face.

"You say one visit can't hurt, but how many times has he sucked you back in? Once is all it takes with him!" A startled look leaped into her eyes. She knew what I meant. I had told her I thought Lance was her heroin. "Better to stay away *completely.*"

But she did not listen. She never listened when it came to Lance.

# June 15, 2005–August 18, 2006

*Rachel's journal art, in negative effect,*
*taken from the back cover of Everything Journal V.*

# "I'm outnumbered"

**June 15, 2005**

I woke up thinking I was still in Arizona, but here it's cold.

I feel better this morning than I thought I would. Still I was scared. I put on Christian music and hoped I was worthy enough to have His grace cover me for the day. I tried on my two favorite dresses, and they almost fit.

"Well, you can work on this," my mom said, in reference to the pouch I was lamenting over after the party.

Father, be with me . . . I'm so scared. This house is like a cemetery to me, though it needn't be. Help me to keep my eyes on You all day. Help me to cling to you. Please don't leave me alone. How easily I will go back to my old ways and attitudes.

**July 17, 2005**

There was a girl sitting in front of me at church today. Small. Most likely a zero. She was in love with her husband, who looked a little like Lance. He was everything Lance should have been, everything I wished him to be: supportive, a deacon, smiling, in church. I couldn't stay behind them, so I got up and left. I felt anger at being denied her body, that man. My anger came with involuntary tears.

**June 21, 2005**

I woke up with a blood sugar of sixty-five. I didn't eat a lot, but I ate about two cookies I found stashed in the freezer and a bowl of bran flakes. Hmmm, still low, I see. Matt had to have known something was up; he was following me around.

About five minutes after I'd thrown up, Mom walked by and asked, "Have you had any of your episodes?" I said yes, and she asked me when. I told her, "Just now" because I had been low, and she asked where I had done it. She told me to clean the toilet immediately because bacteria was growing on it, then yelled upstairs for Krissy to clean everything in the bathroom except for the toilet.

I don't know what I expected, but it wasn't that. She made me feel like a dog. Dirty, disgusting, and contaminated, and I'm too low about the whole thing to try to make her understand. They'd have reacted very differently in Arizona. They'd have said, "Come here," and they'd have hugged me. Not that this was what I deserved, but it was what I needed. I might act tough, but in reality, I'm lost and weary and overwhelmed, and my mom's reaction only reinforced this.

## June 23, 2005

Dear Father,

Forgive me for not spending quality time with you today. It was a terrible day as far as body image goes. I suppose if I had spent time in Your Word, I would be refocused. I would realize how fruitless it is to seek fulfillment in my reflection. If I centered my world around You, these things wouldn't hold such clout, but today I put my ED mindset first.

Father, forgive me once again for my pride. It swells up in protest even now. It tells me that to obey You is to let my figure go, accept my present weight. It says, "Now, can you really handle that?" Every voice but one says, "absolutely not," and so I'm outnumbered. Father, the sad truth is that I haven't fully learned this lesson. Not in the slightest, and I'm so sorry. I feel like no matter how hard I try, I can't keep this up. I feel awkward and dishonest in Your presence. Helpless and overwhelmed.

## June 29, 2005

Mom begged me not to go, but I went upstairs to change, only picking out a different black skirt. We prayed before I left. "He's a hard-core drug addict," she reminded me as I walked out the door. The weather was hazy; I took the haunted route but felt nothing. Maybe, I kept it at bay.

I was petting Bullet when he walked out of his room. The first thing I noticed was his cross necklace. Then we had a very long hug. He felt hot and sweaty. We were going to look at the Christian rehab in South Providence. I had to make a decision, but either way was wrong. If I denied him physical touch, he would feel dejected (or so I perceived). If I indulged him, his hopes would be raised only to be let down. I raised them.

He has gotten a lot worse. He has even a shorter fuse, a more dismal outlook. He constantly swears and complains. At one point while driving, I literally thought, as though I were on a horrendous blind date, "Get me as far away from this piece of work as possible. What a miserable human being."

### July 4, 2005

I miss the warm nights in Arizona. Since the sun set, there has been a chill in the air. I shouldn't have goosebumps in July. I change into white pants—pants I wore prior to weight gain when I received lots of compliments. I feel curvy, clumsy. Matt has been pestering me to watch fireworks in Newport with him and his friends. I agreed. Now I don't want to go.

### July 6, 2005

The world seems ridiculously overwhelming, but that is one enormous lie. Because nothing in God's control is out of control, and I have committed myself to His will. The hum in my mind just gets so loud, the options seem so limited, and the easy way out, a numb way, by way of mouth, seems increasingly desirable. Allow more time to pass and it is not only justifiable but wise. Permitting a full-fledged breakdown at work would probably look bad, right?

Oh my God, do I ever want to go for it. I would be so embarrassed if a co-worker were to walk in now. I haven't done anything wrong, but I ate four little bowls of salad in a row. I must look huge.

Dammit. I told myself this wasn't going to happen. I had a plan. I had people who were going to call me: Mom, Glen, and Stan said they'd check on me two or three times. Glen came back at least three times. Stan said he was going to bring me striped bass for dinner. What time was that? I couldn't exactly ask him when . . . it would mean my mind was always on food, now, wouldn't it? So I waited. It got later and later, and I had little snacks, trying to keep it relatively low carb, figuring any minute he would deliver a well-rounded meal. . . . But that time never came, so I decided everyone had forgotten about me. What did it matter if I ate the whole snack bag of peanuts? And since that was calorically more than I'd bargained for, I ate a granola bar too.

Stan came up to the desk to say good night. He asked how I was doing, and I shook my head. "You're not planning on doing anything dumb, are you?" he asked. Tears came. No one ever gives you praise for this job. Not ever. No one gives a rat's ass if you've made it through another day without puking. Big fucking deal. But get skinnier and listen to the applause. Restrain yourself from eating and "What willpower!" No one ever says, "Hey! I just wanted you to know I see you're trying really hard, and I'm impressed! Really proud!" Sadly, even if they did, I wouldn't be able to accept it.

## July 17, 2005

Sometimes I think I may be losing my mind. Even my vision is in this choppy, freeze-frame state where it's difficult to process anything. It's like my physical body is in a coma, and my brain is just biding its time. I look at other girls, at their apparent carelessness, and I am jealous of their seeming ability to disconnect from troubles. I cannot. I try. With food, with alcohol, with drugs, with exercise, with prayer, with sleep.

I don't think I've been touched in days. I feel entirely pathetic about it, but I just really want a hug. I really want to be held just for a minute, but there's no one here, and I feel too ridiculous to ask. No one even sees it, I guess. I feel naked, like I'm missing something. Arms, arms around me. I never ask for it. If I did, people might think I was insane. Moreover, I'd probably burst into tears. I can't even lift my arms.

## August 21, 2005

I have done heroin for the past eleven days straight. Nothing nightmarish yet, just contentment. I can't say if I regret it. I do remember this: feeling productive, motivated to make more money to perpetuate this peace for as long as possible.

Lance knows. (He's in detox, round #4, with plans to go on to a six-month rehab in New Bedford after). Wanda knows, and so does Matt.

The last eleven days, whenever I feel that void, that nagging hole of knowing I have accomplished nothing, well, I've been running to this. I have two dealers' numbers, and I'm fairly confident calling them and driving to Providence myself. I go alone for two reasons: 1) to eliminate the middleman and my chances of getting screwed, and 2) so nobody knows I bought forty dollars' worth or that I've consumed twice as much as I did last week in only two days. My eyes race back and forth in my head. I sweat. I drink wine to enhance the sensation. I like to accomplish menial tasks: errands, work, cleaning, exercise. I have told myself I need to try to go two or three days without it, but the prospect scares me.

With heroin, I get to boss the bulimia around. I get a break. A foolish vacation of sorts, one I assuredly cannot afford to take. But I don't want to spend one more day being held hostage by this ED. I don't want to run crying to God to save me; I want to do it myself. I hate to rely on anybody.

I can't say what appeals to me the most about the dope: the happiness, albeit fraudulent, or the absence of food-related bullshit. I've seen firsthand *the damage this drug leaves in its wake. Would it really steal my personality? Alter my soul? Make me not me after a while? I say no. I say I will never get as fucked up as Lance did. I tell myself it's just fine because even withdrawal sounds decent: lack of appetite and vomiting. I'm already looking forward to jeopardizing my life to drive up tomorrow or Tuesday. It's a thrill. It's an escape, an asinine, deadly one, but anyone who tells me I'm ridiculous can shut the fuck up. Until someone has spent a day in this prison of a psyche, they could not possibly understand how desperate this disease has made me. Or how amazing it is to be able to enjoy a portion of the day amidst what is usually sheer hell.*

*Don't misunderstand. I probably don't know what real hell is until I've experienced full-blown drug addiction . . . but I can say with utmost confidence that it cannot possibly be as godawful as bulimia.*

### September 2, 2005

*I have used heroin every day, save for one, for about a month now. Lance is in rehab. I have lost considerable interest in bulimia but not in the vain pursuit of physical perfection. I do not like who I am turning into, but somewhere, I am inwardly pleased. That panicking, frantic voice that arose when looking in a mirror one to two months ago has subsided to a watchful, ominous murmur: "Steady pace. Nothing rash. You're alright, just stay this course. It won't be like it was last time."*

*I ignore calls from the pastor, his wife, and congregation members my age. Let me do it alone.*

*I know I am a fool. But I do not want to be turned away. I do not want to be rejected. If I remain by myself, at a safe distance from God, family, friends, and lovers, no one can leave me.*

### September 4, 2005

*I have been two days without. It's sick. I've tried to withdraw money from an already overdrawn account. I've tried to cash a check at Shaw's. I've tried calling the credit card company I already owe $5,000 to establish a PIN number so I could withdraw money from an ATM. I took one of my mother's checks. I stole $100 out of someone's purse at work.*

*It feels like the whole world is caving in. I've traded the problem I'm sick of dealing with for a more vicious, costly one that, praise God, has released me from the grip of bulimia for days. It's an asinine solution to a problem I just* cannot beat. There was a safe way to beat it once. Trouble was, it involved trusting and relying upon an unseen force—one I felt uncomfortable trusting completely. Actually, it wasn't discomfort; it was sheer pride. I want to be the one to beat this, to find my way out of this maze. All alone.

I am cold and tired and dizzy, experiencing a low-grade withdrawal. Lance said seven days. I'm sitting here trying to justify heroin as my friend, as yet another but less insidious monster than bulimia. I'm sitting here just as I sat on these steps years ago when every instinct in my body told me bulimia was something too big, too good, too wild to be able to keep in check. One day it would control me. Now my rebellious spirit is saying the same thing about heroin; I don't care. I want this badly enough to accept that I may very well pay beyond dearly for this in the future.

### October 16, 2005

I move methodically, slowly. I feel exposed. All bone and muscle with the occasional belly roll that is impossible to conceal.

I have not written in about two months and am ashamed of it. I haven't attended church or kept in contact with anyone but Lance. I haven't furthered myself. I regard Arizona as little more than a dream. I just exhale a bit more easily at the fact that I can eat a bowl, even two if I want, of Raisin Bran without being overtaken, without bingeing, without purging. And yes, I do consider this an accomplishment. Even if it is the solitary one I have to show for $124,000 worth of therapy.

# "Peace when I die"

## January 11, 2006

It's difficult to continue writing if you are ashamed of what you have become. It's painful to face. I have become someone who would rather hide from everyone else's judgmental eyes and from my own, ten thousand times more critical eyes.

I've been fired. Eight days ago today, and the story I've fabricated is one I almost entirely believe now. I'm extraordinarily lucky I wasn't caught in the act.

Still today was charmed. I was accepted into a free CNA course due to a letter I'd composed from grit, instinct. Dad also composed a letter (Mom did, too) for my boss at Seaside, one that I hadn't the courage to write myself. Dad's forgiveness and acceptance and complete lack of grudge regarding my negligence of our relationship touched me. (How wrenching it must be for a parent to watch a relationship with a child deteriorate.) It provided me with a real-life illustration of God's love, of the way God would welcome me back, despite whatever has transpired.

When Dad said he was going to pray with me for God's will regarding my getting re-hired, I cringed. Knowing the truth of the matter, it felt blasphemous.

## January 25, 2006—1:00 a.m.

Awful, wretched human being. I am driving myself mad looking for "missing" drugs for hours upon hours. Since Lance swore by his innocence, I am convinced that, yes, I did move them, did take them out of the bullet necklace. But I have scoured my room, the living room, even looked in my roommates' rooms. I will risk my stupid loan officer job. I will risk my clean record. I will risk being able to pay rent to find these drugs. I don't care.

Awful, awful bastard. We should be falling together right now. I really loved having him here. I really liked cooking with him, driving with him, showering with him, reading with him, conniving with him. So I keep searching this room for the heroin. Of course, it has to be here! Of course, this is just some terrible mistake. He wouldn't, couldn't betray me for so cheap a price. His tears, his claims—that someone spied on us through the glass door, climbed up the back deck, and took it in the night—were so genuine. Or he sleepwalked out here and accidentally moved it. Last night was foggy—I was drinking. I was using, and I took sleeping pills. I was processing too much information for this new job: mortgages and loan consolidation and refinancing. What magnificent hiding place did I decide upon last night? He said in such a convincing way that he hoped I'd find it first thing.

I can't taste the last of the heroin anymore. I want to find the missing bags, drive back to Tiverton, and get Lance. We'll split it and return to the apartment exhausted but relieved. Lance will go to Providence to buy more. I will make it through nine hours of work. The W-2 will have come, and we'll be swimming in a tax refund by this time tomorrow.

Where haven't I yet looked?!

### January 27, 2006—5:00 p.m.

I quit the job at AmeriFi. Or rather, I just didn't show up. After not sleeping all night, I knew going there at nine a.m. was definitely not happening. So, between MaryBeth calling and informing me of the CNA course beginning Feb. 20th, and Middletown Baptist Church asking me to chaperone a Youth Encountering Christ retreat, I suspect selling mortgage loans was not the direction the Lord intended for me. Chasing large commission-based paychecks would undoubtedly encourage a burgeoning dope addiction. Right now, I just want to take my hands off the steering wheel and allow my Father to drive. I must stay away from Lance, or more specifically, from anything that might lead me to be trapped again. So I found the YEC trip to be a perfect escape, a perfect way to readjust my internal compass.

With a CNA degree, I'll be able to work anywhere in the country. Arizona. I felt like _me_ in Arizona. I certainly do _not_ as of late.

### February 1, 2006

Today I did drugs, ate way too much, made one awkward phone call to secure a reference for a nanny position, and read. I did shower. Right now my belly feels swollen, and I am contemplating eating a bit more and then purging. It isn't late enough, though, and I'd prefer to have everyone in the house sleeping so I can run the garbage disposal in the other kitchen. The one on our side doesn't seem to be working properly anymore.

I miss Lance. My heart fell a bit when I learned from Ken that Lance had been admitted to SSTAR at two p.m. I wanted to talk to him, apologize for the terribly harsh words I screamed at him in his driveway. For pushing him away from my car so I could slam the door and drive off. I'd been trying to make him see that he did indeed have motivation; he overcomes impossible obstacles to get drugs. Why couldn't he channel some of this motivation into trying to find a rehab? I guess he did.

## April 22, 2006

Mom and Dad must be right when they say it's the "evil one" who convinces me that I am not worthy to approach You because I'm not walking with You. I'm not too proud to confess my sins and ask forgiveness; I just, as You know, find it immoral to promise to stop sinning when I know in hours I will do it again. Thank goodness you know my heart. You know why I do things. You know more about me than I know about myself. How do I thank You for Your patience? I feel the peace in working at becoming like You; it's like reaching my hands towards a campfire.

Father, I am afraid of so many things. More than obesity, poverty, or death, I fear emptiness. Every second of the day, I focus on abating it. I jump from one preoccupying task/activity to the next, incessantly asking myself if I am alright in the sense that the overwhelming void is not overtaking me.

Father, please give me the desire to stop using, to seek another way. As my Father, You know my weaknesses and fears, so I drop my burdens at Your feet. Begrudgingly. Because as wicked, deceitful, and damaging as the addiction is . . . I hold it dear. But I know only too well my escape is also my entrapment. Please, instill in me the desire to seek You instead of drugs. I pray for clear thoughts, ears that hear Your voice, my stubborn pride to recede, and obedience.

## April 28, 2006

I've loved working at Dad's house cleaning these past few days. Flirting with the idea of re-establishing myself as a family member with this unlikely collection of people. Or, rather, if I'm drawn in, seeing if I'm invited and encouraged to stay. I move through the rooms polishing everything till it gleams as if to prepare for a new life, wondering if living among them is even a remote possibility.

It's funny to be around my father. No matter how hard I scrub, I cannot erase this lingering grudge, the hurt that didn't heal. Every time Cam looks at me, is she remembering what I did? Opening the closet that had once been my father's but was suddenly filled with her clothes. Running my fingers along the satins and silks in vibrant colors and gorgeous prints. Eventually slipping some on. Weren't my intentions blatantly obvious? Didn't she see that I was just a little girl trying to mimic the exotic beauty of a woman who had stolen my father's attention?

### May 3, 2006

I had a serious meltdown today. Between finding out my driver's license will be suspended in a month due to an outstanding traffic violation, and my bank account being overdrawn by $1,000, and then my unemployment check conveniently being direct deposited into the delinquent account, and then the dope running out with not even twenty dollars to our names, I proceeded to throw a sizable "we might not have any drugs for a few hours" tantrum. With tears streaming down my face over my vast financial woes, I literally ran from the bank to the parking lot where my car was dead. Lance (gasp) called my father for a jump while I desperately tried to piece together a story that might cause Dad to cough up some cash, yet not make me look like a fucking addict.

Mission not accomplished.

When Dad showed up, he told me a detective had questioned both him and my mother about my whereabouts. So tomorrow I have to go to the police station and tell them I have no recollection of my gas theft activities in Warren and hope I am not arrested, held in a jail cell overnight, and lose the medical license I have been working on for the past four months.

My father disgustedly sized me up and told me I look like a junkie. Yes, I am skinny (and quite tired of being reminded of it, frankly), and yes, I was dressed in a tattered, red hoodie. Yes, my face looked frightful after crying in front of complete strangers while begging for any amount of my own (albeit overdrawn) money. Still, my father's words were like a curse, a self-fulfilling prophecy. My precarious water-treading self-esteem plummeted to inaccessible places. I felt like the biggest lost cause.

### May 6, 2006- 6:00 a.m.

I just can't face the authorities. I know in my gut if I go in and tell the truth, it will involve arrest. I will have a permanent criminal record and automatically lose my CNA license, and basically trash my future hopes of becoming a nurse (or doctor?) or 75% of other career prospects. So for three days now, I've been lying low.

## May 9, 2006

Every day is depressingly the same. I try to sleep as long as possible to make the rations last longer. I watch television all day and take little 1/9–1/11 blasts,[92] chain-smoke, eat Starbursts, and paint my finger and toenails. I don't shower. I'll engage in one activity in the late afternoon, a tag-along drug run or trip to the grocery store. Today it was tanning and coffee with Dad.

The last few days I've realized, much to my relief, that one day, even if I can never find my way out of the downward spiraling maze, I'll get to have peace when I die. Today I realized I really wanted to just have God take me. Take me home and away from this.

## May 23, 2006

Lance is talking about quitting. I want the days back when I could have four bags. The other night, after working dry, Lance prepared his cottons for me and gave me my first injection. I was completely against it at first, but he assured me I wouldn't get high, just avoid being sick till the next morning. Instead, I was up all night with no sleep aid. No drugs, no pills, not even any alcohol. It was torture. Finally, at four am, I took half a Suboxone[93] and another half three hours later. I had the chills, the sweats, and an awful craving. I'm expecting Lance to bring some at noon, but I'm guessing it'll be more around 1:30 p.m. Either way, it's seven to nine more hours. Of course, I've turned my back on God again, so I obsess over drugs. There is a definite pattern here:

Begin to draw closer to God

Sin

Feel I can't approach Him because I don't stop sinning and thus cannot truly repent

Distance myself/turn my back

Get desperate and empty

Back to #1

## June 16, 2006

I haven't journaled in weeks. Everything has declined. I will not state what I've resorted to, but when I read this later, I will remember. At this time, I am too ashamed to name these sins.

We have no money or credit cards. Quite mysteriously, we lose incredible quantities of our rations nearly every day. Just yesterday, Lance's bag of four-and-a-half disappeared out of the dresser drawer. I've lost bags as well, and we are far from careless. A few days ago, when the last one I had painstakingly saved vanished, I cried and cried and cursed God, telling Him to stay out of my things. God must be the culprit! I can arrive at no other conclusion. To lose packets of heroin when I KNOW I deliberately hid them in very specific places is beyond maddening.

## June 17, 2006

I don't want to stop.

Lance and I writhed around in bed with no prospects for money. We planned to rob the tanning salon but first attempted to rob the people collecting parking money at the beach. That plan failed because it was already two-thirty, and they'd stopped charging. Dejected, Lance refused to go through with our plan to rob the tanning salon.

The withdrawal symptoms are driving me mad. I can handle being sick. I can handle chills, diarrhea, vomiting, even depression. I absolutely cannot bear the acute restlessness that occurs in my shoulders, arms, and wrists. Two minutes of it, and I'm wildly jerking and flailing, screaming obscenities. It is the most intolerable sensation. It is spiders, itching and trailing over millions of mosquito bites that you cannot itch. It's being strapped down during this unbearable, unrelenting tickling. It's wretched enough to drive you to murder.

Wanda was the angel who rescued me. I didn't want to see her, but when she agreed to pay me back the forty dollars she'd owed me for months, I went to her new job at a Greek deli (where either Lance or I might be hired next week). Wanda was the first person to treat me like a human being and not a drug addict. She asked if I'd been keeping my food down. She gave us a hundred dollars for dope, God bless her, and knew precisely what she was doing. "I just don't want you to be sick," she said. Then she hugged us and told us not to resort to theft but to come see her first.

If she only knew we steal everything: gas, food, cigarettes. If she only knew I've sold myself for forty dollars and welcomed the opportunity. Lance is the only witness to this crime. This is why I avoid my family and have severed friendships. I am a shadow of my former self and ashamed of it. I'd rather be a recluse than keep up these phony appearances. I don't care to share my opinions, learn about other people, or get back in touch with myself. Beautifying myself internally—being content and lit from within—used to be of utmost importance to me. Now it doesn't matter. Nothing does, scary as it sounds, not even the condition of my soul.

### June 20, 2006

So Lance is in detox (again). I'm glad; I feel a burden lifted. I have a whole bed to stretch out in. I can eat food I like, without worrying about him.

"We might never see each other again," he said on the way up.

"Don't be silly," I said, but the idea sounded too good to be true.

I have eight more days till my appointment to start detox. I don't want to go. I told Dad this on Father's Day when we were talking on the deck. "Well, then it has to get even worse," he said. While making him vow never to tell Mom, I admitted I had had sex for money. He said he feared that might happen. He hugged me, but it wasn't a full, loving embrace. And he still didn't offer me money. I don't get this. If I had a daughter using drugs, I would rather give her money than have her subjected to selling her body. My parents refusing to help me financially does not discourage using. It only encourages desperation. I wonder if my mother would still refuse if she knew.

### June 23, 2006

I have been to Providence copping drugs every day this week. I also succeeded on my first attempt at injections the past three days. I'm frustrated; they're not fulfilling. I tell myself this is because I'm snorting too much (which I am). Everything important to me no longer is. Family, religion, exercise, self-awareness, cultivation of my soul, art, expression, relationships.

I'm working at the deli, and I've stolen ninety dollars in the last two days. I cannot afford to lose that job, yet twenty-five dollars a day is pathetic. I want to ask Drakos for forty dollars a day. I just don't think it's worthwhile otherwise; I'm sacrificing much-needed sleep and much-desired beach time, but business is so slow I know it's useless to ask.

### June 28, 2006

I went with Lance up to Providence this morning. Some guy promised we could get something awesome from a new spot on Potter's Street. After nearly an hour, I happily surrendered my last one hundred dollars for five bags. I called Drakos to tell him I'd be thirty minutes late, and he said it was dead and not to bother coming in. Then tonight, he texted telling me not to come in tomorrow. I cringe, wondering if Drakos matched the money missing from the register to my pinpoint pupils.

Tomorrow afternoon I'll have to resort to prostitution, apparently. I can't call Wanda; Drakos fired her. Lance refuses to rob the tanning salon, the fool. I feel crazed with craving. I just want to be high for fifteen minutes.

## July 1, 2006

I haven't slept since Thursday afternoon, but thanks to amphetamines and Vivarin, I feel well. I couldn't sleep because I was worrying about money. I ended up calling Lance's mother and borrowing a hundred and fifty dollars for "rent."

I called my mother to see if she'd help with gas. She said she wouldn't help me until I helped myself. I told her without help, I was driven to do illegal things. What I wanted to say was: "I'm your daughter. I'm choosing to do this whether you help me or not. Your refusals will cause me to resort to prostitution. Do you still think you're helping me?" I didn't say this, of course. I did, however, make the mistake of telling her I really had no desire to live anymore. I couldn't hide my hopelessness. Something in me, which is very, very alarmed, is increasingly willing to speak openly about this.

## July 8, 2006

Dad, the sweet, helpful little man, told Lance's mom that I use. This not only sabotages quite a few "operations" for Lance and me, but it is incredibly mortifying. Why my parents feel the need to stomp my reputation into the ground is beyond me. I will never forgive them for gossiping about my issues. When I realized I had no way to escape my anger here at work, it only magnified. I had no binge food. I couldn't use drugs—I was already beginning to nod ever since I pulled over on the side of the road on my way here and shot up in my car. Any more dope, and I will pass out. Now what do I do?

## July 21, 2006

I'm sitting in my room at a quarter of three a.m., debating whether to take Chantelle's car without permission to go to Stop & Shop. I have no food. Plus, I found her ATM card with her PIN printed on it.

I am officially a junkie.

I crashed my uninsured car into a Jeep three days ago while attempting to shoot dope, using the cord on my cell phone charger as a tie-off.

Yesterday I snuck into the unlocked apartment downstairs to use their phone and searched through a wallet right next to it. I go through any abandoned purse or wallet I come across. I steal roughly thirty dollars a day from the register at the deli. My forearms have green, enormous bruises on them and studded red track marks along the predominant vein. I am terrified of heroin withdrawal since I began injecting; I just know it is going to be worse, and I would prefer suicide to quitting.

Everything negative that has happened to me in the past year has been a result of this. Maybe I should try to get another job at a hotel. I often reminisce about opening those wedding envelopes and pocketing wads of hundred-dollar bills.

I fuck everything up; every secret is out. It's only a matter of time, with my recklessness, before I am found out at the nursing home and stripped of my license. I caught Gloria looking at my arms the last shift. She is street smart. She's seen those marks before. They just don't align with my personality yet. All it will take is for one of the nurses to casually mention the broad spectrum of my pupil dilation, and I'm done. Yet will I stop shooting up around corners of the building two to three times a night to avoid this? I doubt it very much. The ice I skate on isn't even ice anymore. It's like wax paper coated in a thin layer of frost. If I am late to the deli again, I'm done. Then I'll have no spare cash.

I hate being alive lately. My needles are dull, and I am tearing apart the green bruises on my arms to reach the portions of vein that have not yet collapsed.

## August 13, 2006

So this is my first night without. It'd be easier if I knew I was getting more today, but I know it's over unless I go up to buy enough to intentionally OD. It's as I imagined it would be—tedious, empty, the VOID sign flashing. The only thing I have to look forward to is the escape sleep provides. Otherwise, I really haven't the foggiest idea how to live like this. I miss the taste. I could cry at how badly I want to feel thin steel pierce my veins, the faint shuddering of eyelids. Maybe I do need jail. I really don't care about anything; let the tide take me.

## August 14, 2006

For whatever reason, I didn't expect going without heroin to be like this. I see no point to anything. In fact, suicide by OD'ing seems a more viable option than a fifteen-month residential treatment program. This is like déjà vu: the unwillingness to relinquish control and accept much-needed help. I am trying so hard not to crave dope. I feel like if I dwell on the particulars of what I miss, I will go and get it, and then what? It's jail or suicide, the latter being more attractive.

It's only been two days.

I spent the day sleeping and eating. I broke into someone's Jack Daniel's. I caught a buzz and felt just the smallest bit better.

Earlier I dug in the kitchen trash for the bag of paraphernalia I had disposed of after learning the house was under surveillance. Much to my dismay, I remembered flushing the cottons. There was nothing, and I broke down in the kitchen. That's when I started hitting the bottle.

I called my mother crying and told her I wasn't doing well. She wanted to pick me up and take me to her house. Dad says she has things planned for tomorrow. Art projects, completing the paperwork for Mercy Ministries. I have plans too. They involve getting drunk and sleeping through as much of life as possible.

## August 17, 2006

I am pushing my fucking luck. I knew I shouldn't have bought three yesterday for a hundred and fifty dollars. I spent another hundred and forty on the Adderall script.

Yesterday Ethan called Dad because apparently I nodded out on the kitchen counter—twice—and was mumbling incoherently. My father called my mother, who rushed over with a jug of OJ. He showed up moments later; both were alarmed as all hell, fearing the absolute worst.

"I almost called an ambulance!" Dad ranted. "What is your blood sugar? Check it right now in front of me!"

It read high—translation: above six hundred.

Dad peered into my room. "Is Lance here?"

I blamed it on the ridiculously severe hyperglycemia and extreme sleep deprivation. Obviously, I didn't mention the Klonopin or the three bags I shot in the Dunkin' Donuts bathroom.

## August 18, 2006

I want it so bad right now I'd risk jail to get it. I'm trying so hard to avoid even thinking about it . . . fearful that I'll be driven mad, running from this nursing home to the filthy streets of Providence.

It's so hard to have nothing to look forward to except court, a likely license suspension, and Teen Challenge, this god-awful residential facility with no cigarettes. How can I be expected to comply with this bullshit? I fucking hate myself for the nights I took for granted when I snuck out of here during a break with a pocket full of pre-filled syringes. What I wouldn't give for just one of those now.

*July–August 19, 2006*
*age twenty-two*

# Tough Love

Perry and I did not learn about Rachel's heroin addiction until ten months later when Matt's roommate, Ethan, found her unconscious at their kitchen table.

In June of 2006, before starting his first semester at the University of Rhode Island (URI), 18-year-old Matt had moved into a four-bedroom, two-bathroom, and two-kitchen apartment in Middletown with two friends. He offered Rachel the fourth room. I had discouraged the move, especially for Matt, for whom it would be costly, non-conducive to studying, and inconvenient—URI was twenty miles away. However, Matt wanted "the full college experience," which included sleeping with his pretty new girlfriend, Chantelle.

I could not fathom why neither Matt nor Rachel called. All summer long, I did not receive one invitation to see their place. If I phoned them, they were short.

My grief was compounded by losing thirteen-year-old Ryan, who had just moved in with his dad. I didn't think it would last. When at thirteen Matt had tried living with Perry, Matt had phoned that same night, coughing and wheezing, begging me to deliver him from the dust and dog hair. To my chagrin, Ryan stayed. We still had Krissy, but she had quite a social calendar. I used to dream of this day when the kids would be gone and silence would reign. When it came, I felt surprisingly hollow.

One day, I packed a grocery bag with fruit, paper products, and Rachel's favorite canned soups and rang their bell. I heard raucous male laughter and heavy metal music. Matt cracked the door, the chain latch still attached, and I was assaulted with a blast of mingled cigar and pot smoke. I saw only half of his face, and it was not smiling.

His voice was flat. "Mom, you need to call first."

After that, I left them alone.

Eventually, Rachel phoned to tell me that Matt was sleeping with Chantelle. She saw pink pregnancy wands in their wastebasket. She said the boys were slobs. They constantly drank, smoked, and played poker but never washed dishes or picked up their clothes.

Days later, I talked to Matt about the sex when he stopped by to borrow our cooler. He scorned every admonishment I proposed. Like the pot, he had it under control.

Then Rachel informed me that Matt was *selling* marijuana.

I drove back over, enduring his frowning half-face behind the cracked door.

"I want to talk to you, Matt. Let's go to the parking lot." He followed without protest.

I cut to the chase. "I know you're selling drugs."

His face reddened, I thought because he was ashamed.

"Did you know Lance has been living here, holed up in Rachel's room?" His eyes glared at being ratted out by Rachel, whose heroin addiction, I would soon learn, he'd been hiding for months.

"This is about *you*, Matt. If you get caught *using* pot, it's a hand slap. *Selling* pot is a whole different ball game. You could go to prison. Then you can kiss your future goodbye. This is *serious*, Matt!"

"I swear, I'm so careful, Mom! I only sell to people I know."

"Don't be ridiculous! All it takes is one cop to see one deal. Moreover, it's *wrong*, Matt. You're helping other kids break the law. Why would you do this?"

"I need the money for college, Mom! I'm stressed out, having to pay for rent and school. My Chili's job is just not cutting it. I'm not getting any help from you or Dad."

It was true. I had helped Matt apply for scholarships, as well as co-signed a high-interest loan, against my better judgment, but I had not contributed to his tuition. Our finances were tight, and whatever we did for one child, we had to do for all.

"Matt, I'll try to scrape up some cash for your tuition, but you have to promise to stop this *immediately*."

"I'll think about it, Mom," he said, nodding. "I really will."

✦   ✦   ✦

THE DAY I RECEIVED Matt's urgent call that Rachel had been found unconscious at their kitchen table, I rushed over to the apartment. Perry arrived moments later. Rachel was still at the table, rallying around, trying in a garbled voice to pass her condition off as low blood sugar. She looked skeletal in her gray gym shorts and pink camisole. Her hair was twisted into a messy bun, revealing the knotty vertebrae of her spine. Her eyelids were half-drawn shades. Quasi-aware of our presence, she fought to keep her eyes open and keep her bobblehead erect.

Perry and I hoisted her up, one of us on each side, her back and arms so frail, and guided her into bed. That day, Lance was not there.

Rachel agreed to see me the following day before she left for work. I was stricken again by how thin she looked in her periwinkle scrubs. Five months earlier, she had gotten her certified nursing assistant (CNA) license after being fired from the Seaside Manor for theft, an allegation she vehemently denied. With her hair in a tight ponytail, her head looked enlarged, like a starving Biafran baby's. The vein on her forehead was now a constant fixture. She had finally achieved her goal, and she looked terrible.

I wanted to ask her why she would resort to the drug that had taken Lance down—*why, why, why* after the horror she had seen. But Lance was there, stretched out on her double bed, wearing a wife beater and black running shorts. An air conditioner rattling in the window beside him ruffled his black hair. After acknowledging me with a solemn hello, his eyes returned to his noisy cop show. I would ask her that question later, at different times and in different ways. Her answer was always the same: Heroin took away her hunger.

That day I simply asked her to stop. Asked her to let me get her help. She said no. She was not ready to. She wanted to keep using a lethal street drug though her life had already begun to topple.

The Seaside Manor was not the only job she lost. She also had to resign from her nanny job. After learning about her addiction, I met with a drug counselor, who agreed that she could not be trusted to care for her two small charges, ages four and six.

Eventually, Rachel prostituted herself for drugs. She told Perry, who told me—a visceral punch. *My God, how much lower could she sink?* And I couldn't utter a word because she had made him vow never to tell me. What would I have said to my daughter anyhow? What did I know about that level of back-alley desperation?

On July eighteenth, Rachel crashed her uninsured car into a jeep while driving to Providence to buy drugs. She said it happened in the second she looked down to switch radio stations. No one was hurt, but her car was totaled. She was arrested and forced to pay a hefty fine for driving without insurance.

Days later, Rachel was caught buying drugs in Providence and arrested again. Only this time, she was incarcerated for possession and scheduled for arraignment the next day. However, when a Red Cross medic noted her raging blood sugars and severe withdrawal symptoms, she was transferred to Rhode Island Hospital for three days while her sugars were stabilized and she was detoxed.

On the third day, as the attending physician prepared to discharge Rachel, I panicked. I informed him that only days earlier, Rachel had totaled her car while going to buy drugs. Diabetes and drug addiction were the least of her problems, I explained. She had been battling bulimia for years.

Clean cut and thirtyish, Dr. Ledger stared at me intently through silver-rimmed glasses. Retrieving a pen from the pocket of his medical coat, he began writing notes on her chart while I recounted Rachel's rehabilitation and relapse.

"That's why she uses heroin. To quiet her urges. Otherwise, she binges and purges multiple times a day. If you release her, I *know* she'll start using again." I paused, preparing to voice fears I had never told anyone. Dr. Ledger was staring now, his pen still.

"My daughter's a danger to herself. She's *not* well. She needs more treatment. *Right now.*" Near tears, I admitted, "I'm afraid she's going to kill herself if she doesn't get help."

Nodding, Dr. Ledger agreed that Rachel's co-occurring issues could be dangerous. He recommended that she be transferred to St. Joseph's, a dual-treatment in-patient facility for substance abuse and psychiatric issues in Fall River, Massachusetts. He made a call and informed me that they had one available bed. They would take her today if Blue Cross approved, which miraculously they did.

My heart soared. Rachel was finally going to get help, and not just for her addiction, but for whatever psychological issues were driving her self-destructive behavior. I had begun to believe that she needed to be in a locked facility until someone figured out what was wrong.

"Now we just have to get Rachel onboard," Doctor Ledger said.

I deflated. "Can't we just transfer her over there?"

He shook his head. "Dr. Fischer, our psychiatrist, has found her mentally competent. Because she's an adult, she can't be admitted against her will."

Rachel declined to be transferred to St. Joseph's, opting to be treated at CODAC, an outpatient center for substance abuse in Newport. No amount of coaxing from Dr. Ledger or me could change her mind.

Driving home from the hospital, Rachel and I hardly spoke. As I merged onto I-195 South, I tried to relax. I loved this stretch of highway. Bordered by trees on both sides, it was beautiful in any season. Today the sky was an impossibly beautiful blue with puffy white clouds. The sun shone majestically through emerald leaves, creating a scintillating tunnel of green.

*Embrace this day. July's nearly over. Before you know it, the cold'll creep in.*

But I couldn't see anything but red. I was furious that Rachel was sitting beside me when she could have been tucked safely in a hospital bed at St. Joseph's. Livid that a heroin addict with a severe ED who had just crashed her car for the second time in weeks had been released. On *what,* pray tell, had Dr. Fischer based Rachel's mental stability? Oh, she could spin a pretty story, fooling people with her vocabulary alone.

Rachel was angry, too. Not only for being "forced into treatment," but also for finding seven hundred dollars missing from her wallet when we retrieved her belongings from the Providence Police Department, cash the police had confiscated during the arrest and had given me to hold until she was clean. We rode home in stony silence, Rachel staring out the window.

Opposed as I was to Rachel's treatment choice, I drove directly to CODAC in downtown Newport to get the process rolling.

As Rachel signed in, I recalled my own visit to CODAC weeks earlier when, not knowing the first thing about heroin, I had sought guidance there.

I was paired with a counselor named Rob. Tall, slim, and fiftyish, he had greeted me in the waiting room with a grin and a firm, warm handshake. His thinning sandy hair was camouflaged by a spikey youthful cut. He wore a white linen shirt, Khaki shorts, loafers sans socks, and a small gold hoop in one ear.

Rob led me down a narrow hall into a cubicle-sized office where books abounded in cases and on shelves. His tidy desk was pushed against a wall. Above it hung three framed diplomas, including a Ph.D. in psychology from Harvard University. Rob gestured me toward the only chair next to his.

"What can I do for you?" he asked, his vulnerable blue eyes magnified by wire-rimmed bifocals.

Rob's eyes appeared even larger when I confided that my heroin-addicted daughter was working as a nanny. "She needs to resign," he said. "Of course, you'll want to encourage her to do it herself, with the understanding that if *she* doesn't, *you* will." After a few awkward moments of silence, he asked, "What else can I do for you?"

"I—I just want to keep my daughter safe," I stammered, my voice cracking.

Nodding, Rob reached over to open the lowest drawer of the file cabinet in front of me, I thought, to grab a notepad. Instead, he stretched out his long legs, using the drawer as a footstool while settling into his black leather executive chair.

"Tell me, are you very affectionate with your daughter?"

I was taken aback. This was an odd question.

"Probably not enough," I confessed, studying the tassels on his shoes.

Though I had lavished my kids with affection when they were silken infants and chubby-cheeked toddlers, as they grew, I hugged them less. And for some reason I couldn't explain, I felt especially uneasy embracing Rachel.

"Why do you think that is?"

My throat started to ache, my eyes to leak.

"Did your mother show you very much affection?"

Tears were falling now. I had felt her hand only in anger, her stinging slap on my arms or face, though sometimes she favored a fly swatter or a wooden spoon. How foreign was the hand of my aunt Ginny tenderly stroking my sweaty back as I retched into her toilet, having caught some nasty bug while visiting her at age ten. I did not want her to see or smell this mess. At the same time, I was desperately grateful for her loving touch that magically quelled my nausea, convincing me I wasn't going to die on her bathroom floor.

Rob nearly toppled the file cabinet, scrambling to pass me the Kleenex. As I blew my nose, he offered to support me through these unchartered waters with Rachel. I readily accepted.

Rob would become Rachel's counselor months later when my therapy had run its course and she had become disgruntled with her counselor, Ann-Marie. However, the first day, Rachel followed Anne-Marie down the same hall, returning in what seemed like minutes with a plan to commence methadone therapy in one week.

Afterward, Rachel said she needed something from Stop & Shop. I dropped her at the door, parking in a space nearby. While waiting, I called Perry, who was taking a break from Rachel, galled that she had "turned into a junkie" before he had put a dent in his Remuda bill. This would become his pattern. His support would wax and wane, depending on her gratitude or compliance, but he always wanted intel.

I waited five, ten, twenty minutes. Rachel could lose herself in grocery stores. Sighing, I went in to find her. After scanning aisle after aisle, teeth chattering in the sub-zero temperature, I spotted her emerging from the restroom. As she meandered through Produce, I noticed her holding something—a pint of blueberries, on which sat what looked like an open package of shoestrings, one white lace dangling. *What was she doing with shoestrings in July?* As her dazed eyes and droopy lids came into focus, I gasped. She'd shot up in the restroom.

✦　　✦　　✦

I DECIDED I'D BEEN a rotten mom. How else could this have happened? I hadn't hugged or played with Rachel enough; I hadn't tried hard enough to crack her teenage silence. I only had two hands, and I probably addressed the boys' needs first. They demanded my attention. When I was distant, Matt would take my face in his two small hands, turning it toward him. At thirteen months, Ryan had tugged on the hem of my pink silk robe, a gift to myself to replace my threadbare flannel one, until I removed it and gave it to him. Henceforth, I couldn't pry it out of his dimpled hands; he slept swathed in pink silk while I returned to my flannel. The boys seemed more needy, maybe because Ryan was the baby and Matthew spent a good chunk of his child-hood in an oxygen tent due to his asthma. Rachel was strong, independent. She could take care of herself. Or so I thought.

I resolved to change. I would become the best mother I could be right now. It wasn't too late. Hadn't Mom taught me that? She had turned into a loving mother when she was forty-six and I was twenty-four. I would do the same for Rachel. Support her in this crisis and from now on, no matter what.

The first order of business was her health. She had been complaining of numbness in her left foot. On August first, I took her to a podiatrist, who diagnosed her with *foot drop*. He said this temporary condition was often related to a larger problem. He referred us to a neurologist who saw Rachel the next day.

"You have neuropathy, nerve damage, in both feet," the neurologist told us after performing a battery of tests. "Do you take care of your diabetes, Rachel?"

She shook her head.

"Prolonged high blood sugars probably caused the damage."

"Is it reversible?" I asked, swallowing.

"Unfortunately, the damage is done, but Rachel can prevent further injury by maintaining tighter diabetic control. You should follow up with your endocrinologist."

Exiting the doctor's office, I felt ill.

Rachel appeared undaunted. It was lunchtime, and she wanted to eat.

We walked to a noisy, crowded deli next door that smelled like pastrami. In a daze, I ordered two boxed lunches that we brought to the car.

"This is really good," she remarked after a few bites of her turkey-avocado wrap. "I had no idea how hungry I was." She ate some kettle chips, her crunching audible in the silence.

"Why aren't you eating, Mom?"

I had spread a napkin in my lap, placing half the wrap on it. At her prompting, I took a bite. While I was chewing, tears fell down my cheeks. One dangled from my nose.

"What is *wrong* with you?"

"I'm sick!" I erupted, wiping my face with my napkin. "Didn't you hear what he said? Your feet have irreparable nerve damage!" While I spoke, I stuffed the wrap back in my box.

It seemed like some cruel fluke. Neuropathy happened to older people who'd had diabetes for decades and stopped taking care of themselves. Rachel was only twenty-one. No doubt she'd been neglecting her diabetes since she'd been using heroin, but that had only been several months, way too soon for complications. Little did I know that by then she'd been restricting insulin for over seven years.

"So what?" she said, biting into the second half of her wrap.

On August eighth, I sat in Dr. D.'s waiting room while Rachel had blood drawn. She was way overdue for her A1c test. Wearing pink scrubs and purple Crocs, she walked back from the lab as if in slow motion. The poor thing was probably exhausted after having worked third shift the night before. When I had picked her up from Rest View Nursing Home that morning, she dozed all the way to Providence. Now, though she tried to read a *Vogue* magazine, she kept nodding out. Only when a nurse called her name did Rachel snap to attention.

"How are you doing, Rachel?" Dr. D. asked, smiling as he always did when he entered the examination room. If he was concerned about her blood work, he did not show it, nor did he flinch at her appearance, though she weighed one twenty-five, nine pounds less than her last visit.

Rachel told him straight out about the heroin. He didn't scold; however, he did mention that heroin raised her sugars while making her apathetic and thus less inclined to manage her diabetes.

Dr. D. informed us that Rachel's blood sugar was 571, and her A1c was 15. There was no need to interpret those numbers for her. He knew that she knew they were grotesquely elevated, healthy sugars being between 73 and 113, and a good A1c under 7.

"Rachel, I'd like you to aim for tighter control by testing at least three times a day and increasing your insulin."

"That's going to be tough, Doc," Rachel said matter-of-factly, "since Blue Cross just dumped me. Test strips are pricey even *with* insurance."

Eyebrows raised, Dr. D. turned to me. Nodding, I confirmed that our application to the Navy for continued health benefits for an adult child incapable of self-support had just been denied, though we were currently appealing it.

"I'd be happy to write a letter on Rachel's behalf to advocate for continued health benefits," Dr. D. offered.

"That would be so helpful," I gushed, but he waved it off.

"Excuse me for one moment, please," he said, exiting the room.

Dr. D. returned, juggling multiple boxes of test strips, vials of insulin, and a glucometer, still in its box. Smiling, he handed these to Rachel, like a diabetic Santa Claus.

"Don't *ever* not take care of your diabetes because you can't afford supplies," he said, looking into her eyes. "Come see me. I'll give you anything you need."

Rachel smiled for the first time in weeks. My eyes welled at his kindness.

While I paid the bill, Rachel rifled through her red backpack, making room, I figured, for her new supplies.

"My journal's missing!" she suddenly announced. "I think I left it at the neurologist's office. We hafta go back'ngedit." Her words slurred together as she fought to stay awake.

"Wait here while I get the car." The way she was weaving, I didn't want her walking far.

✦  ✦  ✦

RACHEL DROPPED INTO THE passenger's seat. In seconds, she was snoring.

She had sworn she was not using, but I was starting to wonder. The cause of her car crash had also continued to gnaw at me. Had she really rear-ended that jeep because she had looked down to switch radio stations, or had she been high out of her mind on heroin?

Once I got to the neurologist's office, I locked Rachel in the car while I retrieved the journal. Reaching under the counter, the smiling receptionist handed me the notebook. I thanked her. Then, with my heart drumming, I ducked into the ladies' room where I broke my own rule: I read my daughter's journal.

Flipping it open, I frantically scanned the entry dates for July eighteenth, the day of her car wreck. There was no entry for that day, but on July twenty-first, she wrote, "I crashed my uninsured car into a jeep three days ago while attempting to shoot dope while driving. I was pulling my cell phone charger onto my forearm to use as a tie-off."

I gasped but could not think about this now. I had to press on to learn if she was still using. Though it was irrational, though Rachel was probably in a deep, drugged sleep, I worried she would burst into the restroom, lambasting me for this breach of privacy. No matter how justified I felt in reading her journal, she would view it as the ultimate betrayal. Her mouth would be frothing, so I read as if the room were on fire. In seconds, I learned that Rachel had stolen cash to support her habit; she was now *shooting* heroin; she was using at work; and she was suicidal.

But that entry was written seventeen days ago. She literally had no means to buy drugs. Her car was totaled, and I was still holding her cash. Moreover, she had started methadone three days ago. I drove her to CODAC daily, myself, and watched her drink red syrup out of a shot-sized plastic cup. Rob had told me, and I'd read it online, that Methadone blocked the effects of heroin; one could *not* get high on heroin while taking Methadone. Still, Rachel's behavior surpassed normal fatigue. The passages I'd just read implied that she would stop at nothing to shoot up. I flipped to her most recent entry, written nine days earlier.

### July 29, 2006

*I'm already beginning to seethe at the mere thought of it: all the fucking ridiculous, stupid, STUPID shit I've done to reduce me to one fucking bag and forty dollars. If Wanda doesn't save my ass tomorrow, I am royally fucked. I have no ride, no money, and no credibility.*

I recalled that Wanda had recently phoned and confessed to lending Rachel her car. When Rachel wrote that entry, she was desperate for drugs. I realized with a sickening pang that she was probably still using.

Closing her journal, I returned to my car, where Rachel was fast asleep. She didn't flinch when I got in and shut my door. Her large black bag lay open on the floor by her feet. I placed the journal inside it and paused. *Do I dare?* My right hand made an executive decision. While backing out of my parking space, I felt around for an inner pocket, the most likely place she would conceal contraband. With my eyes fixed on Rachel, I undid its zipper, dipped in my fingers, and pulled out a small package wrapped in cellophane. Heart racing, I stashed it under my seat.

After dropping Rachel off at her apartment, I sped home. Fortunately, Ryan was at Doreen's, and Krissy was visiting her cousin in New Hampshire. I couldn't wait any longer. The moment I parked, I reached under my seat to retrieve the package. Peeling away layers of cellophane, I discovered four smaller bundles fastened with rubber bands. Removing one of the rubber bands, I counted ten cream-colored, tissue-thin pouches the size of Sweet 'n Low packets. Peering inside one pouch, I saw a beige herb-like substance. I'd never seen heroin before, but I had a hunch I'd just confiscated forty bags of it.

*Now what?*

Rachel would be frantic when she found her drugs missing, but how could she question me without incriminating herself? If she had a quandary, so did I. She would be outraged if she knew I'd searched her purse and taken her drugs. Like my reading her journal, she would view it as the ultimate invasion, but hadn't her lies and crimes and dangerous behavior driven me to it?

Soon Rachel phoned, claiming she had lost some money.

"I'll check the car," I offered, walking outside. I held my cell by the car door so she could hear me opening it while I feigned looking around.

"Nothing in the back. Let me check the passenger's seat where you were sitting. Nope. Oh, wait a minute. What's this? I found something wrapped in cellophane on the floor."

"Mom, don't open it. That's the money. I wrapped it so I wouldn't spend it."

"It doesn't look like money." I faked opening it, crinkling a paper bag that was in the car. "It's packages of something. What—what is this?"

"Mom! No! *Don't!*"

"Oh, my word! Is this *heroin*? I don't believe it! You told me you quit!"

"Mom, it's not that easy! You can't quit heroin overnight." She paused and said more calmly, "Listen. I need that back."

"Are you *crazy*! Do you really think I'm going to return your heroin so you can trash or even *kill* yourself? What kind of a fool do you think I am? I'm going to flush it as soon as I hang up!" In truth, I had no idea what I was going to do with the lethal bundle that I had stashed in my sock drawer.

"Those drugs cost me a lot of money," she said, her tone suddenly cold and measured. "I had to do dangerous things to get them. If you don't give them back, I'll do whatever it takes to get more."

I swallowed, struck by my stupidity, the implications of my actions seeping into my consciousness like water in a sinking car. I had thought that by taking her drugs, I was protecting her, but I had forgotten the obvious—she was an addict who would risk anything to replace them. *Oh, God! What had I done?*

When I didn't answer, Rachel tried another tack.

"Listen, if you give me back my drugs, I'll sign a paper for in-patient drug rehab."

"Like I could trust you to follow through. You've been lying to me this whole time!"

"Then you leave me no choice but to do whatever I have to do to get more." I heard a click, and then the line went dead.

I felt ill.

Now that Rachel knew I had her heroin and was not returning it, what *was* I going to do with those forty packets?

"Call the Middletown cops," Perry urged when I phoned to report what had happened. "If you don't want to, I will. I'll even drop the drugs off myself."

That sounded harsh. Rachel already had one possession charge. Her arraignment was in three days. I did not want her to incur a second felony, especially by my hand.

"Flush the drugs," Phil replied without hesitation when I called him.

That sounded too soft. Discarding the heroin was like saying I never found it; the problem didn't exist.

While pondering this dilemma, I mechanically vacuumed the carpets. My briefcase was bulging with student essays, but I couldn't focus on anything else. As I was filling a basin with hot water to scrub the kitchen floor, my cell rang. The woman identified herself as a drug counselor from Perry's church. Apparently, he had enlisted her help. She said that a teenage client of hers had recently died from a batch of heroin cut with strychnine. She urged me to report the drugs. It was the safest route. It would force Rachel to get clean.

"Some parents think this is too extreme. They flush their kids' drugs. Then when their kids overdose, they never forgive themselves."

"Are you one hundred percent sure this is the right thing to do?" I asked.

"I am."

I thanked her and hung up. Though leaning toward calling the police, I was still deeply conflicted. I poured ammonia in my basin, my eyes stinging from its pungent smell. Kneeling on all fours, I dipped a scrub brush into the sudsy water and began scouring the cold ceramic floor. A judge might waive one felony for a first offense, but probably not two. I scrubbed hard, making wide, circular motions. I did not want Rachel to have a criminal record. Her young life had already been so hard. Though I did not know one-tenth of her turmoil then, I knew she suffered from diabetes, bulimia, and now a drug addiction, not to mention a dysfunctional boyfriend. A criminal record would only wring more hope and happiness out of her life.

The phone rang again, causing me to jump. Coincidentally, it was Rob from CODAC, asking how we were doing. When I updated him, he entreated me not to report the heroin but to wait until our session next week to discuss some alternate plans. I told him I'd consider it. Rob had decades of experience working with addicts. I respected him a lot. But I was sitting on forty bags of heroin. This was urgent.

Again, I was confused. My decision would affect Rachel for the rest of her life. It had to be right. Silencing my cell, I went upstairs to pray. Kneeling by my bed, I poured out the contents of my heavy heart, telling God what He already knew but still wanted to hear: my confusion, anxiety, fear. *Lord, I'm in a dark, dark place, drawn into these shadows by my daughter, who is so lost. Please help me to help her. I cannot find my way.*

A Bible verse from Ephesians came to my mind: "Do not participate in the evil deeds of darkness, but even expose them." The drug in my drawer, I realized with sudden clarity, had not only killed people, but people—addicts and dealers—had killed for this drug. It had caused Rachel to lie, steal, and prostitute herself. It would eventually destroy her. Heroin was that potent, that evil. I wanted it out of my drawer, my room, my house. By turning Rachel in, she might end up with a criminal record, but at least she'd be alive.

Without divulging my name or Rachel's, I phoned the Middletown Police Department and reported the heroin. To my disbelief, the officer informed me that my daughter could not be charged because I had no right to search her bag. I explained that she was a menace to herself, having recently wrecked her car while driving under the influence. I told him about her arrest for possession in Providence. He suggested they pick up the drugs and file a report, which, coupled with her previous charge, might get her court-ordered substance abuse treatment.

It was the ideal solution.

Minutes later, a police car pulled discreetly into our driveway. Phil, who'd just removed his work boots, answered the door. The officer was fortyish, tall, with broad shoulders, short black hair, and penetrating brown eyes.

Removing his hat, he introduced himself as Detective Riccio while firmly shaking our hands.

We sat in our sunroom. The detective retrieved a pen and small, spiral notepad from the breast pocket of his tan uniform. Clicking the pen open, he asked how I'd found the heroin. As I spoke, he scribbled notes. Within minutes, he stood up.

"I think I'm all set." Closing his pen, he returned it to his pocket with the notepad. "If you could just show me the drugs."

The detective's jaw dropped when I returned with the four bundles.

"That's a *tremendous* amount of heroin."

He undid one of the bundles and counted it, as I had; then, eyeing me soberly, said, "I know you were told your daughter wouldn't be charged, but the sheer volume of the heroin changes everything." He hesitated. "I'm afraid I'm going to have to arrest her."

I was just beginning to relax, relieved that I had done the right thing without threatening Rachel's future.

"In fact, it looks like she may have been dealing. *No one* buys this much heroin, and it's packaged to sell."

I eyed the uniform packets, my heart now pumping wildly, erratically.

"You don't know my daughter, Detective! She has an eating disorder. She does everything in excess! I assure you she's *not* dealing!"

"That's right," Phil added. "Rae was squirreling it all away for herself."

"I'm going to take both your word for that, but I still have to arrest her for possession. I'll need her name and address." He sat back down, retrieving notepad and pen. "And I'll need you to write and sign a statement, Ms. DiPasquale."

"How do I know you won't nail her for dealing?"

"I just gave you my word, Ma'am," he said, looking directly into my eyes.

So had the officer on the phone. Yet there was something different about this man. He wasn't tough or cocky, like some cops. I decided to tell him everything—how diabetes had triggered Rachel's ED, which had led to her heroin habit. He nodded sympathetically while I gushed out the whole story, along with my misgivings about turning her in.

"I feel that by giving you her contact information, I'd be striking a match to her future."

"I understand, Ma'am. I have kids, too, but I'm telling you, this is the right thing to do. It's called *tough love,* and it will save your daughter's life."

"I feel like I'm damned if I do and damned if I don't."

"You're more damned if you *don't*," he said, his dark eyes glinting with conviction.

Because his words resonated in my gut and echoed not only my prayer but the Christian drug counselor's advice, I gave him Rachel's name and address.

"Fifty Cardinal Street!" Detective Riccio slapped his creased pant leg. "We've been watching that place for months. I *knew* they were dealing drugs out of that apartment."

As Detective Riccio looked down to record the information in his notepad, Phil and I exchanged panicked glances. I trembled, realizing what I had done.

"Wait, Detective Riccio!" I said with a halting hand. "I can't believe I have to tell you this—frankly, I can't believe *any* of this—but my eighteen-year-old son also lives at that address. He's a college freshman, a good kid, but he started smoking pot in high school, and I recently found out he's selling it."

Detective Riccio regarded me with an odd expression of sympathy and shock. In a desperate attempt to bolster his sympathy, I almost told him Matt was going to be a dad. Matt had dropped this bomb two weeks after reporting Rachel's heroin habit. But fearing this information might have the opposite effect, making Matt sound even more delinquent, I decided against it.

"I confronted my son as soon as I found out," I continued, "begging him to stop because I know the consequences are much stiffer for selling."

Detective Riccio nodded while he listened, breaking eye contact only to write notes.

"I even sent his former youth pastor over there to talk some sense into both kids. Matt said he stopped." I recalled the cryptic note Matt had left in my mailbox, in his backhand script: 'I just got rid of everything, and I'm stopping that game.' "But, Officer, I've been too wrapped up in Rachel's crises to confirm it. I honestly don't know if he's still selling or not.

"But I don't want two kids to go down!" I blurted out, near hysteria after the stream of stressful incidents that day.

Phil picked up my hand, lacing his warm, calloused fingers through mine.

"Listen, Ms. DiPasquale, I'm not going to charge your son. We want the heroin. You need to make sure he scours that apartment because it will be searched. If we find one pipe or bud of pot, I can't guarantee what will happen. Now, may I please get that statement from you?" He was standing again.

With shaking hands, I wrote and signed the statement.

# WASTED GRACE

I watched Detective Riccio back out of the driveway, his headlights like two blinding eyes. The dusk sky, a tranquil pink and orange watercolor, was almost a mockery. I called Matt, explaining what had happened. In days, his sister would be arrested, and their apartment thoroughly searched. He and his roommates would have to remove every vestige of marijuana, or they could also get arrested.

"Oh, man!"

"They were on to you, Matt, long before this went down."

"What are you talkin' about?" he asked, suddenly defensive.

"You selling drugs. The cops saw cars coming and going. They *knew.*"

"I *stopped,* Mom, right after you talked to me!"

"I hope you're telling the truth."

"I *am,* Mom! I *swear* it!"

"Good, because I begged the detective not to arrest you. He agreed to let you go in exchange for Rachel." As I said this, I felt viscerally ill, like I had sacrificed one child for another.

"Oh, wow," Matt whispered.

"I hope you see this for what it is, Matt, pure grace you don't deserve. You've been breaking the law for years. You need to straighten out, especially now that you're going to be a dad."

"I will, Mom, I promise—but what about Rachel?"

"Maybe these arrests will wake her up," I said, but my stomach churned.

For the next two days, I jumped every time I heard the screech of a siren, picturing Rachel getting seized and cuffed. I also fretted about Matt's apartment being searched. What if they found something, and he was arrested, too? What if both kids ended up with criminal records? But the police combed the apartment and found nothing.

Moved by Rachel's legal and medical problems, Perry was back in the picture. Since her neuropathy diagnosis, I'd been driving her to and from CODAC each morning, as well as to Warren several times a week so she wouldn't have to walk the four blocks from the bus stop to Restview Nursing Home. Now, to my relief, he agreed to share the driving.

On August 10, Perry took Rachel to Superior Court in Providence for her arraignment. He said the judge was harsh, ordering random drug testing and threatening Rachel with a five hundred dollar fine and prison if she got caught using again in Providence. She wept.

We felt bad for not warning our daughter that a second arrest in Middletown was looming. Maybe if she'd shown some remorse. But driving back from court, Rachel told Perry she'd keep using if she could get away with it.

That evening at nine p.m., while Rachel walked the short distance from the deli to her apartment, she was stopped on West Main Road for the heroin I had reported. She was handcuffed and jailed overnight. While searching her, officers found another bag of heroin, resulting in an astonishing *third* felony charge.

The next morning, Rachel was arraigned in Newport court for the possession of forty-one bags of heroin. She told the judge that she was being treated for substance abuse at CODAC. He released her on her own recognizance, subject to random drug testing in Newport while she awaited her sentencing.

Now Rachel was being monitored for drugs in two towns.

EACH MORNING AT SEVEN-THIRTY a.m., I picked Rachel up from her apartment and drove her to CODAC to get "dosed." She always wore gray sweats or blue scrubs with her red pullover sweatshirt, hood up, fists stuffed in its front pouch. Always tired, she dozed there and back.

Rob had told me that Methadone is a man-made opiate. Though a potent narcotic, it did not get patients high; rather, it *blocked* heroin's euphoric effects, making them less inclined to use while taking it. A long-acting drug, methadone stayed in clients' systems for up to thirty-six hours, relieving their cravings and painful withdrawal symptoms.

CODAC's Opioid Treatment Program offered two types of care: methadone maintenance—some clients took it indefinitely—or medically supervised withdrawal. Rachel chose long-term withdrawal, which should have lasted thirty-one to one-hundred-eighty days; however, she stayed on methadone for *two full years*. During this time, her life stood still. Even her journaling dwindled. The one thin volume that captures those years has huge gaps. Of the existing entries, more than one begins in her neat penmanship, but the words get progressively smaller and more misshapen, eventually trailing above or below the line and stopping mid-sentence. Rachel routinely nodded out in the car, at the table, in front of the TV. Once, she passed out on our new aqua sofa while eating eggplant Parmesan. I entered to find Phil furiously scrubbing red stains out of the seat cushions. Another time, we found her sitting cross-legged on her bed, face down in a large bowl of popcorn, a scene that might have been comical under other circumstances.

Concerned that Rachel was being over-medicated, Perry and I researched optimal methadone dosing. We learned that doctors usually upped patients' dose until their heroin cravings stopped. Most responded to sixty milligrams or less, though some needed substantially more. Two months into the program, Rachel's dose was a whopping one hundred-twenty milligrams and still climbing.

Rachel's fatigue was a mystery back then. Fortunately, her journals expanded my view. I learned that during her two years of methadone therapy, she was using heroin and other substances prohibited by CODAC to create potent cocktails that, at the very least, would have knocked her out but could have also killed her. She popped benzodiazepines or "Benzos"—Xanax, Valium, or Klonopin—like breath mints, washing them down with hard alcohol, a little trick that, I would discover, stoned methadone users out of their minds.

How Rachel got away with using substances that CODAC screened for, I don't know; however, she received very few positive urines, according to their toxicology reports.

Rachel was also taking Adderall, another key ingredient in her cocktails and, ultimately, in her demise. It had been prescribed by her doctor a year earlier as an appetite suppressant to control her bulimia. Initially, CODAC had banned it, along with benzodiazepines, in a formal letter to Rachel.

Pacing, she had fretted, "How am I supposed to beat a heroin addiction on top of bulimia without help? Going off Adderall is asinine and unrealistic."

My heart flew to her corner. It was true. Both addictions were brutal.

Rachel must have worked on Rob, too, because shortly after, CODAC reversed their decision.

Days later, I was in the produce department in Stop 'N Shop, selecting tomatoes, when a cart pulled up beside me.

"Rachel should *not* be taking Adderall with an opiate addiction."

I looked up to see the familiar face of Rachel's former pediatrician—high, fair brow, wire-rimmed glasses, ponytail of rusty curls.

"Oh, hello, Dr. Newman. How are you?"

Smiling tightly to acknowledge my greeting, she added, "You know, Adderall is an amphetamine. It's *highly addictive.*"

Before I could blink, much less speak, Dr. Newman had pushed her cart halfway across Produce, and I was staring at her shrinking red ponytail.

I had told Dr. Newman about Rachel's ED and her drug addiction and treatment at CODAC. Though she had stopped caring for Rachel years ago, she always asked about Rachel while treating Krissy or Ryan. I had *not* divulged the Adderall. Either Dr. Newman was still being copied on Rachel's health care, or news traveled fast in the medical community of a small island.

"Why don't you tell that witch to mind her own business?" Rachel spewed when I recounted Dr. Newman's concern. "Though I'm technically going against medical advice, CODAC's allowing the Adderall. What's it to her?"

CODAC's approval made Adderall okay, but Dr. Newman's warning rang in my ears.

✦　✦　✦

Since Rachel's first arrest, I'd been seeking legal advice from my brother-in-law, Dale, a real estate attorney who owned a Wisconsin law firm. On hearing the latest, he said it was time to hire a lawyer who knew Rhode Island criminal law. I swallowed hard. How was I going to afford this? As if he could read my mind, Dale offered not only to find a talented attorney but also to pay his legal fees, a gift that flooded me with relief. I thanked him profusely, but he dismissed it.

"I just want Rachel to get better. I don't want you worrying about anything but your daughter right now."

Dale referred us to Tom O'Leary, a tall and lean attorney with sharp hazel eyes and wavy russet hair. He wore a starched white shirt, cobalt silk tie, pleated khakis, and loafers that looked like he had lifted them out of the box that morning. Carrying a leather-bound portfolio and a mug of steaming coffee, he led us to a large conference room, the smell of java trailing behind him. A wall of windows overlooked the firm's parking lot on Belleview Avenue in Newport. Drawn by the ocean breeze, we sat beside an open window at a massive walnut table.

Pen poised over a legal pad, O'Leary asked Rachel to recount what happened during her Providence arrest. As she spoke, he jotted notes, pausing only for swigs of coffee.

Rachel summed up her story by saying she was stopped for no reason.

O'Leary looked up, his brow furrowed like an accordion.

"It says here in the police report that you failed to use your right turn signal."

"That's a lie," Rachel said. "I *always* use my turn signal."

"That may be true, but a judge is never going to believe you."

"So it's okay for a cop to lie, for me to get arrested under false pretenses? What a crock of shit!"

O'Leary's eyes shot darts. "Look, Rachel, I don't know if you used your blinker or not, but who do you think the judge is going to believe, a police officer or someone buying drugs?"

Rachel flushed. I couldn't tell if she was going to retaliate or cry. Instead, she swallowed and said nothing. The interview continued, with O'Leary questioning her education and work history while she gave clipped replies.

Next, he quizzed me about finding and reporting the forty bags.

Rachel shifted in her seat, mumbling, and huffing as I recounted the events. When I mentioned searching her bag, she blurted, "I don't fucking believe you! You said you found the dope on the floor of your car! *You fucking lied to me*, not to mention violated my privacy!"

"You were passing out! *You* lied to *me* about not using. I had to find out."

O'Leary held up his hand to halt us both, his gold cufflink glinting.

"I understand you're upset, Rachel, but I need this statement from your mother."

"Fine!" she snapped, crossing her arms and slouching. "I'm done with this bullshit."

When O'Leary finished, he turned back to Rachel.

"Having three felonies on your record at twenty-two is very serious. I can see you're an intelligent young lady. A criminal record will limit your potential in every area of your life."

Now, her bottom lip trembled. Her blue eyes welled.

"I'm going to ask the DA to consider you for the Diversion Program. This is a special program for first offenders who are educated and come from good homes. You may have to participate in a substance abuse program, but if you stay clean for six months, you bypass prison, and those felonies are dismissed."

My heart fluttered like a pinwheel at the prospect of this gift. "She's already being treated at CODAC," I offered.

"That's good," O'Leary nodded, never diverting his eyes from Rachel. "Usually, their rule is one felony, one town, but you're more educated than most. Believe it or not, your mother reporting your drugs works in our favor. It shows you come from a good family. I think we have a decent shot."

Walking to the parking lot, a mild breeze caressed my bare arms. The sun was bright, the sky blissfully blue. Rachel was quiet, probably still seething at my betrayal.

"Well, what do you think? Isn't this *amazing* news?"

She had lit up a Kool Lights when we stepped outside. Now, as we reached the car, we both leaned against it, our eyes closed, our faces tilted toward the sun. She inhaled deeply, blowing menthol smoke over her opposite shoulder that never failed to snake its way back to me, filling my nose and throat.

"I think that guy's an asshole, that's what I think."

"He may be arrogant, but he's highly qualified." Opening my eyes, I faced her. "Rachel, he's offering you a ticket out of prison and a *clean slate.*"

"He made me feel like *dog shit.*" Her eyes were electric. She shielded them with one hand while pulling deeply, almost desperately, on her cigarette.

"I know he did, Rae, but you have to suck it up." Another heady gust of smoke rushed up my nose; I tasted mint on my tongue. "This is going to be a long, grueling process. You have to play the game, cooperate to get what you want. Putting up with a cocky lawyer is a small price to pay for your freedom. But, listen, you can't talk to your lawyer like that. Your language was *way* out of line."

As much as I despised Rachel's swearing, I sensed that she loaded her sentences with expletives because she felt so small. Cursing amplified her voice, gave her brawn.

"I'm furious that he justified that cop's lie!" She flicked embers on the ground. "You think that was okay?"

"Rachel, you can't take the high road with people while walking on the low road." I sighed. You've got to clean up your life first. This is your chance. Please *don't blow it.*"

Our next stop was the apartment. Rachel and Matt's lease was nearly up, and it was time to start packing. Now that Matt was going to be a dad, he wanted to move back home to save money. They both did.

I worried about taking Rachel in. What if she was still using or started up again? I did not want Ryan and Krissy exposed to drugs—or cussing. Rachel's foul mouth had gotten worse. One morning, on the way to CODAC, she pelted me with such a string of expletives that I drove her to McKinney Shelter, which was just down the street. However, when I saw the run-down building and the desperate types smoking outside, I was deeply relieved when the toothless receptionist told me their beds were filled. I still had serious reservations. But hadn't I vowed to help her, no matter what? How quickly I forgot the moment she showed her fangs. I was starting to realize that my daughter had never needed me more. I agreed to take her in with the same terms I'd given Matt: a twelve-thirty a.m. curfew (except for special occasions), no sex, and absolutely no drugs under my roof.

That night, Dale called to tell me O'Leary had dropped Rachel's case. Evidently, he overheard her call him an "asshole" through the open window. Dale said he'd gone to great lengths to find this lawyer, who was offering her the "opportunity of a lifetime." He couldn't fathom why she was being so "obstinate and ungrateful." Until she was ready to cooperate, he was pulling his support. I thanked him for what he had tried to do.

As I hung up, defeat spread through me like poison. Now Rachel would be relegated to a public defender, whom Dale had said would not fight for her as a retained attorney would. We could probably kiss the Diversion Program goodbye.

✦　　✦　　✦

PERRY AND I UNDERSTOOD that Methadone therapy was a process. CODAC's doctor said withdrawal couldn't be rushed. However, Rachel seemed content with the status quo: getting dosed, sleeping all day, crawling out of bed only for CODAC or work. This could go on forever.

We were convinced that our daughter needed a different type of therapy, without an opioid component, synthetic or not. It had to be live-in and long-term. Now, though, Rachel had *two* serious addictions. It was hard to tell which to address first. The heroin seemed the most urgent, but hadn't bulimia driven her to it?

Teen Challenge (TC) made the most sense. Residential and faith-based, the program dealt with serious addictions of *all kinds*. Despite its name, it treated adults, eighteen years and older. TC lasted twelve to eighteen months, during which time "students" learned biblical principles that challenged and eventually replaced their harmful thoughts and behaviors. There was a women's TC right in Providence.

Most importantly, TC's eighty-seven percent success rate was unmatched. According to TC graduates, transformation came from surrendering their lives to Jesus Christ, who gave them new life—fresh thoughts, attitudes, goals—but also, in no small part, from living with staff. TC graduates themselves, leaders showed amazing patience and love in their interactions with students, proving by their reformed lives that recovery was possible.[94]

With goosebumps, I had glimpsed this transformation myself. The women's group in Providence had been performing at Middletown Baptist Church for years. On the first Sunday in August, they would file into our sanctuary, wearing white blouses and knee-length black skirts. Some had tattoos and dark hair roots, but their eyes were clear and their smiles real. In between singing worship songs, some spoke about their former lives as alcoholics, prostitutes, and drug addicts, who had lost everything until a judge ordered treatment at TC. Now they were rebuilding their lives, excited about their futures.

In recent years, my eyes ran freely as I fantasized about my daughter completing this program and telling her story on stage. If only Rachel could hear these girls speak. I had invited her before, but she always declined, claiming she needed to sleep on Sunday mornings after working third shift. Rachel wanted no part of TC. She scorned its "ridiculous rules," likening its twelve-month program to a "prison term."

Still, Perry and I kept nudging her in that direction.

## August 19–November 12, 2006

No one looks at me and sees beauty.
There is no one who knows me.
No one to say my name.

And most strangely, in these times, I picture the Lord,
the only One present any longer.
And I raise my jaw to Him. Not in defiance,
but to hold all the shattered little pieces in place.

# "I DON'T RECOGNIZE RACHEL"

### August 19, 2006

I admit it. I was stubborn and argumentative, and difficult with that lawyer today. Mostly because there is probably no way to avoid residential treatment, and my skin crawls at the thought of no methadone, Adderall, caffeine, or cigarettes. No coping mechanisms whatsoever, except for God.

Now, I'm no fool. I know I don't stand a chance in beating any addiction, much less heroin, without God, but let us not forget I'm still not interested in giving up heroin. In truth, I do fear a reprise of what happened when I was discharged from Remuda. Of course, one could argue that my discharge was premature, and had I been able to stay longer, recovery may have been attainable. The main thing to take away from it, I guess, is that I felt ill-prepared to deal with the real world because life at Remuda was so sheltered. How much more so will I feel that way if I'm kept under lock and key at Teen Challenge for twelve to fifteen months!

A huge fan of TC, Dad said on the drive in tonight, "Sometimes God just wants to test us to see if we're willing to do whatever it takes."

### September 12, 2006

No one would believe the crazy things that have been happening since Dad has been letting me use his van. It has been so wonderfully nice of him to let me take it overnight while I work third shift. It has made my life much easier, and I love being able to drive again. Then last Monday, I used the van again to run some errands for Dad while he was working. At three-thirty, I picked up Bobby, my dealer, and we copped in Pawtucket. I didn't even really want dope, but whenever I do crave it, I have no vehicle. Plus, I knew I'd have a drug test with pretrial services on October 11th when I meet with Savon. So I figured this was my last window before the testing began.

I bought four bags, having to pay Bobby one. I did half with him, and it was very good, cutting through the methadone much better than anything I've tried since going on it. I dropped the other half in the mess of dad's van when a cop pulled Bobby over for running the first two seconds of a red light. We nearly had heart attacks: With lightning speed, Bobby stuffed his bag in his rear end! I hid my two in my eye shadow compact. The cop didn't end up searching us, but I was so shaken up after we drove away, I made Bobby hold my hand for about fifteen minutes.

I was about twenty-five minutes late coming back from Providence. Dad was waiting at the deli for his van. He informed me Pre-Trial had contacted him and told him they tested randomly by color, and my color was silver. I needed to call every evening to see which color they were testing the next day. He said when he called at four p.m., the color was gold, but I should double-check later to be sure.

I was in a good mood. I had found three hundred dollars under the passenger-side floor mat in the van, and I had the night off to enjoy my spoils. For once, I didn't have to fake being in a carefree mood with Drakos. Until about six p.m., that is, when I called the color line and discovered that the color for tomorrow was silver! I lit a cigarette and began to pace behind the building. What?! I wait and wait to hear from these people—a month goes by—and now I finally get my color assigned and must be drug-tested tomorrow after I had just used for the first time in three weeks! When I went back inside, my hands were shaking, my eyes were wild. When I told Drakos I had to leave, the idiot said, "So more important that you lose job here! This is business!" Oh my God.

## September 23, 2006

I hate and I love how tired I get. On the one hand, I can fall asleep whenever I want to—use dope as a sleep aid to turn in at a normal hour without being plagued by insomnia or as an escape. However, for the most part, it's impossible to shake this feeling of general malaise. Adderall combats it. Blessed Adderall lifts me from the doldrums of dope; on both, I can get quite a bit of work done.

My attitude is awful; lately, nothing but poison comes out of my mouth. It literally feels like a demon has taken over my psyche, an implacable, rage-ridden demon. Any casual observer would look at me and say, "Oh, don't mind that venomous front; what she's actually feeling is a desperate, overwhelming sadness." But not my mother. She is convinced she's been "duped" by a "phony" for the past two weeks and says we're stopping by the McKinney homeless shelter after CODAC. I don't even attempt to change my bitchy behavior. I hate myself for attacking my mother, but that's how my sadness has been manifesting itself lately, by yelling and cursing at her.

I detest this car situation. I hate relying on others for rides and not being able to run errands when I want to. I hate having to fuck around with busses after I've been working all night. I hate my mother making stupid comments every other fucking day, like, "Well, if you didn't have your drug habit, you'd have a car, now, wouldn't you?"

I hate always feeling tired and miserable. I hate having nothing fun to look forward to. I hate that I am turning into a fat, disgusting pig whose only comfort is in food.

Bobby says it's going around that I busted his man Alex, which is absolute garbage. They apparently think this because I have three counts against me and am not yet in jail. "Rachel, I have never heard of someone receiving three possession charges and not going to jail," Bobby says.

To make matters worse, Dad has more shit to dole out. He said he talked to both Dolores and Dale tonight, and they asked if I'd be willing to take this lawyer's advice, no matter what. Would I quit my job and enter residential treatment? Apparently, he told them he didn't think so—I was nowhere near that type of commitment. Dad can be such a bastard.

### September 28, 2006

I love how Ryan feels compelled to instruct me on proper Christian etiquette.
In church: "Rachel, you can't write in the Bible."
At his Christian school: "Rachel, you can't swear in here."
At youth group: "You can't smoke while you're talking to the pastor."

### October 4, 2006

I elected to come into work on my night off due to a pervading sense of emptiness, which, coupled with having slept around twenty hours, was a recipe for insomnia. It's maddening to want dope and be unable to sleep. So here I am.

I feel guilty having tried to explain this to Mom, how nothing seems to fill this void. When it gets like this, I'm beside myself. Praying, writing, talking, eating . . . nothing but sleeping lets me escape. That, and taking amphetamines, so I'm so busy I no longer think about dope; I can always find something to do on amphetamines. I feel useful.

I hate to say it, but shoplifting does it for me, too.[95] I lifted four shirts from the Gap today, as well as a leather belt for Mom and a pair of socks. It's rather amazing what I can fit into my black bag. A few weeks ago, Mom and I went into Express. I only paid for a pair of jeans, but I walked out with four pairs of earrings, five shirts, and a pair of black leggings: $275 worth of stuff. Three weeks ago, it was Gap at Providence Place: two turtleneck sweaters, a lacy pair of underwear, a Gap body-fitted gray tee.

### October 18, 2006

I'm sick of my cravings. I'm sick of my own words and thoughts. I don't want to hear myself talking anymore. I'm more and more certain that I'm a waste. A waste of grace.

It's so hard to complete the simplest task: showering, taking antidepressants, dialing seven digits to find out how much of a disaster I've summoned in ignoring a possible court date.

Today is like so many other days. I carry my aching limbs to CODAC. I cry in front of the physician because of my perpetual fatigue from taking methadone, and I'm told, yet again, that I'm undermedicated. Up the dose goes to 120 mg, with another ten mg increase scheduled in a couple of days. (All because my pupils are dilated?) I tell them, and my mother, it makes no sense for me to be increasingly tired. If I'm getting closer to the ideal range, why am I more exhausted now than I was thirty mg ago??

### October 26, 2006

We received the date for Superior Court, and I was shocked to learn it was only two weeks away. I was relieved to discover it was only the arraignment . . . which just affords me more procrastination time. More time to sleep. More time to worry that the only way to save my life is to go to the god-forsaken Teen Challenge Dad keeps yelling about. Oh, my dear Lord, please allow a different way.

### October 29, 2006

I am too fragile to go to work and be excluded again: the odd wheel out, the poor drug addict. I cannot think straight about what I ought to do anymore. I have been nagged over going to Teen Challenge so many times that maybe I am meant to go there. Or maybe I should just cop one last time and be done with it. I have inhaled this space, damaged it, and now I wish only to leave. I'm cursed—trapped in this body, these thoughts, this life.

### October 31, 2006

So, it turns out I accidentally left the last journal entry on the kitchen counter. The one where I wrote about how I could barely think straight. I'd typed it after getting home from work, then took a shower and went to CODAC. My mom thinks I subconsciously left it there for her to find and read to my father. In reality, I had meant to transfer it into the journal while waiting for group to start. Either way, it incited enough concern to get the antidepressants.

I arrive home to hear my mother's side of their conversation as she grips the phone.

"I know eighty milligrams of Methadone is already a high dose." Long pause while she nods, black lines between her brows. "I don't know. It might be making her tired, getting her down—" Another pause, in which I can actually hear my father ranting. "Perry, Perry. Calm down. I know, but the doctor says a higher dose will stop her urges. The right dosage is supposed to help her feel better all around. I know, I know," she softly assents. "Yes, I'll talk to him tomorrow."

Yet another chapter in the rally against methadone because someone in Albany told Dad it was illegal to dose someone over a hundred mg. I hear this and enter into a mild state of panic, which prohibits sleep. How can I relax when I'll surely go to jail and ruin my life if I don't go to TC?! And now Dad'll never help me get my car or have my hair fixed unless I agree to start a damn detox.

I resolve to get closer to God because I've gone long enough (in penance) without Him. I tell myself I will not steal anything from the grocery store so I can "be in His presence" today. Yet, I do because I can't afford everything I need. I ring things up incorrectly at the self-checkout in Shaw's and slip two mini angel food cakes & one sugar-free pudding pack into my black bag.

### November 12, 2006

I have such an impossible time doing anything: getting out of bed, showering. I am always cold, except at work when I always feel overheated.

I'm supposed to go to church with Dad. I sit on my bed, looking at my open closet, realizing I don't have anything to wear that doesn't make me feel fat. I put on a gray turtleneck and gray sweatpants.

I drive to the hotel parking lot near the church and park the car three spots over from Dad's van. Planning to put on makeup, I adjust the rearview mirror to see my face. I don't recognize Rachel. I see shadows, sadness, pale sickliness. And I think, what is the point? I manage to conceal my under-eye circles, but I do not go in. I restart my car, drive back home, and return to bed. I dream about Paul not loving me because of how ugly I am.

At a quarter of ten, Matt comes home from his retreat and comes up into my room. He sits on my bed and hugs me. He thanks me for the letter and tells me it meant a lot to him. In the letter, I had told him I missed him. I distanced myself because I wanted someone who made time for me; I didn't want to be the third wheel with him and Chantelle as I was with Dad and Cam. I apologized for screwing up on the "exemplary older sibling" role.

Dad calls after service this morning, suggesting I write out a list of things I was grateful for. Right now, I'd be thankful for drugs, sleep, or death. Also, getting off the hook in court. Outside of these things, I can't find what else I'm thankful for. Instead, I list the things I've lost:

· my health
· a close, trusting relationship with my dad
· the peace of mind I felt before drugs
· self-respect
· trust in myself
· financial independence
· drive, motivation, security, innocence, privacy, confidence, freedom, control, friends, time, integrity, dignity, inspiration

*September 6, 2006—November 11, 2007*
age twenty-two to twenty-three

# THREE STRIKES

THE BRASS NAUTICAL BUTTONS on Peter Dubois' navy polyester suit jacket had strained at his waist the first time he reached out to shake our hands.

"Call me Pete," he said, smiling to reveal straight, if stained, teeth.

Rachel's public defender (PD) appeared to be fiftyish, with pure white hair shaved into a badly nicked buzz cut. His shoulders were dusted with dandruff, his pale blue eyes red-rimmed. But those eyes radiated warmth and optimism.

We had been meeting with Pete for several months in the PD's cramped office on the third floor of the Newport Courthouse in Washington Square. He always offered us coffee from a dingy, half-filled Mr. Coffee carafe before pouring himself a Styrofoam cup. Smiling and thanking him, we always declined. Huddled in his cubicle, we learned to tune out the cases being discussed behind flimsy partitions and the receptionist's perpetually ringing telephone.

Pete got Rachel's Providence and Newport court cases consolidated. Now, he was her sole attorney, and he handled both cases in Newport. Confident that Rachel would qualify for the Diversion Program, he put in a good word with the district attorney, who was in charge.

How wonderful to get another crack at this program. I wanted this for Rachel so badly. A criminal record would cripple her life. I was learning this firsthand, having recently volunteered to write grants for *Turning Around Ministries*, an aftercare program for ex-offenders in Newport. Unable to find even menial work, most returning citizens ended up sleeping in shelters and eating at soup kitchens.

On January 22, 2007, a frigid, overcast morning, Rachel was sentenced in Newport Superior Court for three counts of heroin possession. My heart fluttered, like the wings of a trapped moth, as I sat on a wooden bench in the spectator section, awaiting my daughter's fate. To my elation and relief, the judge admitted Rachel into the Diversion Program. She would have to refrain from criminal activity for six months while continuing her substance abuse treatment at CODAC. Mandatory meetings with the DA would be scheduled in his Providence office. If she broke any law, she would have to pay the full penalty for her crimes. If she behaved, the three blots on her record would be expunged.

After court, Pete walked us down the broad courthouse steps into the brutal cold so Rachel could smoke. He wore a black wool overcoat, its shoulders flecked with dandruff. I was surprised when he also lit up. Pete smoked furtively, his back to the courthouse door, taking quick puffs before dropping his cigarette hand to his side. Meanwhile, Rachel smiled widely, blowing smoke rings into the air.

We thanked Pete for everything he had done.

Pete grinned. "Just doing my job." He flicked his half-smoked cigarette on the cobblestone walk, squashing it with the worn toe of his brown wingtip. Rachel would smoke hers down to the nib.

"Remember, Rachel, you have to follow their rules to the letter of the law."

Pete had told us that the Diversion Program was extremely strict. Because they were giving first-time felons such a break, they did not allow mistakes. Now, with a sober face, chapped from the cold, he warned her again to keep clean and never miss a meeting with the DA.

Days later, Rachel helped me wrap a gift basket for Pete Dubois at the kitchen table.

The homemade chocolate chip cookies had been her idea. I bought two bottles of good wine. It still seemed inadequate after everything he'd done. We added gift certificates to Yesterday's Restaurant and Ocean Coffee Roasters, popular places in Washington square. Now, as Rachel guided the crackling clear cellophane around the contours of the basket, she looked doubtful.

"Do you really think I can do this, Mom?"

What a question. In my mind, the court was asking precious little of Rachel while offering her the moon.

"Of course you can, Rachel. Why would you think you couldn't?"

She shrugged. "It's a long time." She grasped the cellophane ends above the basket handle like a nosegay while I secured them with royal blue ribbon that I looped into a festive bow.

"No, it's not," I said, gripping her eyes. "Don't even allow your mind to entertain the possibility that you cannot stay clean for six months. You can *do* this."

She nodded, but her expression didn't match.

✦   ✦   ✦

ROBERT MCCAIN WAS A direct, affable man who warmly welcomed Rachel into the Diversion Program. He said that typically he only accepted candidates with one felony who had been arrested in one town. He made an exception for Paul Dubois.

"You've been given an incredible gift, Rachel," he said, looking deeply into her eyes. "I hope you use it to turn your life around."

Two weeks after Rachel's sentencing, she was arrested for shoplifting in Shaw's grocery store. She told me she had switched stickers to buy items at a reduced price after being declined treatment at the dentist because her A1c level was too high.

"*Why, oh why,* would you do that with everything you stand to lose?"

"Mom, they wouldn't even clean my teeth because of my diabetes!"

Rachel called Robert McCain, tearfully explaining what had happened.

I braced myself for the worst.

Miraculously, she was not expelled from the program. However, McCain said he was required by law to report her crime to the Board of Health since she worked in the medical field. We held our breath, hoping this would not affect her CNA.

Since the kids had moved back home, our food and utilities had doubled. Phil wanted to charge them rent. However, next month when Matt's baby was born, he would be slammed with expenses; though we'd given him some cash for college, he was still paying most of his tuition. Rachel didn't earn much as a CNA. She had to pay for CODAC, court, and diabetes supplies.

Though I was actively seeking work, since I'd recently switched careers from teaching to writing, getting an interview, much less a job, was even more challenging.

"I found you a job," Phil announced one day after work, all dimples.

Phil had come home with some interesting items he'd scavenged from remodeling jobs—marble vanity, rainforest showerhead, pedestal sink—but this was a first.

"Yeah, right." I grinned.

"It's a proofreading position for a contracting company that works for the Navy." He handed me a paper. "Here's the manajah's numbah. Lori Benson's a regulah customah of mine."

Apparently, while Phil was replacing her faucet, she asked if he knew anyone with an English degree. She needed to hire a proofreader ASAP.

"I already applied for that job. They interviewed me but never called back."

I could guess why: Rachel had done my makeup that day. When she offered, I had hesitated. But she had never asked before—how could I say no? Closing my eyes, I enjoyed her soft touch, the flutter of brushes on my face. With a few light strokes of various wands, she turned my eyes electric blue. I guess that was okay. But I gasped at her lipstick choice. "Relax," she said, outlining my lips in blood red. "It complements your charcoal suit and white silk blouse." She also talked me into high heels— "Your legs'll look killer." Staring in the mirror, I had to admit, if bold, I looked good. It might even bode in my favor if a man interviewed me

But Marge Prichard interviewed me, a woman in her late forties, with a high, intelligent brow; wire-rimmed glasses with thick lenses; straight gray hair; *and not a speck of makeup.* In her clogs, she might have been five feet tall. As she escorted me to the interview room—I felt like a circus clown on stilts—she explained that she was the lead proofreader. I would be working *under* her.

I gave what I thought was a strong interview, but Marge Pritchard never called back, I explained to Lori Benson when I telephoned about the job.

"Oh, don't worry about Marge," she said in a booming voice. "It takes her for-*ever* to hire someone. I've got a business to run. I've checked your resume. You're more than qualified, so if you want the job, it's yours."

On March seventeenth, the Board of Health notified Rachel that her CNA license would be suspended for one year, effective on March 31, 2008.

Rachel was devastated. Despite her grievous negligence when she was stoned on the job, she had grown to love her patients. I reminded her that in a few months she would graduate from the Diversion Program. Maybe once her record was clear, they would reinstate her license.

OUR COMPANY SUPPORTED GOVERNMENT editors in the Tech Pubs Department of the Naval War College. Most of our "docs" were classified; therefore, we worked in "the vault," a large, locked room with no windows, natural light, or fresh air. Industrial fans roared. We had personal safes. God forbid if we got up to go to the restroom or get coffee without securing our docs.

The proofreaders had our own alcove in the back, with Marge occupying the front desk. There were two other "proofers," twenty-two-year-old Hubert, fresh from college, and fifty-year-old Norma.

We had to perform three different levels of proofreading, depending on the task. Though the docs were diverse, ranging from Naval War College Reviews to 500-page warfare manuals, they were all highly technical, and each utilized a different style guide, so the rules were constantly changing.

By her own admission, Marge was not the best teacher. She gave vague instructions and often contradicted herself. However, questions vexed her, disrupting her proofreading work.

Between the shifting tasks and Marge's nebulous directions, I was often confused. I could either botch the job or request clarification. Though Marge had been patient for the first two weeks, now she met my questions with sighs, frowns, or comments like, "Go ask Hubert. He got that in one day."

Hubert was her "golden boy." He was a sweet kid, wiry and polite, with black, horn-rimmed glasses. He was also a loner who read on his lunch break and probably reminded Marge of an earlier version of herself. In any case, she praised his every pen stroke.

And she began openly criticizing my work, within earshot not only of the proofers but plenty of other employees. Night after night, I came home beat up.

Henry's birth, on March 21, 2007, punctured my gloom like a sunbeam through storm clouds. It wasn't just new life, his flawless face, and fists. A deeper joy I had not foreseen came from watching my son's parenting. Matt had always been tenderhearted; I knew he'd be a good dad. Still, his bond with Henry flabbergasted me from that first night when Rachel and I tiptoed into the birthing room, and I saw him, acne still on his handsome square jaw, cradling his newborn son.

It hurt Matt that he couldn't take Henry home. He wanted him to sleep in the bassinet beside his bed; wanted to see and hold him first thing. I explained that Henry needed to nurse at all hours; right now, he needed his mom.

When Chantelle resumed working, Matt watched three-month-old Henry several days a week. Between Krissy, Rachel, and me, there was no shortage of female hands reaching out to help Matt feed, bathe, or change Henry. Matt insisted those were *his* jobs. Unless Henry was howling for milk and Matt was scrambling to heat it, he would not fork Henry over. That baby was fused to his heart. Still, knowing that I ached to hold him, Matt slipped Henry into my arms nearly every visit, if only for a few moments.

◆　　◆　　◆

By April, Marge had harassed me long enough. In a private meeting, I expressed my concerns about being publicly corrected.

"Criticism is how you learn," she said coolly, her voice echoing in the conference room.

"That depends on how it's given." I eyed her directly. "You can be pretty abrasive."

Marge swallowed, appearing suddenly so vulnerable with her thick glasses. Why did she have to do this? Why couldn't we be friends? There were things about her I truly admired—her strong editing skills, her independence as a single woman.

"I don't mind criticism, Marge. I want to excel here, but *please* take me aside."

We had peace for two weeks. Then she started back up. Coworkers who overheard her caustic remarks consoled me with a look or a word as we passed in the restroom or kitchen. I learned she had driven out every proofer before me. I needed this job, not just for the cash but also for the experience. With a queasy pang, I realized I would have to go over Marge's head.

✦　✦　✦

Lance was released from prison in early February. Since he had been incarcerated for stealing from his parents and banned from their house, he moved in with his grandmother. Rachel was forbidden to see him. Not because of prison—she was inches from incarceration, herself—but because they were a toxic pair. They needed to focus on beating their respective addictions and rebuilding their broken lives.

However, within six weeks, they were secretly seeing each other. Rachel was dealing with the same old money problems, drug suspicions, lies. On June fourth, just weeks before she would have graduated from the Diversion Program, she was arrested again for shoplifting in Shaw's grocery store.

To our amazement, Robert McCain forgave Rachel again; however, he extended her probation period until mid-September. She would have to "keep a clean nose" three months longer, which would not be easy with Lance back in her life.

✦　✦　✦

Tattling on Marge turned out to be a big mistake. On Monday, we had a cordial meeting in the conference room, airing our gripes to Lori

Benson. With Lori's goading, we agreed to shake hands and start over. But for the rest of the week, Marge did not give me one job. She handed out docs only to Norma and Hubert, passing my desk as if I did not exist.

When I pulled into the driveway on Friday, I was so dejected I could barely breathe. Then I saw Matt sitting on the deck with Henry in his lap, wearing only a diaper and swinging his chubby legs. On seeing me, a sweet smile lit Henry's face. Suddenly, the meanness melted away. In that instant, I felt I understood Marge's cruelty. She'd never married. Without the man, you didn't get kids or grandkids. I had it all. Maybe that was why she hated me so much.

I tried to show Marge kindness despite her claws. Prior to her carpal tunnel surgery in July, I offered to help her cook and clean. She politely declined. However, she accepted the Merry Maids and Mama Leone's Pizza gift certificates I handed her after collecting money from everyone in the vault.

While Marge recuperated from her surgery, she left Norma in charge for six glorious weeks. Morale in the Proofing Department soared. However, when Marge returned on August thirteenth, she said we had done nothing right. Now she had more work. She lashed out at everyone, especially me.

The same week, Lance chucked a rock through his parents' window and stole checks that he forged to buy drugs. Then he pitched a tent in the woods behind their house and shot four bags of heroin. I found out before Rachel did. Barbara called to inform me the police had found Rachel's "missing" wallet among Lance's things.

Rachel willingly submitted to a home drug test. As she peed in a cup, her eyes welled. "He took enough to kill himself, Mom." Rachel passed her test, but over the next few days, her outlook only darkened. It was no wonder she did what she did on August seventeenth, the same day I made the grave mistake of asking Marge a question.

"I can't believe you'd interrupt me for something so obvious. Can't you see I'm buried in work?" Behind her thick glasses, Marge's eyes were cold, muddy beads.

I fought to steady my voice.

"In our meeting, you agreed to answer my questions." Lori had stressed that it was her job to answer unlimited questions, but I never presumed upon that, posing only those that were vital.

"Intelligent questions, yes. You better learn this stuff pretty soon if you want to keep this job." She returned to her document while I stood there with my question dangling.

"And you need to learn how to treat your employees," I said, returning to my desk.

Marge leaped out of her chair. "You can't talk to me like that! I'm your superior!"

*Only in this pathetic place*, I wanted to blurt.

Instead, I said, "This is bullshit," and I started packing my things.

✦    ✦    ✦

I KNEW FROM MATT'S frown—never mind his failure to notice I'd come home three hours early—that something was terribly wrong. Sitting in his highchair, Henry also looked solemn, but that was his natural expression.

"Rachel called Henry a brat. She told me to keep my *brat* quiet so she could sleep."

"Matt, Rachel *adores* Henry. Something must've happened!"

I took the stairs to her room two at a time. Rachel was sitting in bed journaling, red blotches on her face.

When she told me she had been arrested for shoplifting again, I wanted to shake her. "What is the *matter* with you? You were days away from graduating from the Diversion Program! Why would you sabotage that?"

"I don't know," she said, dissolving into tears. "Maybe because I don't deserve it."

I had a sickening, helpless feeling in my stomach that something besides bulimia and drug addiction was seriously wrong with her. *Who sabotages their own progress?*

I would learn that Borderlines do.[96,97]

"Maybe we can still fix this! I'll go to Stop & Shop! I'll beg the manager for mercy!"

Reeling around, I pounded back down the stairs and flew out the front door.

The Stop & Shop manager listened while I explained Rachel's problems, daring back to her diabetes diagnosis; however, even when I appealed to him as a parent, he would not drop the charges. With steel eyes, he said he was tired of people robbing his store.

Rachel was dropped from the Diversion Program.

Though I expected incarceration to follow, Rachel was given a second chance. On October 22, 2007, she was accepted into Drug Court, another program offering non-violent criminals with addictions rehab in lieu of prison; however, Drug Court was much stricter, requiring a twelve-month commitment and frequent court to keep the judge informed, hence its name.

On November 11, 2007, Rachel pleaded no contest to her drug charges. These would be dismissed if she kept court dates and obeyed the law. However, if she broke the contract, there would be stiff consequences, as she discovered eight months later when she failed a drug test. This time, there were no second chances. After a court-ordered methadone detox at Butler Hospital, Rachel was transported directly to the Adult Correctional Institution to serve ninety days of hard time, followed by five months of home confinement.

Miraculously, she wasn't kicked out of Drug Court. She could still get her felonies expunged.

## August 10, 2007–August 13, 2008

*I have no excuses for what I've done.*
*Obviously it was incredibly stupid, reckless, wasteful, asinine.*
*All I can say is that every act I've committed,*
*like the bingeing and like the heroine,*
*was because it quieted something in me.*

# "I've put a life to waste"

**August 10, 2007**

*Fool that I was, I hadn't even known he was using. I never saw him fucked up. It makes me second-guess everything he ever said. Every promise, every act, every last word. He was probably only keeping me around for pleasure and comfort. He never loved me. He loved his precious drugs far more.*

**August 12, 2007**

*I am so low, so severed. He knew, damn him, that his actions would separate us for years. How could he? I'm at the beach right now with family, but trust me, I am alone.*

**August 14, 2007**

*I sleep all night and all day. I don't remember what I dream. Don't know the day. I try not to think about Lance. Since this depression set in, I don't give a fuck about anything.*

**August 17, 2007**

*I was arrested in Stop & Shop today for shoplifting. There is no way I'll be permitted to stay in Diversion, this being the—what?—third time.*

*I really am a piece of shit. Even the politeness, the needless decency of the policemen towards a worthless criminal, made me feel worse about myself, the reason, I think, I couldn't stop crying.*

*I've wasted my life. Wasted my gifts, my second, third, fifth, tenth, eightieth, chances just to fuck it all up once again.*

**October 28, 2007**

*I have been aware, for weeks now, of the presence of disordered eating. I want to eat all the time, though hunger is not a variable in this. It seems unfathomable this could start up again. I realized yesterday that my kidneys aren't invincible; I* have consistently abused them for over a decade now. Any moment they could fail me, and I'd have to resort to vomiting as the only means to control my weight.

I notice myself thinking a little more about drugs since starting the medically supervised withdrawal, but I suppose I could be imagining this.

Late yesterday afternoon, I got a letter from Lance, the second in a row. It was only a paragraph. He said he was out of jail and writing from his grandmother's house. He asked me to call him as soon as I received this letter. I miss him, but I never called. An almost parental feeling came over me, like I needed to protect myself. I'm so terribly susceptible to doing foolish things. If I fall back into this, it would only further detach me from myself, resulting in even more stress that I couldn't tolerate now.

Lance has taken too much already. He's repeatedly demonstrated that he will not take care of me; he will lie and connive when under the influence, and I'll always be suspicious. I just . . . Oh, man. It makes me feel defeated to even consider it. Here we go again. No car, so I'd have to drive. No job or finances, so I'd have to pay for everything.

I don't want any of it, and I can't handle being disappointed again.

I'm shocked those fools let him out so prematurely—what happened to the mandatory rehab upon release? And what'll he put his poor grandmother through if he relapses under her roof?

See, I know these things. I may have forgotten the atrocities I committed while using and living with him, but I haven't forgotten the wrongs done to me.

I will not betray myself.

### November 24, 2007

The day before Thanksgiving, I got a formal letter from the Board of Health. They have officially revoked my nursing license. Well, it expires November 28th. I am devastated, and not just because this was my livelihood, but also because this type of work gives my life meaning. It makes me feel as though I matter. Without it, I worry what will become of my mental health.

### January 25, 2008

I suppose when a lapse of this degree occurs in my journaling, it indicates a stagnant life, one that induces shame and defensiveness.

I miss Lance with an intensity that is borderline alarming to me. I never imagined falling back in love with him. What I stand to lose, the complications that undoubtedly would follow . . . would be nothing short of utter devastation.

*He would, could, ruin me. The more difficult thought to reconcile is that should we fail, the last eight or nine years of my life (dare I say it?) will have been in vain.*

### February 24, 2008

*I'm about to crawl back into bed for the thousandth time since I lost my job. My head and my face ache. I honestly don't know if I have a sinus infection or have just sunk into a deeper depression.*

*Still, there's something relaxing about being sick. I'm not expected to do anything. I don't have to be job hunting, exercising, anything.*

*Lance wants me to call him back later. I'm going to have to reiterate my distress at the number he's done on his future. How I don't want the burden of being the breadwinner—especially when I have newborns. I refuse to be one of those mothers who dumps their kids in daycare and then misses the precious formative years. The only way this might work was if Lance were able to secure a decent-paying job. Why, WHY did he have to take those checks?? Why not steal from a stranger so you might have a bloody chance in hell of getting AWAY WITH IT?!! What an idiot! Now he and I must spend the rest of our lives paying for it.*

### April 2, 2008

*I am the last one awake in this house. After thrashing rain, the sky regroups and sends down a thick, almost pulsing veil of fog. I feel it approaching, just testing the air. I can actually shed my sweater. Finally, I can release my grip. The incessant holding on I must do to survive these New England winters.*

*Summer is coming.*

*What makes summer so intoxicating is that it is synonymous with youth and risk-taking: with kissing and touching on blankets in soft air. It is campfires and drinking too much wine. It is skinny dipping among waves and sneaking about in recently mowed dew-covered lawns. It is salsa dancing in short skirts, shaking shoulders and hips while smiling strangers watch and clap. It is fumbling with your keys at five-thirty in the morning when the sky is barely gray, and the glorious July sun hasn't yet given you away.*

### July 18, 2008

*Lance doesn't touch me as much as he used to. I try to keep quiet about it; I want to be that girl who doesn't need such things—doesn't even detect their absence—but that is not and may never have been me.*

A few days back, Lance and I were gallivanting in Newport, riding his motor-cycle down Ocean Drive. When we ride, the rhythms of the motor sedate me. I alternate between attempting not to fall asleep and letting the wind rush about my skin. I like to raise both arms, but Lance finds this a tad nerve-wracking. That day, while passing waterfront mansions and expensive cars, I started imagining how it would feel to not have to fret over money. I wondered if I was attractive—and shallow—enough to date a man for his wealth. I fantasized having beautiful clothes and a live-in cook. I could see myself doing it for a while, but I certainly wouldn't marry someone I didn't love. Lance took this very moment to touch me. He ran his hand lovingly on my left leg, and I knew that somehow he had picked up on my thoughts. It reassured me, this crumb of affection, that he didn't want me to leave.

### August 5, 2008[98]

The doctor looks at me. His eyes are pale, faded. I want to take everything he says at face value. But his expression suggests he isn't exactly jaded but has taken the truth and fashioned it into something more palatable for those sitting across from him. In this case, me. I decide it would be wise to listen.

After hearing my history, especially my recent transgressions, he pauses, then tells me I'm underachieved. I'm smart, articulate, sophisticated, and I need to break free and become what I have the potential to be. I cannot excuse my cigarettes because I know he is right. Perhaps I'm just clinging to the nicotine because I'm scared to tap that potential. Do I want to continue this aimless path? I should think about this while I'm in this hospital detoxing.

### August 9, 2008

I checked into the hospital to detox Tuesday evening. I've been here six days, not that it matters.

I didn't think fast enough. Forfeited my pills, my ciggies, my phone. What a fool. I already crave something between my lips, though the back of my throat burns.

Night has fallen in my hospital room. It's always cold unless I'm in the fever cycle of the detox.

### August 10, 2008

I have my first tablet of Suboxone dissolving under my tongue.

What are the stages of loss again? 1. denial 2. anger 3. bargaining 4. depres-sion/grieving 5 acceptance or something along these lines. At any rate, I am definitely at stage one! Not accepting this breakup. I know I register disappointment in myself for giving all of me away. Aren't you supposed to dance as though no one's watching, love as though you've never been hurt . . . if you want to experience great love? I suppose the key is to withhold the pearls—cling to them in my case—until someone comes along who genuinely wants them. Lance never did. Still, I gave him all my pearls. I should have held some back. I need to learn how to do this. If I had, I would not be in this state. I feel like he's walking around with everything I own, as though I've allowed a thief to come into my home and in a fog told him, "Yes, yes, take whatever you like. No trouble. Just shut my door when you leave; I wish to go back to sleep."

### August 11, 2008

There is a man here, named Lenny, who is fifty-six years old. He is older than my father, though he could easily pass for forty-five.

Lenny told me in his younger days at rehabs, he would try to get the most attractive girl there to meet him upon discharge. He said, "I always used to say that the best therapy I got at Butler was in the parking lot."

I want someone to be falling asleep with me in this little bed. I'd rather it be Lenny than Lance. I told him I wanted to nap with someone because I knew I was going to be physically uncomfortable from the Suboxone. I actually grabbed his arm and headed towards my door. I told the workers standing there, "Turn your heads; you don't see this." We aren't allowed to enter other patients' rooms or make any physical contact with them. I think Lenny said, "She'd do me in; she'd kill me," so I let go of him.

Stupid Lance. I wonder how much more difficult this breakup will be for me because we lost our virginity to each other. I'll never ever be able to make that claim again, and my chest is heaving at the knowledge that this means more to me than it does to him.

### August 12, 2008

There is nowhere to escape. I can't talk to someone if our rooms are off-limits. I cannot yell without appearing to have a breakdown. The bulbs are so bright everyone can see my feelings. The batteries have died on Ryan's iPod. I can't smoke. I can't even eat because these nurses are trailing me to see how many carbs I've ingested so they can jack up my insulin. Which is _not,_ I repeat, _NOT_ happening. There aren't even tissues in my room, and he just discarded me like trash. What a fool I am.

### August 13, 2008

Today I am one-week nicotine-free. If it weren't for the lack of cigarettes and the nine to ten pounds I gained, I'd be content to stay another week or two.

I want to be clean and sober more than I want to be drunk and high. Because I lost myself. It happened gradually . . . Why did I start drinking in the first place? To be free? But happiness still eluded me . . . it was always one drink away. Honesty is a better place I can only find when I'm sober.

*August 31–November 17, 2008*
*age twenty-four*

# ACI

THE TOWERING CHAIN-LINK FENCE capped with curls of barbed wire commanded my attention. Glinting in the August sun, still strong at six p.m., it was all I saw. I couldn't ponder what it meant. How those steel thorns pertained to my daughter. I pushed that down, way down. Kept my eyes dead ahead.

Mom had gone with me the first time to the Adult Correctional Institution. As we approached the women's division, her head snapped back to take in the imposing fence. "Geez," she said.

We waited for clearance to visit Rachel for over a week. When the phone rang, we had just sat down to dinner. Rising from the table, I started packing homemade spinach and feta pizza, the heavy, garlicky squares still warm. Phil also stood up, prepared to drive me. Matt begged me to stay, but I told him Rachel would be aching for company and good food. She'd told me they scheduled visiting hours during dinner so inmates could eat with guests, who were allowed to bring meals.

Mom stood up, looping her handbag around her shoulder.

"Don't you go too, Grandma!" Matt pleaded. "I got Henry for two extra hours to see you."

Hearing his name, fifteen-month-old Henry smiled. Ryan and Krissy, who had been chatting and laughing, continued eating in silence. Phil resumed his seat.

"Sorry, Matt," she said, wrapping her pizza in a dinner napkin for the road. "This might be my only chance to see Rachel. I've got to go."

A FEMALE CORRECTIONAL OFFICER, sitting in what looked like a bulletproof booth, looked us up and down. "Sandals and earrings are not allowed. Neither are underwire bras." She spoke through a golf-ball-sized hole. "Read the rules yourself." She pointed to a notice on the wall.

We had disrupted a family dinner. Driven fifty minutes one way. To get in, I'd have to break rule number one: All visitors MUST wear undergarments.

In the car, I removed my under-wire bra, along with my earrings, swapping my sandals for the Nikes I kept in my trunk. Meanwhile, Mom, who was wearing flats and had retired her "rib-jamming underwires" years ago, removed her earrings and was ready to go.

Passing successfully through the metal detector, we were directed to a large basement room where female inmates were dining with their guests at aluminum picnic tables. It might have been a church potluck, people smiling and chatting, the smells of chicken and beef in covered dishes and crock pots competing with pizza, Chinese, and burgers people were eating out of boxes, cartons, and bags, if half the guests hadn't been wearing blue uniforms.

Rachel smiled sweetly when she saw us, embracing us both. She sat beside me, seemingly unfazed by her surroundings. But seeing my daughter in prison garb was another visceral punch.

As Rachel bit into her pizza, I saw some guests and inmates already hugging goodbye. Visiting hours ended in thirty minutes, according to the wall clock.

"This is so good," she crooned as if it had been months rather than days since she'd tasted my cooking.

"How's the food here, Rae?" Grandma asked.

"It's pure starch—potatoes, pasta, Wonder bread. Their idea of vegetables is canned corn. I'm already gaining weight," she said matter-of-factly. "But I'll lose it when I get out."

"The good news is I can't binge in here," she said in between bites. "I get three meals a day. And I get tested and dosed regularly."

She was insinuating, as she had in a recent letter, that she couldn't practice her ED or mismanage her diabetes in prison.

"I wish you'd bring one Milky Way and one Snickers or Milk Chocolate Dove bar each visit. You can bring ice cream, too, if it's sealed. I like Ben & Jerry's Chocolate Fudge Brownie. I want to reiterate that I'm sent to the nurse immediately following visiting hours and am always given insulin coverage, so you don't have to worry about purging."

However, her requests for extremely specific sweets smacked of ED behavior. Her repeated pleas for quarters were also suspect. "PLEASE bring eight quarters or two dollars so I can get two diet sodas when you come," she reminded me in every letter and call.

I slid a baggie with eight quarters across the table. Before coming, I had stared at my homemade brownies, the smell of chocolate tempting me to cut

Rachel a big square. Instead, I packed her cubed watermelon and cantaloupe, which I now handed her.

"Thanks, Mom," Rachel said, reaching for the quarters and starting to rise.

"You visit with Grandma. I'll get the sodas."

I deposited four quarters, sweat dampening my brow. The first can tumbled noisily into the bin. As I picked up the icy Fresca, I regretted not bringing more change to buy cold drinks for Mom and me, but purses, like underwires, were not allowed. After inserting the remaining coins, I popped the soda and took a pull while can number two banged down the chute.

I should have given one Fresca to Mom, who looked flushed. Since Rachel had insisted on two sodas per visit, I obediently set both before her.

"It's a bloody inferno in here, isn't it?" Rachel swigged from the open can. "Why didn't you guys get drinks?"

"In my panic to get in, I didn't even think of it. Now our purses are locked in my car. Along with my bra and sandals." I explained how I'd flunked the visitor dress code.

Chuckling, Rachel passed the open soda to Grandma. "You guys share this."

"Thanks, Rae. It is warm in here." Mom slugged the drink, then offered it to me, but I passed.

"Welcome to Shangri-la. The air conditioning constantly breaks." Rachel popped the second can, tipped her head, and drank. "I was so hot last night I slept on the cement floor—or tried to till I felt a rat scurry over my hand." She cringed, recalling the incident.

Mom and I gasped. "What!"

Seeing our reaction, a smile skipped across her face.

"Can you believe it? I felt its tail slither across my wrist!"

"Uggghhh!" We shuddered in unison.

"Five more minutes," the security officer announced.

Shifting gears, I leaned in and asked, "Rae, what are the inmates like?"

"I can't talk about that now," she said, glancing around, though only two inmates remained, and they appeared locked in conversation. "I will say I have a great cellmate. An older Christian lady who knows the ropes and looks out for me."

*Thank you, God.*

"What are my chances of getting assigned to a cell with another believer?" she said, looking from me to Mom. "I know God put me there."

"Two minutes," the officer warned.

"I've heard there are Bible studies here, good ones," Rachel continued while rising. "I'm going to use this time to get closer to God." Gathering her trash, she tossed it in a can. "Otherwise, I won't last another week in here, much less three months."

Huddled in a little circle, we whispered fervent prayers for Rachel's protection, peace, and spiritual growth.

Exiting the prison, Mom and I agreed that Rachel's situation could be worse. Despite the rat in her cell and the potentially hostile inmates, she had a Christian cellmate. Most importantly, she was open to God. With a Bible and countless hours to reflect on her life, she might just turn it around. It happened in hard places like this.

August 31, 2008–December 8, 2008

# "Your mercies never cease"

**August 31, 2008**

Dear Father, thank you for allowing me to visit with my mom and grandma tonight. Thank you for mom's prayer: "Dear Lord, I pray that you give my daughter a distaste for anything that is not of You. . . ." Please apply it to my life. Make it stick, indelible as my tattoo.

You are revealing my deception around food: lying about not bingeing and purging; lying about glucose levels to the nursing staff so they'll lower my insulin; refusing testing and/or insulin doses. . . . This must be sin because it perpetuates disordered eating and there is absolutely no question as to whether it separates me from You.

Father, you know I don't want to be sent to a rehab for a whole year. I would rather go to the Salvation Army but _not_ if it would only "fix" me partially. Help my stubborn heart accept the most effective program, whatever that might be. I know You understand how dear Lance is to me. Please, please, please keep him safe. Please soften his heart so that he might know You. I realize this was _my_ responsibility, and I failed miserably. I am going to get the insulin—or attempt to—because I trust that You will keep me safe. Safe from whispers of demons, safe from myself especially.

**September 1, 2008**

ED Pros vs. Cons:

| PROS | CONS |
|---|---|
| 1. Passes time | 1. Separates me from God |
| 2. Numbs anxiety | 2. Induces guilt |
| 3. Numbs unwanted emotions | 3. Wastes money |
| 4. Relieves (if briefly) urge to eat | 4. Wastes food |
| 5. Helps regulate weight | 5. Complicates diabetes |
| 6. Generates some excitement | 6. Perpetuates cycle |

7. Induces lying + distancing from family/friends

8. Requires inordinate time and planning

9. Prevents exploring/solving root of problem

10. Can precipitate drug relapse

11. Leads to depression

12. Leads to using RX (amph), alcohol, and pot

13. Prevents enjoying life

14. Harms inner child/relationship to self

### September 2, 2008—Tuesday

Mom and Phil visited last night; she felt guilty about being late and/or distressing me yesterday. She brought a turkey burger on a whole wheat bun, sweet potato fries, sauteed broccoli, and a snack-size bag of semi-sweet chocolate chips.

I hadn't anticipated their coming and had already eaten a hefty dinner: baked potato, carrots, milk, three slices of bread with butter, and two portions of chicken breast. After they left, I don't recall if I vomited before or after going to the dispensary for my shot. Vomit spotted my thin blue robe.

The next morning, due to the Humalog coverage on an empty stomach, I got my first jailhouse hypoglycemia. I remember eating ramen, a stack of crackers, a Milky Way, a Snickers, and two Swiss Rolls. Because there was no way I was going to ingest any goop from that Palmolive-green semen glucose tube. Wow. What the hell. So, two binges. I do not think I vomited again, though.

Today I finished Sebold's book, got some more skin cancer. I tried reading the Bible till about 1:40 p.m. Upon learning in the book of Hebrews about people abandoning their faith, I asked God for salvation once again. Now I know I've done this enough times to question my own sincerity, but I realized something today. Except for one other time, I don't know that I have ever entirely trusted in my professions of faith, nor in my ability to be saved because of the many times I've failed. The only time I remember it being different was when Matt's room was mine. I recall hanging my head because of my sins. Then I literally felt my chin being lifted, as if by God's finger, and Him saying, "You are my daughter. I have removed your sins, be not ashamed." I didn't hear these words as much as I sensed them. My whole body felt electrified. That day I felt forgiven. I felt saved. Since then, I've questioned my sincerity in requesting forgiveness. I don't know if I do it solely out of obligation or fear of the direction I'm heading because it doesn't seem to stick. I keep misbehaving. This time, I am almost certain, is different. One, because I know I will exert the effort due to my desperate circumstances. In here, reading the Word, attending services, and prayer are a must. Second, I am determined (if not forced) to trust Him entirely because I know that without His intervention, I will end up incarcerated for years. Without Him, my old demons will overtake me.

### September 4, 2008

Good morning, Father. Despite my frustration and confusion, I must praise you for bringing me through another day. Thank you for the amazing Bible study and for the selfless woman who taught it. Thank you for the material in the study, which I know was meant for me—you know how badly I needed to hear it. How can I begin to thank you for the incredible parents you have blessed me with, for their patience, forgiveness, direction, and compassion. I don't think I ever realized what an enormous gift having such parents is. I don't deserve them.

Please soften my heart. Open my ears and eyes. Make me your clay, so I can learn to trust you without hesitation and accept your holy word without distraction, seeking your will first. I have so much to make up to you.

### September 6, 2008

Here I sit, really imprisoned now, in the general medical ward where we are allowed no visits, no mail, no phone calls, no TV, and no time outside.

I was accused of squirting glucose tubes into beverages for a sweetener because my sugars are running so high. This time I'm innocent, a fact they were supposed to explain to Dr. Hart. I was told they would move me here after dinner so I could still see Dad. Expecting this to happen, I ate a red tray in my room: ham, sweet potatoes, lettuce, three slices of white bread. I ate the third slice of bread smothered in creamy peanut butter. Then I faced a dilemma: my soaring blood sugar might seal my guilt, ensuring my admission to medical. I needed to get rid of it, especially since I wanted the pizza dad was bringing. Not sixty seconds after I vomited, I was paged to the control room.

### September 7, 2008

Matt is coming. He said he would bring pizza, Chinese, peanut butter cookies, Dove chocolate, and a small Milky Way. Forgive my weak, greedy flesh, but I couldn't say, "Don't bring sugar." Instead, I told him to omit a sweet and choose between pizza or Chinese. Thinking back, I might have mumbled it.

### September 13, 2008

Oh God, oh God. I can't do it. I can't do this. I CAN'T. You're allowing an impossible situation. Pasta for dinner, no insulin to cover it, no yard to walk in? And now I know that other girls know. They see everything: how long I'm in the bathroom, my red eyes, my guilty demeanor, is there a CO coming to get me?? Fuck! I know I didn't even get it all up, and God help me . . . I want to do it again . . .

 I didn't ask for much help.
 I prayed before eating, but did I really hand it over??
 Nope.

### September 15, 2008—ISOLATION

Dear Father, I'm discouraged and scared. I understand why you had me go through the trial last night: not taking away the urge to binge or having me fall asleep to escape it. I must take a step of faith for the spirit to work. I also need to reach out. Isolation worsens my disease. You knew I needed Fellowship; I must learn to ask for help.

 But in reading The Purpose Driven Life just now, I feel like my whole life will be this hard, that the whole reason for being alive is to shape my character in preparation for Heaven. I can't survive a lifetime of circumstances being this hard! But! I can honestly say I'd rather be where I am now, even though it's the most challenging experience I've had thus far, because I'm near to you.

### September 17, 2008

I looked in the mirror ten minutes ago when I went to brush my teeth. I'm disgusted by my reflection. My face is swollen, ugly, and round. I look like such an obvious glutton. I feel as if everybody is staring at me and saying, "See her? If she throws up her food, why is she getting so damn FAT?" I miss Newport Hospital, where there were no mirrors.

 Lord, shelter me from self-deprecating thoughts. I'm trying to understand the impossible fact that you love me exponentially more than I ever loved Lance.

That your love is flawless and lasts forever. I just cannot get my head around it. I <u>know</u> I'd feel better if I trusted you, which leads me to suspect that I'm sabotaging this by telling myself I'm unworthy to receive something so priceless. I'm a filthy prostitute and IV drug abuser who has defiled every good thing you gave me, and I was given so much. I know Your love is undeserved. Pure grace. Realizing that doesn't make the present any simpler to unwrap, though.

Oh Father, how can I accept your forgiveness if I am unwilling to forgive myself?

### September 18, 2008

Almighty Father, thank you for everything you have helped me accomplish today: getting to speak to Dr. Clark about morning insulin, not really bingeing, an awesome visit with Dad, Dad bringing safe food, getting sneakers (possibly), and feeling complete acceptance at being here because it doesn't matter where I am if I am within you.

### September 19, 2008

I accomplished nothing of my own last night.

Yes, I hated it at the time. I rocked in overwhelming stress, bit my nails, and kept checking if the closet was locked. He watched the whole time. He heard me cursing myself for being obedient. He read my thoughts while I imagined ways to finagle food from someone else, but I didn't, and it was all God.

### 9:30 pm

Father, I don't want to write to you or pray right now. I don't want to read the Bible or what I wrote earlier today. I want to eat. I'm like the heroin addicts who deliberately check into SSTAR because they know once they leave and use again, their tolerance will be lowered, and the dope will be as good as when they first started using. I know the food will taste amazing. The only thing restraining me is knowing I'll forfeit your rest. That's not entirely true. This morning, I remember how badly I wanted to please you, to reciprocate Your Love through obedience. Please help me to stop using food to fill my empty, panic-attacked soul.

### September 23, 2008

Things I will REMEMBER about Lance:

Always feeling like I wasn't enough to keep him loving me.

Not being emotionally supported, EVER.

Being forgotten on birthdays, anniversaries, holidays.

Having to pay for everything for years, except for the last few months.

Knowing he didn't know me and didn't care to.

Never asking if I took my shots. Or caring enough about my health to EVER ask about it.

Never being thanked for the thoughtful things I did: cleaning, cooking, sewing, buying whatever he needed, building him up, trying to know him, forgiving him.

Refusing to attend church or read The Purpose Driven Life despite his many promises.

Knowing when it came to my needs and desires, he'd let me down.

Only being given two things for no reason over seven years.

Only being given flowers once.

Putting me at risk when he/we used drugs.

Seeing how he looked at prettier women.

Watching him take such care of his motorcycle and wishing he felt that way about me.

Oh Lord, forgive me for choosing to focus on some foolish boy rather than the joy from your perfect love.

Help me surrender
my self-deprecating tendencies.
I need to accept myself
for I am good in Your sight.
You love me.

I surrender to You my relationship,
lay it at Your precious feet.
I surrender my eating disorder,
my desire to control and be self-reliant.
I surrender my appearance to you, Lord.

I don't want my will anymore.
I can't trust my own flawed judgment.
It scares me that I did for so long,

I don't see any good,
anything worth keeping in myself anymore.
Save my creativity, wit, and writing skill,

But these, I believe, are gifts from You.
Strip everything else, Lord.
Make me like You.
Because
I'm gluttonous,
selfish,
stubborn,
proud,
deceitful,
foolish,
masochistic,
fearful,
Oh, I could go on.
But I must stop.
If I dwell on these flaws,
I'll refuse your love.

### October 4, 2008

I need your help. I want to binge.

### October 23, 2008

Dear Lance, I will never be reckless with my body for you again. I will not walk in public with you, wondering if your eyes are wandering. I will never lay next to you or any man who makes me feel so unloved, wishing silently for you to want to know me, for you to ask how I feel about anything.

I remember how I always thought before I spoke, choosing just the right words so you'd inquire further, fall in love with me more. Oh, the fantasy I chased. You wouldn't even smile.

Why did I feel that I deserved this? I think I wanted someone to reaffirm my worthlessness. If I were "good" enough, pretty enough, charismatic enough, perfectly loving enough, then, of course, you would reciprocate. If you had given me love, I'd probably have left your ass because I was convinced I wasn't good enough yet. A constant pursuit—like reaching the perfect weight that I deliberately engineered to be unattainable.

Why am I so hateful toward myself? What a conflict—my inner self wants to protect me, but my outer self is intent on sabotage.

### November 1, 2008

To my little inner Rachel Grace:

I don't want to lie to you or avoid you any longer. I don't want to treat you like a separate entity. You're not. I've tried to forget you, smother you, kill you, but it's not your fault. You were only trying to warn me.

Rachel, I'm sorry you did not receive what you needed when you were diagnosed. I'm sorry I ignored your cries for help. Sorry I did everything I could to drown them out and you, for that matter.

In truth, we have diabetes. Our Dad knew this when he made us. He deliberately allowed our pancreas to peter out at fourteen years old. Yet we must trust Him. Does it suck? Yes. Has it caused ceaseless dilemmas and disorders? Yes, but He gave us many other gifts to compensate; there's no denying that.

I remember the greenish hospital ward with its juvenile paintings, watching rain streak windows like so many tears. I was too young to process what was happening. I remember the nurses trying to teach me how to prick my finger, explaining the meaning of a honeymoon period,[99] lightly asking, "Do you want to try giving yourself insulin today?"

It didn't seem permanent. But when the certified diabetes educator came to the house the morning after my discharge, it began to sink in. How dare this disease barge into my life and boss me around?

It was then I began your slow burial. My silent pact to kill you.

I'm so sorry. I abused, neglected, plotted death against a child.

I know I don't deserve forgiveness until I change my ways. I know you're on to me. You know I haven't fully embraced you because you still frighten me. But I'm willing to listen. Do you want to destroy me too, or do you desire love, acceptance, nurturing? Talk to me.

i hate you. how could you be so dense? so selfish. so cruel. how could you not take care of me? you hurt me so much with all your eating and throwing up. never mind all the dirty things you let men do to you! don't you see, i'm here to help! all I wanted was for you to listen when I told you 'be careful! i'm scared!' why did you turn away?

I'm sorry. You must believe that I never set out with the thought, "Hey, let's torment our inner child." I knew you were in need but didn't have a clue how to provide. I still don't. You probably need love. Acceptance. The healing of your heavenly Father. We must end this war. We need to make peace and come to an understanding, a common ground so we can flourish. I ask your forgiveness,

*little Rachel. I will heed your warnings and stop the abuse. I've gagged you long
enough. Do not hide. You know where secrecy gets us.*

*Sincerely,*

*Rachel Grace*

*P.S. Dear Father, I plead with all my heart for you to heal my inner child.
With my extremely limited wisdom, I don't know how to fix myself. I am terrified of the destructive forces within me that I tend to turn loose on myself.*

# "Failure is all I really know"

### November 17, 2008—First day back home

I wanted to transcribe all the journaling I did in jail from the crappy store-order notebooks to this hard-bound journal. I figured if I recorded the lessons I learned neatly and chronologically, I'd be less likely to repeat my errors. But life doesn't wait.

Oh, please, Lord, remain steadfast in Your patience. I hold all the pieces in my hands. I almost understand, but I STILL think I can navigate with partial blinders on. My past haunts me like the living dead. I reminisce about my sin and ACTUALLY BELIEVE EVEN NOW that there was beauty in that broken, anxious existence. I see a waistline, fire in a woman's eyes, hips . . . and I think: you were that once. I recall the way men looked at me. I fooled them, but I didn't fool myself. She never fell for the charade.

I romanticize the wild things I did: the rush of drugs to my system, the small clothes—I was always so surprised to reach for the zero. I sit in the cinema of my mind, every demon in Hell in the audience with me, saying, yes! Now that you're spiritually aware, if you can just get your body back, you'll have the WHOLE package—you'll be so FULFILLED! Once you get comfortable in your own skin, you can think about God, but, honestly, would you need Him? You've matured enough so that you surely won't lose your way.

When will I stop my FUCKING SHIT? I cannot serve two masters. I lay awake last night, wondering if God were looking down at me shaking His head. What if this is an encore of Remuda? If prison didn't do it, will death be the final teacher? Father, I grieve that I cannot have both. I covet the inner beauty You supply, but wretch that I am, I tell myself it's not enough. I want to be outwardly beautiful, too. But chasing beauty cost me dearly. And who profited? The men I fucked, believing that at least in their memories, my body was beautiful. It was never enough for anyone to love me as desperately as I have wanted to be loved.

Can I not now walk out of the prison?
My Father has undone the shackles.
He has opened the gates.
Yet I remain in the cell,
crouched and fingering the cuffs,
seeing if they still fit.
Oh, Father, if it were just me and You.
Could I?
You already know,
but the realization sickens me—
I love and worship the counterfeit over You.
The most nauseating and certain thing is this:
Once I feel tolerable in my body
(never comfortable, mind you)
there is nothing in me.

I am empty. I am ugly.
I memorize. I mimic.

I have only ashes within.

### November 18, 2008—3:00 a.m.

Father, I will confess my sins to you alone. I have lied to my parents. I have taken medication to control my appetite rather than rely on You. I have sworn and taken your name in vain. I have not taken any short-acting insulin since coming home. I have sought attention, wasting the beauty you've given me on witnesses.[100] Please forgive me, Father. Thank you for taking care of me today.

Father, help me to not crave witnesses. It isn't that I do not trust You to provide a husband. Why, then, do I long to be noticed? Why can't I learn to be content with just You? After all, I've realized that no man can love me like you do. A man's adoration leaves me sickly dependent upon it . . . Sometimes I long for utter solitude. If I lived alone in the woods, I'd be able to hear Your voice so clearly. No mirrors, no media. No eyes, save for Yours.

### November 24, 2008—4:03 a.m.

Last night I was given a dream. In the dream, my eyes seemed to belong to Matthew, and I was watching Henry. Less than a year old, Henry was crawling across the floor of a prison cafeteria for male inmates. The men were unruly. At any moment, Henry risked being trampled or hit on the head by heavy dishes that were falling off wooden tables. No one saw him because he was so small. Henry was oblivious to the danger of the crass, dirty men. I, being Matthew, felt panic and dread, as if I were watching my baby crawling in an earthquake with boulders tumbling around him, but I couldn't reach him due to the ruckus and congestion. Meanwhile, Henry kept crawling further and further away.

"This is you," the Lord said, "You haven't the remotest concept of the dangers lurking around you. Please, let me protect you. As your father, I long to keep you safe, but you must TRUST me."

I am in a complete state of disbelief that I did not eat tonight. Only the Lord could have enabled me to make it. I'm not entirely surprised because I believe He told me He would take care of me if I obeyed. If I took my insulin and held my food.

My stomach is incredibly distended, though I anticipated this. I stare at it in the mirror and hold it. It is wretched as a stomach but breathtaking as a womb, and I am transfixed by it.

### 8:30 a.m.

I am sitting in the courthouse, early. I have this foreboding that I've failed to do something and will be sent back to prison. I suspect I am afraid to be out of the house, even if the activity has been cleared by Home Confinement. I do not want to stand before this judge. Will he ask me yet again what I have learned? If I thank him for sending me to prison, will he send me back for failing to complete the screening process by now? I ought to have worn white socks.

I'm remembering last night. How desperate I was to be witnessed. How detrimental witnessing is to me in the long term. In the short-term, I feed (at a combustible rate) off men's eyes, off their wanting.

### December 8, 2008

Ah. Writing and smoking. A favorite past-time far too long neglected.

Night is so damned long when you can't sleep. In the winter? Forget it.

I get so nostalgic on the cusp of seasonal change. There is patchy snow on the grass from the first snowfall. I hate it. I desperately want to run away but to where . . .

A bar? A dealer? A buffet? Back to him? There is no escape.

*"i hate you," she says. "i dont want to be around you."*

*I both sympathize with her and shake my head at her fury. I raise my hands in defeat. It seems I have two choices: I can remain in this muck, allowing my foolish judgment to send me backward, deeper into the downward spiral. Or I can surrender again. A thousand times, over and over and hope God is not so exasperated with me that He will discipline me further.*

*The demons aren't helping. They have pitched camp again in my subconscious, telling me I'm a fool to blindly trust Him. Dear God, we never learn. I am stubborn, habitual, and rebellious. A bad combination. Or maybe it's my inclination to sabotage success. Because failure is all I really know. Rethink, Rachel. The time is now to rethink, kid.*

From: Miles Nash mnash345@hawks.rwu.edu
Subject: Dear girl on the bus . . .
To: recklessgrace84@yahoo.com
Date: Wednesday, January 7, 2009

Hi Rachel,

I got your note and I haven't stopped smiling since. It was truly amazing because when I spotted you on the bus I couldn't stop thinking about how many opportunities I miss by not taking a chance. Honest to god! So when you gave me that note I was inspired because you did something I didn't have the guts to do. Well allow me to introduce myself. My name is Miles. I am 22. Just last month I graduated from Roger Williams University. I live in Westwood, MA (suburb of Boston) though I'm finishing my rent in Portsmouth for the rest of the year. We should keep in touch. I would like to take you out sometime. At the very least keep this email thing going. If you would like to get together tonight or tomorrow afternoon gimme a call/text at 555-541-8819 or write back before the nights end. Again thank you for being so courageous. You made my day!
   -Miles

*November 17, 2008–May 13, 2009*
age twenty-four

# HOUSE ARREST

It was late November, and so cold Rachel could see her breath. Still, she wanted to be outside to smoke. Her ankle bracelet was attached to a field-monitoring device linked to our phone line and electrical outlet. Home Confinement gave her a seventy-five-foot leash. If she set one toe over our lot line, she was busted.

Rachel followed the sun. In the morning, she sat on the front steps with her coffee and Bible. When the sun climbed over the roof, journal in hand, she moved to the deck, dragging a chair to the sunny perimeter. Wearing her red hoodie, sometimes she journaled for hours, puffing on a running cigarette.

At our last prison dinner, I had asked Rachel to quit.

"You're no longer hooked. Why not give them up for good?"

She paused. "I really should."

But the day she was released, spotting a butt near the courthouse steps, probably one of Pete Dubois's, she stooped to pick it up, chuckling as she fumbled to light it.

Rachel's problems met her at the door.

"None of my jeans fit!" she reported, emerging from her room in gray sweatpants. Patting her rear end, she added, "The girls in prison call this 'junk in the trunk.' *They* think it's sexy. *I* hate it."

I gave her five pairs of my jeans; two fit perfectly. We found more at thrift stores.

Discovering Lance's girlfriend was the next blow.

"Why do you care? You said it was over, that he had nothing to offer you anymore."

"It still hurts. I go to prison, and he discards me—after *seven years*!"

Then there was Rachel's debt. I'd gathered quite a stack of bills while she was gone, and it kept growing. Apparently, she'd maxed out several credit cards on binge food and clothes. Now, with inflated interest rates, she owed over $20,000. Creditors constantly phoned. Lately, they were threatening lawsuits. The last thing Rachel needed was more legal problems. But she seemed unperturbed. She kept her bills in a shoebox in her room; after a while, she didn't even open them. When bill collectors called, she calmly explained her situation. Once they realized they couldn't bully her, they began to negotiate, slashing her debt way down. She agreed to pay once she found work.

Employment or continuing education was a condition of Home Confinement. Willing to do nearly anything, Rachel applied for countless jobs. However, with questions about criminal convictions standard on most job applications, she didn't receive one call.

By January 2009, when Rachel was still unemployed, she applied for Supplemental Security Income (SSI), government aid for disabled people with limited incomes. She had to declare herself homeless and mentally impaired. I was stricken, realizing it was true. My twenty-four-year-old daughter would be on the street if it weren't for me. Her bulimia and substance abuse *had* hindered her work. She *was* incapable of self-support.

Home Confinement (HC) allowed authorized activities. Rachel took the city bus to CODAC, medical appointments, church services, job interviews, as well as regularly scheduled meetings with her HC officer.

One afternoon, Rachel returned from a string of appointments smiling.

"I met a boy on the bus today," she told me while unbuttoning her maroon coat. "I actually wrote him a note, scribbled on a ripped-out page from my journal. Passed it to him like a schoolgirl." She chuckled while draping her coat on the back of a chair.

I had advised my daughter not to date until she recovered; otherwise, she would drag her issues into the relationship and sabotage it. She never listened. Then again, her problems never let up; they accumulated, like her bills. She had been in a holding pattern for years.

"Well, you certainly look happy. What did he say?"

"Don't know yet. Just gave him my digits and email address," she added, smirking. "I'm pretty sure he'll contact me. He wasn't the cutest, though he did have an interesting look. Dark eyes, alert."

"What about your ankle bracelet?" Dating was one activity I was certain HC did not allow.

"I can work around that." She smiled. "I've only got a few more months."

After several attempts, Rachel was accepted for SSI. I agreed to manage her funds as her "representative payee." She was eventually awarded a monthly allowance of $1,200, as well as a back payment of $26,000, which she would use to settle her debts and get an apartment.

Until this cash came in, she was penniless. Since I was working full-time as a technical writer, I paid Rachel's bills in exchange for light housekeeping.

She kept the house spotless. I came home to the welcoming smells of Windex and Lemon Pledge. Vacuum tracks on pristine carpets. Clear kitchen table and counters. Sparkling porcelain in the three bathrooms. Folded laundry at the foot of our beds.

One Saturday, when I was washing clothes, Rachel showed me how to fold bath towels more compactly to fit in our cramped linen closet. She taught me to store extra basket liners in the bottoms of wastebaskets, things she probably learned working as a CNA. I appreciated the tips. Still, I felt a pang—the same feeling that seized me every time she pulled out her worn bus schedule. That my daughter was reduced to riding the city bus and accepting SSI when she should have been driving her own car and gainfully employed made me viscerally ill.

✦   ✦   ✦

DURING RACHEL'S INCARCERATION, SHE had shown remarkable spiritual growth. We thought she had turned a corner. Of course, I had seen inklings of Rachel's ED during our visits—her glee at getting those quarters, her fleeting frown when I failed to bring sugary treats—but I swatted them away, like flies at a picnic. As her faith grew, I believed she would care less about her looks and more about pleasing God. Her grip on her ED would relax until she would finally let go, marveling that it had taken her so long to do so.

When Rachel and Matt began attending New Beginnings, a new local church that catered to young adults, I expected her faith to flourish. She would make friends, maybe even find a nice boyfriend.

But Rachel's vibrancy didn't last. She became quiet and detached, which I attributed to her circumstances. She was dealing with the fallout of her crimes. Literally tethered to our house, her days were filled with tedious tasks. When she did go out, it was for therapy, drug tests, or home confinement business. It was a hard phase that had to run its course, I told her. Once it did, things would improve. The clouds would part, and the sun would shine again.

Four months later, on April 9, 2009, Rachel returned to prison. This time, she was technically innocent. Desperate for treatment, she had tried to admit herself into Pioneer, an ED facility in Massachusetts, only to be turned away due to hyperglycemia. Convinced she had sabotaged her admission, the judge gave her thirty-four days without bail in maximum security, a hellish place, as she described to her friend Amanda in a letter:

**May 1, 2009**

*This wing is known as the armpit of the ACI, I'm assuming because the high turnover rate makes people not give a shit about being disgusting. They don't close the stall door while they're taking a crap. There is no end to stealing, to drama in general. Lesbianism abounds—oh, you'll love this: they call their girlfriends their "hersbands." A few days ago some classy broad smeared shit all over the bathroom walls.*

*I'm heartbroken over missing another summer. This time of year is my absolute favorite: when spring melts into summer. There's a bitter taste in my mouth. Yet again imprisoned in more ways than one due to this [eating] disorder. I don't have the will to fight it anymore. I'm pretty much resigned to the bondage now that I've had it for ten years.*

Rachel was released from maximum security on May 13, 2009, at which time she was expelled from Drug Court. Though I was not surprised, it was still disturbing. Now she would have a criminal record for ten years.

But my dear mother, who'd gone to court with Matt to pick up Rachel, gave me the good news first: She had signed Rachel up for a fifteen-month program at Teen Challenge (TC)! I'd told Mom the day before while driving her back from the airport that Rachel's addictions were out of control. She desperately needed a long-term program, preferably TC.

My mouth gaped. "How did you manage *that*?"

"How do you get anywhere with Rachel?" she said with a wry smile. "I bribed her with a carton of Kool Lights."

Mom told me they drove directly from court to the women's TC in Providence, where she made the down payment. Rachel was scheduled to start in one week. Of course, I regretted her expulsion from Drug Court, but what good was a clean record if she was ill? TC had an unparalleled success rate. If Rachel stayed the full term, she had a good chance of recovering from her drug addiction and her EDs.

## May 22–July 4, 2009

It's her.
She's nervous. And she wants to rush the inevitable.
Is she my soul?
This broken emptiness?
This gaping ravenous hole
swallowing everything?
These fragments overpowered by vanity?

# "My soul and my flesh warred"

## May 22, 2009

I cannot believe I am here . . . I am freaking out over so many things, it is unreal. I feel completely and utterly abandoned. My fucking middle is already filling out nicely thanks to the 10 units of unnecessary insulin I took for the physical.

During the intake process, TC made me sign the paperwork agreeing to abide by their rules—they search outgoing mail, allow only one ten-min phone call every two weeks. When I reached the portion stating a willingness to remain for the entire program—"MINIMUM 15 MONTHS"—I thought I was going to vomit. I can't believe I will be allowed no contact with Miles Nash, the boy I met on the bus. He's such a comfort to me. Why am I freaking out to this degree?

## May 23, 2009

I didn't shower last night because the only vestiges of his smell were in my hair. I understand now why we are denied photos, letters, calls. They're distracting. I live in the Hawks hoodie Nash gave me.

The women here, except for one or two, are huge. Their guts, their asses, their arms, even their calves. Their monitoring of medical procedures is shoddy— they do not check the syringe to see if I've drawn up the accurate amount. They do not watch me while I'm injecting. There is no verification of carb counting or accurate testing. Everything is done on the honor system, but my relief is bittersweet. This house is charmed. God whispers into the ears of these leaders . . . how long before He squeals on me? I want nicotine and sin, liquor, and false promises.

I have this haunting image: I am lithe, clad only in underwear, endless tan limbs crossed, arm attached to a hand, delivering a cigarette to my lips. I am in front of a window. A man crazily in love with me—maybe Nash—witnesses this scene.

Only two things call like sirens, causing me to keep one foot out the door. A lovely thin body and Miles Nash. Once I get bigger, he will not want me.

## May 24, 2009

*This morning was spent in the ER, presumably because TC leaders found my directions for managing my diabetes questionable. They wanted a doctor to document how many times per day I ought to be testing . . . they basically wanted a type 1 diabetes handbook because they must have realized that I couldn't be trusted. JoBeth sat me down and told me they weren't sure they could keep me—weren't sure they were medically equipped to accommodate my co-occurring issues. I nodded and looked out at Adelaide Avenue from their windows and wondered if I would ever know I was where I belonged.*

*At chapel tonight, I wept and wrestled with God and maybe my demons. My soul and my flesh warred, threatening to tear me apart. How desperately I longed to have nothing in my heart but Jesus, to release this bondage and anxiety and receive life and joy which I tasted once, in prison, of all places. Oh, but how my flesh uprises at the sight of the dancing bodies of overweight girls here.*

*Even if I test the waters, telling myself, "If you can't live with the weight, it isn't as if you don't know how to get back to this size!" I know this is the real deal. If I commit to this, I will not turn back. Oh, how I wept.*

## May 27, 2009

*At ten p.m. last night, I found myself in Pastor Cheri's office, being told I was going home because Teen Challenge didn't consider themselves medically able to meet my needs. They still wanted me to sleep in a staff bedroom. Muffled by the sound of my fan, I was able to sneak out of the room at around two a.m., whereupon I adopted the mindset of "fuck em" and proceeded to raid the kitchen. I took an apple (really, now, are you serious?), two Auntie Anne's pretzels, and a few thumbs of peanut butter. I then moved on to the b-day cake I had begrudgingly denied myself two days ago but now cut myself a big slice. It was a weird spice-cakey affair. Afterward, I went into the first-floor bathroom to vomit (something I hadn't done since walking through the doors of TC), but to my horror, nothing came up except cake. Both huge pretzels—as I'd expected—were clinging to the floor of my stomach for dear life. In the morning, I ate Flax cereal + coffee and followed their ass-backward directions of waiting one hour after eating to test and dose. I was the only one unfazed by the high glucose reading. When I refused the seven units to correct it (what for?! I'm going home anyhow), Sister Lisa said it was either insulin or the ER.*

*I took five units of Humalog and squirted the other 2u into the carpet. They still insisted that I go to RI Hospital.*

*I never could see myself sticking it out for fifteen months. Still, yesterday, I felt my soul delight in being fed for the first time in one year. I was anticipating the structure, the clear conscience associated with obedience, a purposeful future, not to mention learning how to eat like a normal person. I recalled that last serious prayer session when I was alone in the conference room, yelling at God for His faithfulness, for His unwillingness to let me go. Why do I flee from everyone who tries to help me?*

MY HEART STOPPED THE morning of the 28th when I received word at work that Rachel was being discharged from TC only days after starting the program. The supervisor who called said they were prepared to ride out Rachel's bulimia, having moved her into a staff bedroom to avert her nocturnal binges. Her diabetes was another matter. She routinely refused her full insulin dosage and had been caught spitting in her blood sample.

I powered down my computer, grabbed my purse, and drove to Rhode Island Hospital. I found Rachel in a hospital bed in the ICU, refusing IV insulin. With chilling impassivity, she said she was tired of needles and pain. Since she could no longer clear her record, she had nothing to live for. She admitted she had hoped TC would work out. Being released only proved she was a lost cause.

A red-headed nurse tried in vain to reason with Rachel. Moments later, a fetching young doctor in scrubs whisked in. Rolling a squeaky stool next to Rachel, he sat down and mentally walked her through the sobering diabetes-related health outcomes if she continued this course. She still refused. For hours, I pleaded, prayed, wept. Nothing I said or did mattered.

It was night, eleven hours after her admission, when Rachel finally accepted IV insulin.

### May 29, 2009

*I am bargaining Ativan for IV insulin here in the psychiatric ER of Rhode Island Hospital, where I have been a prisoner for ninety-nine straight hours. They just gave me ten units of Humalog, which means I'm up to fifteen so far today. Unacceptable. This meal is so getting barfed back up.*

## May 30, 2009

*I'm repressing the call wherein my suspicions were confirmed that Nash is done with me. With us. Maybe we are not so similar; I never could abandon someone precious to me. I am dumbstruck by his caustic tone and comments. "You think I'm gonna wait for you? Be faithful to you for a year?" The whole world fell away. "I loved you. I cared about you." As if love could be flipped like a light switch.*

*I reek of vomit. There is no one to see me. There is no one to talk to. Nowhere to run. How detrimental to have your self-esteem contingent on someone else's view of you. Had I money, connections, a car, I'd be checked out of this hospital and shooting dope into my veins.*

## May 31, 2009—12:30 a.m.

*Still in Rhode Island Hospital. I am hoarding my meds: Ativan, Xanax, Valium. I just snorted a Valium, and if I could get a needle, I'd attempt to get a crushed pill through this IV line. No one is monitoring anything save for my blood sugar. I go into the kitchen multiple times per day for discarded patient meals, peanut butter tubs, saltines, graham crackers, ice cream, and dry turkey sandwiches from those appetizing box lunches. Yesterday I filled an entire pitcher with lasagna from the trays waiting to be dumbwaitered down to wherever they wash the dishes. It was classy.*

*My skin is broken out. I catch sight of my expanding frame in windows and glass doors when I sneak outside for a cigarette and freak the fuck out. I have no friends anymore. I wish for someone to talk with, and though I am moderately certain God is waiting on the sidelines, it is actual dialogue I crave. No one understands. Mom and Ryan visited yesterday, and even as I bemoaned my rapidly expanding waistline and the fact that my whole body is jiggling, I was met with nothing but criticism. "Stop focusing on negative thoughts. The things you worry about are so stupid," my mother says, sitting there, all grace and dancer's physique.*

*I've put on twelve pounds in one week—I was weighed; I'm not imagining this shit. It occurs to me that if given the choice between being thin or having other things that bring me joy, I always choose my dysfunction. Every time. I hate my recklessness. Why can't I treat myself just a little gently?*

**June 1, 2009**

*Due to a blood sugar of sixty-six yesterday (because a sandwich was delivered one and a half hours after the Humalog was administered), my IV was reinserted, and they refused to let me leave the floor. Since the restriction was imposed, I've snuck out at least four times. I walk down to Eddy Street, craving witnesses, begging for someone halfway decent to offer to take me out of here.*

*I know you are moments away from giving up entirely. But what if it really is possible to be free of the obsessive, plaguing thoughts about food? What if life were enjoyable, peaceful, rather than a constant uphill battle to escape anxiety, desperation, and fear? Don't you deserve to find out?*

ON JUNE 2, 2009, Rachel was transported by ambulance from Rhode Island Hospital to Pioneer, the same ED facility in Massachusetts that she had tried to check herself into months earlier. I followed the ambulance in my Corolla, thankful that this was done sans siren and flashing lights.

Recommended by the ICU doctor, Pioneer seemed to have a good reputation. Their website boasted multiple levels of care, starting with twenty-four-hour hospitalization for seven to twelve days or until patients were mentally and behaviorally stable, at which time they would be placed in a lower level of care. Since Rachel was a wreck, mentally and behaviorally, I assumed they would keep her in lock-down for a while. Pioneer's intake person assured me on the phone that Rachel's treatment would last at least three months. This was not nearly long enough, but I was running out of options.

I found Rachel sitting on a bench, awaiting her admission. I sat down beside her. A few female patients floated by in thin hospital robes, looking like Auschwitz victims.

"I'm jealous," she said. "Seeing those girls makes me want to do whatever it takes to look like them."

Driving home, I willed my shoulders to relax. Rachel was in good hands. If she could get her EDs under control, the TC director had assured me they would take Rachel back into the program. When I told Rachel, something like guarded hope flashed across her face.

Three days later, Ms. Murdock, Rachel's caseworker from Pioneer, called, informing me that Rachel was doing well and was ready to be discharged. Was this a twisted joke? I told her that was impossible. My daughter was seriously ill. She had a long-term ED that had never been adequately treated.

Ms. Murdock was firm. She said the doctor had already signed off on Rachel, essentially discontinuing her insurance coverage, a fact I verified after hanging up.

My face burned. How dare a doctor make this determination without even bothering to consult with Perry and me. I wondered if he had even read Rachel's full medical history. I doubted it very much.

With trembling hands, I phoned Perry. He said he would call Blue Cross and get to the bottom of it if he had to go all the way up to the top dog.

The next day, Ms. Murdock called back. She said that though Rachel did not qualify for residential treatment, their next level of care, our Blue Cross covered outpatient care. I declined, claiming that Rachel needed supervision.

"In that case, we'll prepare her discharge papers. You can pick her up today."

"I can't take her back until her ED is under control. I have other kids. She's been self-medicating under my roof."

"Then you leave me no choice but to drop her off at a homeless shelter."

I felt like she had slapped my face.

"Excuse me?"

"If you decline to pick her up, we have no other recourse," she asserted.

I dialed the facility's Chief Medical Officer. Explaining the situation, I begged him to keep Rachel until I could find another program. He agreed but then reneged the next day, claiming he could not help me. Why would he change his mind? What would I do now?

Meanwhile, Rachel called, anxiously echoing Ms. Murdock's threat: "Mom, they're going to bring me to a shelter if you don't pick me up!" She further informed me that, per Ms. Murdock, I was being charged $1,200 for each day she stayed.

✦   ✦   ✦

### June 3, 2009—Pioneer

*I'm the biggest one here. Strangely enough, being surrounded by beautiful, thin girls has cured my urge to binge.*

*I am alone with myself, and I do not like it. I want to call Nash. But his gutting words still ring in my ears, reminding me he is too young for the unconditional love I need.*

### June 5, 2009

*Oh. Oh. Oh. It is very possible they will not accept me into the residential portion of Pioneer courtesy of (huge shocker) my defunct pancreas.*

## June 8, 2009

*I was informed that Blue Cross definitely doesn't cover residential programs.*

*I have been checking my meds to snort in the privacy of my room and barely escaped a shakedown that occurred after Angelina got caught smoking in the shower room. I haven't opened my Bible or the Christian ED book since my arrival. All I care about is my narcotics—my cigarette supply is dwindling—and the way I look.*

*I spent the afternoon sobered by the sight of my new roommate, Wendy, stumbling around, literally intoxicated by meds (some Pioneer supplied; others came from her private reserve). I'm taken aback by how pharmaceuticals are offered in lieu of actual therapy here. I'm disgusted and horrified by the realization that I'm steps away from being in Wendy's shoes.*

*What if I truly began to believe I could do this. Could survive. Well, I know I can survive. What if I could learn to live.*

## June 11, 2009

*So it would seem as though the likelihood of being dumped at a shelter is low, though when I called Mom with the hope of quelling my anxieties on this front, she told me that if I were allowed back home, both my iPod and Facebook would be prohibited. Furthermore, she flat-out refused to mail me cigarettes and told me to "just stop" being anxious. Her lack of understanding with regard to emotional management made me want to scream.*

*"You can't always pray or crack a Bible, especially when problems pass a certain point," I said. When I do, my nerves worsen. If another patient hadn't bought me smokes, I would be having a full-blown panic attack by now.*

*She is positively infuriating. Of course, Christ is ultimately the only way I'll beat this, but sometimes you need a plan B, C, D, and E. Trouble with me is, I save Christ for Plan Z. Seriously, though, her ignorance over the trauma of weight gain in the ED individual blows me away. Just stop it! Dear God!*

Murdock was ratcheting up the pressure. She wanted to discharge Rachel within the next two days. As wary as I was of taking Rachel back in, I could not stomach sending her to a shelter. Just as I was preparing to capitulate, a solution presented itself. Another patient, forty-year-old Amy Banks, who was also being discharged, offered Rachel the spare room in her apartment in Salem, Massachusetts. They would coach each other in their recovery. Murdock was all for it. So was Rachel, who, sensing my qualms, put Amy on the phone.

"Rachel and I are kindred spirits," Amy chuckled with a gravelly voice. Smoking, I gathered, was one thing they had in common. "I know I'll enjoy her company—she's a hot sketch—but this will also help our recovery. We'll keep an eye on each other."

Rachel and Amy were discharged the next day, with no aftercare in place, except the name of a local outpatient program.

Amy was tall and stick-thin, with green eyes, fair skin, and wispy red hair. I learned she had bulimia and anorexia. She smiled, maintaining eye contact while we chatted in the sunroom. Rachel ducked in and out of view as she hauled boxes and bags to Amy's red Volkswagen.

Rachel had told me that Amy did not want rent money, only help with food and utilities. Uneasy with that arrangement, I questioned her again.

"Let's not talk about rent yet. Let's wait a week or so and see how this works out," she wisely suggested.

The next day, Perry called me, all excited. Due to his persistence, Blue Cross had extended his benefit. He'd just received written notification that Rachel qualified for residential treatment. Ms. Murdock had been verbally informed the previous week.

When cornered, she confessed. "I'm terribly sorry. It's—it's just that Rachel had been noncompliant since day one. She blatantly broke rules, and other patients followed her lead. We must maintain order here."

*Why do you think she was in treatment?* I wanted to scream.

Instead, I terminated the conversation. I could have insisted they take Rachel back, especially with Blue Cross in my corner, but how did I know they would not mistreat her? I no longer trusted this facility we had turned to in our desperation, only to be deceived, contributing to our confusion and anxiety. At the same time, I felt stabbed by my daughter, the rebel and hell-raiser, who had once again sabotaged her recovery.

✦   ✦   ✦

### June 17, 2009

*I am vacuous. Lonely in my own company. It alarms me on a level I disguise with liquor and prescription medication. My heart tells me where I belong. My physical body resists—intent on its demise, it seems.*

*Do I feel this way because the boy I love is so distant?*

*I want to know him. I want to correct my mistakes, but do I even have a partner in the affair? I cannot stand to be left out. Excluded from even the hurtful unveiling. I need to know him, doubts, pain, disappointment. The connection sustains me. I feel a piece of me reaching out, begging for soul conjoinment. Relief at the genuine. Always. Hands down. Slow dancing in a burning room.*

### June 23, 2009

*Remember the concern of two eating-disordered cohabitants either being able to support or enable one another? Yeah. I mean, having access to someone who speaks my language, polices me, genuinely cares, and is financially supporting me is awesome. Still, there are definitely toxic elements to this bond. We drink every night. We chain smoke. We spend money recklessly. We abuse prescription medication. We procrastinate like motherfuckers. We are both homebodies. We aren't proactive enough in terms of locating a treatment program. Neither of us is following the established meal plan. I threw up twice the day before yesterday and didn't come clean to her. I polished off her granola bars and a whole box of cereal. I'm so polluted at bedtime I don't even remember what I've said, done, or eaten. The sundown effect is killing me. Depression mounts. Last night we both passed out on the couch, and I burned a hole in my Hawks hoodie.*

### June 30, 2009

*I do not belong here. This environment is not good for me. Or maybe I am the one that has poisoned this environment. I don't even feel better while drunk anymore. My anxiety level is at the point where there's nothing I wouldn't do or use to escape from it. I can't even write about it because I don't trust that this journal will go unread.*

*I unfriended Nash the night before last. Then (and this very well may be chronologically off because I'd taken a whole Xanax and been drinking), I made myself sick on the side of the apartment complex because I knew Amy had passed out. Afterward, I came upstairs, ate tons of food, and purged in the toilet.*

*I hate relying on people; it leaves me defenseless and vulnerable.*

RACHEL AND AMY HAD been living together for about a week when I drove to Salem with Mom and my sister, Dolores, who were visiting. Amy was ready to discuss a more permanent arrangement.

Her apartment was located on a quaint side street in a decent neighborhood. It was bright and spacious. A magnolia candle was burning, its fragrance wafting through the tidy rooms. We sat in her living room on a mauve sofa and loveseat. There was an open Bible on the oval coffee table, and a televangelist was speaking on the barely audible console television.

Under the guise of seeing Rachel's room, I asked her how it was going. On the phone, she had said it was fine, but I wanted to see her eyes.

"We smoke too much," she said, moving her journal from the twin bed to the white nightstand so we could sit down, "and we haven't even started looking for a program." Rachel's eyes finally found mine. "But she watches me like a hawk, Mom. It makes me think twice about bingeing. When I do, she gives me grace, which makes me want to try harder."

I had sent Amy a check for food and utilities. Now, I wrote her a $300 check for July's rent.

"Did either of you smell booze?" Dolores asked as we drove away from the apartment.

"I did," Mom admitted, biting her lower lip. Mom's olfactory senses never failed.

I made a U-turn, tires slightly screeching.

Rachel answered the door, carrying a tall drink.

Verifying that it was vodka, I dumped it in the kitchen sink. Glancing into the living room, I noted that the TV had been turned off. Smoke hung in the air from the snuffed candle. Amy, who was just entering the kitchen, flushed deeply.

"We were just so nervous about your visit," she stammered.

"Give me a break! You two were trying to snow me so I'd finance your party." My eyes spun from Amy to Rachel, who was struck dumb, her face a palette of shock and guilt. "What about helping each other recover?"

I turned back to Amy. "Keep the check, but it's the last one."

"Let me know when you're serious about getting help," I told Rachel on my way out.

✦    ✦    ✦

### July 2, 2009

*Nash is here, and I'm so lonely.*

*I did everything I knew I ought not to do. I pursued when I prefer to be chased. I pressured him when he expressed little to no interest in coming over. I bit my tongue when I needed to talk it out. It's a touch masochistic. Even in* the act, there is (I imagine) a funny smile on my face at knowing how foolish I am—knowing outcomes and yet still risking her.

I sit back a little with this expression and stare at the boy. What can I do to make him feel the way about me that he used to?

He is falling asleep on the floor of my room. He will not look at me, and it makes me feel so low, so disgusting. Being a glutton for punishment, I make sexual advances that aren't reciprocated. I fight the knowledge that this is the last time.

I whisper, "I'm sorry, Nash."

He either ignores me or is already asleep, for he says nothing.

## July 4, 2009

I am morbidly depressed. Never thought I'd see the day when suicide seemed a viable option again. The only time I feel okay is under the influence of prescription meds and hard liquor. The Lord will not rescue me because I will not avail myself of him. When I was with Lance, I do not remember being this bad. I remember hopelessness, but this isn't the same. this is inability to function. this is unimaginable, inescapable anxiety and restlessness. this is being an utter stranger to myself. this is not even being able to cry. this is running out of words. this is being the living dead. entirely vacuous and giving up.

July 5–15, 2009
age twenty-five

# INANE RESCUES

WE WERE LIVING ON the top floor of a three-story tenement. The kids were young—Rachel five, Matt three, Ryan unborn. Perry was not in the picture. Tenants occupied the first and second floors. I was setting the table when I heard a boom and felt the house shake. Glasses tipped, plates slid. Walls cracked, creating giant black fissures. Plaster dust rained from the ceiling. The kids screamed, their eyes like crazed horses. Matt howled, holding up his arms. I scooped him up and held him close.

Suddenly tenants were banging at our door. "Let us in! We can't get out!"

For some reason, no one could escape through the front door. We were trapped inside a collapsing building, and I was responsible for everyone. While the kids and tenants were running amok, I called 911.

In moments, we heard a shrill siren. From the third-story windows, we watched a long fire truck with flashing red lights and blaring horns pull into our driveway. What followed was an insane series of futile rescue attempts. First, firefighters blasted water toward our non-burning house. Realizing their folly, they quickly switched tactics. Holding up a large, circular net, they motioned wildly for us to jump, but I saw, to my horror, that there was a huge hole in the mesh.

The house was rocking now. We were hysterical, thinking we were going to be crushed alive. Finally, the firemen produced a ladder. Just when we thought we would be saved, we saw that it was ridiculously short, reaching only to the second floor.

In my panic, I did not see Rachel hanging over an open window until she fell to her death on the pavement below.

I bolted upright in bed, my heart charging. Next came tears—deep, choking sobs. I felt Phil's solid chest against my back, his arms encircling me.

"What? What did you dream?" Pressing his warm, stubbly face against mine, he whispered, "Tell me."

I relayed the dream to him in spastic sobs.

He kissed my cheek, my hand. "Thank God it was just a dream."

"But it wasn't!" I wept.

✦    ✦    ✦

IT WAS JULY FIFTH, Rachel's birthday, and she had called from Amy's apartment in Salem. I was in New Hampshire at a family graduation party. We'd already talked that morning, but now she was crying into my ear. I left the shade and laughter of the tent, making my way past lush, perfumed flower beds to talk in my in-laws' quiet driveway.

"I'm twenty-five years old, and I have absolutely nothing to show for it!"

There was a note of despair in her voice I had never heard.

"You can change that. We just need to find a good, long program so you can work out your issues. Once you resolve those, you can do anything you like. By your next birthday, you could have an entirely different life."

"That's not true, Mom," she said in between sobs. "I have a criminal record. I'll never get my nursing degree. All that time and money is gone."

"Then you'll find something else. Psychology or education."

Despite my pep talk, I was quaking inside.

Desperate, I dialed my dear friend, Susan. I hated to do it. I knew she was already overloaded, not only supporting her husband, who was headmaster at Ryan's Christian prep school, but also serving as president of their board of trustees. I begged her to counsel Rachel. A clear thinker with a sweet spirit and vast scriptural knowledge, Susan had studied biblical counseling and had helped friends and family members resolve personal problems and crises. Without hesitation, she agreed, as did Rachel, though she hardly knew Susan. I was deeply relieved. If anyone could guide Rachel back to God, it was Susan.

Rachel returned from Salem the next day following a run-in with Amy she didn't elaborate on.

I knew she was abusing prescription drugs, trading one addiction for another. I told her more than once. She swore her "meds" were all "legit," prescribed by doctors. She was also drinking hard alcohol. I found a bottle of vodka under the bathroom sink, and Ryan uncovered another in a laundry basket in the basement.

On July fifteenth, we tried to admit Rachel into Cambridge Eating Disorder Center (CEDC) in Cambridge, Massachusetts. If she met their criteria, they would take her that day, pending Blue Cross approval, which for some reason could not be predetermined.

Rachel packed her bag, and we drove to Cambridge, with Ryan in tow. It was his seventeenth birthday. I planned to entertain him in Boston while Rachel did her intake.

When I dropped Rachel off at eleven a.m., I was told to keep my cell phone close. They would call with the verdict in a couple hours.

I found a parking garage in Boston, and Ryan and I set off on foot, emerging from the cool, dark structure into the arms of a glorious day—bright sun, blue sky, mild breeze. I wanted to show Ryan a good time, not just because it was his birthday. I was painfully aware that I had neglected him, indeed all the kids, during Rachel's crises.

We visited the Mapparium at the Mary Baker Eddy Library. We'd seen it before, but who could resist walking through that giant stained-glass globe again? Next, we viewed the observatory on the fiftieth floor of the Prudential Building. What views. I loved the juxtaposition of old and new, mirrored skyscrapers beside ancient churches and brownstones; how the Charles River snaked elegantly through the cityscape; streets and buildings appearing so tidy and geometric from that height.

We ate lunch at Au Bon Pain—turkey and cheddar on crusty baguettes—under a big red umbrella. While we were tossing bread scraps to swooping, cawing seagulls, laughing at their audacity, my cell rang. Rachel qualified for CEDC! Now we just needed to wait for insurance approval, which gave Ryan and me more time to explore.

Next, we strolled along the Charles River, a breeze tossing our hair. When our feet began to ache, we sat on the grassy riverbank, watching tilted sailboats. Ryan chatted about his passion for music and art and his plans to start CCRI in the fall and transfer to URI once he finished his general education courses. What an opportunity to bond with my son. I smiled and chimed in, but inwardly, I was wringing my hands. What was the holdup? Rachel desperately needed help. Blue Cross had to deliver.

Tingling sunburns drove us to our feet. Ryan mentioned needing guitar strings. We crossed Longfellow Bridge, quickly locating a music store on Newbury Street that smelled like incense. While strumming a guitar, Ryan struck up a conversation with a guy in dreadlocks, who was also sampling the merchandise. As they started jamming, my cell rang. I went outside to answer it and was instructed to pick up Rachel. Blue Cross had denied coverage.

Wearing black sunglasses, Rachel was sitting on a bench in front of the CEDC, smoking. I popped the trunk. Leaning over, she carefully snuffed out her half-smoked cigarette on the sidewalk, returning it to her pack. She dropped her suitcase in the trunk, slamming it shut, then slipped into the passenger seat Ryan had vacated for her. On the way home, she barely spoke.

# "Ill Poetess"

### July 7, 2009

Amy and I smoked pot the night of my birthday. I had run out of Adderall. Then somehow, I "lost" eighty dollars—money allocated for diabetes meds—after which I had a total meltdown. Amy told me I had to leave under the curiously convenient excuse of Section 8 discovering I'd been there for over two weeks. Horseshit.

I am directionless here at Mom's without the Adderall. I took Xanax like it was candy yesterday, and I truly believe that its sedating effects combined with the amphetamine withdrawal are the only things keeping me from a nervous breakdown. I found some of Ryan's Concerta[101] in Mom's medicine cabinet but am unable to gauge its effectiveness because I've had 4-5 cups of coffee already, binged and purged at eight a.m., and had half a Xanax. So who the hell knows.

### July 11, 2009

I feel like reverting to the code we used in seventh grade because some snoopy family member might discover my dirty secrets. Dad's condemning voice rings in my conscience: "What have you gained by journaling? You invest so much time into it, yet you haven't grown."

Probably true, but it remains a cathartic exercise for this burdened soul. I must chart myself because I forget her. Dad minimizes the benefit of venting, even if doing it on paper poses enormous risk. If I can't purge my mind in an uncensored way . . . it's maddening. I resent having to debate with myself whether to journal; these pages are MINE.

Last night, I had my first episode of feeling seconds from death from some life-threatening mix of substances: Valium and two hundred milligrams of Seroquel. Today I had my second, caused, I suspect, by taking Adderall very late in the day. Ryan and I were in the kitchen when I collapsed on the floor. My skull hit the ceramic tiles hard; my glasses were badly bent. I recovered in nanoseconds, but he was alarmed enough to wake up Mom and Phil. They got me a chair while I tried to appear as coherent as possible. But it felt like there was cotton plugging my ears; their voices were so distant. Sweat poured down the small of my back, and droplets soaked through my green T-shirt from Nash. I tested and blamed the for-once healthy blood sugar on a possibly faulty glucometer. Mom started digging in a kitchen drawer for the instruction manual as I furtively wiped the sweat glistening on my forearms.

Ryan blew my cover about the Adderall. I talked over him and continued to insist I was low, blaming it on the walking we'd done and having failed to eat immediately after dosing. I said I was fine but felt unable to stand. They began a scavenger hunt in the kitchen for something sugary to leave at my bedside. As I suggested honey, I made my getaway, hoping they wouldn't witness my drenched T-shirt. I climbed the stairs as fast as possible, but my vision was rapidly fading. I begged myself to press on, all the while foreseeing an ambulance ride. I'm still shocked I made it. Still shocked there was no shake-down of my bedroom.

### July 13, 2009

God, how I wish for a kindred spirit to know me in detail and I them. Yet. Oh yet, yet, yet. I shouldn't be putting such stock in anyone of this world. How can I even be surprised by complications that are almost assuredly a result of the loving, intervening hand of my Father? Love should feel safe. It's supposed to make you feel better, not worse, the opposite of how Miles makes me feel lately.

The other day Angie scooped me up to crash at her apartment in Fall River. After two glasses of Sangria and two Xanax, I, of course, engaged in my stupid-ass habit of buzz-dialing. I wanted Nash to ask what I was doing because, for once, I was out socializing instead of him. I don't even recall if it was Ang or me who jokingly told him to come by for some action. He couldn't have thought we were serious, but either way, he came over.

I'm pretty sure he only had two drinks. I'm trying to remember what insti-gated this. Oh yes, Angie came up to me and said, "Should I try and, like, seduce him?" And I said yes. Wanting to see what he'd do. Hoping, expecting he'd say no. I will not write what happened next. I'm shaking now, like I did after nearly losing my virginity to Lance when I had lied and said I had to leave because I was having a hypoglycemic episode. Shaking with the knowledge of the threshold I'd almost crossed.

I don't remember how Nash left this morning. He was still sleeping while we were having coffee. The next memory I have is looking down from Angie's third-story window and seeing his car gone. I am feeling this odd type of

paralysis . . . like something cataclysmic has taken place, and I am just waiting
for the shock waves to hit me.

## July 15, 2009

Blaring subconscious alarm
tries to reach disabled eardrums.
The whole world sleeps,
but I will myself
to receive these screams
while holding them at bay.

I wrestle with regret
that these are the final hours
I will not be entirely consumed
with hatred for my earthly tent
and would enjoy July's temporary hue
on skin I can only partially claim to own
I will take in legs and arms
aware that I will miss them
more than the sweetest lover
in a mere hour's time.

Tangled impossible maze of thought
disorder,
if I cannot make sense of it
no soul ever will.
I crave to be understood,
accepted
yet cannot accomplish the feat.

Thus why do I persist,
clinging to the familiarity of torture?

How can this be my home
if I never have peace
never feel settled
am vagrant in my very self

*the doublemindedness*
*is enough to slice me in two.*

### July 17, 2009
### Things I Am Thankful For:

Parents that genuinely love me and have not given up on me.

My brothers.

A merciful, loving Father who showers me with grace and has a purpose for my life.

Susan Bailey.

My ability to write, be articulate.

My creativity.

Being allowed back home.

Being approved by Medicaid

The summer.

Being off Home Confinement and out of prison.

Having strangers pray for me.

My mind, though it tortures me on a regular basis.

Being off methadone.

Not having the means ($, car) to binge as often as I otherwise would.

Awareness that I <u>can</u> make it through the night without throwing up.

Still being able to have kids someday.

Being here to help my mom out around the house.

Aaron.

### July 20, 2009

Blustery today, with traces of autumn that I shrink from. The highlight of my day was taking the bus to Superior Court in Providence. Then back home to spend another interminable weekend with Mom and Phil hovering over me. Desperate for company, I called Aaron (Lance's friend who I'd met once). Aaron jumped at the opportunity to come over. He's not the most thrilling guy. We spent a predictably quiet, uneventful afternoon on the deck. I miss loud music and stupid jokes that make me practically scream in laughter. I didn't feel that with Aaron. Is this depression or the depressant effects of alcohol?

### July 24, 2009

I've been hanging out with Aaron a lot this past week. Though his awkwardness and loneliness made me leery at first, I'm really starting to enjoy his company.

He's not the conversationalist Nash was, but the kid tries. I think he genuinely tries to understand and help me. The only benefit so far is his rescuing me from this house at night.

### July 28, 2009

I am the embodiment of regression. I am making the same mistakes. I cannot find a job, and I'm freaking out over being broke and unable to finance my chain-smoking habit. After a fruitless job hunt, I called Aaron, and we had drinks at the bar by OverFlo's. I am kicking myself for not asking him to buy me cigarettes. I am beyond disgusted by anyone who is attracted to me physically because I feel like my inner vacancy is so painfully obvious to absolutely everyone. I hate being awake.

I also hate being asleep.

Last night I dreamed that I disposed of the mutilated body of an elderly uncle (who I did not recognize). I thought it was real to the degree that I woke up with this burdened foreboding that persisted until I was on the toilet and realized I wasn't an accessory to murder after all. I started bingeing anyway, I was so disturbed. Even after snorting half an Addie, I kept eating. Then I wasted another day being anxious and plucking stray hairs in the sun.

### August 2, 2009

Aaron took me out to dinner. I really cannot get over how inexplicably awesome he was with me. I mean, for years I've believed that restaurants are better off avoided, ESPECIALLY at dinner hour. The guy let me talk it out—the dysfunction and fear in my head. Through the process of ordering and eating, he let me ask silly questions like, "Am I eating this at a normal pace?" He also asked me specifics, which to me is the hallmark of genuine concern. I don't mind if someone is not able to 100% "get it" as long as they care enough to make an effort. I don't hold the unrealistic expectation anymore of being "saved" by some male admirer, but I've never had someone convince me so fully of their concern and desire to not only help but also to understand. What a gift.

### August 9, 2009

Aaron and I went to church together this morning. The message couldn't have been more perfect for me: mental battles and conquering the flesh with scripture. He even said, "You better pay attention to this."

Yesterday Mom asked if Aaron and I were seeing each other as more than friends. When I said no, she asked why not. She plainly likes him. He's the only one who's allowed to take me out at night. This is beyond shocking because it's only been, what, three days since Ryan discovered a bottle of vodka upon knocking over my basket of laundry. Mom also somehow found out I'd had the Xanax prescription filled and sold all ninety pills. Since then, I've been pretty much put on house arrest until I'm accepted into a program. I only ended up staying in for two nights, the second of which Aaron came over, and we watched a movie. That was the only night we have ever spent sans alcohol, and it doesn't even count because I had at least two pills.

But when she asked why I didn't like him romantically, I hesitated. I said I didn't know, but I do. I'm still in love with Nash.

God, how often am I with Aaron and wishing he was Nash. Or that Nash had Aaron's personality. Running silly errands. No awkward silences. The support. The ceaseless concern. The affection. The tears. The handholding. The songs. Aaron is everything I've ever, ever wanted in a man, but he is not the one I want this treatment from.

Damn myself. I do not accept me and my behavior right now, so there is something undeniably repulsive in the fact that Aaron does. When he tries to kiss me, I close my eyes and pretend it's Nash.

I am sitting in Aaron's driveway. He is apparently more intuitive than I thought because he is staying away, busying himself with something as a pretext to grant me space. God, he listens. Why do I do (almost) everything imaginable to push him away? I drink. I smoke. I make few, if any, excuses for myself. I let them see me for what I am, and when they don't run in the opposite direction, I am stricken with confusion or revulsion.

This is love, is it not?

I had a phone intake yesterday with Renfrew, that ED rehab in Philadelphia, Pennsylvania. They asked who my support system was. Only Aaron came to mind. Three scant weeks and he is undeniably my closest, dearest friend. I trust him wholly. It's beautiful.

### August 13, 2009

I'm getting worse. I tell myself it is because my admittance into Renfrew is imminent. I'm pulling my usual pre-rehab shit: losing as much weight as is humanly possible before entering to buy more time for the inevitable weight gain.

Depression is seeping in, fueled by alcohol and stubbornness. I meet my eyes for a moment in the mirror. "You know this won't work. Are you sincerely out of 'fight'?" I hear the devil whispering into my ear, like a jazz DJ, talking me into sleep, only the sleep is death now.

**August 16, 2009**

Wow. Three days sans entry. Aaron and I are in New York. I love it here. I feel safe in this little old, cluttered house. I haven't binged. I haven't purged. I've been doing as well as could be expected with anxiety and insulin before entering a facility. Why? Aaron is 100% vigilant but has often said that if I have to do it, I have to do it. Why am I so safe with him? It's because I know I'm loved, isn't it? Last night, I stifled the urge to say, "I love you." I think I love the way he makes me feel loved. I have bared my soul and experienced the relief and exhilaration of acceptance. Yet how well do I know him? I sense he's still on his best behavior though I've seen glimpses of his flaws when he is drunk.

**August 17, 2009**

It's Monday. An admission into Renfrew is not happening tomorrow because apparently, my labs have yet to be faxed to them. Meanwhile, I feel I am burdening and boring Aaron as we pass the 72-hour mark of uninterrupted time together. I sense an infinite sadness in him. We are definitely in sync on some mental plane. He answers questions before I ask them; almost clairvoyantly, he does the things I wish for. There is a connection that surpasses anything I've experienced.

**August 19, 2009**

At Aaron's house, I feel more comfortable without the presence of his mother, who is watching his great-grandma recuperate, post-stroke. His mother has done nothing to make me feel as self-conscious and uninvited as I do, so maybe I am projecting the judgmental tendency of my own mom.

Shockingly, Mom hasn't called to ask where the heck I am. It blows me away how much she trusts and claims to like Aaron. Never in the past have I spent time with a guy without interrogation and chastisement. The lack thereof is even more curious, considering she is aware I've spent the past five nights with him unsupervised. I keep bracing for a severe reprimand. Perhaps she's washed her hands of me in one maternal flourish, believing her conscience can rest because I have two treatment centers lined up—at least in her mind.

**August 20, 2009**

I am aware that I am merely running in place here, biding my time. I notice in photographs that I look at least twenty-five and appear to be on the verge of tears. I notice when I smile, I am usually faking it. Yet I am embracing the break from bingeing, from purging, from judgmental looks, be they perceived *or actual, from the parental units. From comments on my laziness, my lack of employment, my falling back into old routines, from being a general waste of oxygen altogether.*

### August 22, 2009

*Aaron is about loyalty. This guy is mine, hook, line, and sinker. Mine for the taking—or the destroying. "Don't mess this up," Mom told me. Ahh. The sabotage element. Maybe unconditional love and support in the face of my flaws demands a second, far-closer look.*

### August 27, 2009

*I do not want to go to Renfrew Monday morning. I sense autumn creeping in. It makes me want to cling to summer, squeeze every second out of it. I am in love. I feel the rushing air. Hear every note of music. Goose flesh prickles my skin.*

*I lean over, kiss Aaron's cheek, and thank him.*

*"For what?" he asks.*

*"For loving me."*

*Do I have reservations? Assuredly. Is he fun, entertaining? No, but a million guys are. Aaron's qualities are far rarer. He is loyal, nurturing, considerate, patient, loving, stable. All the things that I am not, and I find myself able to live in the moment for the first time in my life.*

### September 1, 2009

*I was up the whole night before my Renfrew admission date. We left New York for Philadelphia at about four a.m. I drank en route; I didn't care whether inebriation denied my admittance.*

*The campus was secluded and very nice. We were separated while I received an EKG and breathalyzer. My blood sugar was 317. The psychiatrist evaluated me briefly. With disapproving clucks, she discontinued my Adderall, Valium, and Xanax and put me on Librium for alcohol withdrawal. I told her that I am legitimately an insomniac with an anxiety disorder. She said it went against everything in her to allow the downers with my history of substance abuse, and aside from that, she does not prescribe anyone Xanax. However, she allowed me twenty milligrams of Adderall because I told her failure to do so was a deal-breaker. She prescribed me Seroquel, too, though it failed to sweeten the deal.*

*I left to find Aaron, who was allowed to attend a meeting with my would-be therapist. He was so lovely, rubbing my neck continuously. The therapist asked if I wanted to get better or if I was still running away, willing to die. I was cry-ing again, and I said that of myself I was not inclined to try, but Aaron made me want to get better. Yet, even as I spoke, I felt I was betraying Nash, who, if truth be told, I miss the ghost of. But a ghost is still a ghost.*

*I can't say why I left. Whether it had to do with giving up Aaron or my meds. Maybe it was both.*

### September 2, 2009

*I am soaking up the September sun in Aaron's backyard. I awake just before seven when Aaron's alarm buzzes, and no matter how badly I want/need additional sleep, I can't. I make instant coffee in one of their huge mugs and sit outside with a few cigarettes and my magnifying mirror. After an hour, I get bored and hungry, and wanting to be productive, I crush Adderall in their bathroom and snort it. Usually, I eat a tapioca pudding beforehand. When the sun starts shining, I change to a bikini top, put on self-tanner, and set up my "station." This consists of a beach chair, iPod, journal, smoking paraphernalia, mirror, book, coffee, cell, and manicure crap. I feel lazy and stagnant. I am not a contributing member of society or this household.*

### September 3, 2009

*A hundred and thirty-six pounds as of this morning. Funny thing is, I can't remember what I was a few days ago. The day before yesterday, Aaron said I looked a little bigger than when we'd first met. While I appreciated his honesty, I cannot help feeling disappointed in myself. I don't know if it's part of the body dysmorphic disorder that makes my clothes feel tighter and my upper arms, thighs, and stomach seem larger. It's maddening to be incapable of seeing oneself objectively.*

### September 7, 2009

*Sometimes I feel I cannot take this. Do I prefer living here over a treatment center? Yes. But Aaron still overwhelms me with all these demands. He, albeit gently, hints at testing, insulin, eating, not purging, not drinking, not taking certain meds, not making derogatory comments about my weight and appear-ance. He tells me to stop scratching my head, biting my nails, smoking so much, being anxious, being self-conscious, changing clothes so often, even wearing my waistband too high, for God's sake.*

*Today I'd just about had enough. "If you want to change every last thing about me, why are you even with me?" I snapped.*

*The comment hurt him, but I will not apologize. Because it's true, and it hurts.*

Today Aaron asked me to teach him how to draw up and administer insulin because apparently I was drunk to the point of belligerence the night before and refused to take the Lantus. He said I passed out at the kitchen table, the pre-drawn syringe having fallen to the floor. He had to carry me to bed. He said if it ever happened again, he'd have to inject me. I am ashamed of these stories I don't even recall.

### September 14, 2009

Yesterday, Aaron surprised me with a brand-new, state-of-the-art easel. He pinned me against the counter and said, "See? Even though you were bad last night (he'd found out I'd relieved myself of two marinara sticks I'd purchased at Lee's), I got you a present. So somebody does love you."

When I talked to Mom last night, she spoke about Aaron in such a way that leaves little doubt she would like to see us married. Tonight, his mother jokingly referred to the way we argue over certain things like an old married couple.

### September 15, 2009

I weighed myself this morning and discovered I'm 137.5 pounds. I couldn't believe it. I'd been 134 several days earlier. When Aaron came home for lunch, he walked out to the backyard where I was painting and asked if I was coming in to eat. I said, "Absolutely not." When he asked why, I told him, "Because I weigh a hundred and thirty-seven and a half pounds, that's why."

I took photos of myself today, holding a paintbrush as though it were a Cruella de Vil–type cigarette. Upon viewing them, I was taken aback by how haggard I looked. I'd applied make-up and thought I looked moderately acceptable in the bathroom mirror, but no. The alcohol and stimulant abuse have aged me considerably. I don't feel sexy or attractive anymore.

### October 22, 2009

I no longer journal; I paint. Or rather, I repress through painting. It's Adderall during the day and vodka at night. My life reeks of stagnancy. I cannot believe I have become to Aaron what Lance was to me. I am struck by the unbelievable role reversal. I've become the lazy, helpless, aimless soul Lance was when I supported him.

### November 4, 2009

*Not much to report. Except that Aaron's mom happened upon a bag of puke a few days ago, and now she's thrown me out. She called me a "parasite." The shame was enough to raise my temperature. After packing my things and checking the basement to retrieve, yes, you guessed it, the only lingering bag of vomit I was storing there till I could dispose of it, I returned to Mom's. Aaron drove me there and stayed late—till almost ten p.m. because he didn't want to see his mom. I remember him saying as he fought tears, "This is the last night we're gonna be together before you leave for Renfrew." He spooned me on the couch, and I passed out immediately.*

*I was up at four a.m., cold and terribly lonely. I went upstairs to bed, where I tossed and turned till five-thirty at least. I am terrified of going into Renfrew, most specifically at the prospect of having no one with me at intake. It makes me want to cry just thinking about it.[102]*

### December 7, 2009

*I'm lonely in this institutional room, and I miss you. I miss being touched. I could cry (and am fighting the urge) just thinking about how bad I want a really, really long hug.*

*Last night, when we had that transparent moment where I asked if you'd be willing to "put up" with me if I got as big as I was in that photo, all I wanted to hear was, "I'll want you and love you no matter what happens to your body." I know when you said, "That's how you're supposed to look," you meant, "I want to see you healthy." I just wanted to hear it that other way.*

### December 26, 2009

*Keep my heart as shards of ice*
*Keep the lies close*
*Keep the cold confusion*
*until black settles in the elixir*
*of funeral soil*

*Keep me sure there is something:*
*A multi-faceted jewel of a soul*
*Ill poetess*
*A time and a place for*
*Hope*

*That this girl realizes what a drab place*
*this world would be without her*

◆　◆　◆

RACHEL DIDN'T LAST A month at Renfrew. According to her December fourth Facebook post, "I dubbed myself the Angelina Jolie rebel[103] of this concentration camp, trust me, you'd agree!" On December thirty-first, she bragged, "Rachie is discharged for repeatedly sneaking out of the window and smoking at night. I missed the memo on Renfrew being a nicotine rehab as well as an ED rehab. Oopsies."

Without saying it, Rachel and I both knew this was the end of the line for her. Renfrew was her last rehab. She wasn't going to rehabilitate. She would have to live with her disorders, as she had for the last decade.

Below is Rachel's final journal entry.

◆　◆　◆

### March 11, 2010

*I don't know what I am anymore. I used to feel I had time. That God had special plans for me. He'd tolerate my screwing around and wasting time until I straightened out.*

*Only I never did. I only succeeded in slipping further and further away. There is little to me anymore. How foolish to fantasize of a quasi-fulfilled existence painting and doing Adderall in solitude. Because now I am lonely in my own company. An empty shell. My family are veritable strangers, and it hurts to imagine what they must think of me. So I think instead of the boys or men I have granted portions of my heart to, how I hold pieces of each of them dear enough to ache for but never the whole.*

# Part IV

May 2010–November 7, 2012
ages twenty-five to twenty-eight

# THE APARTMENT

THE NEWPORT APARTMENTS WE viewed were in charming Victorian homes, like those on the covers of Christmas cards. Inside, they smelled of fresh paint. The hardwood floors gleamed. Of course, they creaked, but I thought that gave them character. Rachel liked the modern kitchens and large, energy-efficient windows, flooding the spacious rooms with light. She said she could see herself painting there. Smiling widely, she filled out several applications.

However, Newport landlords performed background checks. Not one called her back.

Now that Rachel was getting SSI, she could afford her own place. She even had cash to furnish it, thanks to a fat back-payment check.

Finding one was another story.

On May thirty-first, 2010, Rachel moved into a rundown three-bedroom apartment in Bristol. Except for new paint, nothing had been updated. The hardwoods were scratched and stained. The antiquated windows stuck, as did the original kitchen cabinet doors. The chipped Formica counter was only three feet long. Off the kitchen was a rusty fire escape. Cracked windows, overgrown grass. The whole six-unit building screamed, "slumlord."

At least, Bristol was a safe, quaint seaport. Rachel's apartment on Wood Street was a stone's throw from Turner Avenue, where she grew up. With her ingenuity, I knew she would transform that shabby unit into a lovely space.

Rachel's art flourished. She turned one bedroom into a studio. She had bins of acrylic paints, her preferred medium, though she also liked watercolors; and scores of brushes, some with only two or three short, stiff hairs for her pointillism pieces. She learned how to layer paints to achieve unique textures and found that intricate stencils created ethereal backgrounds. As her confidence grew, she gravitated toward larger canvases. When these were scarce, she painted on cardboard, chalkboards, wood, glass.

I was thrilled that Rachel's art had taken off. Work and love gave life meaning, according to Freud. If Rachel couldn't have a conventional job, she needed a gratifying pastime that drew her out of bed each morning, pushed her to excel, and got her recognition. Painting did it.

Love was another story. Rachel leaped from guy to guy; she had lovers galore. Yet true love, the kind that grew sweeter and sweeter, like Phil's and mine, eluded her.

In June, Rachel's latest boyfriend moved in. Nine years Rachel's senior, Grant was a moody Greek fisherman with dark hair, bushy brows, and gorgeous green eyes. Hard work had muscled his thin frame. His hands were calloused and strong. Grant smoked like a fiend. While framing Rachel's watercolors or repairing their windows, he'd be puffing on one cigarette, with another tucked behind one or both ears. When he was home, smoke engulfed their flat.

Grant constantly accused Rachel of cheating. He stalked her on Facebook and confiscated her cell, interrogating her for hours over harmless texts and posts to male friends. Meanwhile, he bought her beautiful dresses and jewelry. Two pairs of Uggs. At Christmas, he surprised her with a terrier pup she named Lola.

"Did he ever hit you?" I asked when she reported his latest rant.

"No, but he punched a wall. Left a hole the size of a softball that he still hasn't fixed." She shook her head.

"You know, there's something to be said for living alone, Rachel. It gives you time to figure out what *you* need before bringing a guy and his issues into the mix." We'd had this talk before, but this situation warranted revisiting it.

"Oh, I have plenty of time to think. He's out to sea for weeks at a time." Staring at me, Rachel's skillfully made-up eyes looked like blue jewels.

"But this situation is obviously bothering you."

I was referring to the open sore on her chin. Rachel's face occasionally broke out, but never like that. The sore had appeared shortly after Grant did and only seemed to heal when he took extended fishing trips.

"Dealing with this drama distracts you from your own issues. Rachel—I'm worried sick about your neuropathy."

I hated to change subjects when there was plenty more to say about Grant, but Rachel was always juggling multiple crises. Our time was limited. It came down to triaging her issues.

That her neuropathy "worried" me was an understatement. Since she'd told me she was shorting her insulin, I feared she would lose her feet. It was my constant dread.

"I don't want to talk about it, Mom," she said, averting her eyes.

"But you're in pain. I saw it the day you moved in."

On our umpteenth trip up the three flights of filthy stairs in her apartment building, she had admitted that her feet were throbbing. She was wearing her Aldo flip-flops with the abalone discs. Noting that her feet were red, I made her sit down.

"Is there anything you can do to stop it?" I'd asked her that day.

"Taking all my insulin stops the pain," she confessed.

"Then for God's sake, take it, Rachel!"

"Then I gain weight. I've *told* you this, Mother!"

Indeed, she had explained her twisted rationale for restricting her insulin: "I want to feel good in my skin now. I'd rather live a shorter life thin than a longer life fat."

"But look what happens when you don't!" I said, motioning toward her inflamed feet, my voice rising in panic. "If you keep this up, you could lose them!"

"I don't think so. I'll die long before that happens," she said, smashing my heart.

This time when I broached her neuropathy, she made light of it: "Don't worry, Mom. When my feet ache, I lie down—or take meds if it's really bad."

"But you're treating the *symptom* rather than the *cause*. Your body needs insulin!" Beside myself, I added, "Think about losing your feet—never being able to walk again!"

Rachel eyed me evenly, the infected sore marring her pretty face. Then she gutted me again. "Mom, I've been abusing my body for years. I'm not going to live that long."

Weeks later, I revisited the subject, trying a different, admittedly desperate, approach. "You know, if you end up in a wheelchair, you'll *really* pack on the pounds."

"I'd off myself before that ever happened," she coolly countered.

After that, Rachel ignored my calls and texts. I backed off. For one full month, she made no contact. Those five weeks felt like a year. Then I received a clipped text. Our neuropathy talks were "too real, too painful." She never wanted "to go there" again.

I got the message. If I wanted to see my daughter, I'd have to look away while she slowly destroyed her organs. It was beyond heinous, a tacit agreement too terrible to speak about. I never told anyone, not even Perry, Mom, or Phil. I numbly went along with it, reasoning that a dysfunctional relationship with Rachel was better than nothing at all.

Grant lasted fifteen months. One day while he was out to sea, Rachel decided she was done and changed the locks. Grant broke down the door. It cost her four hundred dollars to replace it, "Money well spent to be rid of him," she said.

By December of 2011, Rachel was dating Josh, a twenty-three-year-old premed student at Roger Williams University who lived in her building. She described him as a tortured soul who'd been in therapy for years due to some unspeakable family abuse. She omitted his addiction to pills. I couldn't fathom why he lived in that slum when his father was a doctor and his mother a lawyer. I would learn that he was there for the same reason as Rachel: no background checks.

Soon, Josh moved into Rachel's apartment with his eighty-pound golden retriever, Red.

After that, Rachel withdrew, not just from me but also from her father and brothers. I guess at twenty-seven, she deserved her space. Sometimes, she'd text late at night. Even if I was asleep, I thrilled to see her name on my screen. Her messages were light—news about Lola, her latest painting, a request for cash from her account—but they kept us connected. I cherished every crumb.

# SURPRISE

PURPLE TULIPS AND YELLOW daffodils danced in our flower beds one blustery Saturday in April of 2012. After an interminable winter, the leaves and grass had sprouted overnight, the lime green trees and lawn appearing fluorescent in the full sun. The air was perfumed with new blooms, the day so divine that Rachel and I wanted to sit on the deck, but the chill chased us indoors.

Rachel had called that morning, asking if she and Lola could visit. She wanted to talk.

We sat at the table, watching Lola through the slider race laps around the yard while the coffee maker sputtered and hissed. At that speed, Lola was a black blur. Phil stood watch. "Lola!" he'd holler if she strayed too far.

"She loves it here," Rachel said. "It's the only time she gets to go outside without a leash."

"You should bring her more often. We miss you, Rae."

Starbucks Sumatra tinkled into the carafe, its heady aroma filling the room. I poured two mugs, setting Half-&-Half and Splenda beside hers.

Rachel's smile faded as she turned from the glass. She prepared her coffee in silence.

"I-I don't exactly know how to tell you this," she stammered, forcing her eyes to face me. "So, I'm just going to come out with it."

I nodded, not sure what to expect. Hadn't she done it all? I mean, really, what more could she tell me?

"I'm pregnant, Mom."

I was taken aback. Women with bulimia were often unable to have children, as were women with poorly managed diabetes. Since Rachel had been sexually active for ten years, usually without using birth control, we had both deduced, without saying so, that she was probably infertile.

"Are you *sure*?"

Nodding solemnly, she unzipped her backpack. "It's just been confirmed with a blood test." She handed me a folded paper. "Here's my ultrasound," she said, unfolding it. "I was pregnant with twins, but I lost one. The other one is viable." She pointed to a blob in a sac on the mottled black and white report.

"Oh, my stars!" My heart skipped a beat. First, at hearing she'd had *twins;* then at the loss; then the wondrous news that one fetus was alive! Rachel had conceived a child!

"How far along are you?" I asked, breathless.

"Just a couple of months. I conceived on February twentieth."

It pinched that she hadn't told me then—she'd waited two months.

"I must say I'm stunned."

"Frankly, you're taking it a lot better than I thought you would."

Of course, I would have preferred to hear this news nine months after she had married a loving, stable man. Rachel was now the third of our five kids to conceive out of wedlock. Nikki had had a son with her then-fiancé a year after Henry was born. Each time I felt sucker-punched. Having a "love child" hardly raised an eyebrow anymore; however, I still believed in the institution of marriage. But once the deed was done and a tiny life forming, what could I do but rejoice?

Quite honestly, in Rachel's case, as she'd failed program after program, and especially after learning of her insulin restriction and how it was advancing her neuropathy, in my desperation, I'd begun to wonder if an unplanned pregnancy might save her. Wouldn't she *have* to take care of herself if she knew she were harboring life?

"How do you feel about it?"

A shadow eclipsed her face.

"I'm concerned about some of the meds I was on before I found out."

"But you've stopped them, right?"

"Yes, and I even quit smoking—well, I went from a pack to only two a day, which is major for me."

"I'm happy to hear that."

"But then there's my hyperglycemia." Rachel broke eye contact. "High blood sugar in the first trimester is extremely unhealthy for a fetus. That's when its organs are forming."

"But you can do something about that."

She nodded. "I'm taking all my insulin now, but I can't undo the damage that was done before I knew I was pregnant." Fear flashed across her face.

"You don't know that the fetus was damaged, Rachel. But let's get you checked out. There are OBGYNs at Women & Infants Hospital who specialize in high-risk pregnancies. I'll find one. I'll drive you there."

She continued as if she hadn't heard a word, her eyes far away. "And then there's Josh."

Oh, yeah—Josh. With her history, I figured he'd be long gone before the baby came.

"How does he feel about this?"

She bit her lip. "I think he's freaking out."

"Rachel, he's just a kid. What do you expect?"

"I expect him to step up to the plate," she snapped, her eyes refocused and fiery. "Matt was four years younger than Josh when he became a dad. This is Josh's last semester of pre-med school, so his situation could be worse. Yet, he's carrying on like his life is over."

"What do you mean?"

"Let's just say he has more of a drug problem than I thought. It didn't bother me as much when he was my boyfriend. It's different now that he's going to be the father of my kid."

"How do you know he's using?" This was news to me.

"He's been hanging out with the guys across the hall." Rachel's eyes swirled the room as she added, "They sell drugs."

That building, I was beginning to realize, was drug central. Rachel was surrounded by users and dealers. Yet, I felt oddly relieved. Didn't her concern over Josh's habit imply that she, herself, was clean? She wouldn't be pointing out his drug problem if she were using, would she?

"Can't he get help?"

"His father's trying to get him into a program, but he's resistant."

The next evening, I was sitting in bed with Phil softly snoring beside me, praying for Rachel's pregnancy, when she texted. As usual, I felt a pulse of joy to see her name lit on my cell. But her text arrested me: "I feel like getting rid of this baby and then offing myself."

Leaping out of bed, I telephoned her.

She instantly answered.

"What's going on, Rachel?" I asked, descending the carpeted stairs into the dark living room, where I began to pace.

"I don't have a good feeling about this, Mom. I've been sick too long. This baby is going to have serious problems—I just know it. Josh and his dad agree." She hesitated. "We have an appointment to go to Planned Parenthood tomorrow. His dad said there's some pill I can take to naturally abort it. It costs five hundred dollars, but he'll pay for it."

*Of course, he'd want to eliminate this "problem" for his son.*

"Rachel, that's your *baby* you're talking about, your flesh and blood!"

"But, Mom, it doesn't have a chance with the garbage I've exposed it to! If it were just the meds and the booze and the cigarettes, I might risk it, but hyperglycemia in the first trimester is nothing to fool around with! It causes *serious* birth defects!"

"Don't make a decision based on fear! You're assuming it's going to have problems, but you don't know that for sure. Plenty of unhealthy women have perfectly healthy babies. It happens a lot. God seals fetuses in their little sacs, protecting them from all kinds of harm."

She was crying now.

"Oh, Mom, I just could not stand to have a deformed baby! It would remind me every day of what a failure I am, how I did this to myself and my kid! I caused the defect by not taking care of myself!"

She was probably right. How could I refute that? What could I possibly say without sounding pat? She had ignored doctors' orders, defied every shred of advice I'd ever given her, broken every rule. Now she was backed into a corner, with very real, indeed horrendous, consequences threatening her.

Dumbfounded, I started to pray, asking God to remove Rachel's fears, give her wisdom, and protect her baby. As I heard myself speak, I was appalled at how wooden and hollow my words sounded. My heart was not in that prayer. Of course not. I was cowering in that corner with Rachel.

After we hung up, with trembling hands, I called Dolores, explaining what had happened and how I had failed to effectively counsel or even pray for my daughter. I begged my sister to call Rachel back.

Dolores talked to Rachel for an hour. She had the insight and largesse to offer to take Rachel's baby if it was mentally or physically impaired. Dolores's offer, coupled with her kind words and gentle reminder that life and death were God's domain, calmed Rachel down. She agreed to cancel her appointment at Planned Parenthood.

Two days later, Rachel called to tell me she had miscarried. She let it slip that she had gone to Planned Parenthood. I didn't know what to think. Had my daughter aborted her baby? Had she taken that pill? I couldn't prove anything, but inwardly I felt a dark, heavy weight.

Rachel texted me that she was in serious pain, crying so hard that her eyes were slits. She had not left her bed for two days.

I did not instantly respond.

If she had miscarried, I wanted to rush to her side. But if she had terminated her pregnancy . . .

I had accepted my daughter's lies, drug abuse, theft, and imprisonment. *Even her prostitution.* Taking life, *her child's life,* was a different matter.

I prayed and prayed, on my knees, in my bed, while I jogged, showered, dressed, my oppression slowly lifting. I never did discern if Rachel had miscarried or aborted her child. Suddenly, it just didn't matter. What rose to the surface of all that suspicion and confusion was the unalterable fact that Rachel belonged to me. She was my daughter, my blood. I loved her unconditionally and would never stop loving her, no matter what she had done.

I immediately drove to Bristol. I brought Rachel a pair of my pearl earrings that she had coveted and broccoli-cheddar soup from Panera Bread.

Barking, Lola greeted me at the door that Rachel had left open. I found her in bed, her face blotchy and swollen. A wastebasket overflowing with crumpled Kleenex. As I pulled up a chair, Lola hopped up on the bed, curling up beside Rachel.

"How are you feeling?" I said, kissing her forehead.

Rachel's eyes welled, triggering a lump in my throat.

"The pain's finally starting to subside. I never knew a miscarriage could hurt this bad."

"You mean physically?"

"Both. It shreds your body and your heart."

Tears sprang to my eyes. Seeing the magnitude of her distress, I wondered again if she had terminated her pregnancy. Losing a child by her own hand would have affected her much more than miscarriage. It would have slayed Rachel.

"I'm really sorry I didn't come sooner," I said.

"It's okay. Lola never left my side." Hearing her name, Lola lifted her head and looked at Rachel. Not getting further orders, she yawned, flashing her sharp teeth and curled tongue, and lay back down.

"I hope Josh has been helping."

"He cooks and walks both dogs." Josh's spastic dog, Red, had not stopped barking since I arrived. Josh left him in the spare room when he attended classes.

"He must be relieved."

"No doubt about that," she said, stroking Lola.

"What about you? You've had lots of time to think."

"Oh, I had some very real talks with God. I know He tried to bless me with a child. I understand that was a precious gift." She stopped to pluck a fresh tissue and wipe her welling eyes. "I wasn't able to receive it because I didn't take care of my health. I have to own that."

My heart swelled with hope.

"And what does that involve?"

"Well, for starters, taking all my insulin. Also, knocking off the booze, the nicotine, and most of the pills. Generally, cleaning up my act.

"Because the thing is . . ." Now her face folded, and her tears flowed, setting me off, too. "What I realized through this is that I want a kid," she finally choked out.

"Then follow your plan." I pulled a tissue and wiped my tears, then leaned over and hugged her. Feeling the bed shift, Lola stood, wagged her tail, and then nestled back down.

"In the meantime, be careful. Now that you have that pregnancy hormone in you, you're more fertile."

She blew her nose. "That's an old wives' tale, Mom," she said in a stuffy voice.

"I don't think so."

After Rachel lost the baby, I resolved to visit her weekly. Since I had flextime, I told her to choose the day and the activity. I didn't care if we did chores. I just wanted to spend time with her. Some days we grocery shopped; other days, we drank coffee in her apartment while I admired her latest paintings. One day, we were having lunch at the Beehive, her favorite little offbeat restaurant in Bristol, when she leaned in and told me she was pregnant again.

"Are you serious?" I thought she looked a little peaked for August.

I lifted my index finger to halt the waitress who was heading toward us with menus. She doubled back to the service station.

Rachel nodded. "I did a home pregnancy test. Plus, I'm constantly nauseous. Oh, and my tits kill."

I smiled. She did look a little chestier in her white spaghetti strap camisole, though her stomach was still flat under her pink cotton maxi skirt.

"How far along are you?"

"Only a few weeks."

"But you're happy, right?" I searched her eyes for truth.

"I am . . . I just want it to be healthy." Her eyes dropped. She lifted her water glass and took a long drink.

"I thought you said you were going to take better care of yourself. *Get clean,*" I added, leaning in and lowering my voice.

She shifted in her seat. "It isn't that easy, Mom," she whispered. "We're talking three major addictions."

"Well, what about your blood sugars? Are they at least in a safe range?"

"They're—uh—not what they should be." Her eyes broke from mine to scan the dim restaurant. "Where's our waitress? I swear, I'll drop this kid before she takes our drink order!"

I couldn't believe it. She'd gone right back to her old ways.

"It's early. You can start over right now. I'll take you to Women and Infants to see that OBGYN."

"I'd like that," she said, locking eyes with mine. "I want you to know that I stopped drinking and smoking and cut way back on my meds."

"I'm thrilled to hear that, Rachel." I hailed the waitress. My daughter needed fluid and food.

As the weeks passed, Rachel became more positive about the pregnancy. Josh, who had completed a one-month program for substance abuse, also seemed more optimistic about becoming a father. He took Rachel to see the high-risk OBGYN, whom she told me was top in his field. She had an ultrasound that showed one viable fetus with a strong heartbeat.

Again, I dared to hope.

# AGAINST ALL ODDS

MY TRILLING CELL FINALLY penetrated sleep. I felt around my nightstand, but by the time I found it, the caller had disconnected. It was one a.m. I sat up and listened to the message.

"*This is Doctor Jones. I'm calling to inform you that your daughter, Rachel, has just been brought into the ER by ambulance unconscious. Please call me immediately.*"

Hands trembling, I called him back.

"Do you know why Rachel might be unconscious?" His voice was calm but concerned.

"No, I don't."

"Do you think she would want to hurt herself?" he gently asked.

"No. She's three months pregnant, and she wants this baby. She lives with her boyfriend. Why don't you ask him? He would know more."

The doctor hesitated. "He's not here. She came in alone," he replied, to my consternation.

I told the doctor I'd get some answers and meet him at the hospital.

"What happened?" Phil asked, sitting up. This wasn't the first time we had been roused from sleep because Rachel had fought with a boyfriend or was stranded on the road.

"Rachel's at the hospital unconscious. Josh sent her in an ambulance alone."

"There's something seriously wrong with that kid," Phil said, shaking his head.

When I phoned Josh, he answered on the first ring.

"I just talked to an ER doctor who told me Rachel was unconscious. What *happened?*"

"Holy shit! I *knew* something was wrong. Saturday she wasn't feeling well."

That was true. I'd driven there that day to drop off some soup, calling from the parking lot to see if she'd invite me up. She had recently met with her new OBGYN, and I wanted to hear all about it. But she said her feet throbbed, and she needed to nap.

"She slept for a long time," Josh nervously continued, "nearly the whole day. When I tried to wake her, she wouldn't come to, so I threw a glass of ice water on her, and then she started screaming, but after she had something to eat, she was okay and started acting like herself again but then today—"

"Slow down, Josh!" I interrupted. "I can barely understand you."

"Yeah, so again she slept all day, well, we both did—"

"You mean Sunday, right?"

"Yeah, Sunday, but when I woke up, I noticed that her arm was in a really weird position. I shook her and shook her, but she wouldn't budge, so I tested her blood. It was twenty-nine. That's when I called 911."

"Why didn't you go with her?"

"When the paramedics were carrying her down, she peed on the stairs. I had to mop it up. She also wet the bed, so I had to change the sheets."

"But you're going now, right? The doctor needs information."

"Yeah, sure. I'm leaving right now. I'll see you up there."

As I hastily dressed, I visualized my daughter being carried down the three flights of filthy stairs in a gurney. That she had urinated not once but twice indicated that she must have been unconscious for some time.

I felt viscerally ill.

"You want me to come?" Phil asked, yawning.

I hesitated, knowing it would take hours. Though we both had to work that day, I could go in late, whereas he started at seven a.m. sharp. Yet, not knowing what to expect, I nodded.

He was up and dressed in moments, the irony piercing me: Though I'd given Phil no children, his devotion was bottomless, whereas the father of Rachel's child could not be bothered to follow her ambulance.

JOSH WAS IN THE ER waiting room when we arrived.

The three of us were immediately admitted into a small, curtained room where we found Rachel intubated, looking pale and lifeless. I felt numb. The nurse questioned Josh about the cause of Rachel's unconsciousness. He repeated what he'd told me, omitting one minor detail.

"We found cocaine and amphetamines in Rachel's urine," the nurse announced.

"*What?* But she's pregnant!"

Reeling toward Josh, I barked, "What do you know about this?"

"She was out of Adderall. I think she might have gotten coke from the guys across the hall, but I'm not sure—"

"I need the *truth,* Josh!"

"Yeah, I know . . . I'm pretty sure she got it from them . . ."

"And you approve of her using cocaine while she's pregnant with your kid!"

I had to step out of the room. I was getting far too caustic.

"That kid's covering something up," Phil said, leaning against the corridor wall beside me as I took deep breaths.

"You *think?*"

An orderly wheeled Rachel to a room in the ICU, with us following.

Wanting to get a better picture of Rachel's condition, an ICU nurse questioned Josh again about the events leading to her coma. He maintained eye contact until she asked what quantity of drugs Rachel had taken and how long she was unconscious. Then his eyes hit the floor; his shoes became the most fascinating things.

The next day, at Dr. Jones' prompting, I phoned Josh to ask how long he thought Rachel had "fallen asleep." I knew they'd both taken drugs and passed out, but I used neutral language, hoping it would yield truth. He admitted that it could have been twelve hours or longer.

Rachel's total lack of response since her hospitalization was already a bad sign. Now doctors ordered an MRI to rule out—or confirm—brain damage.

The following morning, I was sitting at Rachel's side, holding her hand. She had a clear tube down her throat that was connected to a ventilator. This machine, along with several others positioned around her bed, was keeping her alive.

Suddenly, a doctor breezed in with his unbuttoned medical coat sailing behind him, along with a flock of medical students. He wore a tie and dress clothes and looked sixtyish, with a gray combover and silver-rimmed glasses. He stopped at the foot of Rachel's bed, the students in blue scrubs fanning out around him.

"I'm Doctor Johnson, Chief Medical Physician in the ICU. We have the results of your daughter's MRI," he said, scanning his chart. "Unfortunately, she has sustained extensive trauma to the brain." He hesitated, staring at me, along with at least twelve other sets of sober eyes.

I swallowed. "What exactly does that mean?"

"She has irreversible brain damage. She's in a vegetative state from which she will not recover."

My mouth went dry. My face burned, but I clenched my stomach.

"Do you always deliver parents such devastating news with an entourage?"

He blinked multiple times but did not answer. Shock might have immobilized him. Feeling all those eyes still on me, I added, "Please leave me alone."

✦   ✦   ✦

I SPENT THE NEXT few hours in a small family room, curled up in a ball, crying.

When I called Phil, I could not even choke out the words.

"I'm leaving right now. I'll be right there!"

My friend Lu eventually joined Phil and me. I had texted her requesting prayer. When she asked if I wanted her to come, I told her I didn't know. I was in alien waters. She arrived an hour later, with a bag from Au Bon Pain, her expression so tender. Lu was Cuban, with large chocolate eyes that saw and felt everything. That day her pretty, naturally pouting lower lip protruded even more.

"I bought black bean soup and baguettes," she said, setting the bag down to hug us. She was one of those friends who would have known we hadn't eaten all day.

"Bless you, Lu. Let's go see Rachel first."

We tiptoed into her room, lit only by the lights from the life support machines. Lu gasped, whether at Rachel's immobility or the whole wretched affair, I don't know.

"Dear Jesus," she whispered, leaning over and kissing Rachel's pale, inert forehead.

Walking out of the room, she squeezed my hand. "I'm in this for the long haul, Baby"—Lu always called me "Baby" or "Babe"—"here every day, as long as you want."

That evening, Dr. Cohen, the ICU's other Chief Medical Physician, requested a meeting with our family. Perry and the boys were already there. Lu took notes. We crowded in that small family room. Just as Dr. Cohen was closing the door, Josh slipped into the last chair.

Dr. Cohen looked to be fiftyish. Trim physique, tanned skin, intense brown eyes. Short, almost shaved gray hair. He didn't carry a medical chart. With hands clasped loosely in his lap, he asked, "What do you plan to do about the fetus?"

Except for Lu's frantic note-taking, the room was silent. We stared at him, dumbfounded, all, no doubt, still drifting on separate clouds of unreality.

Still trying to process the shattering fact that Rachel was gone. She would not leave that bed. Never crack another joke. Never talk, laugh, or cuss again. In our shock and grief, we'd forgotten about the fetus.

Now Dr. Cohen told us that "against all odds," it was still alive.

"In my thirty-year career, I've never seen a fetus survive a brain assault of this magnitude," he said, scanning the group. "And, quite frankly, we're scratching our heads. We've been calling our colleagues around the country to figure out how to proceed, depending, of course, on what you decide to do."

After a candid question and answer period, my resistant mind finally grasped what the tactful doctor was trying to say: there was little hope for Rachel. If she regained consciousness, she would not be able to recognize or interact with us. If she did *not* come to, at some point we might have to consider stopping life support. *What horrible options!*

"However, pregnant women in a vegetative state have been known to successfully give birth . . ."

My heart quickened. *Was I hearing right?*

"We've never seen this happen," he continued, "but our colleagues around the country and world have successfully performed C-sections on women in your daughter's condition."

*Oh, what a sweet prospect! How wonderful if an infant awaited us at the end of this nightmare.*

"That's absolutely amazing," Perry said.

"But would the baby be healthy?" Matt asked.

"Right now, all we know is that it has a strong heartbeat."

*A strong heartbeat—after Rachel had been comatose for over twelve hours!*

"If you want to explore this option, and it looks like you do," he said, noting our enthusiasm, "I'll schedule a meeting with the OBGYN and Neonatal teams at Women & Infants' Hospital. As we get more facts, you can decide how you want to proceed. Whatever you choose, we will support you one-hundred percent." Standing, Dr. Cohen shook each of our hands.

If the first chief medical physician had flattened me with his callous delivery of this crushing news, his tactful cohort had given me hope. I knew there were no guarantees. For Rachel to carry a healthy baby to term in her condition and with her extensive health issues was a long shot. Our prospects were not good. Still, Dr. Cohen's willingness to support us when the outcome appeared so grim was like a candle in a blackout. A sip of water in a drought. I wanted to hug him.

"I expect you'll want to keep it," Josh said, coming up beside me as we walked down the hall to kiss Rachel good night.

"Yes, I do, if you don't mind."

"Of course. I mean, I figured you would. I need to finish med school anyway."

That was the last meeting Josh attended. He sat beside me in a large conference room at Women & Infants Hospital for the next one. But while we were waiting for the teams to arrive, he asked if he could keep Lola. When I said no, he walked out. I never saw him again.

In our meeting with the neurologist, we learned, to our devastation, that Rachel's brain injury was vast and irreversible. The MRI revealed severe cortical damage. Though her brain stem was still alive—she might eventually twitch a limb or open her eyes—these movements were purely random. Her higher brain functions—voluntary movement, thinking, perception, and the *expression of individuality*—were wiped out. What made Rachel "Rachel" was gone. She was in what he called "a persistent vegetative state."

The condition of the fetus was not as cut and dried. We wanted to know if it had a fighting chance, but after multiple meetings with the ICU, OBGYN, and NEONATAL teams, the doctors unanimously agreed that it was too early to tell. A brain deficiency, among many other potential health issues, could not be detected until birth.

What concerned the NEONATAL team was Rachel's hyperglycemia in her early weeks of pregnancy. A healthy A1c for a pregnant woman was six percent. Rachel's was 11.2. High blood sugars in the first trimester could cause birth defects, they informed us, echoing Rachel's fears. Diabetes *alone* made Rachel's pregnancy high risk. Even diabetic women with good control and healthy A1c's had more babies with physical problems, like heart defects and holes in their spinal columns.

These were sobering things to hear. We listened. We nodded. We restrung the same questions with different words, hoping to get more heartening answers; however, the verdict never changed: this fetus was *ultra* high-risk.

In the last few years, the chronic stress in my life had taken its toll. By age fifty-three, I had been diagnosed with osteopenia, advanced arthritis, and basal cell skin cancer. I had shattered my foot twice, had bones removed in both thumbs, and had multiple Mohs surgeries.

In my physical condition, caring for a *healthy* infant would have been challenging. What if this infant were mentally or physically impaired? Would I be able to care for it?

And yet . . . this fetus should not have survived. Despite Rachel's abuse of her body, its tiny heart was steadily ticking. It must be a fighter. Of course it was. It was Rachel's, indeed, the only living part of her left.

To the astonishment of the specialists who advised us against it, we chose life.

And, true to Dr. Cohen's word, every single one of those medical teams stood behind us.

The earliest they could take the baby was twenty-four weeks. Lu and I hunkered down for a thirteen-week wait. Rachel was moved from the ICU to the Respiratory Intensive Care Unit (RICU), which was one level of care below it; however, first she was given a tracheostomy.

I had recoiled at Rachel being cut. Dr. Cohen assured me that this was standard procedure for long-term protection of Rachel's airway.

When Rachel came out of surgery, I was wearing my reading glasses. In sharp focus, I saw a fraction of her fresh red incision peeking out of the bandage. *My daughter had a hole in her throat. A machine was breathing for her.* Moments later, she opened her blue eyes, but she was not there. Her brain was gone. She was gone. I cried and cried.

Doctors who had heard about Rachel's case stopped by to encourage us. Per my plea, a doctor from the neonatal team monitored the baby's heartbeat daily—normally, they did this weekly. Another doctor brought me Rachel's latest ultrasound. Another, a beautifully illustrated children's book called *On the Night That You Were Born,* by Nancy Tillman, as well as two research studies on babies that had been born to women in vegetative states. I read them multiple times, gaining hope that this could happen. Rachel could give birth to a healthy baby, maybe even a blue-eyed girl that Phil and I could raise as our own.

Lu did not let me wander too far down that road. When I aired these thoughts, she gently reminded me that Rachel was ill. The fetus had been traumatized. If it survived, it might not be well. "Let's pray for God's will, babe."

✦  ✦  ✦

THE RICU WAS MORE relaxed, maybe a little too relaxed. Doctors and nurses were sometimes congregated at the nurses' station, chatting and laughing. Sometimes, we had to press the red Help button multiple times before a nurse or CNA responded. Though Rachel's hair was separating with oil, no one washed it until I offered to do it myself; then a nurse returned with an inflatable shampoo basin that she placed under Rachel's head. It had a hose that, when attached to the faucet, allowed her to fill and drain it in the bed. In moments, Rachel's long hair was floating in water where she lay. The nurse lathered it twice with baby shampoo, massaging it into Rachel's scalp and thoroughly rinsing it each time. After a vigorous towel-drying, Rachel's hair was a sheet of snarls. I didn't care; at least it was clean. Standing on opposite sides of the bed, Lu and I gently worked disposable black combs through the tangled knots. It took about two hours, but once Rachel's hair dried, it shone like spun gold.

Most disconcerting about the RICU were the constant room changes. In one week, Rachel was relocated three times. The last move happened on a day Ryan took Lu's place. In that room, the ventilator didn't sound right. Rather than the steady hum I was used to, it was sputtering. The nurse said that the "trach," or tube inserted into the tracheostomy, just needed to be suctioned of Rachel's mucus build-up, a process that required us to step out of the room. Apparently, a plugged trach could hamper or even halt Rachel's airflow. Once the nurse suctioned the trach, the familiar hum returned, but by the end of the day, the machine was crackling again. I made sure she corrected it before Ryan and I left.

That evening as I was getting into bed at about twelve-thirty a.m., I received a frenzied phone call from a doctor in the RICU, informing me in a heavy accent that Rachel had had a heart attack.

"What? I was just there! She was fine!"

"Please come quick!" he urged. "She's not doing well!"

I called Perry, who said he would meet us there. Phil was already out of bed, pulling on his Levi's. I repeated the news to Matt and Ryan, who were both still awake in their separate rooms. "We need to leave *now*. Dad's already on his way."

They sprang to their feet. We grabbed our coats and flew out the door just as a light snow started falling.

As we drove, the snow picked up. Perry was just entering the hospital when we arrived. Together, we rode the elevator up to the fifth floor, rushing past the nurses' station en masse to reach Rachel.

We stopped short inside her door. Surely, this was not the room. There was not a single machine in sight—no heart monitor, no feeding machine, no respirator, not one glowing number or blinking light, no hums, fans, beeps. The room was completely quiet and utterly bare, except for a bed, with

Rachel in it, as pale as the crisp white sheets that covered her small form. Her hands, free of tubes and catheters, were folded on her chest. *Oh, God!* Just as my brain grasped what had happened, Ryan collapsed on the floor, sobbing. Perry was already breaking down while Matt and Phil were still frozen, still trying to process the surreal scene before them. I dropped to my knees, shielding Ryan with my body while we both sobbed.

A doctor waited in the hall until the tidal waves of shock and grief subsided. Then he beckoned us into the lobby. We sat on brown leather couches arranged in a square. He remained standing.

"I'm Dr. Shurwrong. I'm terribly sorry for your loss," he said. It was the same voice I had heard on the phone. Tall and lanky, with black eyes and brows, he was one of the doctors I'd seen fraternizing with the nurses. "Your daughter was already gone when I called, but I couldn't tell you on the phone."

Was this some perverse answer to prayer? In this impossible situation, I'd started praying exclusively for God's will. Was this a disguised kindness, God's way of sparing me from a number of horrible outcomes? Now, I would not have to make the unthinkable decision of discontinuing life support if Rachel didn't regain consciousness. Would not have to watch my brilliant daughter rot in some nursing home. Would not have to raise a mentally or physically impaired child. All these dreadful scenarios had just evaporated. But so had the sweet prospect of gaining a grandchild.

"Something went wrong with the trach," Dr. Shurwrong explained.

"That machine was making noises all day," I retorted. "Isn't it the hospital's responsibility to maintain life support machines, for heaven's sake?"

"I tried to replace the trach," he continued, ignoring my question, "but that didn't work, so we re-intubated her. That worked, but it caused her to go into cardiac arrest." He paused, looking at me as if appealing for pardon. "We usually only resuscitate for five minutes, but because of the pregnancy, we worked on your daughter for over thirty minutes."

I imagined the violent chain of events—panic, commotion, blood—that had preceded the peaceful scene we had just walked in on. Was this supposed to console me? Was their extra effort supposed to make up for what sounded like negligence and ineptitude?

"Isn't this a *hospital*? What do you mean, you 'tried to replace the trach, but it didn't work'? Aren't you a *doctor*? Isn't this your *job*? And who wouldn't have a heart attack after that horror show!"

"Mom, Mom, calm down!" Matt said, gently adding, "You can't bring her back."

No, I couldn't. My tears began to flow. Now I had lost them both.

When we left the hospital, the snow had turned heavy, coming down like it never had in early November. The world was completely white, wooly flakes falling, covering our hair and coats. After hugging me tightly, his hair dredged with snow, Ryan left with his dad, not wanting him to be alone. Phil, Matt, and I trudged through inches of cold, powdery snow. It entered my shoes, chilling me. The parking lot was pure white, the vehicles frosty mounds. Furiously falling flakes glittered like fairy dust in the parking lot lights.

How Phil found our car, I do not know. After unlocking my door and starting the engine for heat, he and Matt began scraping the windows. I got in, dropped my head on the dash, and to the rhythm of their scraping, released the floodgates. Since we had opted to keep the baby, I hardly thought about Rachel. Understanding that her mind was gone, I regarded her more as a vessel than a person: her body was keeping the fetus alive. Indeed, the fetus had stolen my attention. I had hoped that life would right this nightmare. Now that I had lost them both, it was *Rachel* I longed for. The only reason I had ever wanted the baby was to preserve her.

I cried and cried for the daughter whose blue eyes were gone, whose jokes and feisty laugh I would never hear again; but also for the daughter I did not know and now never would; who had lived such a short, tortured life that she had to bury it in the pages of her journals. I wept for her pain. Though I glimpsed only a fraction of it then—illness, a string of stinging romances, loneliness, untold loss—even that was way too much for one young woman. I wept for what was over—our talks, our jewelry swaps, our nocturnal texts, our treasure hunts at yard sales and thrift stores. She would never give me another painting or pedicure; I would never make her pizza or eggplant Parmesan. She would never announce, "I just saved your birthday again," then describe the tacky gifts Phil or her brothers had nearly purchased before she intervened. She would never conquer her EDs and substance abuse—never give that victory speech at our church. Most heartbreaking, she would never taste true love. She missed out on two of God's greatest gifts: marriage and children. I cried thinking of her horrible end, dying of a heart attack with her unborn child, whom I would never see or hold or watch grow. There was no end to my tears. They fell and fell and fell, like infinite snowflakes on the windshield.

July 2018

# New Eulogy

*My Dearest Rachel,*

*Your first eulogy was not for you. It was for the hundreds of people who packed into Middletown Baptist Church on November 17, 2012, to grieve your tragic passing on November seventh. So many sad eyes, staring at me as I stood behind that podium, trying to help people comprehend why a lovely, bright young woman had died.*

*However, I did not understand it myself. I had witnessed some things, but the biggest things you hid from me. I knew that the pith and truth of your story was buried in those journals that I had not yet read. So, I did the best I could; I gave the Dick 'n Jane version of your demise. Walking away from that podium, I felt like I had failed you. I **had** failed you.*

*Therefore, I decided to write a new eulogy. This one is for you. This one is true. At least, I believe it comes closer to conveying the actual circumstances that took your life way too soon. It has emerged only after years of perusing your diaries— reading them so many times that the pages are worn, and my tears have blurred some of your words; researching your illnesses until I thought my head would burst; and, indeed, writing this memoir, a daunting project I doubt I would have finished had you not asked me to.*

*Do you remember? You were eighteen when, fearing you wouldn't live long enough to pen your memoir, you passed the task to me:*

I miss my mother.

I miss what I never had, someone to entrust everything in. I want to be close. I can't carry around these secrets anymore. In a sense, doesn't she own me? My father has never owned me, but my mother gave me life, and I lived in her. And in the soft warm hum of shared blood, I breathed her, became a broken off piece of her.

I always think that she knows my thoughts.

That at her core, she would understand.

I picture myself telling her everything someday.

I would let her have my words in this book,
and I can see her furiously working at publishing it.
From here on,
this belongs to my mother.
Only at her discretion
will anything written escape
these pages or the confines of her mind.
This book is the most priceless
article I own.
Upon my death, I leave it to my mother.
January 2, 2003

*That you felt you had to get your affairs in order at eighteen . . .*

*That you were so ill . . .*

*and I was so blind . . .*

*I have spent the last seven years laboring to understand and document what I did not see then.*

*Rachel, this memoir is your new eulogy.*

*I hope it reflects your true life and why it ended so soon. I hope it pleases you.*

*At the same time, I hope your story serves a larger purpose, warning parents that their young teen down the hall can be severely ill without their awareness; but that son or daughter needn't suffer and self-medicate. There are good treatments today. Adolescents with mental illness can live and thrive if they get help right away.*

*I hope your story softens all readers' hearts, as it did mine, making them slower to judge those who seem to make unsound choices, repeat their mistakes, or seek solace in substances. More people struggle with mental illness than we might guess, some fighting simultaneous battles lasting years or decades. Therefore, let us embrace the unembraceable. Let us treat them with respect, patience, and love. Let us give them grace.*

*Your loving mother*

# ENDNOTES

### Diabulimia

1. The Ophelia Fund is a donor-advised endowment of the Rhode Island Foundation for the research, prevention, and dissemination of information about eating disorders.

2. The Partial Hospitalization Program for Eating Disorders was an outpatient treatment program at Hasbro Children's Hospital that Rachel attended prior to and following her hospitalizations.

3. Dada, Janice H. "Understanding Diabulimia—Know the Signs and Symptoms to Better Counsel Female Patients." *Today's Dietician,* vol. 14, no. 8, 2012, p. 14, www.todays dietitian.com/newarchives/080112p14.shtml (14).

4. Daneman, D., et al. "Eating Disorders in Adolescent Girls and Young Adult Women with Type 1 Diabetes." *Diabetes Spectrum,* vol. 15, no. 2, 2002, pp. 83–105. *Crossref,* doi:10.2337/diaspect.15.2.83 (91).

5. Goebel-Fabbri, Ann E. "Diabetes and Eating Disorders." *Journal of Diabetes Science and Technology,* vol. 2, no. 3, 2008, pp. 530–32. Crossref, doi:10.1177/193229680800 200326 (531).

6. "Shocking Trends of the New Year: Kaytee, Michelle, Wanda." Dr. Phil, Peteski Productions, Inc., 20 July 2008, www.drphil.com/slideshows/shocking-trends-of-the -new-year-kaytee-michelle-wanda.

7. Jones, J. M., et al. "Eating Disorders in Adolescent Females With and Without Type 1 Diabetes: Cross Sectional Study." *BMJ,* vol. 320, no. 7249, 2000, pp. 1563–66. Crossref, doi:10.1136/bmj.320.7249.1563 (1565.)

8. Goebel-Fabbri 530.

9. Daneman et al. 84.

10. "Influence of Intensive Diabetes Treatment on Body Weight and Composition of Adults with Type 1 Diabetes in the Diabetes Control and Complications Trial." *Diabetes Care,* vol. 24, no. 10, 2001, pp. 1711–21. *Crossref,* doi:10.2337/diacare.24.10.1711.

11. Newer insulin analogues show promising evidence that weight gain may no longer be such a risk. Goebel-Fabbri, Ann E. "Diabetes and Eating Disorders." *Journal of Diabetes Science and Technology,* vol. 2, no. 3, 2008, pp. 530–32. *Crossref,* doi:10.1177/ 19322968080020326 (532).

12. Janice Baker, registered dietician and certified diabetes educator says honesty from the outset is vital for type 1 diabetes patients: "Individuals should be told they'll gain weight with the initiation of insulin . . . and a mental health professional should be seen at diagnosis to support body image concerns" (Dada 14).

13. Dada 14.

14. Daneman et al. 91–92.

15. Goebel-Fabbri 531.

16. An A1c (also called HbA1c) test gives patients a picture of their average blood sugar level over the past two to three months. An optimal glycemic control level is generally less than seven percent.

17. Goebel-Fabbri (531) and Daneman et al. (93).

18. "Diabetic Ketoacidosis Overview." Mayo Clinic, Mayo Foundation for Medical Education and Research, www.mayoclinic.org/diseases-conditions/diabetic-ketoacidosis/symptoms-causes/syc-20371551. Accessed 7 Oct. 2021.

19. Daneman 93–94.

20. Goebel-Fabbri, A. E., et al. "Insulin Restriction and Associated Morbidity and Mortality in Women with Type 1 Diabetes." *Diabetes Care*, vol. 31, no. 3, 2007, pp. 415–19. Crossref, doi:10.2337/dc07-2026 (417).

21. Steel, J. M., et al. "Clinically Apparent Eating Disorders in Young Diabetic Women: Associations with Painful Neuropathy and Other Complications." *BMJ*, vol. 294, no. 6576, 1987, pp. 859–62. Crossref, doi:10.1136/bmj.294.6576.859.

22. Wing, Rena R., et al. "Subclinical Eating Disorders and Glycemic Control in Adolescents with Type I Diabetes." *Diabetes Care*, vol. 9, no. 2, 1986, pp. 162–67. *Crossref*, https://doi.org/10.2337/diacare.9.2.162.

### "I Haven't Been Myself in a Long Time"

23. Dr. Abraham was Rachel's child psychiatrist, with whom she had private weekly therapy sessions from September of 1999 to June of 2000.

### Broken

24. Anderson, B. J., et al. "An Office-Based Intervention to Maintain Parent-Adolescent Teamwork in Diabetes Management. Impact on Parent Involvement, Family Conflict, and Subsequent Glycemic Control." *Diabetes Care*, vol. 22, no. 5, 1999, pp. 713–21. Crossref, doi:10.2337/diacare.22.5.713 (719–20).

25. Wysocki, T., et al. "Deviation from Developmentally Appropriate Self-Care Autonomy: Association with Diabetes Outcomes." *Diabetes Care*, vol. 19, no. 2, 1996, pp. 119–25. Crossref, doi:10.2337/diacare.19.2.119 (123).

26. It didn't take long for Rachel to misuse this skill once she discovered that reducing her insulin resulted in weight loss.

27. Traditionally, needles used in insulin therapy were 12.7 millimeters (mm) in length; however, today smaller 8 mm, 6 mm, and 4 mm needles are just as effective, and people are less likely to inject shorter needles into their muscles. Tubiana-Rufi, N., et al. "Short Needles (8 mm) Reduce the Risk of Intramuscular Injections in Children with Type I Diabetes." *Diabetes Care*, vol. 22, no. 10, 1999, pp. 1621–25. Crossref, doi:10.2337/diacare.22.10.1621.

### SOS

28. According to Doctor Mary Pipher, adolescent girls expose only a fraction of what they're feeling, submerging their larger issues. Pipher, Mary. *Reviving Ophelia: Saving the Selves of Adolescent Girls.* 1st ed., Ballentine, 1995.

29. The Eating Disorder Examination (EDE) and the Eating Disorder Index (EDI) were two effective tools used to detect the presence of eating disorders in 1999.

### "Not Doing Too Well Today"

30. Arrythmia is an irregular heartbeat. While underdosing her insulin, Rachel often journaled about her racing heart rate, among other frightening symptoms. Severe hyperglycemia or diabetic ketoacidosis (DKA) may result in rapid heart rate. Barry, Jennifer. "How Does High Blood Sugar (Hyperglycemia) Feel?" *Medical News Today Healthline Media,* 11 Mar. 2019, www.medicalnewstoday.com/articles/313138#_noHeader PrefixedContent.

31. This disturbing mindset is not uncommon among young females practicing diabulimia. According to ED psychologist Marion Olmsted, "Patients may feel angry that diabetes either prevents them from reaching their eating disordered goals or brings a price that those without diabetes do not have to pay. The fear of disability and premature death is an almost universal underlying theme, although it is frequently disguised by neglect of diabetes management and disregard for the consequences." Daneman et al. (100–101).

### Oblivious

32. In this excerpt, gleaned from a college essay, Rachel fantasizes about the prospect of living with a functioning pancreas: "In the near future, I hope to get a pancreas transplant. This would leave me dependent upon anti-rejection drugs for the rest of my life but would render my body ordinary. As I sit here staring at the very word 'ordinary' on my screen, I am absolutely struck by it. To be ordinary, normal, to have everything working as it should. Sometimes I'm in awe of people's flawless bodies, how every one of the hundreds of intricate systems they have are functioning normally. Yet they have no idea how blessed they are. If they appreciated what this meant, they would never cease to give thanks. This I know: if my body is ever relieved of diabetes, I would never be able to stop rejoicing."

33. An experimental treatment for type 1 diabetes that involves separating islet cells from a donor pancreas and transplanting them into a person with type 1 diabetes. Once transplanted, the islet cells begin to produce insulin, actively regulating the level of glucose in the blood. "What Is Islet Transplantation?" Diabetes Research Institute Foundation, www.diabetesresearch.org/what-is-islet-transplantation?gclid=CjoKCQjwwYLBh D6ARIsACvT72PoqSlAvLHTjC3dFtLT9xSoLg7MDepVsCRkoex2QpOEuavbF588e3. Accessed 11 Oct. 2021.

### Bittersweet Sixteen

34. Rachel read *Brio* for four years, learning about women's intrinsic worth. Meanwhile, pop culture was pushing the opposite view—that looks were everything. The media was

bombarding adolescent girls with images of thin, sexy women, brainwashing them into believing this was the norm (Wolf, Naomi. *The Beauty Myth: How Images of Beauty Are Used against Women*. New York, Morrow, 1991). Girls who fell short were driven to change themselves, according to Mary Pipher. The healthy ideas Rachel gleaned from *Brio* were probably washed away in this flood of false ideas, of which beauty magazines were the most detrimental (Field, A. E., et al. "Exposure to the Mass Media and Weight Concerns among Girls." *Pediatrics*, vol. 103, no. 3, 1999, p. e36. *Crossref*, doi:10.1542/peds.103.3.e36; Field, Alison E., et al. "Relation of Peer and Media Influences to the Development of Purging Behaviors Among Preadolescent and Adolescent Girls." *Archives of Pediatrics & Adolescent Medicine*, vol. 153, no. 11, 1999, pp. 1184–89., doi:10.1001/archpedi.153.11.1184).

Fortunately, I noticed a heartening shift in these trends around 2019. Today, female news reporters, commercial models, and actresses are not all thin. That false body type hasn't been shelved, but at least on television we now see a variety of sizes and shapes that represent real women.

### Falling Down

35. "Eating Disorder Statistics." *ANAD*, National Association of Anorexia Nervosa and Associated Disorders, www.medicalnewstoday.com/articles/7504#causes. Accessed 11 Oct. 2021.

### Girl with Snarls

36. Larrivee, Marie-Pier. "Borderline Personality Disorder in Adolescents: The He-Who-Must-Not-Be-Named of Psychiatry." *Dialogues in Clinical Neuroscience*, vol. 15, no. 2, 2013, pp. 171–79. *Crossref*, doi:10.31887/dcns.2013.15.2/mplarrivee.

37. Larrivee 172.

38. Amy Wiggin. "What Does 'Axis II:799.9 Diagnosis Deferred (Threatened Personality)' Mean?" *Quora*, 13 Oct. 2018, www.quora.com/What-does-Axis-II-799-9-Diagnosis-deferred-threathened-personality-mean.

39. The Global Assessment of Functioning is a scale in DMS-IV used to rate the severity of mental illness. It measures how much patients' symptoms affect their daily lives on a scale of 0 to 100, 100 representing ideal functioning. At sixteen, Rachel's score was 45–50, reflecting "serious" symptoms that could—and in her case, did—result in shoplifting and suicidal thoughts. At twenty-four, her score had plunged to 30, reflecting behavior "considerably influenced by delusions . . . OR serious impairment in judgment (e.g., sometimes . . . acts grossly inappropriately, suicidal preoccupation) . . ." Smith, Matt. "What Is the Global Assessment of Functioning (GAF) Scale?" WebMD, 26 Feb. 2021, www.webmd.com/mental-health/gaf-scale-facts.

40. American Psychiatric Association. *Diagnostic and Statistical Manual of Mental Disorders*. 4th Ed, Text Revision. Washington DC: American Psychiatric Association. 2000.

41. American Psychiatric Association. *Diagnostic and Statistical Manual of Mental Disorders (DSM-5)*, 5th Ed. American Psychiatric Association, 2013 (663–64).

42. DSM-5 (665).

43. DSM-5 (663).

44. Drew Westen et al. "Identity Disturbance in Adolescence: Associations with Borderline Personality Disorder." *Development and Psychopathology*, vol. 23, no. 1, 2011, pp. 305–13. *Crossref*, doi:10.1017/s0954579410000817.

45. Westen et al. 311.

46. Westen et al. 308, 311.

47. Whitfield, Charles L. *Healing the Child Within: Discovery and Recovery for Adult Children of Dysfunctional Families*. Health Communications, Inc., 1989 (9).

48. Winnicott, D. W. "Ego Distortions in Terms of True and False Self." *The Maturational Processes and the Facilitating Environment: Studies in the Theory of Emotional Development*, vol. 64, International Universities Press, 1965, pp. 140–52. https://www.sas.upenn.edu/~cavitch/pdf-library/Winnicott_EgoDistortion.pdf (144–48).

49. Whitfield 10–11.

50. Winnicott 148.

51. Alice Miller. *The Drama of the Gifted Child: The Search for the True Self*. 3rd ed., Basic Books, 2008 (21).

52. Whitfield 2.

53. Whitfield, Charles L. *Co-Dependence Healing the Human Condition: The New Paradigm for Helping Professionals and People in Recovery*. Health Communications, Inc., 1991 (5).

54. Masterson, James F. *Search for the Real Self: Unmasking the Personality Disorders of Our Age*. Free Press, 1988 (51–54).

### "Heal Me, O Lord, the Hope of the World"

55. Rachel was referring to her disordered eating. How she coined it in her journal depended on what aspect of it she was describing. For example, when she fantasized telling people her secret, she would write, "I'm a bulimic," or when she spoke of it clinically, she called it an ED. However, when Rachel recorded her struggles with bulimia or diabulimia, she objectified her EDs, often shrouding them in pronouns such as "this" and "it" to keep her secret, secret.

56. Rachel's deviant behavior may have stemmed from her personality disorder. Many Borderlines with identity disturbance "have a self-image that is based on being bad or evil" American Psychiatric Association. *Diagnostic and Statistical Manual of Mental Disorders, 5th Edition: DSM-5*. 5th ed., American Psychiatric Publishing, 2013 (664). This tendency to project a bad boy/girl image is particularly true of adolescents according to Westen, Drew, et al. "Identity Disturbance in Adolescence: Associations with Borderline Personality Disorder." *Development and Psychopathology*, vol. 23, no. 1, 2011, pp. 305–13. *Crossref*, doi:10.1017/s0954579410000817 (311).

### Ravenous

57. Miller, Alice. *The Drama of the Gifted Child: The Search for the True Self*. 3rd ed., Basic Books, 2008 (12).

58. Whitfield, Charles L. *Co-Dependence Healing the Human Condition: The New Paradigm for Helping Professionals and People in Recovery*. Health Communications, Inc.,

1991 (67).

59. Winnicott, D. W. "Ego Distortions in Terms of True and False Self." *The Maturational Processes and the Facilitating Environment: Studies in the Theory of Emotional Development*, vol. 64, International Universities Press, 1965, pp. 140–52. https://www.sas.upenn.edu/~cavitch/pdf-library/Winnicott_EgoDistortion.pdf (150).

### "She Looks Like Deception to Me"

60. Researchers have found a link between EDs and petty theft. In one large study, women with bulimia were four times more likely to be convicted of shoplifting—especially food items—than their healthy peers, possibly because frequent binging adds up. Those with coexisting disorders that included an impulsivity symptom like Borderline were even more likely to shoplift. Yao, Shuyang, et al. "Risk of Being Convicted of Theft and Other Crimes in Anorexia Nervosa and Bulimia Nervosa: A Prospective Cohort Study in a Swedish Female Population." *International Journal of Eating Disorders*, vol. 50, no. 9, 2017, pp. 1095–103. *Crossref*, doi:10.1002/eat.22743. Accessed 5 Jan. 2018.

61. Rachel may have been referring to the burning pain she felt in her stomach when she deprived her body of insulin and became hyperglycemic.

### "Why Can't I Just Give Up on Him?"

62. Bingeing and purging.

### Doves Make Feeble Mothers

63. The Jesus Movement was a powerful campaign that swept the nation from the late sixties to the late eighties, reviving many individuals and churches with its focus on spiritual gifts and pursuing a personal relationship with Jesus Christ.

64. Pipher, Mary. *Reviving Ophelia Saving the Selves of Adolescent Girls*. 1st ed., Ballantine, 1995 (135).

65. Pipher 12–13.

66. Pipher 23–24.

67. Wiseman, Rosalind. *Queen Bees and Wannabes: Helping Your Daughter Survive Cliques, Gossip, Boyfriends, and the New Realities of Girl World*. 2nd ed., Three Rivers Press, 2009.

68. Matthew 10:16.

### "There Is Vomit on my Shirt"

69. Rachel identified the quandary many young women with diabetes face: they cannot achieve their weight goals while correctly dosing their insulin, the reason some throw health to the wind. In such cases, parents and treatment providers are inclined to enforce the rules. But researchers warn that a more relaxed approach may better serve insulin-phobic patients, who might, for example, be more likely to take two rather than four daily insulin shots, the rationale being that any improvement in metabolic control reduces the

risk for diabetes-related problems. Daneman, D., et al. "Eating Disorders in Adolescent Girls and Young Adult Women with Type 1 Diabetes." *Diabetes Spectrum,* vol. 15, no. 2, 2002, pp. 83–105. *Crossref,* doi:10.2337/diaspect.15.2.83.

70. Warren, Rick. *The Purpose Driven Life: What on Earth Am I Here For?* Zondervan, 2002.

## Weighty Matters

71. Even well-meaning comments are not well received by people with EDs. When Rachel was severely underweight and I or others tried to tell her the few pounds she had gained filled in her face or gave her some flattering curves, she panicked, feeling like she had failed.

72. Hudgens, Jessica. "Eating Disorders and Competition, Comparison." *Healthy Place,* 20 Mar. 2014, www.healthyplace.com/blogs/survivinged/2014/03/comparison-competition-and-eating-disorders.

73. Current studies show that even when people vomit directly after bingeing, about 1,200 calories remain in the body. It's likely that bulimia, the risky method Rachel trusted to control her weight, was not as effective as she thought. "Bulimia Nervosa. A Contemporary Analysis." *National Centre for Eating Disorders,* eating-disorders.org.uk/information/bulimia-nervosa-a-contemporary-analysis. Accessed 13 Aug. 2017.

## Christmas Tat

74. Rachel was likely dealing with "impulsivity," another core Borderline symptom. To meet the clinical criteria for this symptom, one must display "potentially self-damaging impulsivity in at least two of these areas: spending, sex, reckless driving, binge eating and substance abuse." Rachel engaged in them all. American Psychiatric Association. *Diagnostic and Statistical Manual of Mental Disorders (DSM-5).* American Psychiatric Association, 2013 (663).

75. Rachel wanted to stop hurting herself; however, her recklessness only intensified. She would continue down the same path—the same deadbeat boyfriend, the same destructive coping mechanisms—that had misled her countless times. A person's inability to alter her thinking and behavior, even in the face of evidence that it doesn't work, is the hallmark of mental illness, *DSM-5,* 763.

## "There Are Drug Addicts in My Cinema"

76. Street name for Klonopin (Clonazepam), a controlled benzodiazepine drug used to treat seizures and anxiety.

77. SSTAR (Stanley Street Treatment and Resources) is an affordable, holistic health care facility in Fall River, Massachusetts, that specializes in addiction treatment.

## Interference

78. *Alcoholics Anonymous,* 4th ed., Alcoholics Anonymous World Services, 2001.

79. *Alcoholics Anonymous* 46–48.

80. *Alcoholics Anonymous* 28.

81. *Alcoholics Anonymous* 50–51, 281–559.

82. While reading the memoirs of other ED victims, I noticed a similar trend, not unlike the Stockholm syndrome, for young women to speak positively about the very disorders that trap and torture them. Recalling her history with diabulimia, one woman wrote, "Though it was my worst enemy, it also became my best friend . . . the constant in my life while everything else was changing" (118). Marcle, Amy Lynn. *Slow Suicide: Living with Diabetes and an Eating Disorder.* CreateSpace Independent Publishing Platform, 2013. Following her recovery from bulimia and anorexia, another wrote, "I miss it. It hurts like a sonofabitch. It's disgusting, but it was my safeguard, my sure thing, my security, my life for all those years" (121). Hornbacher, Marya. *Wasted: A Memoir of Anorexia and Bulimia.* HarperPerennial, 1998.

83. Whitfield, Charles. *Co-Dependence Healing the Human Condition: The New Paradigm for Helping Professionals and People in Recovery.* Health Communications, Inc., 1991 (5).

84. Whitfield 60.

85. Whitfield, Charles L. *Healing the Child Within: Discovery and Recovery for Adult Children of Dysfunctional Families.* Health Communications, Inc., 1989.

86. Whitfield, *Healing the Child Within* 12.

87. Whitfield, Charles. *Co-Dependence Healing the Human Condition* 20.

### Teaspoon of Therapy

88. Now that Rachel was being properly dosed, she was probably experiencing *edema,* the bloating and water weight that can occur when insulin is restarted; however, it is generally not permanent. Goebel-Fabbri, Ann E. "Diabetes and Eating Disorders." *Journal of Diabetes Science and Technology,* vol. 2, no. 3, 2008, pp. 530–32. *Crossref,* doi:10.1177/193229680800200326 (532).

89. Enmeshment can occur in families when parents divorce and the opposite sex parent relates to a child as a surrogate husband or wife. When a father exploits his daughter to get his emotional needs met, this puts a heavy burden on her, resulting in an unhealthy co-dependence. Pease Gadoua, Susan. "When Parents Make Children Their Friend or Spouse." *Psychology Today,* 24 July 2011, www.psychologytoday.com/us/blog/contemplating-divorce/201107/ when-parents-make-children-their-friend-or-spouse.

90. It was tragic that the one time Rachel was open to long-term treatment, she was not able to receive it for lack of financing. Had she been able to remain at Remuda Ranch for an extended period through a work-study program, for instance by helping with art therapy classes, she might have received the care she desperately needed. Remuda doesn't offer such a program, but maybe they should.

### Free Fall

91. Aaws. *Alcoholics Anonymous.* 4th ed., Alcoholics Anonymous World Services, 2001.

### "Peace When I Die"

92. Just as heroin is measured in grams or fractions of an ounce for street sale, Rachel is measuring her intake in fractions.

93. Suboxone (Buprenorphine) is a prescription medication for people addicted to heroin or other opiates used to relieve the symptoms of opiate withdrawal.

### Wasted Grace

94. Kenney, Andrew. "Teen Challenge's Proven Answer to the Drug Problem. A Review of a Study by Dr. Aaron T. Bicknese. "The Teen Challenge Drug Treatment Program in Comparative Perspective." Northwestern University, 1999, pp. 1–12, acadc. org/wp-content/uploads/pdf/NW_study.pdf.

### "I Don't Recognize Rachel"

95. Rachel might have been using shoplifting as a coping mechanism. Coping mechanisms are compulsive activities that serve as outlets for the profound emptiness and other intense emotions that plague Borderlines. These can include any obsessive behavior from fantasizing, overeating, and unfulfilling sexual liaisons to alcohol and drugs. Masterson says, "these pathologic activities function like a kind of armor to protect against the emptiness, helplessness, and depression that would otherwise consume them." Masterson, James F. *Search for the Real Self: Unmasking the Personality Disorders of Our Age.* Free Press, 1988 (73–74).

### Three Strikes

96. According to the DSM-5, "Individuals with Borderline Personality disorder may have a pattern of undermining themselves at the moment a goal is about to be realized." American Psychiatric Association. *Diagnostic and Statistical Manual of Mental Disorders (DSM-5), 5th Ed.* American Psychiatric Association, 2013 (665).

97. Masterson says Borderlines sabotage their progress out of fear. They're afraid, not only to manage their own lives, but especially to succeed as this requires activating and asserting their real selves. Borderlines are not "adaptive," they're "defensive." All they know how to do is to defend themselves from pain through unhealthy coping mechanisms. Masterson, James F. *Search for the Real Self: Unmasking the Personality Disorders of Our Age.* Free Press, 1988 (12, 23).

### "I've Put a Life to Waste"

98. On August 5, 2008, Rachel was sentenced to prison for failing a drug test while in Drug Court and sent to Butler to detox from methadone. One week later, she was transported to the Adult Correctional Institution (ACI), medium security, in Cranston, Rhode Island.

## "Your Mercies Never Cease"

99. The early period following a diabetes diagnosis when a patient does not need as much insulin because the pancreas is still producing some. Fletcher, Jenna. "What Is the Honeymoon Phase of Diabetes." *Medical News Today Newsletter,* Healthline Media, 28 Mar. 2019, www.medicalnewstoday.com/articles/320842.

## "Failure Is All I Really Know"

100. In Rachel's world, "witnesses" were men who were attracted to her, those who wanted a good time, as well as those who sought a relationship. Perhaps because her weight fluctuated, she craved witnesses to see and appreciate her body when it was toned and thin. Rachel's obsession to be witnessed might have been related to her identity disturbance. Whitfield says when one's true self is repressed, one feels empty and tries to fill oneself from the outside, turning to people or things for happiness and fulfillment. Ultimately, this leads to addictions and disorders. Feelings of emptiness can only be remedied by healing one's true self and connecting with one's Higher Power. Whitfield, Charles L. *Co-Dependence Healing the Human Condition: The New Paradigm for Helping Professionals and People in Recovery.* Health Communications, Inc., 1991, pp. 33–34.

## "Ill Poetess"

101. Concerta is a stimulant medication used to treat attention deficit disorder (ADD).

102. Phil and I had both taken time off work to drive Rachel to Renfrew. We were looking forward to taking this road trip with her. More importantly, we wanted to ensure that she was actually admitted. However, Rachel rejected our offer, opting to travel alone.

103. Angelina Jolie played a rebellious character in *Girl, Interrupted,* a movie based on Susanna Kaysen's best-selling memoir about her experiences in McLean Mental Hospital in Belmont, Massachusetts, where she was treated for borderline personality disorder. In truth, Rachel had more in common with Kaysen, played by Winona Ryder, who was impulsive, promiscuous, and suicidal.

# WORKS CITED

Aaws. *Alcoholics Anonymous*. 4th ed., Alcoholics Anonymous World Services, 2001.

American Psychiatric Association. *Diagnostic and Statistical Manual of Mental Disorders (DSM-5), 5th Ed*. American Psychiatric Association, 2013.

———. *Diagnostic and Statistical Manual of Mental Disorders, Text Revision (DSM-IV-TR), 4th Ed*. American Psychiatric Association, 2000.

Anderson, B. J., et al. "An Office-Based Intervention to Maintain Parent-Adolescent Teamwork in Diabetes Management. Impact on Parent Involvement, Family Conflict, and Subsequent Glycemic Control." *Diabetes Care*, vol. 22, no. 5, 1999, pp. 713–21. *Crossref*, doi:10.2337/diacare.22.5.713.

Barry, Jennifer. "How Does High Blood Sugar (Hyperglycemia) Feel?" *Medical News Today*, Healthline Media, 11 Mar. 2019, www.medicalnewstoday .com/articles/313138#_noHeaderPrefixedContent.

"The Big Picture: Checking Your Blood Sugar." American Diabetes Association, www.diabetes.org/healthy-living/medication-treatments/blood-glu cose-testing-and-control/checking-your-blood-sugar. Accessed 23 Dec. 2021.

"Bulimia Nervosa. A Contemporary Analysis." *National Centre for Eating Disorders*, https://eating-disorders.org.uk/information/bulimia-nervosa-a -contemporary-analysis/. Accessed 13 Aug. 2017.

Dada, Janice H. "Understanding Diabulimia—Know the Signs and Symptoms to Better Counsel Female Patients." *Today's Dietician*, vol. 14, no. 8, 2012, p. 14, www.todaysdietitian.com/newarchives/080112p14.shtml.

Daneman, D., et al. "Eating Disorders in Adolescent Girls and Young Adult Women With Type 1 Diabetes." *Diabetes Spectrum*, vol. 15, no. 2, 2002, pp. 83–105. *Crossref*, doi:10.2337/diaspect.15.2.83.

"Diabetic Ketoacidosis Overview." *Mayo Clinic*, Mayo Foundation for Medical Education and Research, www.mayoclinic.org/diseases-conditions/ diabetic-ketoacidosis/symptoms-causes/syc-20371551. Accessed 7 Oct. 2021.

"Eating Disorder Statistics." *ANAD*, National Association of Anorexia Nervosa and Associated Disorders, www.medicalnewstoday.com/articles/7504 #causes. Accessed 11 Oct. 2021.

Field, A. E., et al. "Exposure to the Mass Media and Weight Concerns Among Girls." *PEDIATRICS*, vol. 103, no. 3, 1999, p. e36. *Crossref*, doi:10.1542/ peds.103.3.e36.

Field, A E., et al. "Relation of Peer and Media Influences to the Development of Purging Behaviors Among Preadolescent and Adolescent Girls." *Archives of Pediatrics & Adolescent Medicine*, vol. 153, no. 11, 1999, pp. 1184–89. *Crossref*, doi:10.1001/archpedi.153.11.1184.

Fletcher, Jenna. "What Is the Honeymoon Phase of Diabetes?" *Medical News Today Newsletter*, Healthline Media, 28 Mar. 2019, www.medicalnewstoday .com/articles/320842.

Goebel-Fabbri, A. E., et al. "Insulin Restriction and Associated Morbidity and Mortality in Women with Type 1 Diabetes." *Diabetes Care*, vol. 31, no. 3, 2007, pp. 415–19. *Crossref*, doi:10.2337/dc07-2026.

Goebel-Fabbri, Ann E. "Diabetes and Eating Disorders." *Journal of Diabetes Science and Technology*, vol. 2, no. 3, 2008, pp. 530–32. *Crossref*, doi:10 .1177/193229680800200326.

Hornbacher, Marya. *Wasted: A Memoir of Anorexia and Bulimia*. Harper-Perennial, 1998.

Hudgens, Jessica. "Eating Disorders and Competition, Comparison." *Healthy Place*, 20 Mar. 2014, www.healthyplace.com/blogs/survivinged/2014/03/ comparison-competition-and-eating-disorders.

"Influence of Intensive Diabetes Treatment on Body Weight and Composition of Adults With Type 1 Diabetes in the Diabetes Control and Complications Trial." *Diabetes Care*, vol. 24, no. 10, 2001, pp. 1711–21. *Crossref*, doi:10.2337/diacare.24.10.1711.

Jones, J. M., et al. "Eating Disorders in Adolescent Females With and Without Type 1 Diabetes: Cross Sectional Study." *BMJ*, vol. 320, no. 7249, 2000, pp. 1563–66. *Crossref*, doi:10.1136/bmj.320.7249.1563.

Kenny, Andrew. *Teen Challenge's Proven Answer to the Drug Problem. A Review of a Study by Dr. Aaron T. Bicknese.* "The Teen Challenge Drug Treatment Program in Comparative Perspective," June 1999, https://acadc.org/wp -content/uploads/pdf/NW_study.pdf.

Larrivee, Marie-Pier. "Borderline Personality Disorder in Adolescents: The He-Who-Must-Not-Be-Named of Psychiatry." *Dialogues in Clinical*

*Neuroscience,* vol. 15, no. 2, 2013, pp. 171–79. *Crossref,* doi:10.31887/dcns
.2013.15.2/mplarrivee.

Marcle, Amy Lynn. *Slow Suicide: Living with Diabetes and An Eating Disorder.*
CreateSpace Independent Publishing Platform, 2013.

Masterson, James F. *Search for The Real Self: Unmasking the Personality Disorders of Our Age.* Free Press, 1988.

"Mental Health by the Numbers." *NAMI National Alliance on Mental Health,*
Mar. 2021, www.nami.org/mhstats.

Miller, Alice. *The Drama of the Gifted Child: The Search for the True Self.* 3rd
ed., Basic Books, 2008.

Pease Gadoua, Susan. "When Parents Make Children Their Friend or
Spouse." *Psychology Today,* 24 July 2011, www.psychologytoday.com/us/
blog/contemplating-divorce/201107/when-parents-make-children-their
-friend-or-spouse.

Pipher, Mary. *Reviving Ophelia: Saving the Selves of Adolescent Girls.* 1st ed.,
Ballentine, 1995.

"Shocking Trends of the New Year: Kaytee, Michelle, Wanda." *Dr. Phil,*
Peteski Productions, Inc., 20 July 2008, www.drphil.com/slideshows/
shocking-trends-of-the-new-year-kaytee-michelle-wanda.

Smith, Matt. "What Is the Global Assessment of Functioning (GAF) Scale?"
*WebMD,* 26 Feb. 2021, www.webmd.com/mental-health/gaf-scale-facts.

Steel, J. M., et al. "Clinically Apparent Eating Disorders in Young Diabetic
Women: Associations with Painful Neuropathy and Other Complications." *BMJ,* vol. 294, no. 6576, 1987, pp. 859–62. *Crossref,* doi:10.1136/
bmj.294.6576.859.

Tubiana-Rufi, N., et al. "Short Needles (8 mm) Reduce the Risk of Intramuscular Injections in Children With Type 1 Diabetes." *Diabetes Care,* vol. 22,
no. 10, 1999, pp. 1621–25. *Crossref,* doi:10.2337/diacare.22.10.1621.

Warren, Rick. *The Purpose Driven Life What On Earth Am I Here For?* Zondervan, 2002.

Westen, Drew, et al. "Identity Disturbance in Adolescence: Associations
with Borderline Personality Disorder." *Development and Psychopathology,*
vol. 23, no. 1, 2011, pp. 305–13. *Crossref,* doi:10.1017/s0954579410000817.

"What Is Islet Transplantation?" *Diabetes Research Institute Foundation,* www
.diabetesresearch.org/what-is-islet-transplantation. Accessed 11 Oct. 2021.

Whitfield, Charles L. *Co-Dependence Healing the Human Condition: The New
Paradigm for Helping Professionals and People in Recovery.* Health Communications, Inc., 1991.

Whitfield, Charles L. *Healing the Child Within: Discovery and Recovery for Adult Children of Dysfunctional Families.* Health Communications, Inc., 1989.

Wiggin, Amy. "What Does 'Axis II: 799.9 Diagnosis Deferred (Threatened Personality)' Mean?" *Quora*, 13 Oct. 2018, www.quora.com/What-does-Axis-II-799-9-Diagnosis-deferred-threatened-personality-mean.

Wing, R. R., et al. "Subclinical Eating Disorders and Glycemic Control in Adolescents With Type I Diabetes." *Diabetes Care*, vol. 9, no. 2, 1986, pp. 162–67. *Crossref*, doi:10.2337/diacare.9.2.162.

Winnicott, D. W. "Ego Distortions in Terms of True and False Self." *The Maturational Processes and the Facilitating Environment: Studies in the Theory of Emotional Development*, vol. 64, International Universities Press, 1965, pp. 140–52. https://www.sas.upenn.edu/~cavitch/pdf-library/Winnicott_EgoDistortion.pdf.

Wiseman, Rosalind. *Queen Bees and Wannabes: Helping Your Daughter Survive Cliques, Gossip, Boyfriends, and the New Realities of Girl World.* 2nd ed., Three Rivers Press, 2009.

Wolf, Naomi. *The Beauty Myth: How Images of Beauty Are Used Against Women.* 1st ed., Morrow, 1991.

Wysocki, T., et al. "Deviation from Developmentally Appropriate Self-Care Autonomy: Association with Diabetes Outcomes." *Diabetes Care*, vol. 19, no. 2, 1996, pp. 119–25. *Crossref*, doi:10.2337/diacare.19.2.119.

Yao, Shuyang, et al. "Risk of Being Convicted of Theft and Other Crimes in Anorexia Nervosa and Bulimia Nervosa: A Prospective Cohort Study in a Swedish Female Population." *International Journal of Eating Disorders*, vol. 50, no. 9, 2017, pp. 1095–103. *Crossref*, doi:10.1002/eat.22743.

# Acknowledgments

Thanks to my writing group, Newport Round Table (NRT), especially Lisa, Nancy, and Devin, for their camaraderie, constructive feedback, and constant support throughout the formidable process of writing *Reckless Grace*.

Lisa went above and beyond, believing in the importance of this project to the extent that she built my first website and provided legal advice during contract negotiations.

Elisabeth, another NRT member, provided support and friendship during the long, grueling process that we shopped our manuscripts. Her sense of humor while reviewing some of my stilted query letters kept me chuckling through countless rejections.

Special thanks to Melissa, NRT moderator, for her singular feedback and enduring friendship.

I am deeply grateful for the three endorsements I received from former U.S. Congressman, Patrick J. Kennedy, Dr. Ann Goebel-Fabbri, and author Maryjeanne Hunt.

To my mother and sisters, for their intelligent reviews over multiple iterations of *Reckless Grace*, as well as their continual support and prayers throughout the publication process.

To my many dear friends, who prayed me through every phase of this process. I can't count the times a writing roadblock suddenly vanished or I received a waft of energy, clarity, or encouragement out of nowhere. Those prayers helped me make impossible decisions. They provided peace in chaos, shafts of light in moments of despair.

I thank my son Matthew for his astute review of *Reckless Grace* and excitement when I signed with WiDo Publishing. I thank my son Ryan for his artistic contributions, including his sketch of Rachel's tattoo. I thank both sons for their sincere interest in every facet of this project.

I am enormously grateful to my friend, Michael Osean, who out of love for Rachel poured himself into this project. The first to read *Reckless Grace*, Michael raved about it to anyone who would listen. When literary agents snubbed my manuscript, Michael reminded me of its worth. To boost interest, he built my current website and created my video. He photographed all the art in *Reckless Grace*. Michael's lavish contributions to this project cannot be measured.

Jay Gowen deserves accolades, not just for being a brilliant editor but also a decent human being, whose respect, sensitivity, and open-mindedness softened the long, often thorny editing process. A visionary with "superpowers," Jay read hundreds of pages of Rachel's journals, selecting entries to create new "Rachel" chapters that not only amplified her voice, his primary aim, but more importantly, illuminated her mental illnesses. Whereas I had shed a mere crack of light beneath that door, Jay flung it wide open.

I thank my husband, Phil, for anchoring me to the earth after I lost Rachel. I thank him for helping me count the exorbitant cost of writing this book, yet still waving me on. I thank him for his unfaltering love over the seven years that I researched and wrote *Reckless Grace,* routinely scorching meals and rarely changing out of my sweats.

Finally, I thank my daughter, Rachel, whose journals, at once dark and dazzling, inspired this book. Had she not documented in excruciating detail how it felt to live with co-existing physical and mental disorders; writing well into the wee hours, fighting fatigue to capture her thoughts and experiences while they were fresh; often in the brutal cold so she could smoke, there would be no *Reckless Grace*.

# About the Author

Carolyn DiPasquale grew up in Franksville, Wisconsin, graduating from UW-Milwaukee with a double major in English and French. In 1983, she moved to Rhode Island where she raised three children while pursuing her Master's in English at the University of Rhode Island. Over her career, she taught literature and composition at various New England colleges; worked as a technical writer at the Naval Underseas Warfare Center in Newport; and wrote winning grants as a volunteer for Turning Around Ministries, a Newport aftercare program for ex-offenders. She has been an active member of the Newport Round Table, a professional writing group (founded in 1995), since 2013.

DiPasquale currently lives in Richmond, Rhode Island, where she has started working on a sequel to *Reckless Grace*. She has also ventured into writing children's books. In her free time, she enjoys cooking and baking with healthy ingredients, hiking and trapshooting with her husband Phil, and volunteering at the New Hope Chapel food pantry in Carolina, Rhode Island.